Contents

Volume I

FOREWORD

Liam Price spent his leisure hours over many years studying the placenames and antiquities of County Wicklow and neighbouring counties. In his pursuit of both placenames and archaeology he was a tireless fieldworker who always believed in consulting local people on the archaeology and traditions of an area and on the names of places and their pronounciation. His book on the placenames of County Wicklow is a classic that not alone has not been surpassed for Wicklow but does not have an equal for any other county in Ireland with the possible exception of Limerick, with its official county volume produced by the Placenames Branch of the Ordnance Survey of Ireland. His Wicklow volume was a labour of love, the fruit of many years of research, and contains much local history and incidental information on people and places, which makes it a pleasure to consult or dip into.

He was an active member of the National Monuments Advisory Council and the Archaeological Exploration Committee of the Royal Irish Academy, and co-directed the excavation of the Labbacallee wedge tomb, Co. Cork, in 1934 with H.G. Leask, publishing the results two years later. He was also a member of the Irish Folklore Commission and the Irish Placenames Commission but devoted much of his talent and enthusiasm to the Royal Society of Antiquaries of Ireland, whose journal he edited from 1935 to 1949 and again from 1957 to 1963. He also served as president of the Society (1949–52) and presided over its centenary celebrations: the Society was founded in Kilkenny in 1849. He published many articles over the years on placenames and antiquities, edited a book of Austin Cooper's diaries and illustrations, and did much work in indexing and seeing through the printing of Charles McNeill's edition of the Calendar of Archbishop Alen's Register, which was published by the Society in 1950.

His fieldwork over many years was methodically and meticulously written up in a series of small notebooks which provide a mine of information on the archaeology and placenames of Wicklow and nearby counties. Many sites and antiquities which have since been damaged or destroyed are here described, and many placenames which may since have been forgotten are recorded.

Chris Corlett and Mairéad Weaver have done the worlds of archaeology,

THE PRICE NOTEBOOKS

The Price Notebooks

Volume I

Edited by
Christiaan Corlett and Mairéad Weaver

An Roinn Comhshaoil agus Rialtais Áitiúil
The Department of the Environment and Local Government

Dúchas
The Heritage Service

First published in 2002
Dúchas The Heritage Service
Dún Scéine, Harcourt Lane
Dublin 2

ISBN 0-7557-1284-6

British Library Cataloguing-in-Publication Data.
A catalogue record for this book is available from the British Library.

Typeset in Ireland by Wordwell Ltd

Cover design by Rachel Dunne

Printed by Colour Books Ltd

placename studies and local history a great service in editing and making more widely available this wonderfully rich source of information.

Conleth Manning,
President,
Royal Society of Antiquaries of Ireland.

Liam Price (courtesy of the Royal Society of Antiquaries of Ireland ©).

INTRODUCTION

In 1864 George Roberts Price married Lillie Hormsby Wright, and together they had a family of three boys and one girl (five other children died at birth or as infants, and another boy died aged 12). Lillie herself died on 22 February 1885, and George Roberts Price subsequently married Kate Askin. On 23 February 1891 their son William George was born. His sister Kathleen was born two years later. During this time the family lived at Leeson Street in Dublin. William did not simply inherit his middle name from his father; he was also exposed to his future calling, both in the legal profession and in historical research. His father had graduated in Classics at Trinity College, Dublin, and was a prominent member of the college History Society, in which he won the Silver Medal for Oratory. He later became a well-known member of the Irish bar, and in 1893 was elected Bencher of the King's Inns. In August 1899 he was further elected to the office of the Registrar of the Chancery Division. He died on 31 October 1915. Liam's mother Kate died on 18 June 1942, aged 88.

Liam went to Aldenham Public School in England and, like his father before him, graduated in Classics at Trinity College, Dublin, where he subsequently qualified as a barrister. At the time of the Easter Rising of 1916 he was serving in Cork with the Army Pay Corps. Ó Broin (1985, 88–92) tells of how he was in Dublin for the weekend and, unable to get back to Cork because of the Rising, he went through the city watching the developments as they unfolded, appalled by the sudden rebellion. Extracts from his first-hand observations of the events of the Rising are preserved in the National Library of Ireland (as are the more complete accounts by his older stepsister Lily). Price began his accounts thus:

> 'Yesterday, Easter Monday, this extraordinary business started: & it is worth putting down what I see of it, as it goes on'.

This introduction is interesting in that it shows that Price realised the importance of documenting people, places and events from an early age. At one point he gives an account of visiting St Stephen's Green immediately after it had been evacuated by the Volunteers, and of examining one of their abandoned trenches:

'saw rifle, and belt and pouch, on ground here — stains of fresh rust on rifle, from lying here all night. Picked up belt & pouch, and took it away under my coat — was looking at rifle, when shot suddenly fired from just above us — rushed off to gate, which would not open — but it was only stiff & had stuck, so pulled it open, & went back — man said volunteers were in Winter Garden's pub; & shot probably came from there. Anyway, I could not have taken rifle, might have been shot carrying it: besides, if I had got it home, Volunteers rifle bad thing to have in house.

In the above account he gives the impression that the shot fired may have been aimed at him. In the version of the same event given by his sister Lily, however, there is no mention at all of a shot being fired. Liam's notes are clearly written by a young, enthusiastic man — he was then 25 years old — and are quite different from the mature and less energetic style of his later field notebooks.

In 1918 he served for a short time with the Army Pay Corps in France during the First World War campaign. Some brief and rather disjointed accounts of his experiences during his time in France are preserved in the National Library of Ireland. On his return he became gradually sympathetic towards the Irish nationalist cause (Ó Broin 1985, 197–8). Known throughout his youth as Willie, he now called himself Liam. During the War of Independence he practised in the underground courts held by the Dáil Department of Home Affairs, and after the foundation of the State he was appointed a District Justice, serving initially in Mullingar and Kilkenny. From 1924 until his retirement in 1960 he served almost exclusively in Wicklow.

In 1923 Price met Dorothy Stopford, a medical doctor and a niece of the eminent historian Alice Stopford-Green who, shortly before, had been the first candidate elected to the Senate by the Dáil. Dorothy herself had been an active supporter of Sinn Féin and, unlike her aunt, had taken sides against the Treaty. During the Civil War, Dorothy served as a doctor in Cork to the men of the Third Brigade who had turned their arms against the Provisional Government. Therefore, despite their common Protestant background, Dorothy and Liam's political outlooks were quite different. Even so, from an early stage they appear to have agreed to differ, and did

Group photo of Liam Price and a delegation of the Royal Society of Antiquaries of Ireland during its centenary celebration (7/7/1949) (courtesy of the Royal Society of Antiquaries of Ireland ©).

not allow such matters to create a division between them. They both had an interest in walking in the Wicklow and Dublin mountains, and Dorothy had a particular interest in fishing. One day during the autumn of 1924 at Luggala, near Roundwood in County Wicklow, they decided to get married, and hurried to her family home at Old Connaught near Bray to break the news. A few days before their wedding Dorothy was presented with a gold watch by Denis Lordan as a token of affection from the men of the Third Brigade in Cork. The day before the wedding, while visiting her aunt Alice Stopford-Green, all her purchases for the wedding and honeymoon were stolen from her car. Alice had everything replaced. On 8 January 1925 Liam and Dorothy were married at St Ann's Church, Dublin (Ó Broin 1985, 199).

An accident during his time at Aldenham Public School had left Liam with a limp for much of his early life. Dorothy now convinced him that a hip operation would relieve some of the discomfort. However, he continued to suffer from a slight limp and to use a walking stick, which was frequently employed as a scale in the photographs and sketches that accompany his field notebooks. Dorothy also introduced Liam to Robert Barton, who later lived at Glendalough House and who was to become an important informant regarding the archaeology and placenames of the area.

In 1924 Dorothy became a visiting physician at St Ultan's Hospital for Children in Dublin. It was during this time that she took a particular interest in the fight against tuberculosis (TB) in children. She learned German and read much German literature on the subject, and from this prepared a thesis on the Continental theories and practices of diagnosis for the disease in children. She also worked as a consultant physician to several other hospitals. In 1937 Dorothy began to write a book on the forms of TB that affected children, entitled *Tuberculosis in children.* The workload was beginning to take its toll on her health, and in 1939 she suffered an attack of muscular rheumatism, which would affect her periodically thereafter. Despite this, she completed her book, and continued to lecture and publish widely. In October 1946 she read a paper at the inaugural meeting of the Irish Tuberculosis Society. Soon after, with the appointment of Noel Browne as Minister for Health, many of the measures she had been advocating were finally adopted. Browne appointed Dorothy as chair of a Consultative Council on TB, and later she was appointed chair of the Central Committee (Ó Broin 1985). The strain of her dedication to the fight against TB eventually caused Dorothy to suffer a stroke in January 1950. This resulted in a partial paralysis and a temporary loss of speech. Throughout Price's correspondence during this time, many of his friends and colleagues asked about the health of his wife. In a reply to one such query made by Michael Duignan, Professor of Celtic Archaeology at University College, Galway (preserved in his papers in the Placenames Branch), Price wrote:

'Thanks for your enquiries about Dorothy; she is fairly well, but not able to move about much; maybe if the weather improved things might be better'.

In 1954 she suffered a second, fatal stroke, and three years later Liam himself published *Dr Dorothy Price; an account of 20 years fighting against TB,* for private and personal circulation. It was described by Surgeon William Doolin as 'a sad but exquisite memoir' (Ó Broin 1985, 225).

Mr Jenkinson from Ballard (from notebook 11 but not mentioned in text).

The diaries of Signe Toksvig, the Danish-born wife of the writer Francis Hackett, provide rare glimpses into the personalities of Liam and Dorothy Price. Following a visit to their home on 11 October 1932, Toksvig wrote: 'Price so straight-forward and shyly sweet and she herself well in hand, was a good hostess' (Pihl 1994, 213).

Price's working career was spent as a District Justice. However, as Joseph Raftery noted:

'his side interests took precedence over his formal work, so that, in the minds of his contemporaries, he appeared to be a scholar of note whose hobby was the law' (obituary, Annual Report of the Royal Irish Academy, 1966–7).

He had an inexhaustible passion for local archaeology, history, folklore and placenames. He was not a fluent Irish-speaker but he acquired a good knowledge of the language (Ó Broin 1985, 201). His research was focused principally on County Wicklow, but his influence at a national level cannot be underestimated. He served on the National Monuments Advisory Council, helping to preserve a large number of archaeological sites, and his participation on the Archaeological Exploration Committee of the Royal Irish Academy influenced much research through archaeological excavation. In some cases his influence was quite specific: in the report describing the excavations at Drimnagh, Co. Dublin, the excavator wrote that 'District Justice Liam Price kindly secured protection for the site' (Kilbride-Jones 1939, 191). It seems that Price may have used his influence as a District Justice to ensure a Garda presence at the site during the excavations. This would also appear to have been the case during the excavations at Ballybrew near Enniskerry. His archaeological excavation, undertaken with Harold Leask, at Labbacallee wedge tomb in County Cork was the first to take advantage of a scheme introduced in 1934 whereby government funds were provided for excavations in areas of unemployment (Herity and Eogan 1977, 14). This was also one of the first Irish excavations to follow the standards set by the contemporary Harvard Archaeological Mission to Ireland. Indeed, Price appears, along with Adolf Mahr (then Director of the National Museum of Ireland), to have been an instrumental figure in the establishment of the Harvard Archaeological

Price (far right, sitting on railing) and unidentified group at Glen of Imaal (courtesy of the Placenames Branch ©).

Mission to Ireland. In January 1944 he was appointed government representative on the Board of Visitors of the National Museum of Ireland. Later Price argued that it was important to 'encourage scientific excavations, not necessarily at sites of the first importance', and added that 'every such excavation should be fully reported; if the results are not recorded, the work is in fact not excavation, but destruction, like that done by the treasure seekers of the past' (Price 1950, 8).

Outside archaeology and history, as a member of the Folklore Commission since its foundation Price encouraged the documentation of oral folk traditions. He was also a patron of the Irish Placenames Commission from 1951 until his death. Perhaps Price is best remembered for his outstanding work on the placenames of County Wicklow. Following his publication of the placenames of the barony of Arklow in volume 46C of the *Proceedings of the Royal Irish Academy*, T.F. O'Rahilly wrote to Price proposing to him that he should publish his research into Wicklow placenames in book form for the Dublin Institute for Advanced Studies. In his letter (dated 21/3/1941 and preserved in Price's papers in the Placenames Branch) O'Rahilly wrote 'I regard your work as a model of its kind'. *The placenames of County Wicklow* was published by the Dublin

Institute for Advanced Studies in seven volumes (1945–67). Following publication of the second volume Michael Duignan wrote:

'What labour, care and patience and skill you have brought to your task' (letter dated 29/1/1947, in the archives of the Irish Placenames Branch).

Price's expertise in Irish placenames was no doubt invaluable in his compilation of an index to accompany the publication of Archbishop Alen's Register (McNeill 1950). Elsewhere he often combined his placename skills with his broader interest in local history, reflected by several important articles on the history of County Wicklow (for example see Price 1949). Realising the importance of local historical studies as a means towards exploring history at a national level, he wrote:

'Do not underrate the value of local history. It can make contributions to every branch of history' (1950, 17).

Leon Ó Broin (1985, 200–1) provides an interesting portrayal of Price during this period:

'Liam was a good-looking man but at first sight somewhat forbidding, which was perhaps the appearance he presented on the bench. He could be gruff, even testy at times, and as a District Justice he was known to have certain prejudices. He was unbending in the matter of getting extension for late night dances which would have meant increased facilities for drink, and he was said to be "hard" in the matter of driving offences. There was an amusing aspect of this, if true, because he was a very fast and rather alarming driver himself, so that when in the car with him, Dorothy was understandably critical. Going through his district alone, his mind was as often as not on something other than the road before him. He was interested in so many things. He might be worrying about a Court case, of course, or the derivation of a placename, or seeking the solution of some conundrum or other he had encountered in the antiquarian field'.

Liam Price and Frank Byrne (pointing with walking stick) (from notebook 23).

Price was elected a member of the Royal Irish Academy in 1933, and subsequently served on the Council for the periods 1940–2, 1946–7, 1955–8 and 1960 4. He also served as Vice-President in 1957–8 and 1960–3. Price appropriately received an honorary degree (D.Litt.) from the National University of Ireland in recognition of his academic contributions.

In 1926 Price was elected a member of the Royal Society of Antiquaries of Ireland, and in 1931 he was first elected to the Council of the Society. From 1949 to 1952 he served as President of the Society, and it is perhaps fitting that he began his term of office during the Society's centenary year. He fully realised the honour of the occasion (Price 1950, 1). At the end of his term and in response to a letter from the then Honorary General Secretary of the Society, A.T. Lucas, complimenting and thanking him for his work as President, Price concluded that:

'Like you, I think the Society is a body worth working for. That is what makes it so gratifying to get such appreciation from you . . . There are plenty of things to discourage us these days, but we will go on working in spite of them' (letter dated 25 January 1953, in the archives of the Royal Society of Antiquaries of Ireland).

Portrait of Liam Price (aged 6), his younger sister (aged 4) and their mother Katie (courtesy of the National Library of Ireland ©).

George Roberts Price (Liam Price papers in the manuscript collection of the National Library of Ireland ©).

Dr Dorothy Stopford Price (National Photographic Archive, Liam Price Collection, album 304, courtesy of the National Library of Ireland ©).

Liam Price in military uniform, April 1917 (National Photographic Archive, Liam Price Collection, album 304, courtesy of the National Library of Ireland ©).

Liam Price on a motorbike at Chester, 1923 (courtesy of the National Library of Ireland ©).

Liam Price and Canon T.E. Young at Aghowle Mountain, 4/7/1933 (courtesy of the Royal Society of Antiquaries of Ireland ©).

Liam Price and a local garda during the excavation of cist 2 at Ballybrew, 28 September 1935 (photographer not indicated, possibly G.F. Mitchell, courtesy of the Royal Society of Antiquaries of Ireland ©).

*Liam Price and then Taoiseach John A. Cosgrove at a reception at Áras an Uachtaráin
to mark the centenary of the Royal Society of Antiquaries of Ireland, 9/7/1949
(courtesy of the Royal Society of Antiquaries of Ireland ©).*

Price was also honorary editor of the Society's journal for 1935–43 and 1957–63. The diversity of his interests and research is highlighted by the impressive range of topics featured in his own articles and notes, which appeared frequently in the journal, and also in the *Proceedings of the Royal Irish Academy*. His notebooks contain much information gathered in the field, which he subsequently used in his articles. Volume 95 of the *Journal of the Royal Society of Antiquaries of Ireland* was dedicated to Price, and in the introduction his friend A. T. Lucas wrote that wherever

'there was good to be done by counsel, persuasion, diplomacy and, above all, by work, he has been there to do it, but so successful has he been in doing good by stealth that even his closest friends hardly realize how pervasive has been his influence'.

Lucas added that Price was

'the most modest of men, abhorring vanity, pomposity and humbug but, though he will deny it, suffering fools gladly for the sake of whatever good there is in them'.

Price's humble reaction to this honour is recorded in his own words in a letter (dated 8 December 1965 and preserved in his papers held in the RSAI) to Helen Roe, then President of the Society:

'It was really quite a shock to me when you presented this special volume to me last night. I had already expressed my gratitude for the honour of having my name associated with a special number of the journal, which really I cannot feel I have altogether deserved, and now I feel rather overwhelmed by this. Well, I am sincerely grateful to you, and I must ask you to express my thanks to the Council. You spoke in too flattering terms last night. There is nothing now but to retire as gracefully as possible, after having read my obituary notice. Something will have to be done to make sure that in future the honour falls on more deserving shoulders.
Yours sincerely,
Liam Price.'

Price died on 23 January 1967. In an obituary Eamonn de hÓir (1968), then Chief Placenames Officer in the Placenames Branch, wrote:

'He was kindly, considerate and hospitable, and was always willing to help others from his own store of knowledge, often going to considerable trouble to do so'.

To these words may be added those from an obituary written by Joseph Raftery:

'He was a man of fantastic modesty, and any form of public notice was anathema to him. He was also a shy man and his efforts to combat this gave him sometimes an air of impatience. He was, however, one of the kindest of men, ever helpful to others and especially to the young. His many unobtrusive acts of goodness will live after him, as he would himself have wished, as private monuments to a man of charity' (Annual Report of the Royal Irish Academy, 1966–7).

The obituary published in the *Journal of the County Kildare Archaeological Society* claimed rightly that

'his passing is not only a loss to our Society, but to the many other Societies of which he was a member' (Anon. 1966/7).

On his death, Price's collection of books was donated at his request to the Royal Society of Antiquaries of Ireland. The collection was so extensive that it had to go into storage, where it was tragically destroyed in a fire on 16 August 1970. According to his will, Price also bequeathed his notebooks, papers and maps to the Royal Society of Antiquaries of Ireland with the request that the Society should hand over to the Public Record Office any such documents as would be considered appropriately held by that office. The records are incomplete, but it seems that the Society decided to donate the notebooks and other papers to the Dublin Institute for Advanced Studies. Shortly afterwards, in early 1968, these were donated by the Institute to the Placenames Branch (currently part of the Department of Community, Rural Affairs and the Gaeltacht), where they are presently housed. This material mainly consists of information collected by Price for the Institute in relation to the placenames of counties Wicklow, Carlow, Kildare, Laois and Offaly. The rest of the Price material held by the Placenames Branch consists of extensive correspondence and manuscripts of collected notes and transcriptions from published and primary sources, and field notes of work carried out in west Mayo in August 1942. Also amongst the material is an important album containing photographs (and their negatives) taken by his sister Kathleen of farmhouses, bridges and landscape scenes of the area covered by the Poulaphuca reservoir scheme. Some of his papers, including some correspondence, photographs and annotated offprints of his own articles, are presently held in the collections of the Royal Society of Antiquaries of Ireland.

Price was frequently accompanied in the field by well-known professional and amateur archaeologists and folklorists, in particular Diarmuid Coffey (best man at his wedding), Harold Leask, Robert C. Barton, Anthony Farrington, Françoise Henry, Patrick Walshe, Seamas Delargy and Edward M. Stephens, as well as Edward O'Toole, Rev. T.E. Young, R.A.S. Macalister, Adolf Mahr, Liam Ua Bróin, Dr E. Flenry, J.B. Malone, Ruaidhrí de Valera, C. Ó Danacháir, Henry Wheeler and Paddy Healy. However, many of his visits were carried out alone, especially on his return from a morning session at the various courtrooms around County Wicklow. Indeed, he frequently used the courtrooms themselves as an opportunity to glean information, occasionally being presented with artefacts or questioning clerks and even defendants as to the pronunciation of a placename. In a letter to Price (dated 9 October 1951 and preserved in his papers held in the Royal Society of Antiquaries of Ireland), Gerald Murphy made the amusing comment:

> 'Would that more legal men spent their free time as you do. You deserve well from the people of Ireland, protecting them by day from drunken motorists in Bray, and by night protecting us from falling into error about our past history'.

Price used a car to drive to and from the various courts, at a time when cars were still luxury items. Indeed, it was about this time that the landscape of Ireland became more accessible than ever before, as a result of the increasing use of the car and the improvement of roads. This gave Price and his contemporaries an advantage over their predecessors in that they had easy access to all parts of the countryside to carry out their fieldwork. Price appears to have recognised the changing face of Irish roads; in several instances he described in his notebooks the condition of roads in Wicklow, and sometimes discussed their potential origins.

Liam Price lived and worked at a time when there were very few full-time archaeologists or historians working in this country, and it is in this context that the value of his extensive research reveals itself. He had quite a methodical approach to site inspections, arguably advanced for its time, and he was capable of analysing archaeological sites of all periods. Effectively, Liam Price single-handedly achieved a comprehensive archaeological survey of County Wicklow. This was acknowledged in his own lifetime by his friend Harold Leask, who wrote that the Archaeological Survey of Ireland (then under the auspices of the Office of Public Works) was indebted to his 'monumental survey of Co. Wicklow and parts of Kildare', the information from which he freely contributed to the survey (Leask 1942, 13). Price felt that in advance of widespread research excavation it was necessary to carry out a large-scale archaeological survey. He argued that the Archaeological Survey of Ireland was 'a task of national importance, not only for ourselves but for the history of all Western Europe' (1950, 7).

The Field Notebooks also contain accounts of several archaeological excavations in which he was involved, including those in 1932 at the passage tomb at Seefin, Co. Wicklow (Macalister 1932). There is a brief account of an investigation of a cairn on the northern shoulder of the Great Sugar Loaf in May 1933, in the company of Farrington, Walshe and Coffey. This is the only record that an investigation took place at this site. Price also provides a useful description of the passage tomb on the summit of Baltinglass Hill in November 1931, before the excavation and subsequent reconstitution of the site (Walshe 1941).

Price visited many of these sites over 60 years ago, at a time when the social and even the physical landscapes of County Wicklow were quite different. He also recorded a considerable amount of local folklore, history and placenames that would otherwise have been lost with the death of older generations, and several archaeological sites which he visited have since been destroyed. The Field Notebooks contain much information that he used in the publication of *The placenames of County Wicklow*. He often recorded the names of fields and other local names in an area, and he paid particular attention to pronunciation. His notebooks record his opinion of the work of John O'Donovan for the Ordnance Survey in 1838 and 1839. O'Donovan's fieldwork (Corlett and Medlycott 2001) was the most intensive carried out in the county until Price's research nearly a century later. Price was dismissive of his predecessor:

> 'It is a great misfortune for the historian that O'Donovan was sent to investigate the antiquities of this area' (see notebook 23, entry dated 15 August 1949).

During four decades very few archaeological sites or placenames in County Wicklow escaped his gaze, and he concentrated much of his effort on many of the lesser-known sites, as well as searching for previously unrecorded monuments. An independent account of one of Price's site visits is recorded in the diaries of Signe Toksvig. On 17 April 1932, 'Liam Price and Mrs P. came early p.m. to take us to Ballyvolan Fort. We did go. F[rances] and she picked primroses and talked politics behind a gorse bush while he and I scrambled over indeterminate earth-works and rubble-heaps and wondered were they round or angular and was the masonry Norman or pre-. He took photos with my camera' (Pihl 1994, 172).

I would argue that no other county in Ireland owes so much to one person for the recording of its local heritage. The enormous contribution made by Liam Price to the study of Wicklow's local heritage was not fully realised in his own lifetime. This publication of his Field Notebooks complements a similar contribution of his own, *An eighteenth century antiquary, the sketches, notes and diaries of Austin Cooper (1759–1830)*, published in 1942. Price's Field Notebooks illustrate the range and extent of his research behind the scenes, and I sincerely hope that this publication will prove a fitting tribute to and acknowledgement of the energies, commitment and achievements of one man.

Christiaan Corlett
February 2002

THE FIELD NOTEBOOKS

The Field Notebooks presented here were originally held in the National Museum of Ireland, and were later given to the National Monuments and Architectural Protection Division during the compilation of the Sites and Monuments Record for County Wicklow by the Archaeological Survey of Ireland. It is not recorded how they came into the possession of the National Museum of Ireland, though it seems likely that they originally formed part of the Price manuscript material that was given in 1968 to the Placenames Branch. It has been suggested (Dónall Mac Giolla Easpaig, pers. comm.) that Pat Nyhan, who then worked for the Placenames Branch and who had previously worked for the National Museum of Ireland, may have removed all material that he considered to be of an archaeological nature and donated it to the Museum.

The Field Notebooks consist of 28 blue, bound notebooks, containing entries that span the years 1928 to 1966 — the year before Price's death. It is not known when or by whom the notebooks were bound, though it is possible that it was done by Pat Nyhan. They are small, ledger-style notebooks of various sizes, ranging between 10.6cm and 12.5cm in width and between 16.2cm and 18.7cm in height. There are on average 40 sheets of paper in each notebook, though in some cases pages have been removed, probably by Price himself. Notebook 26 is significantly larger and consists of 84 sheets.

These are the notebooks in which Price recorded, in his own elegant handwriting, the information he gleaned from site visits and from talking to local people in County Wicklow. Price also made several excursions into parts of neighbouring counties Wexford, Carlow, Kildare and Dublin. In several instances there are notes taken from published sources during his research, but it has been decided to omit these transcriptions and to concentrate on the publication of the information he acquired in the field. For this reason notebooks 5, 6 and 7, which consist of notes taken from Sweetman's *Calender of documents relating to Ireland*, have been entirely omitted. Price's earliest entries, in notebooks 1 to 4, are quite brief. From notebook 8 onwards his accounts of site visits become more comprehensive, providing invaluable descriptions of archaeological sites as they existed over half a century ago. As well as local folklore, he made every attempt to record local placenames. His notebook entries are predominantly in chronological order, although he sometimes added information to earlier entries after revisiting sites later. Occasionally the precise date of the entry was not fully recorded, and notebook 13 appears to represent a rather haphazard collection of notes made between 1933 and 1934. All the notebooks were used fully except notebook 28, which was only partially used. Indeed, this notebook is unusual in that it contains notes made by Dorothy Price in 1949. Some years later Liam made his own entries at the rear of this notebook.

The following is a list of the notebooks:

Field Notebook 1 — March–August 1928

Field Notebook 2 — August 1928–April 1929

Field Notebook 3 — April–July 1929

Field Notebook 4 — July–December 1929

Field Notebook 5 — notes from Sweetman's *Calender of documents relating to Ireland*

Field Notebook 6 — notes from Sweetman's *Calender of documents relating to Ireland*

Field Notebook 7 — notes from Sweetman's *Calender of documents relating to Ireland*

Field Notebook 8 — January–June 1930

Field Notebook 9 — May–August 1930

Field Notebook 10 — August 1930–February 1932

Field Notebook 11 — February–October 1932

Field Notebook 12 — December 1932–January 1934

Field Notebook 13 — 1933

Field Notebook 14 — February–September 1934 [includes entries up to September 1935]

Field Notebook 15 — February–December 1936

Field Notebook 16 — January 1937–April 1938

Field Notebook 17 — April 1938–1939

Field Notebook 18 — April 1939–November 1940

Field Notebook 19 — July 1941–September 1945

Field Notebook 20 — August 1942–April 1945

Field Notebook 21 — June 1945–November 1946

Field Notebook 22 — April–August 1947

Field Notebook 23 — September 1947–December 1949

Field Notebook 24 — April 1950–September 1952
Field Notebook 25 — January–December 1953
Field Notebook 26 — July 1954–January 1959
Field Notebook 27 — March 1959–July 1961
Field Notebook 28 — 1961–1966

PHOTOGRAPHS AND SKETCHES

The sketches and photographs published here are included in the notebooks; however, several additional photographs are reproduced here courtesy of the Royal Society of Antiquaries of Ireland and form part of a collection of Liam Price's papers. Others are from lantern slides that form part of the Photographic Collection of the Royal Society of Antiquaries of Ireland and appear to have been commissioned by Price and donated by him to the Society for use in illustrating lectures. Price's own photographs in this collection are easily distinguishable by the walking stick he used as a scale. Further photographs have been provided courtesy of the Photographic Section of Dúchas The Heritage Service. These are contemporary with Price, and some were clearly taken by Harold Leask, Inspector of National Monuments, then under the auspices of the Office of Public Works, who sometimes accompanied Price on his site visits.

ACKNOWLEDGEMENTS

The editors would like to take this opportunity to thank Geraldine Stout for bringing to their attention the need for the field notebooks of Liam Price to be published, and we are indebted to David Sweetman for providing the necessary access to these notebooks in order to prepare them for publication. Many thanks also to the Council of the Royal Society of Antiquaries of Ireland for permission to use the Liam Price photographs in their possession, and to John Scarry of the Photographic Unit of Dúchas. Sincere thanks also to Sara Smith of the National Photographic Archive, Noel Kissane of the National Library of Ireland and Dónall Mac Giolla Easpaig of the Placenames Branch for their invaluable assistance and permission to reproduce the photographs from their collections. We are indebted to Con Manning, Siobhan de hÓir, Pamela Bradley, Tom Condit, Mary Tunney and Celine Walsh for their help, and a very special thanks to Alison Bray and Finbarr Bastible.

EDITORIAL NOTE

In order to present the Liam Price notebooks in a format suitable for publication while retaining the diary-like qualities of the entries, a number of editorial changes were made. At the same time to preserve the integrity of the notebooks a house-style was not rigidly imposed.

Little alteration was made to the text of the notebooks. For the most part, what is published here has been transcribed word for word from the original entries. Where necessary, editorial additions have been inserted in square brackets to provide clarification or additional information. In the majority of entries Price's punctuation has not been altered, although spelling mistakes have not been retained.

The spelling of placenames varies throughout the original notebooks, and we have sought here to standardise these in accordance with the index of Price's work *The placenames of County Wicklow* (1967). Where there is doubt about the correct spelling of a name the alternative has been inserted in square brackets after the spelling used in the notebook. Where the text was difficult to read an ellipsis has been inserted. For the most part abbreviations have not been retained, except for points of the compass.

Price was very interested in placenames and often sought to reproduce their pronunciation. He used the symbol • to indicate stress on a syllable, and quite often spelled placenames phonetically. These have also been retained.

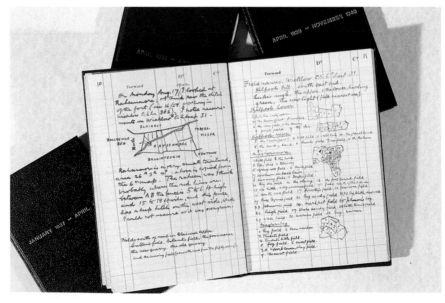

Liam Price Notebooks (photo: John Scarry, Dúchas The Heritage Service).

REFERENCES

JRSAI	*Journal of the Royal Society of Antiquaries of Ireland*
PRIA	*Proceedings of the Royal Irish Academy*
JKAS	*Journal of the County Kildare Archaeological Society*
NMAJ	*North Munster Antiquarian Journal*

Anon. (1966/7) 'Obituaries', *JKAS* **14**, 2.

Corlett, C. and Medlycott, J. (eds) (2001) *The Ordnance Survey Letters — Wicklow*. Roundwood and District Historical and Folklore Society, Wicklow Archaeological Society and Kestral Books.

de hÓir, E. (1968) 'Liam Price', *Onoma* **12** (1966/7), 2–3.

Herity, M. and Eogan, G. (1977) *Ireland in prehistory*. Routledge, London.

Kilbride-Jones, H.E. (1939) 'The excavation of a composite tumulus at Drimnagh, Co. Dublin', *JRSAI* **69**, 120–220.

Leask, H.G. (1942) 'The Archaeological Survey', *JRSAI* **72**, 1–13.

Macalister, R.A.S. (1932) 'A burial carn on Seefin Mountain, Co. Wicklow', *JRSAI* **62**, 153–7.

McNeill, C. (1950) *Calender of Archbishop Alen's Register c. 1172–1534*. Royal Society of Antiquaries of Ireland, Dublin.

Ó Broin, L. (1985) *Protestant nationalists in revolutionary Ireland: the Stopford Connection*. Gill and MacMillan, Dublin.

Pihl, L. (ed.) (1994) *Signe Toksvig's Irish diaries 1926–1937*. The Lilliput Press, Dublin.

Walshe, P.T. (1941) 'The excavation of a burial cairn on Baltinglass Hill, Co. Wicklow', *PRIA* **46**C, 221–36.

Notes and articles by Liam Price published in various academic and local journals

Martin, C.P., Price, L. and Mitchell, G.F. (1935–7) 'On two short cist interments found at Ballybrew, Co. Wicklow', *PRIA* **43**C, 255–70.

Price, L. (1929) 'Note on a rude stone monument at Lackan, Co. Wicklow', *JRSAI* **59**, 68–9.

— (1929) 'Kilcrony church', *JRSAI* **59**, 179–81.

— (1930–3) 'Notes on Feagh McHugh O'Byrne', *JCKAS* **11**, 134–75.

— (1931) 'The Hearth Money Roll for Co. Wicklow', *JRSAI* **61**, 164–78.

— (1932) 'Armed forces of the Irish chiefs in the early 16th century', *JRSAI* **62**, 201–7.

— (1933) 'The Byrnes' Country in County Wicklow in the sixteenth century', *JRSAI* **63**, 224–42.

— (1934) 'The Ages of stone and bronze in County Wicklow', *PRIA* **42C**, 31–64.

— (1935) 'Cremated burial found near Enniskerry, Co. Wicklow', *JRSAI* **65**, 325–7.

— (1935) 'Cist burial at Kenny Court, Co. Kildare', *JRSAI* **65**, 327–9.

— (1935–45) 'Antiquities of Burgage and district', *JCKAS* **12**, 197–9.

— (1936) 'The Byrnes' Country in County Wicklow in the 16th century and the Manor of Arklow', *JRSAI* **66**, 41–66.

— (1936–9) 'The need for a study of Irish place names', *NMAJ* **1**, 29–33.

— (1937) 'The placenames of the Barony of Newcastle, County Wicklow', *PRIA* **44C**, 139–80.

— (1938) 'Cist burials in Co. Kildare', *JRSAI* **68**, 293–4.

— (1938) 'Early Irish silver brooch from Co. Wicklow', *JRSAI* **68**, 145.

— (1938) 'Cist burial at Calary Lower, Kilmacanoge, Co. Wicklow', *JRSAI* **68**, 157–9.

— (1938) 'Flat copper axes at Monastery, Co. Wicklow', *JRSAI* **68**, 305–6.

— (1939) 'Find of flat copper axes at Monastery, Co. Wicklow', *JRSAI* **69**, 50.

— (1940) 'Glendalough: St Kevin's Road', in J. Ryan (ed.), *Féil-sgríbhinn Eóin Mhic Néill, Essays and studies presented to Professor Eoin MacNeill*, 244–71. Three Candles, Dublin.

— (1940) 'The antiquities and place names of south Dublin', *Dublin Historical Record* **2** (4), 121–33.

— (1941) 'Glencolumbkille, Co. Donegal, and its Early Christian cross-slabs', *JRSAI* **71**, 71–88.

— (1941) 'Two bog finds from Co. Wicklow', *JRSAI* **71**, 151–2.

— (1941) 'The placenames of the Barony of Arklow, County of Wicklow', *PRIA* **46C**, 237–86.

— (1941) 'Some unrecorded local placenames in Co. Mayo', *JRSAI* **73**, 74–6.

— (1943) 'Phelim McFeagh O'Byrne and the lands of Ranelagh', *JRSAI* **73**, 50–9.

— (1943) 'Encrusted urn from Agower, Co. Wicklow', *JRSAI* **73**, 152.

— (1944) 'The Manor Bothercolyn', *JRSAI* **74**, 107–18.

— (1945) 'St Broghan's Road, Clonas', *JRSAI* **75**, 56.

— (1945) 'An old graveyard at Ballagh, Co. Wicklow', *JRSAI* **75**, 257.

— (1949) 'Place-name study as applied to history', *JRSAI* **79**, 26–38.

— (1950) 'Four thousand years of Irish history', *JRSAI* **80**, 1–21.

— (1950) 'A Roman coin find at Churchtown, Co. Dublin', *JRSAI* **80**, 97.

— (1950) 'The history of Lagore, from the annals and other sources', in H. O'N. Hencken, 'Lagore crannog: an Irish royal residence of the 7th to 10th centuries A.D', 18–34. *PRIA* **53**C, 1–247.

— (1951) 'The place-names of the Book of Survey and Distribution, and the other records of the Cromwellian settlement', *JRSAI* **81**, 89–106.

— (1952) 'Sweathouse, Co. Wicklow', *JRSAI* **82**, 89–106.

— (1953) 'Bodenstown, Co. Kildare', *JRSAI* **83**, 200–1.

— (1953) 'Powerscourt and the territory of Fercullen', *JRSAI* **83**, 117–32.

— (1954) 'The grant to Walter de Ridelesford of Brien and the lands of the Sons of Turchill', *JRSAI* **84**, 72–7.

— (1956) 'The Barony of Shillelagh', *JRSAI* **86**, 77–83.

— (1958) 'On the distribution of place-names beginning with Dun-, Lis-, and Rath-', *JRSAI* **88**, 83–4.

— (1959) 'Rock-basins, or "bullauns", at Glendalough and elsewhere', *JRSAI* **89**, 161–88.

— (1959) 'Sculptured cross-base at Oldcourt, near Bray, Co. Wicklow', *JRSAI* **89**, 97.

— (1960) 'The name Dublin', *JRSAI* **90**, 89.

— (1963) 'A note on the use of the word *Baile* in place-names', *Celtica* **6**, 119–26.

— (1964–5) 'Pronunciation of Derry- in Co. Kildare', *Dinnseanchas* **1**, 21.

— (1964–5) 'Liss na Calligi', *Dinnseanchas* **1**, 94–5.

— (1968–9) 'Belach Feile', *Dinnseanchas* **3**, 6–11.

Price, L. and Leask, H.G. (1936) 'The Labbacallee megalith, Co. Cork', *PRIA* **43**C, 77–101.

Price, L. and Mahr, A. (1932) 'Excavation of urn burials at Clonshannon, Imaal, Co. Wicklow', *JRSAI* **62**, 75–90.

Price, L. and Stephens, E.M. (1948) 'Bullaun stones near Derrylossary Church, Co. Wicklow', *JRSAI* **78**, 179–81.

The Price notebooks

Price, L. and Walshe, P.T. (1933) 'The stone and bronze antiquities of the Barony of Lower Talbotstown, Co. Wicklow; with a description of the excavation at Haylands Mote, near Blessington', *JRSAI* **63**, 46–67.

FIELD NOTEBOOK 1:
March–August 1928

26th March 1928

At Dunlavin Court examined Tubber old graveyard, fairly recently walled. No sign of a church. I did not see the ogham stone. The large mound appears to have been shaped artificially: it rises in terraces and at the top is a circular platform (grass) about 7 or 8yds in diameter. On the NW side it is most easily approachable, there being only three terraces there. The old ruined house looks as though it dated from late 18th century — there is a long shallow reservoir at the bottom, with place for a sluice, or a water wheel? A fish pond?

There is a field in Knockpatrick which goes by the name of 'Glownshod', the scene it is said of a battle ages ago, article by Lord Walter Fitzgerald.

March 1928

Mongnacool. Cloneen, the house above the dolmen [called] 'the Fairy House' — occupied by Peter Byrne — husband of [a] sister of Mr Justice O'Byrne. There are said to be ghosts about the place, and it is supposed to be unlucky. Peter Byrne bought it on his marriage: his wife is from Kilquiggin (from Dr O'Brien sister of Mrs Fogarty of Aughrim).

11th April 1928

Knockaulin. Two small boulders on the top. The rock shows signs of having been quarried. The view extends along the Wicklow Mountains, Mount Leinster, Blackstairs, Slieve na Mon, Slieve Ardagh Hills (or Devil's Bit?), Slieve Margy, Dunamase, Slieve Bloom, and the Plains of Meath and Dublin.

24th April 1928

Looking for St Bridget's Headstone and Chair. Mrs Wynne (house immediately N of Spinans Bridge) said there was also St Bridget's Well near by at 'Poulnageer' (spelt phonetically). I went into fields behind a galvanized-iron shed not far from Spinans Bridge to SE saw a small standing stone, somewhat pointed — about 3ft high and 1ft wide. This is more like a cattle scratching stone than a stone monument, but it has an old appearance.

I also saw in Cloghnagaune a flagstone surrounded by medium-sized stones round ⅔ of its circumference. The centre one of the surrounding stones has a cross engraved on it by chiselling out the outline of the cross leaving it in relief. A Latin cross about 1ft in length and 8in. in width.

I did not find Poulnageer. Note — the townland Kill is pronounced 'Kyle': presumably 'Coill'.

20th May 1928

Visited Kilranelagh Churchyard. St Bridget's Well inside the churchyard. Not ruined but neglected — overgrown with weeds, and the recesses among the stones at the back of the well hidden by weeds and earth, and empty. The back is built up, in the shape of a half-cylinder, about 6ft from the water.

The wall round the churchyard is a low drystone fence, overgrown and undisturbed: no appearance of fresh stones thrown on it — but round single graves, or groups of graves, are quite fresh lines of stones, about as big as could be comfortably carried in one hand, in rectangles, sometimes 8ft or 10ft square. Nothing else noticeable. The churchyard is still used for burials.

The well [is] round, 3ft across, a place of earth to kneel in front of it, and another of stones 3ft further away, a few inches above level of water. See Joyce's *Social History of Ancient Ireland* vol. 2, p.563, for custom of raising a cairn as a burial mound at a grave, by each man bringing a stone and throwing it on the cairn.

3rd June 1928

Visited Dr Fleury near Oldcourt. She said there is a ghost story about a woman being drowned in Cleevaun Lake. Another connected with a gate on the left-hand side of the road leading from Oldcourt to Ballysmuttan, where there is a shortcut to Kilbride School: an independent story says that at a recent funeral the woman being buried was seen standing at this gate. She gave local pronunciations — 'Killibeg' and 'Balla-h-woultha' — she said the latter was the Marquis of Downshire's property and mentioned a man pronouncing 'Luggacullen' with aspirated 'c' — she could not imitate it. ('Lugachulyeen'?) — also 'Kea-j-een'.

Kavanagh's Camp and Kavanagh's Gap — she said a man near there told her Kavanagh was the leader of the Shelmalier men when they came up from Wexford to Wicklow in '98 [1798]. He was the only man who knew anything about it. There is a cross at Burgage: she heard nothing about it but a vague legend that in one night forty crosses sprang up in different places.

She also said that — Murphy, the farmer who owns the house she is in, when the mare foaled on Whitsunday, cut a slit in the skin of the foal's head, and put in a 3*d* bit: Mrs Murphy said it was unlucky to have a foal born at Whitsun, and that this was done to prevent the ill luck.

10th June 1928

Ballyboy. The ruined house in Ballyboy (near Drumgoff) belonged to Mr Crutchley. An old man in Ballybraid dreamed three times (the third time) that there was gold buried in it, and went and dug there; but he dug in the day instead of at night, and he only found wooden coins (or leather buttons): he dug inside the house walls, near the fireplace.

As to 'the Clóghrán', it is there Art O'Neill was buried — it is on the old road to Glendalough, not on the military road: ¼ mile N from the turn to Ballylow, and 100yds from the main road: near Edge's Rock, a pile of stones: the funerals used to stop at it, and men threw a stone on it.

The farmer 400yds from main road on the turn to Ballyboy, on the right just over the little bridge, told me this.

Clonsast, near Clonbullogue — St Brochan's pattern, 24th August.

June 1928

Ballintober near Hollywood. Cross — (shaft broken off from head) of a single piece of granite on Byrne's land, Ballintober, 200yds to the W of the road from Humphrystown to Johnstown, beside Harristown townland. On the hillside, rough grazing land, about 60 or 100yds from a disused quarry. Story that money is buried beneath it, or (Michael Kelly's aunt) in the field at Harristown just over the townland boundary. There is a holy well about 200yds from the cross. Quintagh, Carrigacurra, pronounced 'Cōntă' or 'Cōntī'.

The Wooden Cross (I think) is the fork where the roads from Valleymount to Granabeg and Glenbride join.

24th June 1928

With C. Dixon and D. Coffey at Art O'Neill's Grave. A man named Maguire of Oakwood or Knocknadroose brought them up and showed it to them. He called it 'Prince Art's Grave'. The girl at Farrington's of Knocknadroose called it 'the Prince's Grave'. It is just above where the Glenreemore Brook divides into two, a large rock or small cliff of granite with two faces making a right angle between them, facing the N — up the edge of the flat ground where the two streams join, just before the mountainside rises from the flat — there is a row of stones, five or six across the [angle?], with two larger stones in the place where a headstone would be.

8th August 1928

Knockpatrick. William Whelan of Castledermot took Frank Stephens, myself and Dorothy to see the stone with footmarks. Granite slab, about 5ft x 3ft, said to be part of the natural rock. Flat, 2ft below surface of earth. Two small cuttings in shape of feet at N end; small round hole said to be for staff, at right-hand side, about 1ft away. Latin cross incised also. Feet about 8in. long. A person standing with his feet on the marks would be facing S.

St Patrick [is] supposed to have stood there and preached to the people in front. Whelan also said St Patrick preached to the people from between the two trees in centre of graveyard. The holy well was outside the wall, towards the W, where the wood is. A stream flowed down towards Graney from it: when it was filled up the stream stopped, and the land is boggy since. Whelan said it was a curious place to make a graveyard in, as there is not more than 2 or 3ft of earth over the coffins, the rock is so near the surface. The wall is round the graveyard as long as he remembers. Haddaway closed up the old passway, which was from the S: a man named Brown gave the present passway (from ESE). The coffins are carried from the gate in the field the graveyard is in. Whelan said one of the Haddaways was in the lunatic asylum: he said an old brother and sister of the name [are] living there now, that it was their father closed the well. He said Corballis or Fraughan Hill ('Frŏchăn') (see Joyce vol. 1, p.485) used to have sports held on it, and they have been recently revived: they were on the second and third Sundays in July. He said sports were also held at Belan Gate, by ¼ mile of wall, bowling was one of the sports there. He pointed to mounds in the field E of Graney village, S of the Baltinglass Road, and said that was where Graney village used to be, as far as the tree with a large stone under it.

12th August 1928

Mullinaveige, Roundwood. The ruins of a house on the E side of the old Long Hill Road, among some beech trees, a mile or more from Roundwood, are the remains of the house of Andrew Price, a magistrate and a neighbour of Holt's. Holt's house was in a field, two fields to the S, on the road, opposite to Murphy's of Mullinaveige: nothing of it remains. The hearthstone is used as [a] hearthstone in Murphy's house. Price's house has gradually decayed: Murphy remembers the walls 8 or 10ft high. He said he found and still has a silver spoon with the initials 'A.P.' on it, dug up near the house.

FIELD NOTEBOOK 2:
August 1928–April 1929

21st August 1928

Sketched doorway of ruined church at Killadreenan. At back of door is slot for wooden bolt: a square hole, about 4in. square — on the right-hand side (facing inwards) the slot is more than 3ft deep.

This is the door referred to at p.181 of Petrie's *Round Towers*. See also p.188 for herring-bone masonry: this is still in N wall. Petrie says date is not earlier than 12th century. Small pointed windows in E and S walls, each with arch cut out of one stone, but the windows are covered with ivy, and the archstones appear to be cracked. I saw no other feature of interest: the ruin is greatly overgrown.

Fig. 1—Sketch of doorway of Killadreenan Church.

22nd August 1928

Baltinglass Abbey. W wall and gate, the S line of pillars of nave. Two large circular arches in choir —? the E window (lancets restored with brick) — the sedilia with ogee arches (three) in S wall of choir. Carving on capitals of pillars of nave: alternate square and round pillars. The rest of the buildings seem modern. Date 'AD 1151' carved at W end of pillars (modern figures). Property of Representative Church Body.

Donard. Saw [Broomfield] dolmen on road to Merginstown, in field to N of road. Three stones standing: capstone leaning on them — a large stone flat in ground, outside the lower end of capstone. The inner sides of the uprights very level and flat, with markings as though the granite was flaking off in large unshaped flat plates. The dolmen is in the hedge.

Mr Drury said John Allen 'the post' knows all about the churchyard at Donard. (The tomb there is St Sylvester's.)

4th September 1928

Rathgall. Inner circle, 30ft diameter. Second circle 100ft diameter. Granite blocks [facing?] each face of wall with rubble interior of granite — blocks not cut or shaped, but apparently chosen for their shape, and walls have the faces perpendicular. Ditch between second and third circle, having the appearance of a fosse between two banks. The fourth and outer circle is destroyed in parts: it is an earthen bank, apparently having grown over a bank of stones. Townland Rath. Owned by 'Mr Lauder' ('Lowther'?), his steward Neill works the lands, lives at Rath House: just to the W of the rath. Local people call it 'the Ring'.

Mr Gallagher, County Surveyor, says that there were arched passages 8ft high in these stone rings, but that they were broken down and the stones taken away in the past 25 years by local people. Mr Lowther stopped this at the instigation of Canon French of Ferns.

He also told me (6th September 1928) that Octavius Braddell of Ballingate near Carnew, an old man, since dead, had collected a lot of information about Wicklow and had intended to write a history of the county with Lane Poole, who used to stay near Ballinacarrig. Where are Braddell's papers? O. Braddell said that iron ore used to be imported from Wales in the 16th century at Jack's Hole, and brought by a pack road to Clash, where it was smelted with charcoal from the oak woods at

Fig. 2—Interior of Ring of the Rath (Rathgall hillfort). On the back of the photos it is indicated that they were taken by Robert Barton and were developed in July 1959.

Shillelagh, and that the smelting-pits still could be traced — he (Gallagher) had seen the line of the old pier, near Hughes' house, when the sand was blown away.

Gallagher said he had seen old presentments in a private house, which had since disappeared — one by La Touche and Lord Meath to build a bridge at Delgany, for £300, about 1800.

He said the Drumgoff–Leitrim Road was in ruin before his time in the county. Referred me to Skinner's Maps made about 1760 by order of the Irish Parliament.

He has no old papers in his office referring to the building of the roads in the Grand Jury days. He says they were sent to the Record Office.

Who were George Francis Savage Armstrong and Edmund F. Armstrong (his father)? The former wrote *Stories of Wicklow* (bad poems) and the latter included stories of Wicklow in his poetical works. *Stories of Wicklow* (p.292), 'De Riddlesford's Castle beside a "lakelet" under Little Sugarloaf'. Where is this?

10th September 1928
Killelan 'Church' near Davidstown, Co. Kildare. Met Mr William G. Doyle, National Teacher of Moone, member of the Kildare Archaeological Society. A well-informed man about antiquities.

12th September 1928
Visited Tornant Moat. … Tornant Moat is on Mr Thomas Fisher's land. The two ramparts have been destroyed to the E, presumably by taking the mound away for sand or earth. About ⅛ of the circumference is gone. There

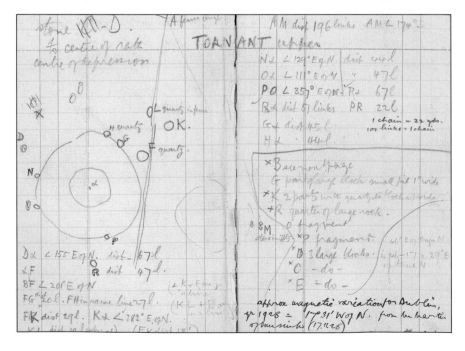

Fig. 3—Notes, measurements and sketch-plan of a kerbed mound, termed by Price 'the rath to the E' in Tornant Upper.

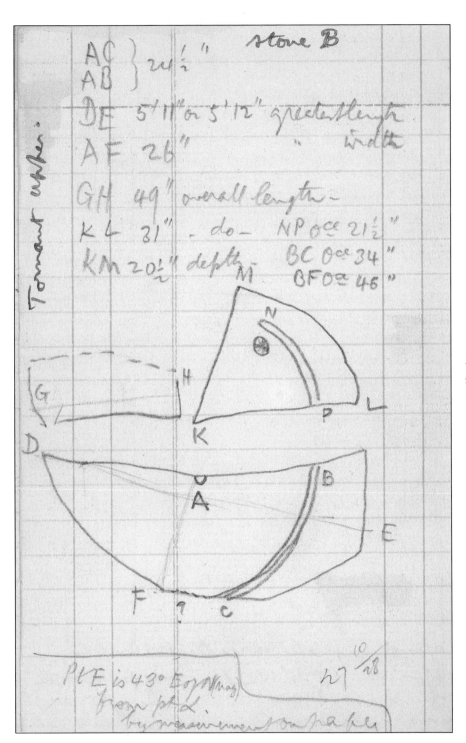

Fig. 4—Sketch of stone with circular groove at Tornant Upper.

are no stones there, but one of Mr Fisher's men told me that there had been stones which were dynamited and removed, that some of the pieces are still lying in the fence [to S].

He said a small flagstone 15in. square had been there, but had been taken away: that it had very old figures or numbers on it. Sand is still being taken out of the outer ring, on the W side.

St Nicholas' Well is below the moat and beyond the hedge: NE from Mr Fisher's house. There used to be a pattern to it in midsummer, but this is disused.

Rath in Tornant Upper — high up on top of the hill — which looks as if it had been cut away for gravel. This rath has one stone on it, with what appear to be incised markings, not spirals, but more like a labyrinth. The stone is lying flat, in the centre of the rath, and at the top. The rath to the E. A small rath. It had stones round it, all but two of granite (of those remaining). It is on Mr Joseph Norton's land. His father drilled the blocks and dynamited them. The marks of the drill are on those which remain.

There are five, or possibly six, stones remaining of the inner and smaller circle, three to NE and two (possibly three) to S. [Including] a block of flint. Five large ones (split) of the outer circle, of these [one] appears to have had a circular groove 1in. wide and about 1in. deep on its upper surface, about 2ft in diameter. The two circles are outside the rath, one on its outer edge, the other 5 or 6ft away.

About 100yds to the NE is a large stone block (split). No marks on it that I could see. This is much the same position (relatively to the circle) as the block which is outside the Hollywood Circle.

I did not see the obliterated road or ogham stone mentioned by Father Shearman.

16th September 1928

At Kilbaylet. The 'churchyard' is on the E side of the road just to the S of the roadway leading to Kilbaylet House, Mr Valentine's — it is never tilled — more than 100 years ago people from Wexford (Rourke?) came to bury a corpse there but could not find the grave, and carried the corpse back to Wexford. There are supposed to be the marks of graves there still — Mr Terence Reilly lives beside it and gave us the information. The old Donard is behind his house and on his land — he calls it 'Knocknakéeráwn', and says a battle was fought there, on Ballymooney townland. His house was Captain Dennis' who was shot in the rebellion at Knocknakeeraun. There was a well on Church Mountain, inside the 'church' he has seen water in it. St Gad's Well — he said he did not know how the stones got there but that he heard soldiers handed the stones to one another up to the top.

30th September 1928

Ballinascorney, Co. Dublin. The dry gap in the hill above Ballinascorney, to the S, is called 'the High Hollow'. A man named Walsh lived in the house the ruins of which can be seen on the W side of this gap — the hole in the fence, E of his house, is called 'Walsh's ice-hole'.

Wicklow placenames: Joyce refers to an 'Inquis. James I' (v. Muskeagh vol. 3).

10th October 1928

At Knockdoo ('Cnoc da dhamh'?) near Colbinstown. Hill 616ft high. An oval hill, appears to be one of the glacial gravel mounds, rounded stones and gravel in fine earth. On the top is a small standing stone, 3ft high (of slate?) — weather-marked — no artificial marks. There is a ditch and mound still surrounding about half the hill, and a wall and ditch on another portion, just at the foot of the hill.

A woman driving cows said it was 'Knock-ă-dou(gh) Hill' (slightly guttural: 'ough' as in 'plough'). She knew no story about it. [She] said there had been a ditch all round. She did not know of there having been more stones than the one. It was a 'comrade stone' to the stone in 'Kill-y-een' (Killeencormaic). There used to be a row of cottages, seven or nine, at the foot to the NE, all inhabited by Pipers. Mud cottages — she said her husband's father remembered three — that might be 60 years ago. Now no traces, only a row of trees.

N.B. Father Shearman writes it 'Cnocadhow' (*JRSAI* xii, 344). One story makes the hound jump there from Killeen.

25th January 1933

Measured the stone [in Knockdoo]. It is 38in. high, breadth 30in., thickness about 1ft. The flat portion of the top of the hill is about 100yds E–W by 30 or 35yds N–S: the stone is in the middle of the long axis, and near the S side of this flat part.

15th October 1928

At Arklow. Up on Castle Tower. The pool immediately below it is called 'Pollacholly', or 'Pollacopple' (on Tancred's authority). The two lanes leading down to it are called 'the Coomies lanes' ('Coome'). It used to be the harbour for the ships. There is a canal on N bank of river which used to bring the ore from Avoca. It was smelted at the Smelting Hill, which is above Lord Wicklow's Hospital. The river used to run out there, but was diverted when the present bridge was built. Arklow Church was ¼ mile to E of Castle. The abbey was further to E. There is also a mound known as 'Chapel Hogan' near Arklow Rock.

16th October 1928

Derrylossary Parish. Story from Father Vaughan, and through him from Father Geraghty of Roundwood, who got it from a book. There are five stones outside the graveyard wall of the church, lying flat. Pagan fires used to be lighted on these. The king of the country built three churches, this is one and another is on the Enniskerry line (at St Kevin's Well and Church, Glasnamullen?) — there was communication between the three, and fires could be seen from one to the other. Derrylossary is an old pre-Celtic word — (*sed qu.*).

4th November 1928

R.C. Barton told me the Reverend Stokes derived it [i.e. Derrylossary] from 'Doyre-lasad', 'the light of the oak wood'. It has quernstones inside the churchyard and outside — one large one — perhaps a font.

21st October 1928

Walked up Mungduff [Munduffe?], Carrig and Keadeen — (pronounced 'Káyjeen'). There is a heap of stones on the neck between the two hills — this seems to have been where Moore the murderer of Mr Hume was gibbeted. There is also a large cairn of flattish stones on Keadeen. Walked down to Rathdangan via Cornan (pronounced 'Cornáwn') — saw Toberowen — St John's Well — it was concreted last year by 'the council'. No tradition of a pattern to it. The tree died within the past 50 years. Rathdangan Chapel was in the SW part of the village — a new hall is built on its site.

22nd October 1928

At St Bridget's Headstone and Chair, Cloghnagaune, near Baltinglass. The Headstone is a large block of stone shaped thus [semicircular], with a circular cylindrical cavity in it. The hole is 8¾ in. in diameter, 10¼ in. deep on the right side and 10¾ in. deep on the left side — the bottom is not quite level, but convex in shape. A man's head fits in conveniently. The cylinder is regular. Mr Hawkins of Spinans Middle, an elderly man about 80, a Protestant, told me people go to it to be cured of diseases of the head. They put in their head and turn it round, and never have a pain in the head again. Hazel bushes and a young ash tree are growing over the stone. There were rags, pieces of string, a bootlace, and a piece of leather tied onto lower branches over the stone. He said there was an old chapel of which the ruins still remain, near the old shed W of the Headstone. These are old butts of walls. There is nothing to suggest a chapel about them.

He said many years ago a man ploughed the field St Bridget's Chair is in, and was clearing away the stones: he stopped him and made him put them back: he had words with him and knocked him down. The stones were disturbed, but were replaced. The land belongs to [Minchin?] who lives at Tallaght. Lord Walter Fitzgerald visited Hawkins and was told by him anything he knew of these stones.

Hawkins' wife's father was an old man named Jackson — Hawkins said Jackson had seen Macalister buried in Kilranelagh Churchyard, and had showed him the grave.

S of St Bridget's Headstone, near the gap in the field fence, and on the Headstone side of it, I saw a raised oblong piece of ground about 5ft x 2ft, with fresh grass sods on it. I could not find out what it was. Neither Mrs Wynne nor Mr Hawkins ever heard of unbaptised children being buried there.

4th November 1928

Woodstock House, near Kilcoole. The 'Druidical Altar' is 300 or 400yds S of the house just above the river. It consists of a number of blocks of stone, moss-covered; at the bottom is what looks like an outcrop of rock — then large boulders in a heap, and on top half a dozen blocks of stone placed in a curve facing S — one has a raised edge to it on the S side, and is otherwise flat and even — the gardener said the druid used to put his book there. Below towards the river the blocks are in the form of a sacred dolmen with four supports and a capstone. Further E there is a fishpond and an (artificially?) antique bridge.

I doubt that the Druidical Altar may also be a fake antique. See for a similar case *JRSAI* 26, p.411, but N.B. 'Clochtogbhala' near Newcastle, *JRSAI* 38, 129n.

From R.C. Barton. In 1798 Thomas butler to Hugo heard Hugo say he would imprison him as a suspect if a rising broke out. On the rising, Thomas went out with a gun of Hugo's, waited for Hugo in the avenue and fired at him — the shot missed, going through the two windows of the carriage. Thomas remained with the rebels. Later he and a rebel named Harmon were betrayed when hiding in a turfpile on Castlekevin. They broke out through the yeomen — Thomas was crossing a bog to the S when he met the Reverend Weekes of Annamoe. Weekes put a ball in his gun and shot him through the leg. He was taken and hanged and his head put on a spike on Rathdrum Courthouse. The spike is said still to be hidden somewhere — Harmon also got away but was captured later and died in prison in Dublin.

Hugo shot suspected persons at sight — Barton's grandfather(?) or uncle? wanted two ash trees cut up, and the men refused to cut them and were dismissed — later these trees were cut up in a sawmill, and two bullets found in one of them — the tradition of the shooting of men against the tree remained — Barton himself found two bullets in another tree, and has them. Hugo shot one man when he met him in the avenue, and after shot his dog on the grave the man was buried in.

The Reverend Graves noted down some of the stories at Annamoe. He excavated the graveyard at Knockatemple, dug up a priest, and died shortly afterwards.

The old road [from] Annamoe to Togher runs past Derrylossary Church.

6th November 1928

Clonmore, Co. Carlow. The castle is a square enclosure, the buildings along the E side — ruin of a tower to SW. Moat still visible on E, N and W, the road is to the S. At NW corner is a roofed-in room, the floor 10 or 12ft above the ground — called 'the Seven Windows' or 'the Six Windows' by the local people. Told there were four 'pooka's heads' on the castle, but only one is left. A passage runs from the castle to the top of the mote. The entrance is now blocked up: it begins in the centre of the W side of the castle buildings (see *JRSAI* 13, p.493n).

The mote is covered with furze bushes and surrounded by a wet ditch and a bank. There are some small trees on the top planted to commemorate the 1916 men. There is said to be a hollow on the top, but it is so overgrown I could see nothing. A labourer told me people had dug into the side of the mote, as a result of a dream, and he thought they found bones — also that some young men had followed the passage from the castle as far as the village (Whelan's) but then had to come up on account of the bad air. I saw a large stone on the W side of the ditch, and two others in a line with it near the drain in the field to the left.

Another man (in Whelan's Pub) said when they made the road bridge over the stream, they came on the big flags of the passage, and the air that came from them was bad. The road was built through the old churchyard. There is an old cross in one part of it and St 'Mōgue's' Well in the other (pattern day was 31st January). And a bullaun stone — a flat stone with three hollows in it — S of the churchyard in a field — these hollows never get dry. I only saw the castle and the mote. Clonmore is 'Cluain Mor Maedhog'.

12th November 1928

Pronunciation of Garryknock in Wicklow Gap — 'G ă rr ə nŭk'; Tiknock, Kiltegan — 'Tĭ-nŏk'; Barraderry (near Kiltegan) — 'Barr ŏ derry'; Borkillbeg, Kiltegan — 'Bork ə l' or 'Bort ə l'. 'Fĕddăn'; (In 1927 — Labbanasigha, Moylisha, 'Lŏb nə sȳe').

1st December 1928

In King's River Valley.

'Moȳ eera', the mountain SE of Kilcoagh (probably Lyragh).

'The Tenters' Fields', in Ballinahown. An old mill used to be there (woollen).

Two raths NW of the Priest's Bridge.

'Grăssy', the W slope of Black Hill.

'Blănăkāy', the N slope of Whelp Rock (perhaps Lugnaskeagh).

'Shĭle shawn', the N peak of Moanbane (see *Namebooks*, 'Ballinastockan').

'Frŏchăn Hill', near the Ballynastockan Brook.

5th December 1928

MacDermot's Castle in Ballynagran, Glenealy D.E.D. and parish, there is a square space, enclosed by the remains of a wet ditch, and of a rampart on the outside. About 40yds (?) square. On the S side, in the middle, just inside the ditch and with the trace of a causeway leading through the ditch is a building of two walls with the remains of the springing of an arch, about 6ft high on each wall. They are about 10ft apart — and look as if they had been the side walls of an arched gateway — the walls are somewhat ruined, there are traces of other walls jutting out from them. This is the only building in the enclosure. It is not unlike in position the remains of [the] building at the W edge of the Newcastle mote.

'Sci Patric' (or 'Sceach') near Tinahely — see Father Shearman in 'Loc. Patriciana', *JRSAI* 13, p.385, from Book of Armagh, and see *Onom. Gaed.* p.415. (Father Shearman says on Gilbert's farm, above a spring...

The Mottee Stone, Crossbane, Avoca. The iron footholds are said to have been put in by Captain Higgins, the manager of the mines. What townland is Bell Rock in? Where is the Spink and Whitsun Hill at Shelton Abbey?

16th December 1928

At Killegar. The slab is in the chancel and the [other] slab at the N side of chancel. The [third] slab is lying loose in the grass, on the W side of chancel, and in danger of being destroyed.

17th December 1928

Michael Browne of the Vale View, owner of Oakwood House. It is the house called 'the Black Dog' — he says there was a story about a black dog that was seen about the place.

Askintinny. Sergeant Mangan, Garda Station, Arklow, says it is pronounced 'A. tenny' or 'A. tanny' and there is a story that a huge eel lived in the marsh, and that there was an appearance like fire on it — it was driven out to sea and left a channel in the marsh, which was filled up with rocks etc. So 'Ask an teine', 'eel of the fire'. *Sed quaere.*

Tighes of Rossana. Mary Blackford, born 1772, probably at Rossana, married Henry Tighe, her cousin, in 1793. *Psyche* published in 1805. Died

1810. Her picture painted by Rowney (in the National Gallery?). Buried at Woodstock, near Kilkenny. *Psyche* is based on Apuleius. She kept a diary of which the manuscript is said to be in existence. (*Irish Statesman*, December 22nd 1928.)

C.G. Thompson, master at Mountjoy, 15 Highfield Rd, Rathgar (names collected by him):

'Lavarnia' (Lavarney)

'Ballanuntha' (Ballynultagh), also on the wood [on?] Prince William's Seat.

'Cloghnagun' NW of Prince William's Seat.

'Castletool' just below it, both outcrops of rock.

'Cleithhāgan', cube of rock E of Tonduff, in the valley.

'Clochnagull(y)een' (Whelp Rock?), the name is given to that rock.

'Beenleegh', off Bendoo, right-hand side of Baravore valley and 'Corranillagh' [Corrasillagh?] is beyond on the left, up the main valley, the hill beyond the Horses' Glen.

Slayfonn.

'Carrig a fayonn' or 'Corrig a feeun', an outcrop of rock on the SE of Camaderry.

'Glanaslagh' pronunciation of Glenealo — the stream on the right is 'Glanaslaghbeg'.

'Lough Firub', Firrib.

The Three Loughs: Corragh pronounced 'Cŏrŭch', 'Glanakeeragh' — the stream E of Glenreemore (out of Lough Firrib), 'Poultandruim' — at the meeting place of two streams by Glendalough.

They call any heap of stones on a mountain 'a molty'. Thompson heard the cairn on Lug. called 'the Molty'.

'Corrigoortna' (Carrigurtna), 'the rock of the field of the ford'?

Ballybraid is called 'Braighe' (pronounced 'brĭ').

'Tramonawigna' near the head of the Liffey valley (between Lough Tay and Sally Gap). 'Ascanabulōg' is on the flat between Eagle Rock and the top of Kippure.

'Boleyhărrigan'.

The top of the road over Lough Tay is called 'the Barr'.

Fancy = 'Fanshee' ('slope of the fairies')?

19

'The Cloghoge Bracket Rocks'.

'Gannagunneen' is the strand at Lough Bray.

'Bearnaveag', 2m [miles?] S of Sally Gap, where the road gives the first view of Tonelegee. Mullacor pronounced 'Mullaghōir'.

'Portándoo', pool on the river between Cloghoge and the Fancy.

'Glennisloran', valley above the waterfall [at] Powerscourt.

Barnamire — 'Keeper's Gap'.

'Dowrnadarrig', the dolmen at Glaskenny.

'Escalower' and 'Askanacrann', streams above the ... water works.

'Moneen', 'the bog ... of the road'.

'Glannach(w)eelia', valley E of Tonduff.

'Mullansoo' [Mullaunsoo?] the hill E of it.

A man called Killegar Church 'Stagóny' to Thompson — distinguishing it from 'Stagonil' (see *Letters* p.2) which he gave as the old name for Powerscourt. 'Barnacreeliagh' [Barnacreel?], [the] bog between Corrig and Seefingan. 'Corriganoura' [Corriganour] is Corrig Mountain.

5th March 1929

Umrygar Moat. Ten paces across the top (diameter), no traces of stone. In the centre of a ploughed field, with ridge 30yds (?) long towards W. No appearance of circumvallations or moat (wet ditch). There is a stream on each side, 100yds and 80yds away respectively. Riddled with rabbit-holes. Circumference at base about 110 paces.

The ridge is a natural ridge of sand and small stones. Thirty yards W of the moat a fence crosses it with what appears to be a right-of-way foot track, running N and S. The ridge slopes sharply on the S face and just E of the fence a piece 5yds long has the sharp slope on the N face also. The ridge continues another 30 or 40yds to the W and the stream then bends round the foot of it. The stream to the N is further away, but seems to be in an artificial channel. Possibly: the ridge originally had a sharp slope on both sides with the streams at the foot, and has been ploughed over, and the streams confined in artificial channels. The ground near the ridge is boggy. There is a sandpit, now being worked, 300 or 400yds W of the moat. The moat seems to be at the E end of the ridge.

18th March 1929

Kilmacrea. The Round Ball is an old rath. Half the circle, towards the SW, has a modern drystone-wall fence built on it — the rest is a grassy bank a foot or so high, with stones under the grass. Near the W point of the circle, inside, is an outcrop of rock. Diameter [of circle] about 54 paces. The NE quadrant is marked out by two lines of grassy bank or stones, which are almost radii of the [circle]. Marked by watch at ten past two, twelve o'clock pointing to the sun. The outcrop is at quarter past two and the two radial lines point to four o'clock and eight o'clock. Their junction is rounded. The wall runs from about ten o'clock to three o'clock.

A flat rounded slab of granite (?) rock, about 300yds SE of the Round Ball, and near an old cart track leading from Kilmacrea crossroads. It has cupmarks on it, at least three near the centre and three more close to the N edge. Length SE to NW about 8ft 6in.; from SW to NE about 7ft. Is this the Cat Rock?

'The Quadrant' — is this a cattle booley? Or is this rath the 'raithin formerly used as a burial ground' mentioned by O'Conor?

29th March 1929

Ballintombay Giant's Grave. To get to it follow the path shown on the 1-inch map (my 1904 ed.) — it becomes a sheep track near the townland boundary, among some newly planted trees. Cross the fence, and the Grave is a rough oblong of stones, about 20ft x 10ft — the inside vacant, just a rough piece of mountain. There is what might have been an entrance on the E side. About 25yds below it, to the E, is what is I think a spring though it is dry today after four weeks dry weather. The Grave is N of the townland boundary, but this looks as if it was newly cut when the fence was put up.

The reservoir in the valley is one of the Rathdrum reservoirs — the stream is the Ballinderry Brook, so an old man told me. He also told me the house in ruins above it belonged to a man named Monks, who lived by himself in it about 25 years ago — had a farm, and also worked drawing ore from the mines to Arklow (the Ballymurtagh mines?). He said they could get no living out of it. He knew the name 'the Giant's Grave' and knew what it was, but had no story about it. He said the young people have given up reading the old histories.

At Ballinastoe — asked an old woman on the road where St Kevin's

Well was. She said there were steps leading to it, a stile in the fence, that it was near St Kevin's Priory, which was at Singleton's View (the house on the crossroads), that there is another well further on towards Roundwood on the left-hand side of the road, it never froze in winter when all the other wells did. It is near the stream which is close to 'the old road to Luggala' — she lives near this old road, her name Kavanagh. She called the stream 'the Stonypass River'.

30th March 1929

Ballymaghroe Graveyard. A circular enclosure in a field — the wall is well built and thick of stone and earth. Some new and some old graves in it, and a broken font, I think of granite. No sign of a church.

Raymond's Castle, Killaveny. As you go W from the Togher crossroads, towards Wicklow Gap, just after you come to the first road junction and before the second one, there is a stile in the fence on the left. Standing on this and looking down into the river flat, in the far corner of a large field, a bit W of N, about 400yds away, is a stony enclosure — this is the site of the castle. There are no remains of building. A large stone on the edge of the stream beside it is called 'Raymond's Po'.

Toberpatrick. A fine, clear cold well, built round with stones, and with a clear stony bottom (covered with weeds), just beside the road. Mr Hayden on whose land it is says he still sees people drinking the water at four o'clock in the morning (on St Patrick's Day?). There used to be 1000 people at the pattern on the lawn on Patrick's Day. St Patrick's Bush is also on his land — go up from Toberpatrick to the crossroads, and turn to the left and it is the single old thorn 40yds along the road on the left-hand side. There used to be a rath but the road was built through it. Hayden spoke of raths 14ft high — I don't know if he was speaking generally or of this one. He said as long as he and his father could remember (50 and 50 years), it, the bush, had always been the same. That the coffins always stopped before the bush, not at the crossroads.

The well water was colder than any well round, even than the one that came 40ft up through rock. That there used to be two trout in it, as big as salmon, and a man caught them and took them away, but wasn't able to cook them: so he brought them back, and lifted up a stone at the side and put the trout back. He said the weeds in it were good for curing people, that his brother a surgeon in Dublin used them, that they'd stay on the stomach when nothing else would and that one was good for the yellow jaundice.

Croghan Mountain: from the bridge over the Gold Mines River go up the lane leading W — when the lane is coming to an end, nearly at the crest, turn SW up the hill, keeping up to a post on the W slope. From the post keep on round, not up the hill, when in five or ten minutes the top can be seen over the slope in front; 1½ hrs from bridge to top (easy going).

31st March 1929

Climbed Lugnaquillia from Toorboy ('Toórwee') — up to the saddle between Lybagh and Slievemaan — passed Cloghowen, which is a large boulder, on the townland boundary, 50yds or so from the stream, about 8ft high, and shaped somewhat like [a dome]: from the road to this is about ¾ hr, from this to the saddle is about the same, and from the saddle to the top of [Lugnaquillia] is another 1¼ hrs (easy going). Keep round Slievemaan, towards the W end of the top of [Lugnaquillia], 2 hrs down.

Kilcromer. Ballynama(áh)noge, near Tinahely. A boy told me it is called 'the Raheen Bank', but did not know any name for it. It is a circular rath with thorn trees growing on the bank inside the rath. The bank of the rath is made of large and small stones. On the W side the field fence makes a second bank parallel to the bank of the rath with a deep ditch between — and elsewhere there are signs that this went all round, making a complete double ring — inside there are signs of earth banks covering the foundations of walls — a square building? There are large stones lying about here and there. An entrance on the S side and what seems like another on the E with a raised bank leading to it, perhaps a causeway crossing the ditch between the two banks? Inside the S entrance is a standing stone (of granite? yes) 4ft high — it has a slight depressed groove on top continuing a couple of inches down the S side — just in the S entrance is a flat stone lying almost square in shape, with a raised edge on the W side (natural). Inside the E entrance on the N side is a small roughly oblong enclosure one side being the wall of the rath — about 14ft x 8ft. Outside this entrance on the N are four fairly large blocks of stone lying loose: part of the outer ring? I could see no markings on the stones except the groove on the pillar stone.

Ra(th)shanmore — there are two large stones in the centre of one of these raths (seen from the road).

1st April 1929

Rampere. Looked for the 'Bull's Foot'. The only stone I could see with a cup-marking on it lies at the foot of a stile on the W side of the road, being one of the supporting stones — it is on the N side of the stile. The mark is on the face turned towards the road, and looks, I thought, natural. I could see no-one to question.

Did not see Rampere Chapel as we passed along the road in the motor. The 'Round O' at Tinoranhill is a rath on the top of the hill, made of stones and earth — a single bank, quite low, about ¾ of it has been arranged as a field fence, with wire on top. The hill is all covered with loose stones. I saw a small standing stone about SW from the rath (towards Baltinglass) about 200yds away or so down the hill but had not time to look at it. I thought it might be a scratching stone, but it is on the furzy part of the hill. Tubbergorry is apparently used for watering cattle.

Ballycore Rath is a very prominent rath on the S end of a hill in the S end of Ballycore townland.

The Ballycore Longstone. To reach it take the byroad from Rathtoole to Whitehills, and at the gate on the left-hand (W) side of the road, just beyond the road to Knockarigg, the stone is about 80yds in in a field. It is 8ft high and shaped much like the longstones at Punchestown and Forenaghts. There are a couple of rough low mounds to the N of it in the field, but no other indication of a rath.

Killeen Cormaic. The excavation by Macalister and Praeger was just completed when we arrived. They found four new ogham stones, and found the gravel mound was undisturbed under the Christian cemetery. They were going on to Tornant Moat, next day (Tuesday 2nd April).

FIELD NOTEBOOK 3:
April–July 1929

No date

Killeen Cormaic. The ogham stone found at Easter 1929 [reads] 'EGN I KO I MAQI MUC' (Dr Macalister adds broken faint 'OI AILNI') and on the fragments with the large scores (i) 'UD' and (ii) 'A'.

Feach Mac Hugh O'Byrne's eldest son was Phelim, and his second son Raymond. Were Phelim's Castle in Ballinacor, and Raymond's Castle in Killaveny, called after them? Yes.

4th April 1929

Newtown, Wicklow — the well is in Doyle's yard, the house just N of Threemilewater E of the road. Doyle said there was an old tree growing over it, that he built the cover over it and the old roots were there. A priest, Father O'Hagan, from Rome told them last year it was a holy well, that it was St Bridget's [Well] and would cure pains and sores: Doyle could give no name to it, and had no story about it. He said some said there was a chapel near the bridge, others said it was 'up in McCoy's field' — (note: this is 'Tobar na Buadh').

Toberaviller in Sheane's farm near his house. He also said there was an old tree growing over it, and showed the roots. He knew no name for it (Doyle called it 'St John's'). Sheane said it always had water in it, and the water was always cold. He pipes it up to the house.

He said some call the place 'Toberaviller' and some 'Toberavilla' but that Toberaviller is right. (The description of Sir Henry Harrington's defeat is in *JRSAI* vol. v, p.428.)

7th April 1929

The old road from Glendalough (Laragh) to Ballybraid. It starts from where the present road crosses the Derrybawn River, and its course then is marked clearly through the heather, cutting off the windings of the new road, and going slightly W of the top of Cullentragh Hill. At the highest point is a rock over the road. Is this Edge's Rock? ... It is just at this point that the old road, as shown on the 1839 OS map, stops and turns back to the new road. The only pile of stones near this seemed to A.F. and myself to be a grouse butt: there were at least two similar structures close by on the slope of Carriglinneen — the path leading from the rock to the new road seems to continue across it and to go down the slope of Kirikee Hill towards Greenan.

17th April 1929

Greystones. The mound W of the church, between Church Lane and the Blacklion Road is being dug away for sand. It is a natural sand hill with a stream running by the W and NW portions of it. I asked the man digging if he saw any bones or large stones and he said 'No'. I saw no signs of any about. The lines in the sand showing the different layers laid down were very clear.

At Blessington Court on 8th April — the name 'Ballinamountra' was produced on a written document. It was the way a party to a case had written down the address given to him by the defendant, and was intended for Ballynultagh.

Fig. 5—Threecastles (courtesy of the Royal Society of Antiquaries of Ireland ©).

Fig. 6—Burgage Castle (courtesy of Dúchas The Heritage Service ©).

21st April 1929

Threecastles. The castle is a well-built and well-preserved oblong building — door on W side — doors, windows, and the angles of the outer walls faced with cut blocks of granite, and granite fireplace on first floor, flush with wall. No stairway up to first floor, but the doorway from this floor to the stairs can be reached, and it leads to the top of the castle and is well preserved. Vaulted roof intact. E and N walls covered with ivy, the N and S walls were continued towards the W, evidently there was more of the building on this side and the corbels for floor beams remain over the door. Stepping stones and a ford across the river close by, leading to Oldcourt. The date? — end of the 16th century. But the walls are 4 or 5ft thick.

Also looked at Burgage Castle — it also has the cut granite facings, but not so nicely finished. It is much more ruinous.

Killerk. The Relicin is near the road [at E]. It is hidden from the road by the hedge. It is a much-battered cross, with, as we thought, a cross in relief on the shaft below the neck which is cut in relief where cross meets shaft. This cross is on the back, or E side, the shaded parts [spandrels] being cut away — but it is not easy to see.

Whiteleas. The stone circle is S of Whiteleas House, about 600yds, and just N of the county boundary. It is a roughly raised circular piece of ground with a number of boulders in disorder about it, and two or more in the centre. A very rough monument. Lord W. Fitzgerald mentions it. The only noticeable thing about it is there are two white quartz boulders on N part, and one on E.

Fig. 7—Doorway at Kilcroney Church.

3rd May 1929

Kilcroney. The old church is about 100yds E of the house. Near it is a very old yew, '1000 years old' Mrs West said, and on the other side a box hedge about 25ft high, said to be Elizabethan. The doorway is of cut-stone blocks with a cut-stone lintel of granite. A place for a door is cut at the back, with bolt-hole. The jambs each rest on a slight step above the threshold. Round-headed window, with head cut in one stone, to E. The window itself appears to be of granite: it is widely splayed, and the stones at the back are full of holes, like pumice. Mrs West said they came out of the Enniskerry River. She said Miss Hall is buried in the church in the SW corner. She made the rockery round it, of stones fallen from the church, and covered up a quantity of bones in the rockery. Her son has made an exotic shrubbery in a hollow W of the house, called 'Dillon's Hollow', because there was a public house there belonging to a man named Dillon; a road used to run there once.

12th May 1929

Knockadreet. Spoke to the old man who lives in the house nearest to the stepping stones on the E side: he will be 70 in August. It is just before you reach the road from Knockfadda to Boleynass. He pronounced it 'Knuck-a-dree-ed', the last two syllables quickly together. The land just W of the stepping stones he called 'Coolharbour': then 'Raheen': then 'Diamond Hill'. He said there was a rocking stone just near his house but they blasted it making the air shaft. N side of house. General Cunninghame was the landlord of his farm — he had no name for the rath near the reservoir in Roundwood. He said the woman who owned the rath 'down there' (pointing towards Annagolan) (Tomdarragh) told her men to cut skeoghs on it, and one of the men said it was unlucky: they did it, and all her cows slipped their calves — of course, that might not be the reason.

Examined the rath (Roundwood) — it had a double rampart, with ditch — the outer rampart only remains on S side and on NW side — at latter it is made into a cartway. Both ramparts are of small stones and earth. A very large stone, with a smaller one to E of it, at N side — apparently some shallow cup-like markings in the large boulder. They are exactly where the outer rampart would have been. (Looked at these later and decided there were no cup-markings on the stone, 1934.) A large thorn tree grows between them.

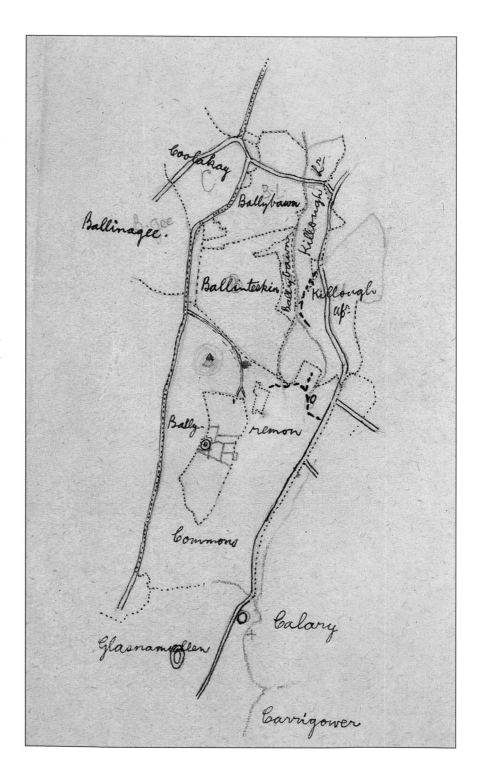

Fig. 8—Sketch-map of Ballyremon Commons.

27th May 1929

Wards of Tober. At point 844[ft], on the top of the hill there is a mound, called 'the Wards Mote' or 'Lemonstown Mote'. It is just inside Lemonstown townland and Crehelp parish, the boundary being on its W edge. It is a grass-covered mound, the top of which is fairly flat, somewhat sunk in the centre, with a deep ditch and fair-sized rampart surrounding it — the rampart is from 3 to 6ft above the ditch at the present time. Trees are planted on the rampart and a few trees are on the mound — the W part of the rampart is cut in two longitudinally, leaving a second ditch on portion of this side, but this was probably done merely to make the fence secure against trespass. No stones on it. A workman said it was well kept and paled in 'the Old Baron's' time, with trees and shrubs on it. Asked were there ever stones on it, he said the surveyors marked a stone with the crow's foot and left it on the top, and then this stone could not be found, so they got another and marked it and left it on top, under the grass; afterwards they found the first one. No stone appears there now. A very wide view from the top. The ditch is filled in towards the NE in such a way as to make a way in: from the centre the bearing of this causeway is, roughly, 59° E of true N. Circumference of mote about 100 to 108 paces; [circumference] on rampart outside ditch about 132 paces; height of mound about 15ft.

2nd June 1929

On Calary Bog, stopped car about 100yds N of Calary Schoolhouse. A road goes off to right (or W), crosses stream and leads to a farm, then goes on about where boundary of Ballyremon Commons is, and leads NE of the hill (point 1072[ft]) and so into the Old Long Hill. About halfway outside the corner of a field fence is a small tumulus, with circular ditch round it, and bank outside the ditch — the field fence corner is made out of this bank. Where 'Knocknandiahab' is shown on the map, that is on the E side of the stream nearest the present main road, and N of the road mentioned above, is a somewhat oval mound, perhaps 20ft high and 30 to 40yds long. It looks like a natural mound. If this is 'Knockdaee' as O'Curry calls it, there is no feature on top of it now. A boy I asked did not know the name. Further S, the mound on E of the main road, and W of the Vartry and NW of Calary Church, is being dug away for sand and gravel. It is a natural little hill of sand or gravel, and I saw no sign of large stones or bones in it. About

¼ of it is dug away. Is this the cairn O'Curry speaks of 'about a furlong S of Knockdaee'? It is more than a mile S.

Scale 1in. to 1 mile [Fig. 8]. The black dots are approximately the old paths. The tumulus is somewhere near the edge of the smallest detached piece of Ballinteskin, about at [where the red dot is marked on the map above] or near it.

A. Farrington has examined the mound marked 'Knocknandiahab' on the 6-inch OS map more than once and says it is a natural mound, naturally shaped.

24th June 1929

Shown by Mr Antony Metcalf a bullaun stone (or small font?) in the centre of a field belonging to Mr Jack Synnott in the SE corner of Crehelp townland. The stone is lying loose in a rectangular portion of the middle of the field — rectangle about 25ft x 20ft (?) — slightly raised: it is never tilled. One other stone [is] visible, no marks on it. The stone in question has a circular basin-shaped cavity worked in its flat surface, about 8in. in diameter and about 3in. deep (estimated). I got no name — you get to the field by a lane leading E from the Crehelp–Kinsellastown road, about ⅜ mile N of Crehelp crossroads.

The Crehelp standing stone. The hole in the stone has the appearance of being made in a doorpost to receive a stout wooden bar rectangular in section. Mr Thomas Head of Crehelp, a man of 76 years of age, says as long as he remembers it was never moved: that the plot of ground round it has never been tilled, it is called 'Crushloe Churchyard' (accented on second syllable). There used to be a 'bun ditch' round the field, and a man was making it into a double ditch, when he found bones near the stone: he made a hole and buried them. There is a row of building stones buried there, but it has not been disturbed. Head said the old people said the hole was put in it for marriages: and Mr Kelly was told the same thing by an old man, a native of Crehelp district, working for Mrs Byrne of Humphrystown. Stone is at map XV. 3.0. Head also showed us what he and Metcalf called 'a cave'. It is on E side of road immediately opposite the lane leading W between Crehelp and Kinsellastown, and about 40 or 50yds from the road. All that is visible is a rounded hump, as though there had been a low round hill in the field — slightly to the N of the top of this hump is a small depression in the grass, full of nettles. Head said this was opened by Baron de Robeck's son and that about 6ft down there is the entrance to a passage, which leads towards the Lodge (now Mr Goggin's house): the passage is in the sand, the sand is like concrete, and very fine and dry: in places you have to stoop and in places it is 6ft high — at about 10yds N of the hole, de Robeck had another small hole dug as a 'porthole' (*sic*). Men went in with candles but did not go much further than the 'porthole'. Metcalf said he saw this opened about 10 years ago, and that there are two other passages, one leading towards the road (and that the road sounds hollow in one place) and another leading towards the standing stone, i.e. S.

There is a 'mote' in Kinsellastown close to the road and on the W side of it, opposite the Lodge: it is called 'Crehelp Mote': you can see Tober (Lemonstown) Mote from it. Also a mote called 'Terry's Mote' which was levelled by a man named Terry: it was towards the W: Head pointed almost towards Friarhill from the cave, and said the mote was on the skyline. He said the old people said they were 'fairy motes', and that 'the three motes were built for the sight', i.e. were in sight of one another.

Kinsellastown pronounced 'Kinsheltown'. Lemonstown [pronounced] 'Lammonstown'. 'Tornant', accent on second syllable. Baron de Robeck's son lived in Crehelp Lodge (Mr Goggin's house). Metcalf knew the Donard ogham stone came from near Donaghmore — he says there is a Piper's Stone at Oldmill (the Castleruddery Circle?). He said also that the iron cross was put on the Piper's Stone at Forristeen at the time of a cattle plague about 100 years ago, and another iron cross was put up near the Crehelp–Dunlavin road at the same time and for the same reason. 'The Spa Hole' is the adit on the E side of the Hollywood Glen road where the water is tinged with iron.

The crossroad where the road by Conlan's Hill meets the Hollywood Glen road is called 'the Fallen (or Fallin?) Waters' — people used to dance there in the evenings on the road (M. Kelly). Metcalf spoke of 'the Frochan Rock' in the same locality.

29th June 1929
At Kilmacurra with A. Henry. Photographed a *Podocorpus* and a *Laurelia* — the latter almost unique in Ireland. The demesne was used by Sir F. Moore of the Botanic Gardens as a nursery, for 40 years or more. Old Mr Tom

Acton was interested in botany. He left no children, except, it is said, an illegitimate son, who was butler or something of the sort in the house. Query, is he alive still? Old Mr Acton restored the old name ('Kilmacurra') to the house. The old drive is quite obvious, on the road leading from Ballard (or Barndarrig Chapel), a grass-grown avenue with large trees on each side; opposite Hill House. We also saw an old line of yews in the demesne, over 100 years old, beside a small stream. Now owned by Mr La Touche who lives at Dunganstown Castle and tenanted by Hon. Mrs Phillimore.

30th June 1929

Up the road leading from the N end of the Upper Bohernabreena Reservoir to the turf bog between Seechon and Corrig. It appears to be a regular engineered pathway with zigzags to relieve the gradient. When the path meets the county boundary it continues as a foot track along the boundary towards the road at Kilbride Camp. No path goes on from the turf bog over Corrig towards Seefinn, though this would be the direct line towards Athdown Ford. All the SW slope of Corrig is a wet marshy place, and would be difficult to make a pathway across.

Note: point 2364ft is Seefinn, pronounced 'Seefing': point 2043ft is Seefingan, pronounced 'Séefingláwn'.

2nd July 1929

Looked at the two raths in Rathshanmore East. The S one is visible from the road, a roughly circular bank of granite stones and earth, (estimated) about 25yds in diameter. Three stone blocks lying inside the circle, but showing no arrangement and with no marks. There are a lot of obviously broken fragments of large granite blocks in the field, in the fences and in two drains which run across the field. There is a small block of granite coming roughly to a point, and about 1½ft high at the NE point of the circle just inside the bank. The other rath is in the second field to the N. Bank of stones and earth, more covered with earth, and a number of thorn bushes on the ring and in the circle — overgrown with bracken. A very large wedge-shaped boulder at the NE of the circle — not standing with the point upright, but in a half-recumbent position. Length about 7ft. There seem to be some other large blocks in the circle but they are entirely overgrown. Estimated diameter of circle, 20yds. A local man I spoke to said he knew of no name on the raheens. He said there was another in Kyle, and another in Knocknaboley. The one in Kyle is presumably the old churchyard of Kilcommon — he pointed to it from the road near Rathshanmore raheen.

4th July 1929

Rathdrum Court. A Garda giving evidence said he met a defendant from Kilmacoo at 'Tippercoo'. Is this a name for Kilmacoo, or is it Tobernaclo, Tigroney? Kilmacoo and Kilmacoo Upper are in Cronebane D.E.D., Rathdrum Court area, and Tobernaclo is in Tigroney West, same D.E.D. (I suspect there was some mistake about this name.)

FIELD NOTEBOOK 4:
July–December 1929

10th July 1929

Horsepass Bridge. In the townland of Britonstown. Turning down Mary's Road from the Humphreystown direction go in by the first gate on the right. The road is now a grassy track still apparently used sometimes by carts as well as by cattle. Near the river there is a row of large old beech trees on the right of the old road, evidently planted in a bank as their upper roots are exposed and bunched together. There was (or is) a ford W of the bridge. The road was embanked up to the bridge: the embankment is there. The pillar of the first arch (S side) remains, with part of the springing of the arch; and it had the common wedge-shaped projection on the E (upriver) side, part of which remains. The masonry is rough, of uncut slaty stone, with good mortar — the arch seems to spring at a slant in a straight line, not curved. There seem to have been five arches. The road curving E round the brow of the hill is clear on the N side, quite grass-grown. The two arches on the N side are quite gone, the stones of the other three remain, forming a sort of breakwater in the river: except in floods, the river runs entirely in a channel where the two N arches were.

22nd July 1929

At Crehelp. Terence Byrne's farm — with Patrick Walsh (National Teacher). (He took full notes.) Terence Byrne showed us, in the second field from the road at the point marked 757ft on the Ordnance Map — the site of a mound — it was 15 or 16ft high, and used to have a car road down it on the W side. His father demolished it for top-dressing 50 years ago, after asking the priest at Dunlavin, who said he might take it down as it was only a pagan who was buried in it. In the centre was a chamber 4½ft long, three upright stones — with one on top — two chambers, bones in the E one, and 'like knives and forks' in the W.

He gave the capstone to Doyle to make a hobstone as his hobstone was burnt away. There was a ring of stones round the tumulus, which they rolled away into a quarry in the SE corner of the field. Byrne also pointed out the position of an oblong cist, in the field under the tumulus, of which he removed and broke up the slabs — and a circular cist lined he said with earthenware 'the same as the pots' and with four urns and an incense cup in it — he broke up the top slabs, and two of the urns, and gave the other three urns to Dr Lyons who gave them to Walsh, they are now in the Museum — Dr Macalister says they are Bronze Age.

Byrne told a story that before the mound was cleared away, people called Mulhall who lived near were always digging in it. One of them dreamed there was money in it, and dug in it; when he opened it a bird, or something in the form of a bird, flew out and struck him in the eye, and he was blind of that eye afterwards. Mulhall went out to Australia, and very soon brought all his people out there too. The old people told Byrne this hundreds of times.

Is this Kinahan's 'Merginstown Moat' (*PRIA* 1901)? (No) and see 'Terry's Moat' (Crehelp) [in an earlier notebook, p.33]. Pronunciation of Plezica — Byrne called it 'Pléssĭcă'.

24th July 1929

Photographed the holed stone at Crehelp.

There is a rath with one rampart fairly complete; a deep moat (ditch) on the E side for more than ¼ of the circumference and the second bank existing for about ⅔ of the way round, in the N part of Merginstown Glen (Map XV. 15. x) on the E ditch of the old road just before it turns E to join the present main road at Annalecky. Depth of ditch (or moat) from top of bank at deepest part, about 12ft. The inside of the rath was tilled — a potato garden, the wide ridges are perfectly clear.

17th July 1929

The Giant's Grave at Parkmore. The field was cultivated, turnips, the ridges running from N to S, i.e. at right angles to the direction of the 'Grave'. The space between the two stones was not tilled, a width of about 5ft being left untouched.

Coolnaskeagh Rath is called 'Mike Doyle's Raheen'. Doyle lives in the house S of the rath.

27th–28th July 1929

The old road from Kilmacanoge to Ballyremon. It forks near the most N point of Killough Upper, both branches are quite clear. One goes on to

Fig. 9—Holed stone at Crehelp (courtesy of the Royal Society of Antiquaries of Ireland ©).

Ballyremon, the other goes down to the left, winding rather to avoid the slope, and comes out on the Long Hill. It is continued then on the other side of the Long Hill by the little winding road which crosses Ballybawn and joins the Old Long Hill road. This branch is now used as a cart road by the farmer who lives on the Kilmacanoge side of the fork just mentioned, up on the hill — the road on the Kilmacanoge side of his farm is only a track, would not be practicable for a cart.

The main line of the old road after crossing the Long Hill goes downhill, passing three houses on the left (E) and two on the right (W). (The last house on the left, a two-storey slated house, was being repaired at the end of July 1929.) Beyond the last house it crossed the stream (Killough River). The road crossing is no longer clear — the present footway crosses 250yds above the house but the road probably went across nearer the house — it was I think banked up — but the embanking here is gone and the

Fig. 10—Crehelp bullaun stone (courtesy of the Royal Society of Antiquaries of Ireland ©).

river is boggy. The road then turns W and goes straight up the steep hill — the stone fences are clear on each side — very wide road at first, then gets narrow near the top — just on the top of the hill on the right are the ruins of three or four cottages with a 'street' between them — the road then turns S again and comes out at the gate in the fence between Killough Upper and Ballyremon Commons, in the S edge of the square recess in the townland boundary. It seems to go straight on S across the commons, but there are a number of paths, and this one would be difficult to distinguish. The 'Long Hill' or new line was only made about 100 years ago — this must have been the road for the people on Ballyremon and Killough to Kilmacanoge — but it was a desperately steep and narrow road. It is the road shown on Fraser's map.

29th September 1929
At Kilbride — on the Goldenhill road. Stopped at the spot where the N

boundary of Goldenhill townland meets the W boundary of Kilbride townland — about 250yds from the place where 'Kevin's Well' is marked [on the map]. I asked a youth where it was, and he said he had never heard of it and that there was no well at all near. He lived ½ mile to the N, and had horses in the field in Kilbride beside where we were standing. He called the little stream on the N side of the Kilbride–Lamb road 'the Lisheens River', not the Brittas River.

There is a rath about 20 or 25yds in diameter just N of the top point of Goldenhill. Almost due E, just outside the entrance are six large boulders, suggesting a passageway by their appearances. There seems to be the remains of a chamber or cist in the centre of the rath — and the surface inside is not even, but consists of a large wide pit 5 or 6ft deep in the centre (containing the stones of the chamber) with six smaller pits of the same depth irregularly placed around — the surface now all grass- and bracken-grown. About NNE and 60 or 80yds away are two large square boulders without marks. It is on Mr 'Yōsses' land and is called a 'raithin' — so a woman told me who passed. There is a raised circular patch of ground on the top point of the hill — no features.

'Yōsses', i.e. Eustace. It belongs to a farmer John Eustace living in Shankill. Dr Mahr believes the circles are hut or camp sites: visited with him 13th January 1930 — he also said the mote at Haylands was much dug away and probably excavated.

12th October 1929

C.G. Thompson gave me some more unrecorded names (see Notebook 2 [p.19]).

His informant about the Glencree and Sallygap neighbourhood was an old man named Cox, uncle of Mrs McGurk of Lough Bray Cottage. It was he who called the Glaskenny dolmen 'Dowina darrig' [see p.20].

Granamore, a hill in the N part of the townland is called 'Carriggower'; it is said that Father Murphy said Mass there in 1798. The highest mountain in this chain is called 'Nira' or 'Noira'. Glashaboy in Ballinagee, called 'Glashawee'. Camenabologue, pronounced 'Cáme-a-múllog' — C.G. Thompson connects it with 'bolg', 'a bag'.

The slope between it and Baravore on the E side is called 'Black Banks'. Conavalla, pronounced 'Cŭnnaválla', or even 'Cŭllaválley'.

Glenflugh in Ballylow pronounced 'Glenflŭch', 'Gleann fliuc'. One of the McGurks called it 'a flat in Brocky', i.e. the neighbouring townland of Ballynabrocky.

Sleanaglogh, near Carrick Mountain, pronounced 'Slāy nă glŏch'. The hill over St Kevin's Bed is called 'Spink'. Trooperstown Hill is called 'Mweeleen', and the valley leading from it down by Glenwood to Cronybyrne is called 'Glenacŏrya'.

Ballycog in Co. Dublin, N of Glencullen Bridge. Joseph Campbell says this is 'Ballycoog' or 'Cuckoo's Town', and hence perhaps the Cookstown River. Joseph Campbell also said there are two 'Lavarney' streams, the E one running down between Gravale and Duff Hill (towards Inchavore River).

1st November 1929

Copied from 'Particulars of Sale' in the Landed Estate Courts, Ireland, in the matter of the Estate of Ralph Crofton Lawrenson, owner; exparte Michael Fowler, petitioner.

Lots 1 to 8 consist of 'Part of the lands of Cullen in the County of Dublin commonly called and known by the name of "Sleighower" as demised by a lease … dated 18th day of April 1820, made by John Roberts to Anthony O'Reilly'.

The map attached [to the particulars] shows that these Lots 1 to 8 consist of the four sides of Grosvenor Square, Rathmines, on which eight houses had been built on the N side and two on the S side, immediately E of the entrance road.

Date on map, 1870. Date of sale 6th May 1870 at the Landed Estates Court, Inns Quay, Dublin — James Blaquiere, solicitor, of 19 Middle Gardiner Street, having carriage of the sale.

30th November 1929

Went with Delargy to Newcastle, interviewed Dick Walker aged 75 (or older?), a Protestant and labourer of Mr Dagg's. He had a couple of folk tales and some riddles, and songs, which Delargy took notes of. He was born at Tomacork, when 5 years old went to Stump of the Castle near Rathdrum, and at 23 years went to Newcastle where he has been since. One of his poems about the killing of Norris' sheep, mentions 'the Glen of Black Bull'. In another he mentioned 'the Danes' Bridge', that is the bridge where the old road from Newcastle to Kilmartin crosses the Chapel River. When I commented on the bridge being called 'the Danes' Bridge', he said something I could not follow about Dunran Castle being 'the Danes' Castle'. (1st February 1930: he said Dunran Castle was built by the Danes.)

2nd December 1929

Chapel, in Redcross parish. The raheen is on a field of Mr Kavanagh's, a circular enclosure with stones heaped in a ring around it. The centre is overgrown with holly trees, thorn bushes, and brambles: no signs of walls are visible. Kavanagh said it was an old burying ground, people used to be buried there long ago: he said there were no ruins of a chapel there. W or SW of the raheen and on the other side of the hedge is a raised bank in the field: Kavanagh said this is called 'the Camp Field', that the soldiers used to be there protecting the priest when he was saying Mass, and that if you stood there you could see invasions coming from all sides. At this place in the field there is a low raised bank about 40 or 50ft long running roughly N and S with another lower bank of the same length running at right angles at each end of it towards the W.

Kilpatrick House — now occupied by a Mr Kingston, previously by people called Byrne. The 'Chapel Bank' (see Dempsey's *Avoca*, p.20) is in Kilpatrick townland on the road leading from Kilpatrick House to Barranisky. Some ruined walls are supposed to be the remains of the chapel, beside the road about 150yds W of the lane leading to Ballymoyle. There was a spring well in the field N of the road, but it was opened and run off by Mr Byrne. A man named Mitchell aged about 60 told me this: he said his uncle was making a fence at the back of one of the chapel walls long ago, and dug up some bits of glass, that might have been hung up over the altar in the chapel. Mitchell thought they were still somewhere about the house. He looked like a labouring man.

3rd December 1929

The ford between Ballymorris and Ballycoog over the Aughrim River has stepping stones, which are called 'the Stone Bridge' (authority: Thomas Tancred). This is where the old road ('sean bealach') crosses the river.

5th April 1932

(Old notes copied off a sheet of paper on which I had jotted them down.)
'Fara·brogue' ('Fèar-a-bróg') is the NW part of Muskeagh.

The mote at the ford near Hacketstown (in the extreme E corner of the townland of Hacketstown Lower) is on the S side of the river, just beside the road. It is called 'Smithers' Mote'. It seems to be a natural hill of gravel which is at present half dug-away for road material.

It has evidently been shaped into an artificial mound, probably as a fortification. Height 20 to 25ft. A step 5 to 6ft wide rather more than halfway up. Diameter at top about 10 or 12ft. Round the base the trace of a ditch and bank very much filled in and obliterated. Gowle is locally pronounced 'Goold'.

Effy's Brook is the little stream running into the Slaney about 250yds NE of Rathmore Bridge, it runs down by Rathmore House. Information given by Mr Peter MacDonnell of Hill View Cottage, Tallow, to Lord Walter Fitzgerald in 1912. (See OS map 1in. = 1 m [mile] (1913 ed.).)

John Maguire of Oakwood — states [that] Hoyles live now in Knocknadroose. Quins [a] relative of his used to live near the shooting lodge in Glenbride. The informer went to the military camped in Marlfield, Carrigacurra.

Blackmoor Hill — Lawrence Hastings of Lugnagun told C. Dickson [M.D.?] that 'the cairn of stones was where Wat Read was hanged'. (Miss Neill of Butterhill said he was called 'Wat Ridd', she supposed that meant Read.) He was speaking of the highest point of the W end of Lugnagun ridge, where Lugnagun Little, Blackrock, and Rathnabo townlands meet.

FIELD NOTEBOOK 8:
January–June 1930

No date

Ballyvaltron. A priest whom I met in Hunter's Hotel told me he had been curate at Barndarrig for about 4 years, but had never heard of an RC chapel or the site of one in Ballyvaltron. Pronunciation 'văl' as in 'valley'.

Keatingstown pronounced 'Céicinŋ stown'. P J. Noonan of Wicklow told me that it is on the S side of the 'Rocky Road' from Wicklow to Rathnew: that is the road which runs from Wicklow towards the reservoir, but forks to the right while the reservoir road goes to the left. Keatingstown is in Ballynerrin according to the spot on the map he showed me. He said the 'old coach road' (that is, the road which coming out of Rathnew is first the same as the Rocky Road but ½ mile or so from Rathnew instead of bending to the left towards Wicklow goes straight on and to the E of the reservoir and so into the Marlton road and on to the Two Mile Water near Bonabrocka) is haunted.

(He pronounced it 'Bŏnabrōōka', first 'o' as in 'gone' — 'oo' as in 'púca').

(If Father McInerney was right this road led past Monishrule which seems to equal Monisharla. Did a remnant of Sir Henry Harrington's force come up this road?)

8th January 1930

Stratford Castle on Ballyhook Hill. It is a small oblong building, walls about 1ft thick, three small splayed windows on each side. An Elizabethan building? No — modern. Never of strength, perhaps built as a look-out building against the O'Tooles etc. in Imaal over which it has a complete view. At the SW end is a smaller square building, walls about 2ft thick, perhaps the remains of a tower. (See *OS Letters.*)

Letter to Dr Mahr from D.M. Doyle as to a cinerary urn found under a flagstone near Baltinglass, and smashed — owner's name (query) Byrne? (To inquire at Tuckmill.)

22nd January 1930

At Baltinglass. 'Vinegar' [a] subdivision of Griffinstown Hill — Michael Coffey (a labourer), Clownstown, Kilcoole.

This man lived in the row of cottages, or houses, on the E side of Kilcoole on the main road, in the middle of the village. He may have come from Clownstown in Co. Meath, as the plaintiff resided in Dunshaughlin; and 'Clownstown' may be merely an addition, to identify him.

25th January 1930

At Kilmartin. We followed the old road from the N. Immediately after leaving the road, there is a stream with a small one-arch bridge over it, like the 'Dane's Bridge'. Then the old road has been fenced across leaving only a stile for foot passengers. The church is on the right just S of the old farm entrance. It is as described by O'Curry except that the lintel-stone, of slate, has come down from over the door, and is lying on the ground: the masonry over the door still remains complete. There is a well just outside the enclosure on the W side. I photographed the church from the W. The door is in the S side and part of a window with sloping jambs can still be traced in the same wall to the E. Continuing up the lane (old road) it has another fence across it immediately S of the old farm entrance: going on S there are frequent gaps into the fields on the W but the gaps on the E seem to have been recently built up. Just before reaching the Shannon Line, there

Fig. 11—Kilmartin church (courtesy of the Royal Society of Antiquaries of Ireland ©).

is a gate right across the road; but it was not locked. One passes the ruin of a cottage on the W. Then over the hill leaving the gap between two rocky cliffs on the W side — (is this the 'Glen of the Black Bull'?). Then past a house, and then the lane leads down to Cullen's of Black Bull (in Barnacoyle).

The 'Dane's Bridge' is two-arched, but the masonry of it and of this small bridge in Kilmartin seem very similar, and the size and width seem about the same.

It was on Tuesday 21st January that I visited and photographed the 'Dane's Bridge' just S of Newcastle Church: I followed the old road towards Ballyvolan. There is an old and elaborate masonry stile at the place where the road bends from W to SW, it is on the N side of the road. A path runs across the fields from it to Timmore House (to which Newcastle is the nearest village), but this stile suggests that originally there was a road from Newcastle to this point, that is that the old road ran direct to Ballyvolan where it forked, the right fork going to Kiltimon and Dunran and the left fork to Kilmartin and Rathnew, etc. Going further along the road, there are two cottages on the right: opposite is another stile, leading to a well, from which one can get down by a path to the track or roadway leading along the bottom of the glen.

Fig. 12—The Dane's Bridge (courtesy of the Royal Society of Antiquaries of Ireland ©).

26th January 1930

The bridge at Oldbridge is dated 1823 on a stone set into the E wall (cf. Holt's *Memoirs*).

27th January 1930

Hollywood. Castle Bank. This is a Norman moat precisely of the type described by Mr Orpen, circular mound, with a ditch round it, and a large

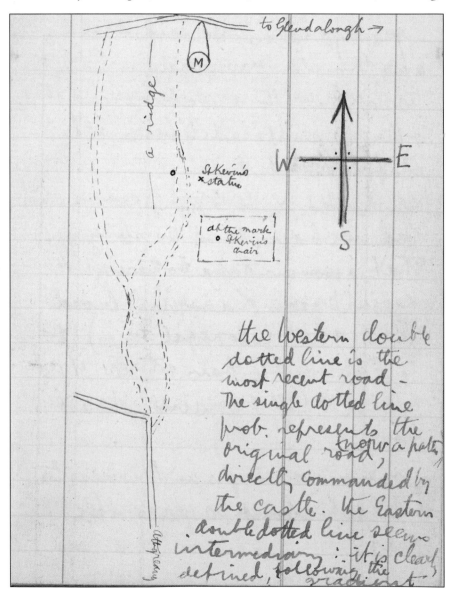

Fig. 13—Sketch-map of roads and tracks at Castle Bank, Hollywood.

platform-like space extending for about 60yds to the N, not so raised as the castle. The ditch is halfway up the site of the mote of the castle. Several large fragments of masonry still lie in the ditch, and the top of the mote seems to be full of stones, and perhaps masonry, covered evenly with grass. The old road led past the castle on the W side, and joined the Athgreany road at the angle.

John O'Toole of Athgreany (?) showed me the Castle Bank. He also told me where Dunboyke Graveyard is. He said there is another old graveyard in Ballybought with a wall round it, and there is supposed to be an old chapel in it.

He showed me St Kevin's Cave, and Bed, and Chair, he said the story is that a woman came bothering St Kevin (pronounced 'Kăhvin', broad 'k' and 'a' as in Donegal 'tá') and he took up the Chair and threw it at her, and it fell and remained where it is now.

This man was 10 years in Minnesota, and is back about 30 years — he is deaf.

3rd February 1930
'Toole's Open' — the name of a lane in Arklow, down the Lower Main Street, near Hugh Byrne's.

4th February 1930
Brought the car over the greater part of the old road from Aughrim to Ballinaclash — entered by the turn to the left next after the turn to Three Wells — past the houses in Crone Beg and up the slope, it is in fair condition, that is, passable for a car, as far as the first gate. After that it became very soft and skiddy — the old road has turned into grass, but the stone road surface remains underneath. At the stream where the road bends just beyond Cloneen the surface was so soft that it was almost impassable for the car, but the momentum on the slope down to the stream carried me up the other slope. After this it again became passable, near the little wood on the right. Just before reaching the grounds of Whaley Abbey (now occupied by Mr Ireland) I found on left of roadway, a pile of broken granite stones, some split by dynamite; and growing among them some old thorn trees and laurel bushes. I asked a boy driving cows what this was, he said it was nothing. On reaching Whaley Abbey grounds I turned to the right and came out by the avenue on to the new road — I could have gone, through

more gates, direct to 'Clash [Ballinaclash]. I passed through five gates altogether, so that the road has very nearly ceased to exist; but about four small farmers in Three Wells still use it as a way to Rathdrum and claim a right-of-way over it, which Mr Byrne of Cloneen, I heard recently, was trying to dispute.

I did not examine the site marked 'Abbey' on the map: I had not time, it was on my left as I went down the avenue to Whaley Abbey gate.

6th February 1930
Examined the old river crossing at Rathdrum. It crosses the river between the townlands of Balleese Lower and Corballis Lower. There is a bridge, of wooden beams, supported at each end on a masonry pillar or platform, and in the middle on iron stanchions, fixed at three places into rocks in the bed of the river. Planks are then nailed across the beams and there are railings at the sides. There do not appear to be any remains of a masonry bridge in the bed of the river: nor are there stepping stones there at present, stepping stones are quickly swept away in these rivers. The river is comparatively shallow above the bridge, and the ford seems to have been there. The road comes straight down from the railway goods station, the track seeming to be still visible in the field beside the hedge. For part of the way lower down it is only a footpath — on the far side of the river there is no obvious trackway up out of the river for carts: the road there must be very long disused. It went to where the footpath starts up the slope, then came back towards the N, and zigzagged back round the top of the slope joining on to the present road — or laneway. The footpath follows a direct track up to the lane. The zigzag of the road has the appearance of having been made in the cliff by cutting, and of having been carefully graded.

The alternative track leading NE seems clear for about 200 or 300yds round the top of the slope outside the field hedge: then it loses itself in the cut through which a little stream flows. I also examined the river at the point where the main road crosses it beside Comerford's mill. It is somewhat deeper here than at the crossing already described. Between the bridge, and the millrace (which has slightly changed the actual course of the river) and the mill building itself, the river is so surrounded and filled with building that it is impossible to say if there was ever a ford there. If so, it would have been a more difficult crossing than the other.

50

Through Comerford's grounds, between Main Street and the main road there is a right-of-way, leading from a point in Main Street almost opposite the Clara Road, to a point in the main road opposite to the way down to the station. At one time this was a road, the cutting away to make it level is quite clear.

12th February 1930

Timolin. The road leading E towards Ballycore. At the top of the cliffs S of this road there is a rath. Central circular platform, flat: a step or platform round it something like that at Tober: then a circular ditch, and bank. Except the central platform which is complete, the works are all destroyed except a small portion on the NE. It looks directly across a river flat to Ballycore Rath. (This must be in the extreme E point of Moone townland).

Ballycore Rath is an ordinary circular rath with thorn trees round it, but at the NE side there is a circular flat-topped platform of earth.

The trace of a road leads up the slope E of the mound or hill on which the rath is situated, reaching the flat space or part of the hill behind (NE of) the rath. Probably the area of this flat part of the hill, with the rath, is what Mr O'Toole's informant called 'a statute acre'. The area of rath and circular platform couldn't be more than about 15 square perch.

Went from there via Kilgowan to Knockandort. After crossing into Co. Wicklow over the stream which is the county boundary, I walked up the lane which leads in to the left. Called 'Bowery' on the map. There is a conical hill, exactly like a large tumulus. It is being dug away, and appears to be a natural gravel mound. Circular. I asked a boy on the road for the name but he could not give it to me — but the man who lives there is called Henry Byrne.

The boy was from Brewel. He knew the stones on the hill, he said a giant threw them there, and that a hound jumped from 'Kyle' to there. Pronunciation like Irish 'Coill'. Is it Knocknagull? There is no townland near named Kyle.

All the country between Kilgowan and Dunlavin is full of gravel mounds of irregular shapes, and here and there pools of water between them. Hence the name 'Usk' ('Uisge')?

Notes from my Rathdrum and Wicklow notes of cases

7th July 1927
Rathdrum. Laurence Mahon charged with malicious damage to turf.

Denis McCoy senior — tenant on Hago's estate, Turbary on Wicklow Gap. He said St Kevin's Road is the boundary between Brockagh and Glendalough. His family [have been] there 'hundreds of years'. Glashaboy, he pronounced it 'Glashawee' Bridge. Lawrence Mahon said he claimed the turf between the highest point on the high road, and St Kevin's Road which he called 'the lane'. It was stated in court there was to be a motion in the High Court for an injunction by Mahon against McCoy.

6th October 1927
Rathdrum. Case of trespass to turf Editha Gardiner's estate, Tomriland.

Peter Mooney, complainant, 72 years of age. His father died in 1897 aged 95. (Evidence as to extent of bank), pronounced Annagolan 'Annagowlann'. Patrick Windsor witness of Tomriland pronounced 'Tom-ɜ-riland'. Edward Timmons of Moneystown aged 68.

It was Mooney who told me about 'Hoult's Walls' at Mullinaveige.

'Coyne's Bank' is the place where the Kilmartin–Dunran road crosses the main road. Is it the slope of the old Ballyvolan road?

2nd August 1928
Charles Lawlor farmer of Moyntiagh near Rathdrum, he pronounced it 'Mōntiăgh' (two syllables).

6th September 1928
Rathdrum. Ballykean near Arklow pronounced 'Ballykane'.

19th September 1928
Wicklow. Simon Brien of 'Ballinameestia' (spelled [on] OS [map] 'Ballinameesda') has a farm at ('Rŭscăh') Roscath.

21st November 1928
Wicklow. Mr Truell owner of lands of Clonmannon Murrough.

Crowlock: gamekeeper to the Wicklow coursing club.

2nd May 1929

Rathdrum. Patrick Byrne of Farbreaga. He pronounced Baltinglass with a sort of 'k' sound instead of 't', as though the whole of his tongue was against his hard palate (a small farmer).

5th December 1929

Rathdrum. Labourer named Jordan — pronounced Ballykillavane 'Ballykillavawn'. Keatingstown near Wicklow 'Kaytinstown'.

Robert Wingfield, proprietor of Dunran.

18th February 1930

The Downs and Woodlands — old church. It was restored by the Board of Works in 1906. The schoolchildren called it 'St Mary's Church'.

There was evidently a village of some importance there at one time. In one place where a field is surrounded by high walls there is about half of a doorway of the 'Queen Anne' type built into the wall and there are other windows and doorways built up in walls nearby. A track seems to have run at one time from the corner of the road leading to the school and old church, SE across the hill, to the point where there is a stile in the E wall of the present main road — this track is cut out as though it had been a road. It is all grass- and thorn-grown.

Ballykinlea pronounced 'Balləkin lay'. This is the name for the land lying on each side of the main road near Mr Henry's house S of Blessington. It is probably the denomination called 'Part of Glebe East' between Burgage More, Burgage Moyle and Glashina.

26th February 1930

'Coolin's of the Long Stone'. This is the house on the E side of the main road, in Ballinacrow Upper, and on the N side of the side road leading to Eadestown. It is at the corner where the two roads join.

The Long Stone stands behind the house on the N side of the stream with two or three boulders near it. It is of granite.

3rd March 1930

The mound which I have so often noticed on the N bank of the Aughrim River is only a few yards W of the 'stone bridge', or ford, at Ballycoog.

Was there a fort of any kind here to guard the river crossing?

I gave a lift to a woman who lived in Kilpipe — she pointed me out the old graveyard in a clump of trees about 300yds E of the road. She said there are no remains of the castle but they say it was in a small field called 'the Castle'; you cannot see a stone there now, but the field is full of hollows.

Quigginroe. Price's crossroads. Three townlands and three parishes meet at this point. In the small field in front of Watchorn's house (Killabeg) on the NW side of the road junction is a stone of white quartz: it stands 6½ft high from the earth to the top, and there is a grassy base round it which is a further 6in. above the level of the field: this grassy base extends for about 12ft in length running N and S, the stone being in the middle. The stone is of an irregular shape, but tapering somewhat towards the top. At a height of 2ft from the level of the field the stone measures 20in. broad from N to S and 25in. from E to W.

This seems too massive for a scratching stone, and it has the appearance of a standing stone ('Long Stone') or boundary stone. There is a local story that a tailor who committed suicide was buried at this crossroads a long time ago, and his ghost is sometimes seen. (Note: there is a small mound in the field immediately E of Price's crossroads, which is partly dug away. Could the pillar stone have come off this?)

The level road leading from Mullinacuff Church to Kilquiggin Chapel was built in the time of the famine by Mr Mumford.

Ballynavortha. A farmer told Reverend Mr Young that there are some old walls in this townland that are called 'the Walls of Troy'.

The graveyard at Springfield. I found from Mr Tom Kavanagh of the Railway Tavern, Arklow, who was born at Springfield, that this graveyard has no name, other than 'Springfield' or 'Ballinabanoge', which is the name of a neighbouring townland. The field has been entirely tilled, so that the position of the graveyard cannot now be seen.

I have not yet visited the place.

George Darcy lately of Main Street, Arklow, a jeweller, had a book relating to the Cistercian abbey in Arklow and about the county generally. He has gone to Manchester to live and has taken the book with him.

4th March 1930
Went through Coolattin Demesne entering from the Greenhall side and

going to Ballykelly House. From Ballykelly House the road leads down a steep incline called 'the Long Hill' to the E side of Deegin's Bridge. Then turns to the left over the next bridge ('Lattin Bridge', but I did not get this name there) and then round by the right towards Shillelagh, but an old track leads up through the trees straight on and this was probably the old road. At the gate opposite the road to Stoops (so pronounced) and Carnew, the avenue leads in at the gate and immediately round to the left (Shillelagh direction) — but there are some old trees leading in a straight line with the old road leading up from the gate, and this probably marks the old road. The demesne is now full of paths and tracks leading in all directions: but the house itself would be practically on the line of the old Carnew road, which would account for its disappearance.

N.B. Drimingall is pronounced 'Drĭm-íngle' ('ingle' as in 'ingle-nook'). But this was by Hopkins, query: has he got the native pronunciation? Yes, Tom Fleming gave me the same.

6th March 1930

Slateroe is the name of the little village of houses on the way down from the main Rathdrum–Avoca road to Ballinaclash, near the gate of the house of Mr Wilson of Ballyknockan. Pronounced 'Slate-row' ('ow' as in 'low' or 'hoe').

Is it an English or an Irish name?

11th March 1930

Co. Kildare. The townlands of Coghlanstown West and Donode Big form the parish of Coghlanstown, W of Ballymore Eustace. The E boundary of the parish is the road leading from Sillagh Ring, and it goes direct to the River Liffey, the S part being now only a track. Where it touches the river there are the signs of a now disused ford. There are the remains of a small platform of rough concrete a few feet from the bank of the river and in front of it there are two small concrete pillars about 6ft apart with wooden posts out of them. I don't know what this was for. The river has clearly been changing its course slowly southwards at this point. The S bank is a high bank of clay and gravel rising out of the river, and being eaten away. Recently fallen portions lay just in the river. The N side is a flat field of grass, a similar bank on the N side being now at a distance from the river;

the point where the road cuts through this bank (it is about 8ft below the top of the bank) is now about 200yds from the ford. The bottom is gravelly, and shallow right across. At a guess I should say it is 4ft deep near the N bank.

The track leads through a white gate on the S side of the road; there is a house built on the actual track of the old road, and a little further on a grass-covered platform cut out in the field on the W side of the road. I should say the site of an old house.

(Is this place 'Greallach Daphil'?)

12th March 1930

Brewel Hill. Circle 68 paces in diameter; about 3ft deep.

Church Mountain 106ft, Bruss 143ft, Hill of Allen 357ft, Galteem 222ft [and] Pinnacle 174ft.

[One of the stones at Brewel Hill] has wedge marks … .

On my way down spoke to a man, like a small farmer's son (I think a parishioner of Father Stafford's), who was going back from the fair of Dunlavin. He and another boy said the marks were made by a greyhound on the stone: they said there are five marks in all. 'Kyle' is a graveyard just W of the main road between Blackrath and Brewel Hill: it has no connection with these Piper's Stones — but Killeen has. (I expect the boy made a mistake meaning Killeen not Kyle.) I pointed to Knockdoo not naming it and asked what it was, he said 'Knockadow', but Father Stafford called it 'Knockadoo'. I asked them about Knocknagull but he had heard no such name. I then asked about Knockandort. He said he never heard the name until he saw it recently on a poster advertising a sale: he had cut meadow there, and it was always called 'The Bowery' ('ow' as in 'cow'), and if you sent a letter to 'The Bowery, Dunlavin', it would be delivered there.

(There is a path leading from Dunlavin to Ballymount across the fields, it leads over the top of Brewel Hill — this is the path he was taking.)

Note — sunrise midsummer day, 47° 21mins E of N. Magnetic variation at Dunsink Observatory 1929, 17° 31mins W. Decrease at present about 9mins a year. From the above measurements, the stone [with wedge marks] would appear to be a pointer for Church Mountain, which is 1° N of true E of Brewel Hill, [this] stone being 2° S of W. [The E] stone does not fit in with any noted monument: Mulleghmast [?] is 10° more E of N (i.e. about 229° E of true N).

[Excerpt] from *The Times* [newspaper] 1948:

'The Bowery
From our own correspondent
New York, Jan. 21
A campaign to change the name of that New York street "famed in song and story", the Bowery, because of complaints that it had "become associated with low-class people," has been abandoned. By a vote of 65 to 64 its merchants have decided to improve the character of the street and leave its name, inherited from the Dutch settlers of three centuries ago — when a *bouwerie* was a farm —alone.'

17th March 1930

Photographed the Castletimon Ogham. I thought the 'I (...)' at the end seemed quite clear. The inscription does not seem very worn.

Peggy Earl aged 9 knew the marks on it were letters — she said they were the name of a giant who was buried underneath it.

I also photographed from the SE the dolmen in Brennan's Field (it is in the townland of Brittas). Peggy Earl said it was thrown there by a giant from the top of Castletimon Hill (see Tuomey's art., *JRSAI*, vol. 3, p.187).

Capstone, approximate length 12ft 6in. E to W, approximate height N to S 11ft 9in.

Fig. 14—Castletimon ogham stone (courtesy of the Royal Society of Antiquaries of Ireland ©).

upper surface presents a broken appearance. It appears to form a chamber in the S side of the dolmen. [Internal measurements: 4ft 1in., 3ft 4in., 4ft 6in.]. Depth of dolmen … approximately 6ft 6in.

I took two magnetic bearings: could not see any others which would be useful:

1. from approximate centre of [the third stone, or backstone] to approximately midway between the inner surfaces of [the first stone and the sidestone], 133° 50mins E of magnetic N = 116° 25mins E of N;
2. a line along the centre of [the third] stone running from SW to NE (the faces are more or less parallel) 61° E of magnetic N = 44° E of N.

I should say that [the third] stone has been damaged by the fall of the capstone. Possibly moved, as Tuomey suggests.

I asked Peggy Earl were there any marks on the stones: she said 'No' — (she was right, there are none). I asked her did she know of any stones except the ogham with marks on — she said 'No'. I asked her did she ever hear of a stone with marks made on it by a dog, she said 'No'.

(A man who was bailiff or keeper at Mount Browne, Carlow, told me about 6 years ago when I was looking at the Mount Browne Dolmen, that he came from Brittas near Wicklow, and that there was a stone there with marks made on it by a dog.)

26th March 1930

At Ballintruer Beg. The castle merely consists of the remains of an oblong tower. The whole base of the E wall seems to be standing, about 15ft wide — it is 8 or 10ft high at the SE corner, and shows a batter from 3ft high to the ground, on both E and S walls. For 18 or 20ft there is from 8 to 6ft of the S wall standing.

Nothing of the N or W walls. The NE corner is not clear, it is only about 3ft high. No feature such as window or door is visible. The owner of the field in which it stands, Mr Moody, was there. He told me people called Doyle of Stratford dreamed there was money in it and dug down until they came to a flag — Did they get any money? No. The hole is there still, in the space between the walls. They had to (partly) fill it in, as a cow fell into it and was hurt. There is the track of a ditch or moat round the castle in the field. It is ploughed up. Moody said he came on three or four nice little flagstones in it, he lifted one but there was nothing in it but water. It was like a 'shore' (sewer).

About half a mile directly S in a field about 200yds from the road is a small raised mound, 12 to 15ft in diameter. No feature. It is called 'the Mote'. It is marked on the map.

Query, is Ballyhubbock Bridge an old bridge?

Fig. 16—Ballintruer Beg Castle (courtesy of Dúchas The Heritage Service ©).

The field in Castleruddery, immediately opposite the gateway of Donaghmore House (the large house in Donaghmore) is called 'the Terraces'. It has a number of rectangular divisions in the SW corner, like old ponds or something of the kind. There are two small, half-destroyed, circles of large stones in this field, on the brow of the hill. ([Sheet] 21, 29.8cm N; 49.6cm E.)

29th March 1930

Ballydonagh. The moat is just W of Holyfield House, in a field which is called 'the Mount Field'. I got no other name, either for the moat or for the spring which is just S of it, and from which a small stream runs down to the W. The moat is a hill of natural gravel, sand and stones, presumably glacially deposited, and was formerly used as a sandpit. It is partly dug away, especially at the SE and at the W side of the top. The sandhill was shaped to make the moat, but it is difficult to distinguish now what its shape was, possibly [terraced].

It does not seem to present any feature of interest; I saw no boulders about.

O'Curry calls it 'the remains of a fine moate'; it must have been more dug away since his time.

30th March 1930

Kilbride, Blessington. Looked for St Kevin's Well. On the slope of the hill S of Glen Heste House there is an old track leading from the back gate of the house. On this track 100yds from the gate and near a ruined cottage there is a large covered-in concrete tank, with pipes leading into it and out, and a small overflow basin — it is a water tank, presumably for supplying the house, though I could not see the pipeline. This tank is perhaps filled from the source which used to supply St Kevin's Well. The side of the hill is wet, but there is now no place on it that could be called a well, or spring. There is in front of, and about 50yds from the ruined cottage, a built-up semicircular well-head, but it is dry and filled up with earth. It has an older appearance than the cottage ruins, being not unlike St Bridget's Well in Kilranelagh Churchyard.

E of the old track, and just outside the back gate of Glen Heste House, there is an enclosure covered with laurels, with some cypress trees and some old high box bushes in it. In the middle is an obelisk of grey stone with what appears to be a tombstone in front: it is inscribed:

'ERECTED TO THE MEMORY OF ISABELLA PRATT WHO DIED THE … 1910.'

(and of two other people). On the E and S edges this plot slopes very suddenly, quite like the edge of a tumulus, or of a natural gravel mound. A path leads into it along the E side of the field behind Glen Heste and through the shrubs. Is this old Kilbride Churchyard? It is much the size of a small early graveyard, but I saw no sign of any other tombstones or of any walls. The nearness of St Kevin's Well suggests a holy site.

6th April 1930

Seefin. S end, stones 2 to 3ft long, roughly flat in shape, and 8 or 9in. to 1ft thick. Fairly uniform in shape. Clear suggestion of closing in a roof as at Newgrange.

Photo of the above taken towards a point 170° E of N. Second photo taken of cairn looking towards point 272° E of N. Breadth between stones, greatest 33in.; narrowest 20in. Length of opening, about 8ft.

The cairn is a large one though obviously much scattered. Round the base is a clear circular line of large stones each 4ft or so long.

This is the point '2043ft' on the map in Athdown townland. There is a square stone on the cairn, obviously an OS trigonometrical point.

12th April 1930

Went to view the furniture at Baltyboys House, saw the owner, Mrs Bradley, daughter of Colonel Graydon-Smith. She was previously married to Captain Stannus. She said the Inchaclare was the fourth bend of the river, as we looked *down* the Liffey from the house. The Castle Inches were immediately below and behind the house, and the site of the old castle was immediately above that, i.e. a very short way SW of the present house. She said her grandfather (or great-grandfather?) built Burgage Bridge — and that there used to be always fighting between 'our' castle and 'McCann's' Castle: by which she meant Burgage Castle. Baltyboys House is a fine early 19th-century house, I should say.

Later visited the Brusselstown Ring, with Dr Mahr, Eamonn O'Toole of Rathvilly, and Professor Eamonn O'Toole of Trinity College Dublin. Mahr's opinion was that from the appearance of the structure one could give no opinion as to its age.

Later we excavated the cist at Knocknatubbrid, Co. Carlow.

15th April 1930

Kilmurry near Newtown. The chapel here was unroofed — that is 'the slates were taken off about 20 years ago' — so a local man told me. The walls are in good preservation, but the plaster has fallen off. The graveyard is used at the present time. The chapel was evidently used in 1839, see *OS Letters*, p.210. O'Curry says the old chapel of Kilmurry was burnt in 1798. The old road in front of the chapel is the townland boundary between Kilmurry and Monalin on the N, and Ballinahinch on the S. It is quite passable for a motor car.

23rd April 1930

Baltinglass. Walked up to the top of Pinnacle, with Patrick Kinsella (local court messenger). We followed a passway which he said led to Coolinarrig, Greenmill (which he said was near Ballinroan) and Kilranelagh. He said when the new chapel was built between 50 and 60 years ago, the stones were got from the top of Pinnacle. Around the top is a ruined wall of stones enclosing (at a guess) about an acre. It is just a ruined heap of stones, overgrown with grass — in places 6 or 8ft wide. The cairn is at the top point of the hill, it is of loose stones. At the bottom can be seen in places the stones which formed a containing circle lying flat and end to end, as at Seefin. There is a chamber in the cairn, partly ruined; it is not all exposed — it seemed to lie S and N, and the S and N ends were visible. The line of supporting blocks was clear at the N end with two covering stones in position — at the S end only a few large flat slabs were visible among the small stones. In 1838 (see *OS Letters* p.94) the *Namebook* says 'on the NE side ... is the evident remains of a stone cave'. This would suggest that the W side was then covered.

Kinsella knew of no name for the rath, and had never heard the name Rathcoran. (Mr Bryne P.C. calls it 'Rathcormuck'.)

He said some ruined houses on the S side were the village of 'Cunniganstown' or 'Cunnigamstown' ('Conynghamstown'?

[Cunniamstown?]). Two hundred years ago the people from it were supposed to have buried the dead in the hill, not in any churchyard.

He also pointed to a spot about NW of the top and said there was coal found there, not coal dust, but hard coal, wood coal, he said.

We went on to Cars Rock, which is just an outcrop of rock. He said that after the 1918 election, at the suggestion of old Mr Conway (an old Parnellite, aged 80 years) the people brought tar barrels up to Cars Rock, and lit them, and rolled about eight or nine of them burning down the hill towards the town, and burned the rest on the top. He never heard of this being done before.

He showed me the well where the Cunnigamstown people had to get water, right down on the passway quite near the old chapel. It now has one side broken out to make a watering place for cattle, but it was then built up all round and covered over.

15th June 1930

Looked again for Sheelah's Well at Kindlestown but could not find it. From the top of Kindlestown Hill the old lane leading across Coolagad, W of Coolagad House, is quite clear — it comes as far as, and joins, the lane leading down to the back of Coolagad House — thence from where it joins it runs a small distance further S, but disappears, and there is no sign of its joining the Blacklion–Delgany road. As it is going in the direction of Kindlestown Castle (which is also visible from the hill), it seems probable it is part of the old road from Bray to Kindlestown.

I also walked the old road through Kilmurry South to Kilmacanoge. On the left there is a distinct hollow between the base of [the] Big Sugarloaf and this road: I would guess that this is the 'Lugroe' of the *OS Letters*, but I have not yet got the name.

In Bray Court, on 13th June 1930. Edward Beale farmer of Killough pronounced it 'Killyōge' or 'Killyōghe', the last sound rather indistinct, accent on 'Kill'.

No date

Taylor and Skinner's Road Maps. First edition 1778 — surveyed 1777. Second edition corrected down to 1783. (Wicklow names in alphabetical order) — [Price lists all the placenames on these maps; they are not reproduced here].

Note, the second edition shows the line of the main road from Blessington to Baltinglass, as far S as Hollywood: so this road must at least have been projected as early as 1783.

The name 'Foulkes Esq.' is shown at Cronawinnia but the latter name is not marked: the house is shown.

The present main road [from] Rathnew to Glenealy did not exist: nor did the Marlton road out of Wicklow. The road into Wicklow from the S was down the hill to the courthouse and Market Square: the road from Wicklow to Glenealy was by Ballynabarny — 'Red Peg's Crossroads'.

FIELD NOTEBOOK 9:
May–August 1930

1st May 1930

At Rathdrum Court, drove home past Ballinderry House — it is locally called 'Grove Hall' and a man named Walsh now lives in it, who uses it as a nursery-garden. A greenhouse against the S gable wall. I do not know if this is Henry Temple's house. I followed the old road which is the townland boundary between Ballysheeman and Ballyhad Upper. There is an overgrown rath, with a spring on the E side of it in the fields in Ballyhad Upper on the E side of this road. No features. This old road is only just passable for a motor: no gates. Went to see Knockrath Castle. Local pronunciation 'Knockray' (as in 'gay') or 'Knockrath'. Its plan is roughly thus (not to scale):

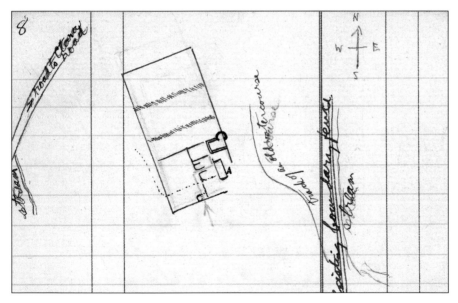

Fig. 17—Sketch-plan of Knockrath Castle.

The rectangle is a piece of rough grazing land surrounded by a ditch 4 or 5ft deep and 6ft wide or more — on the inside there are traces of a drystone wall — it is broken down rather at the SE corner. At A [on plan] a cottage was built perhaps 100 years ago, presumably out of the stones of the castle. The cartway in to this cottage was by the dotted line [from NW turning E]. I think a gap was broken through the outer wall for this purpose

65

and also through the intermediate wall. I could not see clearly where the original entrance was but I thought it was in the middle of the S wall, where I thought I saw the remains of a small gatehouse, with a modern piece of drystone wall built across a gap just E of it. From this the cartway may have gone straight in, and turned to the right between what look like the remains of outhouses, which would have been thatched. Then to a point between the cottage ruins and the castle ruins.

The tower was at the middle E side, with a round tower at the NE corner. Walls of tower or castle proper, about 5½ft thick. Walls of round tower, about 4ft thick. The general level of walls remaining is about 4ft high.

From the castle the old road leading down from Park to Clara Bridge is fully visible for a stretch of about 1½ miles. The nearest point in view is about 1¼ miles away as the crow flies. The castle was probably an outlying fort of the Gabhal Raghnal, intended to guard the road from Dublin to Ballinacor.

The hatching on [the map of] the N part of the enclosure represents terraces, well made and steeply sloped, which look like portion of a scheme of fortification; but why are they only inside the rectangular enclosure?

When was the castle built? and when did it cease to be inhabited? In the *Fiants of Elizabeth* Hugh Duff McDonnell is given as 'of Knockrath'.

An old man from the locality told me that Mr Edge (who used to be the tenant of Knockrath) dug in the round tower for gold. This old man said the castle was called 'King O'Toole's Castle' but that he only heard this name lately.

The castle is very ruinous, most of the walls being only heaps of stones.

6th May 1930

Visited Aghowle Church — the doorway is slightly inclined, being 32½in. wide at top and about 35in. at the bottom. It has a step, chamfered, at the bottom of each jamb, like Kilcroney. It is surprisingly big considering the antique appearance of the doorway.

Note its position, about 1½ miles due N of the 'Lob na saighe' at Moylisha, which is on the slope of the hill to the S.

Followed the old road via Harris' Hill to Kilquiggin. The old cross is in the grounds of the house which is about 500yds from the crossroad near Kilquiggin Catholic Church, on the S side of the road. It is in a large field adjoining the road. It is locally called 'the Crush'. All that remains is a large granite block, roughly shaped to the form of a pedestal with a well-cut rectangular cavity in it. About 12in. x 7in. x 6in. deep. And the head of the cross [is], as in the published photograph, much battered, and weathered.

There is a circular, flat, raised portion in the mid-space between the arms, both at back and front, and on one side the owner of the farm pointed out what he said was chiselling — there are depressions in the circular space, but I could distinguish no design. He has not tilled the space behind 'the Crush', but cleared away a lot of small stones and rubbish which lay on this space, and used it as top dressing.

He said his father-in-law remembered how people used to have to go from Laragh and Kilquiggin round by Boley into Shillelagh — (so neither the famine road, nor the main road was made at the time — perhaps 100 years ago).

Went on by the old road through Laragh and Stranakelly. There is a well called 'the Blessed Well' on the W side of the old piece of road leading from the Tinahely–Shillelagh road to Ballynultagh.

Is this Tober Nahan? I asked two old people for its name, neither could remember it, but one said it had an Irish name.

It consists of a spring coming out over a space some yards square through the grass — a large elm tree, probably 150 years old, growing in the centre of it. No rags on the bushes near. The water is run into a shallow basin made with stones.

Kilpipe. The old church is the ruin of a medieval structure, windows the top of which were shaped thus [like a broad arch], and a fine large arch over the altar with a semicircular recess behind it in which presumably the altar was set. The graveyard is enclosed by a wall or banks partly curved, and partly straight-lined — it might be the circular enclosure of a rath cut afterwards in places, or it might be a modern unshaped enclosure. No new gravestones. One to Benjamin Coates of Ruddenagh, died in 1855.

12th May 1930

Blessington Demesne. Piper's Stones. On coming in towards Blessington on the Naas road, the first townland in Wicklow one comes to is Deerpark. This is on one's left, the road being bounded on that side by a stone wall which is the county boundary. At the boundary between Deerpark and Blessington

Demesne there is a small lane going in to the left; and here the county boundary crosses the road, and runs S, marked by a low stone wall, for 60yds or so, and then E. Between the road and this wall one passes two fields on the right, then a house, then a small gravel-pit; this gravel-pit is in the NW corner of a large field which runs as far as the next small lane on the right; this field is known as 'the Piper's Stones Field', and the farmer who owns it says there used to be old stones in it according to old maps. Part of this field, near the gravel-pit, is quite high; probably the stones were here.

I could see no sign of any stones which looked as though they belonged to the monument in any gate nearby (see O'Conor's account, *OS Letters* p.356). All the walls are made of quite small stones.

Butterhill. The mote. This is the green tumulus which is so prominent on the S side of the Liffey W of Blessington, with a tree growing on it. It is roughly circular and was probably originally flat-topped — but portion of it was dug away in the centre and towards the NE presumably for top dressing, so that it has a rim now towards the SW. The tree is planted in the part dug away: I should guess it to be about 60 or 80 years old. I saw no stones on it or near it. It is supposed that a king is buried under it; Mr O'Neill who lives on the left-hand (N) side of the road about 200yds W of Woodend Bridge told me this, and said that he [the king] was buried in it and the tree planted over him; and that part of the mote had been dug away. This suggests to me that the farmer who dug it out found a burial and stopped digging and planted a tree over the bones or stones; (cf. P. Walshe's account of Friarhill).

O'Neill also said that there is a big stone 'the size of a small house' by the brook under Lugnagun — (i.e. in Lugnagun Great); that if I went to Lugnagun and asked for 'the big stone by the brook' anyone would show it to me. 'It is shaped like a horse's back, and has a step cut on it, and stones cut and fitted under it.'

The man who was hanged on Blackmoor Hill 'is called Rid, I suppose that is Reed'. They had a camp there in '98; there is a well there called the Camp Well; 'it was blessed since'.

Oldcourt. The site where the castle was is the field in the W angle of the four crossroads, where there are lumps in the grass. A man named Halligan pulled it down to build his house. So a man on the road aged about 60 told me, and he said he remembered the walls standing; but it wasn't a castle: (I had asked him first about castle ruins and he said there was none except at Threecastles; then he said there had been a building in the field he pointed out to me, and it was said it was a 'barrack').

Kilbride. The road leading down the hill from Ballyfolan used to continue on towards the river; the green track continues for 150yds or so at present, then it continues as a mass path to Kilbride Catholic Church, turning at right angles by a stile another 200yds on, and crossing the river by a stone and iron footbridge, and by a graveyard up to the church. I could see no traces of a church or building in the graveyard, but it is fairly old. I saw a tombstone dated 1726 and another 1799.

The path went straight on as a footpath to a place where the stream would I think be fordable (no ford there now), and this would make a straight line with the Threecastles road on the other side.

19th May 1930

Arklow. Before the present Protestant church was built the Protestant church stood on the S side of the Upper Main Street where a range of buildings now stands marked 'Church Buildings' [on the OS map] — it was a little bit back from the street. The old graveyard is opposite to it, surrounded by a stone wall. The graveyard is 6 to 7ft higher than the level of the street and surrounding lanes (Kinsella's Lane on W and River Lane on E). It is entirely disused, no doorway into it, and overgrown with brambles and nettles. It contains 19th- and 18th-century tombstones; I saw no older ones, and saw no traces of a building.

Abbeylands. The abbey graveyard is also entirely enclosed — the entrance is by Abbey Lane, but it is bricked up, the iron gate being still there on the inside — a stone cross, granite, stands over the gateway. The graveyard is no longer used, but it is not in as bad condition as the other. It is at the N and E corner of Abbeylands. The town buildings are N and E of it, and a large field S and W. A small field belonging to Mr William Hall, enclosed, some distance S of the graveyard, is called 'the Old Orchard'. Mr Hall planted apple trees in it, but it had the name before that. The tombstones appear to be 18th- and 19th-century. There is no sign of a building in it, but Mr Hall said there used to be a watch tower at the SW corner for watching the graves to prevent bodies being stolen.

A spot just on the border between Arklow and Tinahask Lower is said to have been the site of a chapel; just near Lower Main St. Presumably the RC chapel before the present one was built — the position is in the lower town, called 'the Fishery'. The Upper Main St. is called by the name of 'the Flash'.

Pollacholly ('Poll an ċopaid', 'weir-hole'?) is at the rock at the end of the western of the two Coomies Lanes. Some distance above in the river is a ford called 'the Horse Ford'.

20th May 1930

Newtownmountkennedy. The 'mote' in Mount Kennedy Demesne is just S of the house. Flat top, about 50ft (estimated) in diameter. Halfway down is a terrace, about 12ft wide (estimated). The mound appears to be about 25ft high above the level of the field. It has two arched grottos built into it on its E side (slightly S of E), and a ruined piece of wall with an arch in it built on the top in the centre. These are no doubt 18th- or early 19th-century decorations. The wall on top is leaning over [to] W, as though its foundation had sunk. Possibly the mound was shaped also when these were built. It is called 'the Moat' by the old people about.

(Later) Kilcroney. With Superintendent Casserley and Mr Coster, the steward, who showed us round the demesne. The Pilgrim's Well, near the W boundary, adjoining Glencormick (photographed). He also showed me the old yew tree mentioned by O'Curry, which I photographed with him beside it. I then measured the church further: as follows:

Window in S wall: height 31in., height from base to spring of arch on W 27¾in., on E 28in.

Width at spring of arch 6in., at base of window 6½in. (jambs of window worn). A chamfer all round, including sillstone [length 7in.]. Chamfer about 2in. Height of arch in top stone 3in.

Inside: height 70½in. Measured on inside of splayed window 37½in. (sloped) (this measurement is taken by laying the rule along the splay, from front to back). Depth from front of sillstone 35in. Width 40in. (at the greatest width of the splay). Nine stones in arch — a keystone broken at back and four on each side; symmetrical.

SW corner: squared granite, 124in. from top of wall at corner to the upper level of stone foot or plinth, which is 16in. above present ground level.

Fig. 18—The Pilgrim's Well, Kilcroney (courtesy of the Royal Society of Antiquaries of Ireland ©).

Fig. 19—Mr Coster standing beside the yew tree at Kilcroney (courtesy of the Royal Society of Antiquaries of Ireland ©).

On the S wall the face is set back 3 to 3½in. after going E about 2 to 3ft —
there is no regular line, it is merely a bad patchwork.

Portion of the inside of the N wall near the W end has fallen in since I was
there last. The outer surface of the W wall is quite flat and even, as far
as I could see, all over — no projections. No opening in this wall, nor
any mark of one having been built up.

25th May 1930

At the Sillagh Ring and Donode Moat, Co. Kildare. The moat had a vallum
all round. It, the moat, has been trenched across from N to S, and a building,
I think (all trace is gone), built on the E end — a way for carts seems to
have been made thus [from S–E–N].

The ring is elliptical or oval in shape. Three-quarters of it remains, the
E side is gone. On this E side runs the road from Kilteel and Rathmore —
just beside the ring. Was the road made after the ring? Whether or not, it
seems probable that the E side of the ring was used for road material
sometime or other, i.e. gravel. The W ditch of the road may have been the
ditch of the ring, as there is a slight bend in this ditch, just where the curve
of the ring would be likely to join it. Between the ring and the moat is a
long flat ridge, which would make an admirable place for a temporary
assembly or collection of people. The moat commands it at the S end.

Mullacash Hill (which = 'Caisse'?) is about a mile to the W across a
slight depression.

I asked a boy at Ballinascorney where was Finn's Stone — he said it was
called 'Finn McCoul's Stone' and was 'up there', pointing to Glennasmole,
and that I should go down the hill and turn to the right.

1st June 1930

R. Barton said that Balislam, pronounced 'Băl-eye-lum', was where
Hamilton's house was; and that about a dozen families live in Balislam
[Balisland]: that it is part of Carrigroe. Hamilton's house is in Carrigroe.
Morris of Windgate built the house, and sold it to Guinness, who sold it to
Hamilton.

2nd June 1930

Ballyclogh Lower. At the top of the hill on the old road, on the E side about

Fig. 20—Sillagh Ring, dated 10/10/1936; however, it may date from the excursion of the Royal Society of Antiquaries of Ireland on 3/10/1936 (courtesy of Dúchas The Heritage Service ©).

150yds from the road, is a portion of the field slightly banked up — covered with long grass and of uneven surface — with an old thorn tree growing at each end. This is the site of an old graveyard. A woman to whom I spoke (age about 45) said that her husband's father who was about 90 when he died, remembered people being buried in it.

It is marked on the OS map as 'Site of Church', but there is no sign of a church in it, nor of gravestones — though probably one could find stones under the earth in the lumpy places. The spot is never tilled, nor is it mown — but cattle are grazed there.

This woman also showed me where the old chapel in Ballyvaltron was; the field is called 'the Chapel Field' and there is a quarry in it. It is just NW of her house which is the black spot on the Wicklow 1-inch OS sheet (revised in 1898) immediately in front of (i.e. W of) the 'B' of 'Ballyvaltron' — no doubt an RC chapel before that at Barndarrig was built.

3rd June 1930

Visited Black Tom's Buildings near Tinahely. The ruin is on the N side of the Derry River, in Coolross — facing Boleybawn (al. Fairwood) on the other side of the river. It is about ¼ mile S of Tinahely, and is approached by the laneway which leads off the upper street in Tinahely, to the left at the top of the hill; this laneway is called 'Cellars Lane'. It is on the right of the lane, and one of its walls seems to form the bank.

For the greater part of the surface it is only traces of walls, in some places the stones showing, in others (most) grass–covered. In one place ... there are two rectangular excavations in the ground, like underground rooms, the walls in good condition, of rough stone and excellent mortar. These rooms are about 6ft deep. One is something like 15ft x 8ft and the other say 12ft square (these are only rough estimates). In the square one is the foundation of a hexagonal pillar which may have had an arch at each side of it.

The land belongs to Mr Taylor of Tinahely.

The ruin seems to cover altogether a space of 25yds or so square.

Visited Mrs Smith's of Raheengraney and examined Mr Octavius Braddell's papers.

5th June 1930

There is a 'bullaun' stone on the boundary of the townlands of Aghowle Upper and Sleanaglogh, about 600yds S of Sleanaglogh crossroads, on the E side of the road. This is the boundary between Rathnew and Derrylossary parishes.

[Extract from] *The Irish Times,* 27th December 1930:

'IRISH ANTIQUITIES
Mediaeval Stone Lamp For Museum
Dr. A. Mahr, Keeper of Irish Antiquities, announces that the Irish Antiquities Division of the National Museum, has obtained a very interesting antiquity in an early mediaeval stone lamp of unusual size, of the type which sometimes was supposed to be a cup (chalice) or the like. This valuable object was pulled out of an old wall in Sleanaglogh, Co. Wicklow, and has been deposited by D. Ó Dubhghaíll ... Dublin, to whom the Museum already had been indebted for several other additions. As a result of his connection with the "Wicklow Exhibition", arranged recently by the Wicklow Development Association, several other finds have been communicated to the Museum, and Mr Russell ... Wicklow, deposited in the Museum two stone axes, a very nice diminutive stone axe, and a leaf-shaped flint arrowhead from Co. Waterford ... .'

11th June 1930

Rathmoon. The large double rath S of the road which is marked on the OS map no longer exists — I looked about for it in the fields, and finally asked a boy working on the land and he said there was no 'rá' there, but they called that field 'the Rá Meadow'. The field is the second field W of Rathmoon House ... and third from road. It was in the NW corner/part of this field — possibly part of the field ditch belonged to the ditch of the rath. Otherwise I saw no sign of the rath remaining, but the field rises to its highest point here, and the rath seems to have lain round this highest point.

About ¾ mile NW of this, on the N side of the road, due N of the point marked '546ft' on the map, there is a well-preserved small tumulus — to all appearance untouched. No stones visible, and no part of it dug away — it looks rather as though it had had an outer bank round it which has been levelled. It is on the highest point of the field — and in the NW corner of Rathmoon townland.

Manger. On the right-hand side of the old coach road, about ¼ mile N of Manger Bridge, is what looks like a broken-down and half-dug-away mote or tumulus. Again no stones visible.

Randalstown. There is a small spring just N of the road which comes down from the Stratford road to Whitestown Bridge. It runs under the road, and down through the field on the far side into the old mill-race. Is this 'Tubber a Voster'? It has absolutely no feature of any sort that I could see.

23rd June 1930

Drove up the lane at Sandyhills which is the boundary between that townland and Tober Upper, and walked up to the house in Manofwar, which is just beside the top of the hill (point '813ft' on map). I thought Friarhill Moat was on the top of this hill but it is not. I had to walk across through fields to the W, till I got to Bond's house; and the mote is in the field just behind (W of) the house in Friarhill townland, looking across a slight valley to Forristeen and Brewershill.

The mote has been very much dug away, there being signs of digging all round it. It has no prominent tumulus-like appearance, but looks like one of these rounded gravel hills which are so common in the

Dunlavin–Usk district, only that its surface is dug away and uneven. The place on which the tree is is a small round grass-covered mound. Whether it was always the highest part of the hill it is now impossible to tell, but it looks as if it had been the end of the highest part of a rounded ridge. Presumably in the general digging Mr Bond came across the burial, and covered it in again; the sycamore tree now growing there looks about 30 years old. Judging by analogy, one would guess the burial to have been disturbed. The hill consists of large and small rounded stones — like what I have been told is boulder clay — so that I would think it is part of a glacial deposit or moraine.

25th June 1930
Saw Mr William Henry of Burgage More near Blessington. He has various old books and maps dealing with his locality, and good local knowledge. He says the tower at Burgage is a church tower, not a castle, and that there were living rooms for the clergy attached to the church. He says Ballykinlea is the strip of land adjoining the Wicklow border just below his house; the place where he pointed is part of Kilmalum, and adjoins part of Glebe East. He said the upper part of Glebe East is also called Ballykinlea. There is an old burial ground in Kilmalum, and a field near it is called by the local people 'Mudyéenacrów', or simply 'Mudyeen'.

4th August 1930
Walked from the Red Lane, across the stream which O'Curry calls 'Ath Gabhar' up the hill marked '1152ft' on the 1-inch map. Presumably this is the hill O'Curry refers to as 'Knock Daee'. It is a natural rocky hill, no trace of artificial works about it. It commands a very fine view indeed, including 'Croghan Kinshela', Lugnaquillia and Tonelegee. It might of course be the rounded hill SE of this, but the point 1152ft is much more imposing.

5th August 1930
Walked by Boley and Barnacashel to the lower (NW) point of Aghowle Hill. There is on this point an enclosure very roughly circular, of large stones with a low wall of small stones built on top of them. It is a commanding situation. A farmer in Boley told me these are locally called

'the Churches' but he did not know why. He thought it might have been built by Coollattin for a shooting butt. (I think the large stones are too big for this.) The high point of Aghowle Hill is called 'Stuaicín', Stookeen. This man pronounced Aghowle 'Achowl' ('a' as in 'ah'; 'owl' as in 'howl'), clearly = 'Aċad aḃall'. He pronounced Barnacashel as if spelled 'Bernacashel'. There is a small rath in a field just on the pass dividing Barnacashel from Aghowle Lower; he said it was a rath or fort, but there was no name for it, he pointed out two others nearby, in Boley.

The road leading from Mullinacuff Church past Kilquiggin Chapel to the main road was a famine road, built about 1849 by a Mr Mumford, engineer (authority — Reverend T.E. Young of Coolkenna and T. Fleming of Ballynultagh).

Oaks crossroads in the townland of Killinure. Oaks is a surname which occurs in the books of Aghowle Church (Reverend T.E. Young).

Labbanasigha, Moylisha. The field in which the chapel is built at New Chapel crossroads, a mile N of Waterville, Co. Kerry, is called 'Tooreensaighe' (pronounced like the word 'sigh'): authority Seán Ó Dúḃda of Baile na nGall and M. Keating of Derrynane. They could not give a meaning for it.

11th March 1934

Visited Mr James Farrell of Corrasillagh, Glenmalure a second time. Seamas Delargy, Professor of Folklore, National University, came with me.

Farrell repeated the story about seeing the battle when he was 9 or 10 years old. Delargy says the name of the place ('Lodarrig') is 'log dearg': he heard this distinctly while Farrell was speaking quickly. Farrell said the slope at Cullentragh Park above the Raheen bank is called 'Bore na Crow', 'bóthar na (g)cró'. Delargy suggested from the pronunciation of Cullentragh Park ('Coŏlinapark') it might be 'cúil na páirce'. The place where Cosby was killed is marked by a white stone 6ft high; it is above the slope of Ballinafunshoge.

It was O'Briens who came into the glen first — the trees then were so close you could step from top to top right down to Arklow. Next was a Harney; then the Farbreaga Byrnes; and then Jim Farrell who died in 1798 — he was married to a widow of the Byrnes of Farbreaga. The Farrells came from Longford: they were in Stump [i.e. Stump of the Castle] before they moved into the glen.

He called it 'Glenmùller' [Glenmalure].

Local names in Corrasillagh:

'Coragreinge' ('Cor gréine')

'Bollyemeen' ('Baile? mín')

'Leóawn' (upon the hill) ('Luigeán'?)

'Lugafoot'

'Carrigeenafoōrds'

'Lugcoolmeen' (the ridge E of Lugnaquillia)

'Luggweeer' ('Log dhuibhir') (at the back of Lugcoolmeen, i.e. S of it)

'Beendoo(ch)' (Bendoo in Clonkeen)

'Inchafairdrig' (is where two brooks meet, one coming out of Lugnaquillia and one out of Doyle Street)

'Trommawnmaccartha Brook' (on Farbreaga, coming from the top of Ballinguile, i.e. the stream on the N boundary of Farbreaga, but O'Toole says between Blackrock and Carrigatheme).

Rathgorragh, he pronounced it 'Rawgorrə'.

'Coshgolay' ('Cosgulé') is the whole country from Baltyboys to the top of the Wicklow Gap.

Glanreemore, he pronounced it 'Gleandərymór'. Delargy thought it was 'Gleann doire móir' (it is not: the 'nd' sound must have been a peculiar nasal).

Ballinfoyle, he pronounced it 'Bỏrnàfwile' (or 'Bólnàfwile'). Delargy thought it was 'bóthar'.

He told the story of Macalister's saving Dwyer at Derrynamuck very vividly. Macalister was buried in the ditch outside Kilranelagh Graveyard; they would not bury him in the graveyard itself.

Speaking of Ballinacor, I said to him Kemmis' house was in Ballinacor. He said 'No, I beg your pardon, Kemmis' house is in Drumkitt'.

Drumkitt is evidently a definite part of Ballinacor townland: so is Cawrawn.

FIELD NOTEBOOK 10:
August 1930–February 1932

[There are some disjointed notes on scraps of paper in a pocket at the front of the original notebook which are not reproduced here.]

2nd August 1930
Athdown Mote. Lies S of the present road and just W of and beside the old road which went S through Athdown and across the river into Ballynabrocky. It is circular, at an estimate about 60ft in diameter, with the low remains of a bank round it, and on the SW a deep ditch with a second bank, this ditch being 6 to 8ft deep below the level of the second bank. The surrounding ditch is quite gone on the N side where the field has evidently been tilled right up to the edge of the inner circle. This mote must have been formed (or adapted?) to command the crossing of the river. It is 80 or 100yds from the river, and the old track is on its W edge — it must have been at a very early period that it was used as a fortification, as there is higher ground about 80yds away to the NW.

The old road probably went round by Ballynasculloge to Oldcourt and Threecastles.

17th August 1930
At Castletoole in Oldboleys. It is a natural rock, just similar to those on the Three Rock, on the S end of the Two Rock, and at Prince William's Seat. The county boundary runs to this rock, though it is not precisely on the top of the hill but slightly down on the Co. Wicklow side.

25th August 1930
Spent three days with P.T. Walshe. Ballybought Church — a medieval structure, window of somewhat rounded Gothic remaining in E (or NE?) end. Walshe measured it.

Whiteleas Circle. Fifteen stones remain, of which about six seem to be in position — the raised portion of the field seems to be a circle of about 25yds diameter. Mooney of Knocknastreel [Knocknastreile?] said there were crosses on some of the stones, after we had been there: we did not see them. At Newtown there is a rath with a low bank, and traces of a ditch and second bank.

Could neither see nor hear of any monument, fort or rath in Knocknastreel [Knocknastreile?], though we asked Mooney who lives at Doyle's house in the townland.

There is a mote on the top of the Johnstown ridge, clearly visible on the skyline: it is called 'Chaney Hill Mote'.

The mote at Kinsellastown is just opposite Crehelp Lodge now occupied by Mr Goggin, National Teacher at Dunlavin. It is much destroyed. Roughly oval in shape, 20 to 25yds long by 10yds broad — but quite uneven in outline and in section. It presents no particularly artificial appearance, but it is never tilled, and Goggin said the old people say a young man once went to put potatoes on it, and as soon as his spade went in he fell down in a fit, and died soon after. They also say that the owner of Crehelp Lodge meant to build a house on the SE side of it but the engineer said the foundation was bad as the hill was hollow — and it is supposed that the subterranean passage which has its opening in the field just S of Crehelp Lodge leads under the road to this mote.

In Forristeen there are only two stones remaining, one of which, that towards the E, has the cross in it, in a leaden socket. There is a second leaden socket in the stone, with nothing in it. These two stones are some 200yds S of the Friarhill Mote.

26th August 1930

Went to Grangecon Demesne — Mr D.G. O'Mahony was away: the coachman showed us the urns, all of which he said came from Merginstown Mote about 50 years ago. One was complete, being made of all the pieces fastened together with glue or some such stuff. (The local story is that the cart upset as the urn was being brought from Merginstown to Grangecon, and the urn was broken.)

The surface roughly decorated all over. The other two urns are very incomplete.

Of the third only the base remains. An account roughly written out by P. Mahony describes the cists where they were found at Merginstown: the paper is in the complete urn. With it is a torn envelope addressed to Sir S. Ferguson. It was from Archdeacon O'Regan of Dunlavin that Mahony heard of the cists. He set up two cists in the garden, and the coachman said that a large slab leaning against the wall was the cover-stone of one of them.

The mote is now levelled: it was in the large paddock N of Merginstown House (Fisher's).

Ardsillish Bridge. So spelled on the map — but I asked an old road labourer what the bridge was called and he said 'Āh-sillitch' or 'Āh-sillish' ('ah' as in Irish 'tá'). I think this is clearly the word 'Áṫ', 'a ford'. The place is low-lying, 'Ard' would not apply at all. This man also pointed out the direction of the Bullock Park in Fryanstown [Freynestown?].

I searched for the rath which is shown on the 6-inch map in Freynestown Upper, but nothing seems to exist at that place now and there is no recollection locally of anything there. The Bullock Park is the only place in Freynestown where there was a church, according to the local people: there was a monastery there, they say. It is the field at the extreme E side of Freynestown Upper, just where the road turns S and then sharply NW (Map XXI.I).

'There are bun ditches in it, and old skeoch bushes, and stones lying about it as if there had been buildings' — this is the description given by a young fellow living in the only house in Freynestown Lane, and it is an accurate description. The lines of ditches, and of what appear to be old foundations of walls covered with grass, suggest a fairly extensive range of buildings: but they are not definite enough to indicate a plan. One of the stones is a 'bullaun' stone, or an old font.

The local pronunciation as I got it from the labourer and the young man is 'Frenstown'.

Mullycagh. We went in from the house of a man named Pat Reilly, and crossed into the townland of Kilbaylet Upper — Reilly and a man named Ned Lynch pointed out to us a stone with a hollow in it [shaped like a footprint].

The hollow was nearly full of water. (The weather was very wet.) Lynch said the story was St Kevin was driven away from Church Mountain by the local chief, and he stepped down on to this stone and made the mark of his foot in it. It is always full of water. I am inclined to think it may be a natural hollow. In the W side of this same field is a large natural rock, at the top of a piece of ground where the rock outcrops. It stands about 12ft high — no regular shape. This Lynch said was called 'the Kingstone'; but he knew nothing more about it. He said someone was supposed to have dug at the bottom of it for treasure once.

Reilly had a story of the three raheens which are just on the boundary

Fig. 21—'St Kevin's footmark', Kilbaylet Upper, 1930.

of Kilbaylet Upper and Blackmoor, that an old lady who lived near and was not so very long dead, one night before she died she was talking vaguely and rambling, and in the morning she said she had been out all night in these raheens going from one to the other, and dancing, with a number of people she had known; she named the people, and they were all dead.

Met Dr Lyons of Dunlavin at dinner that evening. He gave me a list of names chiefly on the S side of the Hollywood–Wicklow Gap which he got one evening when he went on a midwifery case and had to stay at the house all night — he got them from Willie Kavanagh of Granamore, who pointed out the places to him.

The two-storey building on the right of the main road from Dublin to Baltinglass in the townland of Ballynatone (E of Stratford-on-Slaney) was Stratford Infirmary, so Dr Lyons said: it is now used as a cow house.

27th August 1930

Photographed the Long Stone in Ballintruer just on the boundary of that and Ballinacrow. ('Cullen's ("Coolin's") of the Long Stone'). Could get no information about it, but we were told that perhaps Dinny Toole of Newtown near Donard could tell us something about it. It stands about

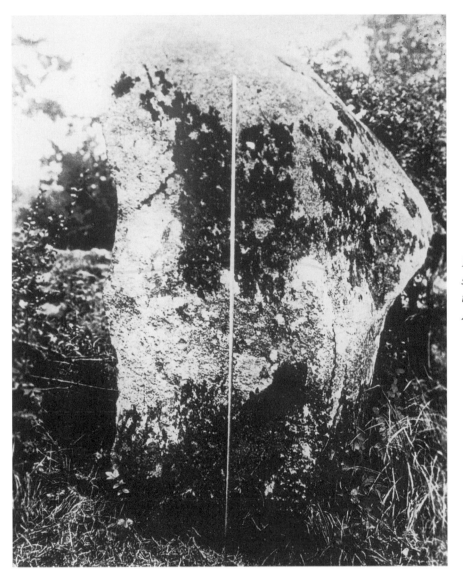

10ft high from the bed of the stream, and has a platform (part of the stone
itself on its SW face) 3ft high from the base [L-shaped].

Went to Terence Reilly's at Kilbaylet Lower. He showed us
Knocknakeeraun which Walshe had not seen, pointed out the so-called
sites of houses to us — and what he called a 'Park' which is on the SE side
of the hill — a flat green space enclosed by a low grass bank, roughly
circular in shape. Also a large stone on the NE side of the hill: he said a man

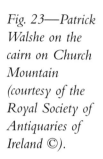

Fig. 23—Patrick Walshe on the cairn on Church Mountain (courtesy of the Royal Society of Antiquaries of Ireland ©).

dreamed three times there was gold under it, and he went and dug under the stone and got another man to help him, and they lifted it, and left it turned upside down — he found nothing but 'some old irons and some dust': people said that it was because he brought another man with him that he didn't find the gold. I asked what was done with the old irons, he said they were thrown away. We then went up Church Mountain, and I photographed the cairn, and the old walls of the church, and two carved stones which Walshe found: they appear to be stones belonging to the jamb of a doorway. Other stones from Church Mountain are said to have been removed to Donard by Colonel Heighington, and to be in his place there.

The well seemed to Walshe and myself to be merely stagnant water in a hollow in the cairn at the W side.

The bullaun stone with the nineteen cup-markings is in Kilbaylet Lower: so was the destroyed one: Walshe said it had only one, deep, hollow in it.

Milltown, near Dunlavin: there was an old water-mill at Mr Deering's; he took out the water-wheel and put in a turbine.

3rd September 1930

Mullinacuff old churchyard. This is a medieval church in ruins — E window remaining. Very similar to the church at Ballybought. Window of granite stone blocks, chamfered as at Ballybought. The top is a slightly pointed arch cut out of one stone. A recent wall has been built round the graveyard which contains 18th- and 19th-century graves, apparently all Protestant.

Just N of this churchyard at the highest point of the field is a mote, partly dug away, but in fair preservation. On the E side of it at the bottom are lying two blocks of granite, one about 3ft long, the other a mere fragment. I do not know if these are of any significance or not: what occurred to me was they might be the remains of a pillar stone that might have stood on the top of the mound. They had no marks.

Lathaleere. Saw the 'cromlech' which consists merely of one large stone only the edge of which is visible, as it is sunk in the ground; it is about 4 or 5ft long, lying E–W. Another small piece of stone is also sticking out of ground on its S side. The field is rented by Dan Kehoe of Baltinglass: he railed in the site and planted spruce trees round it, about 20 years ago. A man named Tom Doran was working in the field: he told me that that field belonged to Robert Park, who died over 60 years ago. Park wanted the monument destroyed: there were then six supporting stones and the cover-stone. Park employed a man named Tom Abbey, who blasted the six supports, and the cover-stone fell to where it now lies. Tom Abbey died almost immediately after doing this. (Doran said that Dr Comerford had described this monument; but it is not in his *History of Leighlin Diocese*.)

Doran also said there were five warriors buried on Pinnacle Hill. He said there was a place called 'the Golden Glin' between Lathaleere and Pinnacle: is this a confusion with the well called 'Golden Well'?

He also pointed out some white stones on the N slopes of Kilranelagh Hill and said they were called 'the Griddle Stones', and there were kings buried there.

7th September 1930

Left car at gate of Powerscourt Demesne which leads to Onagh and Crone — and walked up Glencree River on left (N) bank. In a field about 400yds N of the river, in Onagh, is a large block of granite, at the higher end of the field, lying flat: it has a fairly large basin-shaped hollow (about 6in. in diameter) towards the SE edge of the stone with three, or perhaps four, cup-shaped hollows round it (1in. diameter). Could this be Dourna Darrig?

Fig. 24—Cup-marked stone at Onagh.

22nd September 1930

The ford at the point where the townlands of Broadleas Commons, Whiteleas, and Ballybought townlands meet (near Ballymore Eustace) is called locally 'Carman's Ford'. The road now crosses the river here by a bridge. The local explanation of this name is that it was the place where carmen stopped their horses, or stayed for the night, in the days when this was the main road (that is before 1829). It is however only 1½ statute miles from Ballymore Eustace.

(22nd February 1932: 'Carman's Ford' verified. Not 'the Carman's Ford', and not 'Carmen's Ford'.)

The 'Long Stone' is about ½ mile N of this point almost at the extreme E point of Longstone townland. It is lying down, I think just beside the place where it stood, and I should say that at least 6 or 7ft or perhaps more has been broken off from the top, but I would be inclined to think the lower end is the original butt end.

The road which leads along the S boundary of Ballybought (E end) is called 'the Mill road'.

The old roadway which leads W from the present main road in the townland of Newtown Co. Wicklow is called 'the Mill Lane'. I think these two probably were once continuous; there is what appears to be an old avenue, now grass-covered, leading along the S boundary of Whiteleas.

On the Kildare Archaeological Society excursion of Thursday 18th September Mr Kelly of Rath, an old farmer, age 82, said he always heard Mr Whelan's called 'Rath', and this (meaning the Ring) called 'Rath găl' — this name had not as far as I know been suggested to him at all. He also pronounced the name Knockeen as 'Knickeen' in mentioning the place, without being asked.

24th September 1930

Met Mr E. O'Toole at Baltinglass. He had the following information about Killaduff and Castle Laurence:

Eugene Byrne now of Phillipstown Co. Carlow (Kineagh parish) used to own Killaduff House — he sold it, and the present occupier is Pat Redmond. They showed O'Toole the graveyard. It is through a large field down from Killaduff House on its E side: it consists of a circular ring of earth faced with stones. No trace of graves. There are loose boulders lying inside the ring. The 'church' is 30 or 40yds S of the ring; it is merely a heap of stones; a large thorn bush is growing in the centre of the heap. The field in which it is is called 'the Church Field': it is a small field off the big one; and at the gate leading into it was the place where the cave was supposed to be. There is no trace of it now. It was said to lead to Lugnaquillia.

Eugene Byrne said that he had heard that a tin full of gold was buried in the church or churchyard.

He also said that his grandfather was living in Killaduff House in 1798 — and that when the soldiers were raiding for Billy Byrne of Ballymanus, they came to the house and were going towards the old church. They wanted to break down the fence and make a gap at the end of a barn facing the house. His grandfather had saved some money in gold, and had the gold hidden in this very place — so he told the captain he wanted a gap broken in order to get hay in, and asked him to oblige him by breaking the gap farther down. So they did it and he saved his gold.

Some distance behind Ballymanus House is a field called 'the Castle Field': it is two or three fields from the house. (This I suppose is the site of Castle 'Lawrence'.) Authority for this was John Byrne of Ballymanus, farmer, called 'Jack of the Heights'.

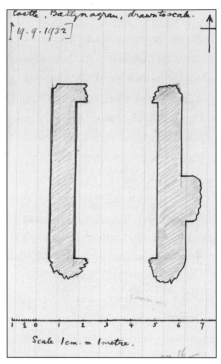

Fig. 25—Sketch-plan of MacDermot's Castle.

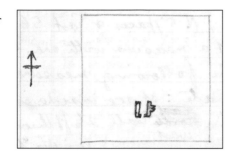

Fig. 26—MacDermot's Castle (courtesy of the Royal Society of Antiquaries of Ireland ©).

1st October 1930

Photographed 'MacDermot's Castle' at Ballynagran near Wicklow. I paced all four sides of the square enclosure on the outer bank. I made the S side 56 paces (44m); W 55 paces (49m); N 57 paces (47½m); E 56 paces (48m). I had not a measure with me, but made the following measurements by estimate: space inside walls 19ft (6.6m) x 11ft (3.45m); W wall 2½ft (1m) thick; E projection from E wall (or was it a buttress) 4ft thick; from ground level inside to spring of arch about 8ft (2.15m).

Three square holes in the wall on each side inside, like bolt-holes about 7in. (15cm) high and 5in. (12cm) across. They are about 5ft from the ground (2.25m, lower edge), or 5½ft. They are not opposite to one another. The doorway or opening on the S side is about 11 paces (5m) from the S side of the enclosure measuring from bottom of ditch.

There are two 'cupboards' or square recesses about 1ft square just inside this 'doorway', one in each wall (E one: 24cm across x 30cm high; W one: 30cm across x 35cm high) top about 5ft (1.3m) below the spring of the arch.

A man to whom I spoke on the road said the field the castle was in was called 'the Briary Field'. I asked the woman who lives in the farmhouse nearby (in Coolbeg), a labourer's wife, if she knew any name for the field, and she said 'No'.

7th October 1930

Saw the Killahokan stone — it is merely a large block of granite about 8ft high and perhaps 25 or 30ft in circumference — standing in the fence which is the boundary between counties Wicklow and Carlow. There do not seem to be any marks on it — the view from it to NW and S is very wide, from Lugnaquillia to Mount Leinster.

Examined Kindlestown Castle. It is very thickly overgrown with ivy and brambles and elder bushes. The N wall is standing, up to the battlements. It is about 60ft long, 6ft thick, and I should say nearly 30ft high at the highest point. It has two narrow openings, splayed, on the ground level, one large opening in I should say the third storey (second above ground storey) which is (estimating it from below) 6ft high by 3ft wide. It has an arched top of the flat type and a small splayed one on the same storey. The wall is damaged at the bottom and at the openings by the stones having been taken out, probably by a pick, as the mortar is good and hard; it is rough, made with large pebbles. Of the E wall a small bit remains — it seems to have been 10ft thick. The staircase was at the NE corner, and the wall inside the staircase (i.e. between it and the interior) was 3ft thick. Huge pieces of masonry are lying about, indicating that the castle was destroyed by being blown up from inside (but perhaps it was merely ruined by weather, ivy etc; see Canon Scott's photograph which seems to represent the NE corner as standing). It had a wet moat round it, the water is now everywhere round the castle.

26th October 1930

Kilbride, near Bray. The two stones, one inscribed with concentric circles (see photo by Mason) and the other with cups, are lying in the field E of the reservoir and stream on the lands of Violet Hill. They are flat and partly covered with earth, moss and grass. The stone with the cups is broken across in at least one place, and I saw no sign of the crosses mentioned by Mr Crawford; but I examined it rather cursorily and did not know at the time that there were supposed to be crosses there. I think however that the other stone is considerably more worn than when Mason photographed it, so this one may be also more worn than in 1913 (the date of publication of

Fig. 27—Rathdown slab at Kilbride (courtesy of the Royal Society of Antiquaries of Ireland ©).

Crawford's paper). The field is used for a pony to graze in, and the marks of its hoofs are all over the field, which probably helps to wear down the stones, which are granite. The old woman in the back gate lodge said the piece of ground where they were had been a cemetery, and that when the reservoir was being repaired some time ago, skulls and bones were dug up, but that Mr Darley (of Violet Hill) had them buried again. She said there was also a small cross, or two crosses, of stone, but that they had been thrown onto the bank of the stream: we looked for them but could not find them. One must be the cross figured by O'Curry (*OS Letters,* p.50).

9th November 1930

The site which O'Curry refers to in Kilmurry South as being called 'Calery' is still pointed out by the local people: it is called 'the Monastery' or 'the Monastery Field'. It is just where the road into Lower Calary branches off from the Red Lane on the W of the road just inside the gate. There is an enclosed space in the field: the space is roughly oblong, enclosed by a bank, which is in places very low, but on the S side about 3ft high. The bank is of earth and grass, but it seems to be over a base of stones and may represent an old wall. At the E end of the S side is a piece of wall, which seems to be a piece of a wall of an old building: it is of stones and mortar. The whole place is greatly overgrown.

I also searched for the site of the cairn described by O'Curry as in Lower Calary (*OS Letters,* p.198). But all I could see was a collection of three blocks of stone about 2ft high, and about 3ft long — rough unshaped blocks, within 10 or 12ft of one another. They are as he describes about a furlong S, or I should say more strictly SSE of the point 1152ft (which I think is Knockdaee). There are at least three long fences running across the mountain here, all built of stones. The mountain generally just here seems particularly free of loose stones. I could see nothing that could be called the site of a cairn.

[Later noted] 18th April 1936

Kilmurry South. As well as the oblong enclosure, there is on the other side of the road the ruined site of an old church, of which the walls, about 3ft thick, can be traced: the church was about 33ft by 20ft internally. It is not enclosed. There is a gap at the W end which may have been the door. In it is a block of granite with a cone-shaped bullaun in it — diameter 14in., depth 8in.

No date

Wicklow Court. I got the following names, still used as addresses of people in Rathnew neighbourhood:

'Charvey', in the SE corner of Milltown North, the lane N of the stream.

'Cuckoo Corner', the road opposite the Glenealy Brickworks, which forms the E border of the townland of Milltown South, between it and Ballybeg townland. Cuckoo Corner is the part of this road which is S of the present main road. This old road seems once to have led to Ballynabarney crossroads, or 'Red Peg's crossroads' which is the local name.

'Yellow Hole', an address in the village of Rathnew.

'Rock' is another address in the village.

16th November 1930

(R.E.G.) The Saint's Knees: a double bullaun stone, which used to be on the road leading from Caher to Ardfinnan: about two miles S of Caher just opposite the byroad leading to Ballymacadam (Co. Tipperary).

Mrs Joan de la Terriere (née Grubb), of Kiltinan Castle (near Clonmel), Co. Tipperary, [is] said to have taken it and put it in the garden of Kiltinan Castle.

15th December 1930

The hill immediately E of Mullacor, ½ mile away, is the one C.G. Thompson heard called 'Slayfonn'. The spur NNE of Mullacor, about ¾ mile away, is 'Middle Hill'. The valley between them he says is called 'Boleylug': the wood on the N slope of Derrybawn Mountain, 'Culliagh' or 'Coolyagh'. 'Carrigagolagh' he says is on the SE slope of Camaderry, fairly high up. 'Ruppla' he says is the name of the bog near and N of Lough Nahanagan. 'Askantriglugh' ('Easca na trí gcloc') is on the S side of Kippure: and he gave 'Asknabullog' and 'Rumpoon' as the names of places near Kippure.

He says Duff Hill is always locally pronounced 'Duffy Hill'. He said one of the McGurks gave him the name 'Foolya' as a place between Fancy Mountain and Cloghoge — (but I suspect this is Nevill's 'Knocknafoalla' near the Crockan Pond: Thompson said the place was merely mentioned in talk, not pointed out to him).

'The Dalty', which a man told him meant 'a fearny place', is the W slope of Cloghoge — and the 'Cloghoge Bracket Rocks' are on its S side, over Lough Dan and the Inchavore.

'Carrigmore' he says is the hill over the Sally Gap road, just E of it and NE of the Sally Gap itself.

December 1930

Mr McGurk told me one day I was up there in the Christmas holidays that the old ruined walls near the Crockan Pond, up on a little hill, are called 'the Crockan House' (pronounced 'Cruckawn'). I have no doubt they are the ruins of Lord Powerscourt's gamekeeper's lodge (see Nevill's map) and they may be what Holt calls 'the grouse house at Luggelaw Mountain' (*Memoirs,* p.39). Powerscourt's new game or shooting lodge, is also now a ruin, the roof being off it: it stands by the side of the road from Sally Gap to Roundwood ('the Churches' road') between Sally Gap and Lough Tay. The roof has been taken off within the last 10 or 12 years.

Doyle's lamp referred to [in another notebook, see p.74] was found in the house of a man named Bradshaw at Sleanaglogh which was previously occupied by people called Fanning. It was put into a hole in an outhouse wall — not built into the wall. Bradshaw knew it was there, walked to the place, put his hand in and took it and gave it to Doyle.

Doyle said there was an almost destroyed cromlech or dolmen on the lands of Murphy of Crone Beg — three stones still standing, and a fourth had been removed years ago.

25th January 1931

[The cup-marked stone in Onagh is in a field called 'Abbeylands'.]

Stone to [Onagh] Dolmen *c.* 348° E of N.

Stone to peak of Maulin *c.* 232° E of N.

Stone to peak of Sugarloaf *c.* 130° E of N.

Stone to top of Crossoona *c.* 103° E of N.

Measurements of the stone in Onagh mentioned on 7th September 1930:

N to S across basin 7ft.

Distance from S end to S edge of basin 20in.

Diameter of basin 12–13in.

Depth 4in.

Diameter of cups *A, B, C* and *D* [four of the cupmarks] 1½in., depth about ½in. Cup E [the fifth cup] [is] not so distinct, diameter 2in.; same depth.

Could these marks be those of a bit which someone was using on the stone with the idea of blasting it and breaking it up?

The central basin however is a distinct circular basin.

A. W cup from edge of hole 10in.

B. NW cup from edge of hole 22in.

C. nearer NW cup from edge of hole 14in.

D. cup E by N from edge of hole 12in.

E. N cup from edge of hole 26in.

Description of stones of dolmen (August 1933).

[Note: these do not run in correct alphabetical order]

A. a small boulder, granite.

B. a small stone.

C. granite upright.

D. slate or shale (?) upright.

E. 8ft high, granite, slopes to E.

G. granite, 6ft high.

H. 5½ft high, white quartz.

J. 6ft high, granite.

M. small boulder, granite.

9th February 1931

After Blessington Court went to see the moat on Chaney Hill. Chaney Hill is what is called 'Kiernan's Hill' on the map according to Michael Kelly of Harristown — I suspect that the name may include the whole ridge from Ballysize Upper to Broughills Hill (pronounced 'Broōchil') but I am not sure. The mote is in the townland of Kiernans Hill, at the point '948ft' on the map. It is circular, about 10 or 12ft high, and about 42 paces round (its outlines are not regular or symmetrical so that it is hard to measure). The usual shape something like a truncated cone; the top is roughly flat but has a large circular depression a foot or so deep in the centre. A number of stones remain around the base of it so placed that they seem to have been originally part of a continuous course of stones in a circle marking its base. On the SE side there are five of these stones still together lying longitudinally and making an arc of a circle — the five extend for about 14ft. The surface is covered with grass and furze bushes now — there are a few small granite stones on the top. The view from it is very extensive. I should say it is a burial mound, not unlike the monument I described on Lugnagun only with a covering mound perhaps of stones still in place.

Walked E from the mote to the border of Johnstown (a fence). Went S of a house on the top of the hill which Kelly said was Toomey's of Ballysize Upper; he said it was called 'Whitebog'. (It is at the mark on the boundary between Ballysize Upper and Ballintober, on map in my notebook [but not published here].) A track leads up to it along the SW edge of the boundary of Harristown between it and Johnstown — this place Kelly said was called 'Berrinclay' (= 'bearna chleithe'?).

From there we walked to the point where Ballintober, Harristown and Johnstown meet, and looked across at the broken cross. It is near the house of people called Byrne, which is called 'Byrne's of the Cross'. The next house just to the N of it (there are two houses) is Byrne's and Burke's; and the well is on their laneway or avenue just at the bend. Kelly said he thought it had been a holy well, and that a track led from that house up the hill, which is called 'St Kevin's Road'. The highest part of Johnstown is called 'Gallowshill' (bordering on Kiernan's Hill). 'Beckonsfield' or 'Bacon's Field' is a field I think in Harristown, near Kelly's house. 'The Mōnyeen' ('móinín', 'little bog'?) is a field in Ballintober. There is a field in Harristown I think between the road and the river called 'Lannahoorey'.

The old road from Hollywood to Ballysize and Killerk is passable still: just as you leave Hollywood there is quite a good bridge over the little river, I should say an old bridge. A track leads from this road up to Kiernan's Hill, where there are a lot of ruins of houses: and this track when it reaches the bounds of Johnstown, branches into two, 'the Johnstown path' and 'the Ballintober path'.

Fig. 28—Rathdown slabs at Killegar (courtesy of the Royal Society of Antiquaries of Ireland ©).

Kelly knows the name 'Lyragh' for the slope above Corach. Also 'the Fair' for the S side of the slope at the Wicklow Gap.

14th February 1931
Measurements taken at Killegar Church by D. Coffey and self. The churchyard had been recently cleaned up and tidied. There is a piece of granite, semicircular in shape and chamfered on the inside, in the graveyard, like the top of a small window.

[Nave internal measurement:] length about 24ft, E end broken, width about 13ft 6in.

[Chancel internal measurement:] length about 13½ft, width about 6 or 6½ paces.

Built in regular courses of medium-sized granite boulders, set in good mortar.

16th February 1931
At Arklow. Went with Tancred to see Chapel Hogan.

Chapel Hogan is a small rough mound, perhaps about 25ft in diameter and about 10 or 12ft, or 15ft, high. On the W side of the top is a little fragment of masonry, about 3ft high — it is a lump of stones set in mortar, the only shape being on the inside (E) where the stones seem to be faced and to form a right angle — but these faces are not now perpendicular. The mortar is good. On the W side of the mound for about 8 or 10ft is the trace of a ditch, and a bank outside it. The top of the mound is flattish, but I would not say it had the appearance of being flattened. Here and there on it there are loose stones, not large, embedded in the earth and grass.

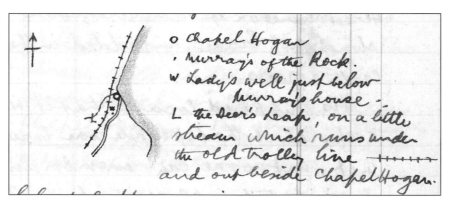

Fig. 29—Sketch of the environs of Chapel Hogan, Arklow.

It is supposed locally that it was a church and that people were buried in it, but no one can remember any burials taking place in it.

'Murray's of the Rock' is the house a little S of it, beside the old road which is quite clear. NW of Murray's and down at the bottom of a field just beside the old trolley track is 'the Lady's Well', a nice small well of clean water, built in with large stones. People go to it on Lady Day in Harvest (15th August) to drink the water, which is supposed to be good for them. It is in Rock Little.

SW of Murray's house and on the far or W side of the trolley track is a pool formed by some rocks on the course of a little stream; Tancred said this is called 'the Deer's Leap'. The stream goes under the trolley track and runs out near Chapel Hogan. This stream is I think the boundary between Rock Big and Rock Little and the Deer's Leap is on the Rock Big side.

22nd February 1931

At Ballyboy, Glenmalure. Walked from the military road in through the ruins of Mr Critchley's house, and along the slope of the hill S of the stream, following the track which runs through the new plantation of trees almost to the top of Mullacor. A short distance below the top of Mullacor is a straight ditch at right angles to this track: the ditch seems to be (perhaps) artificial and it is on the lower side of a cut in the hill made by a little stream. We turned to our left, S, and followed this ditch to the top of the ridge. We (Dr R.D. Joyce and I) came to the conclusion that the track through the plantation is a new track, probably made like that on Maulin at the time of making the plantation. We could see the whole valley as we walked up and as we looked back from the top. There is no sign of a road ever having come up the ridge and across it into Glenmalure: the present road is the old one (probably) and there seemed to be a bit of a continuation on which is now a mere track: but it stops completely. We went on down into Glenmalure, crossing down through Ballinafunshoge, and coming onto the road just opposite the zigzag in Clonkeen.

Carrigurtna is the very prominent rock just W by N of the crossroads at Ballyboy. Pronounced 'Carraig ("corrig") úrtna' (long 'u', broad 'r').

24th February 1931

With Dr Lyons of Dunlavin. Went to the house of William Kavanagh of

Granamore. It is the house that is in the angle made by the Douglas River and the Kings River (on the 1-inch map it is immediately below the 'wer' of 'Lower'). Kavanagh gave me the names he had given Dr Lyons (see map and panorama in Name Notebook [not published here]).

'Crookawnroo' is where there is a labourer's cottage, I think in Corragh, but it is near 'Knocknabōlia' [Knocknaboley].

'Crookawnaraunyeen', 'the K-nops', and 'Luggelaw' are all names in the hollow in Corragh, W of the angle of the Douglas River.

'Lyra' or 'the Scarrs of Lyragh' is the face of the mountain right S, in Corragh.

'Lugnafreechawn' is the hollow just E of the Douglas River in Granamore (between a black line on the hill and this river).

'Caurawn', 'Leeawn' and 'Tromawn' are, from W to E, between Round Hill and the ridge behind.

'White Moss Mountain' is the high part of the ridge.

'Rockamōnyeenamweel' is the knob of a hill.

'The Dry Hill' is just behind it, and so are 'Oram's Holes', a bit more to the E; he said they are holes in the bog, or 'gawgs'.

'The Three Lough Mountain' is further behind.

'Coantagh' is the next ridge or tongue of hill.

'Cor-nagrus' is said to be a graveyard, it is where there is a kind of hollow in this ridge of hill, 'White Hill' is the next ridge.

'Glanreemore', 'Glanreebeg', 'Askawn' and 'Askinbawn' are all near together between the hollow of Glanree and Coantagh.

'The Fair' is the round hill sticking up behind.

'Corrig na mothera' is away behind, nearly in Lugduff.

Kavanagh (a man of 55 or so) said he had heard of Art O'Neill's Grave since he was 'so high'. The old people used to say it was the place where Art O'Neill died. He said the path he'd drive sheep to Glenmalure would be up between Coantagh and Rōckamonyeenamweel, and then leaving the Three Lakes on the left, into Cunnavalla [Conavalla] and so to Glenmalure.

He said the whole King's River valley was sometimes called 'Cooskilay' (like 'cúisciléith', 'cuasachliath'?), 'Cūskilay'. 'Clocanafloan' ('cloch na phailpúin', 'stone of the tent'?) is out over Oakwood. Where Art O'Neill died is called 'the Flags of Glanreemore'.

'Lurgan' is the name of the top of the hill in Lockstown Upper, where there are two big stones.

'Asbawn' is one little place, and 'Askinbawn' is above it: both behind Coanty. 'Lugnafreechawn' is between a black line you can see on the hill, and the Douglas River.

From Kavanagh's we went on and saw Mrs Kate Nolan of Toor (old age pensioner, about 75): lives by herself in a little house. She showed us the Tailor's Room in the Jackdaw's Glen, and the Dalteen Rock, the Hangin' Rock (a cliff), and the Sheephouse. All of them are natural formations of rocks or boulders, round the sides of the Jackdaw's Glen: the Dalteen Rock is a big flat table of granite, about 12ft x 10ft, rectangular, at the bottom of the glen. She said there was a church on Church Mountain, with a holy water trough and a well. There are three saints buried in it, she didn't know their names. All the stones there were brought up in one night: it was a miracle. The people used to go up there in crowds, on the Sunday before the 1st of August, the 15th of August and the Sunday after it: two Sundays

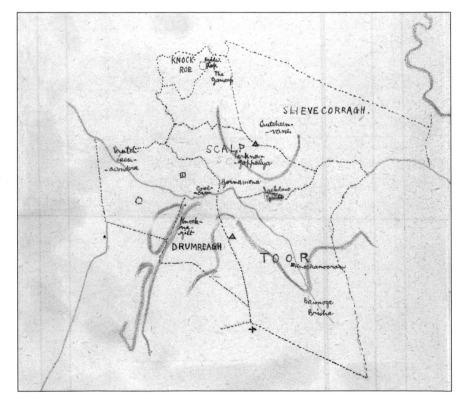

Fig. 30—Sketch-map of Hollywood Glen.

and the 15th. I think she said they went there on a 'thurrus' but I couldn't quite catch it. They went up to pray.

She showed us Coolcawm and called it 'the Madwoman's House' — it seemed to be about at the bend of the stream just S of the word 'Scalp' on the 1-inch map. It is really a little further down the stream, in Dunboyke.

We went on to see Michael Humphrey, a native of Dragoonhill, who lives now in Drumreagh (pronounced 'Drumree'). The house on the E side of the road at the bend in the road at the N end of Hollywood Glen. He was sick in bed: he is over 70. He gave us several names:

'Gornamóna', the two fields adjoining the road this (the Drumreagh) side [of] the Jackdaw's Glen as you go up Scalp, before you go out the Puzzle — in Boyne's (or Byrne's?) garden.

The road from Scalp to Toor is called 'the Puzzle', it is all corners and angles.

'Partnagoppulya' (or 'Parkna-') is on the face of Hegarty's Hill — the SW side of Scalp Rock. A crow could hardly find a place to stand there, much less a horse.

'Crutcheenvane' is the field behind George Newcome's on the S side of the road — (in Slievecorragh SE of Hollywood).

'Glanagūnnyeen' is the glen where Coolcawm Island is, between Toor and Dunboyke: or else another name for the Jackdaw's Glen (I'm not sure which he said but I think the first).

'Levitche's Rocks' are in Glanagunnyeen ('Ledwich's'?).

'The Cooltoges' are in Dunboyke — he pronounced it like 'Dún búic'.

'Knockanooran' is Toor Cottage, that is the ruined shooting lodge, which the Toomeys used to own.

'Bawnoge' and 'Brisha' are over the lodge, where the brook 'here' (that is near his house) rises. (Power, 296. 'Bruise', meaning uncertain, 'a stream'. Probably a form of 'bruis', the debris of underwood, etc., left on a river bank after floods.)

'Knocknagilt' is in Drumreagh, on the left of Hollywood Glen.

'Glanneskin' is in Hollywood Glen (at least I think he said so).

'The Settle Bed' is a rock on Scalp.

'The Gancap' is a place above at St Kevin's Cave, above the statue: beside the Protestant church.

'The Madwoman's Lep' is on the side of the Castle Bank: towards the
    Protestant church. St Kevin threw 'the Chair' at her.

'Cūttheroach' ('Coot-the-rōach') is a pond or well near Hollywood.

'Croŏtcheena coŏndera', a piece of ground beside Joe Whittle's on the coach
    road, W side. Joe Whittle's is the next house S of Rathattin House.
    Perhaps the W end of Dunboyke: or else in Rathattin or Athgreany.

Cheyney lived in Cheyney's Grove at Knockroo up to 55 or 60 years ago.
The name was in it in the rebellion. There are the tracks of bare feet, toes
and heels, on the big stone at the Piper's Stones — they say it was two
devils fought across the cross.

'The Watery Lane' is the piece of the old road leading from Hollywood
to the NW to the main road — the continuation on the other side of the
main road is called 'the Mill Lane'. He spoke of the mote on Cheyney's Hill
as a 'raw' (i.e. rath: note the pronunciation).

A younger man, living in the same house said a ford in Glen Imaal was
called 'Oiltiagh Bridge' (see map) and that there is a place called
'Gowlyawn' to the left of it. I don't think he was very accurate: but this
might be the place called 'Golier' on the 1-inch map, between Brittas and
Stranahely. It was not clear from what he said, just where Gowlyawn is.

5th March 1931

Rathdrum Court. The name and address of a defendant to a civil bill were
Michael Doyle, Knockfin, Glendalough. I made enquiries and found out
that his house is on the road between Laragh Bridge and Glendalough,
about 400yds from Laragh. His is the only house there of which the address
is Knockfin, but on the Annamoe side of Laragh Bridge it is also called
'Knockfin', near where the old barrack is.

This is evidently Holt's 'Knockfinn Bridge', but I did not know the
name was still in existence.

Ballycreen — was pronounced 'Ballagh-reen' or 'Ballachreen' by a
labourer from Crone Beg. This seems to suggest 'cr' followed by a broad
vowel.

Old forms of the name are 'Balliecreerie' (1606/07), 'Ballicreiry' (1605),
'Ballicreer' (1617): it is spelled 'Ballecreenery' on the Down Survey barony
maps: perhaps this is a misspelling of 'Ballecreevery', and the modern form

'Ballycreen' may be a corruption: originally 'Baile craobhaire' or 'Baile a(n) chraobhaire'? meaning 'a place covered with bushes' (Joyce, i. 501). But perhaps Hamilton's '**Baile crionaigh**' is better.

15th March 1931

At R. Barton's. He gave me the following local names:

in Drummin:

'Drumray', the ridge running from Scarr E to the point marked '1171ft' on the map.

'Annaray', the piece of bog on the S side of this ridge just where 'Drummin' is written on the 1–inch OS map.

'Ceocha's Brook' ('Kyŏkha', two syllables): the stream which runs down from Scarr through Annaray and into the river at Annamoe.

'The Brusher Gate', a gap in the fence which divides the mountain from the enclosed land about ½ mile W of the old road at the back of Glendalough House, and just N of the track going from the old road up towards the mountain.

'Annaclochyalla' or 'Annaclochyanna' (Ath na gcloch geala, see Joyce, i. 20): a name which a priest told him he had heard for the place on the S boundary of Drummin where the main road crosses the stream, just near Glebe. Barton himself called this place 'the Goat's Bridge', so did Ned Harding of Killafeen.

He said the local pronunciation of Scarr was sometimes 'Scāh' ('a' as in 'rather'). He had heard Bellanagrana pronounced by a local man 'Boulnagraina scunce' ('scunce' meaning a sort of a ditch).

We visited Killafeen. The raheen was on the land of Ned Harding of Killafeen, in the field on the NW side of the bridge crossing the Annamoe River between Laragh East and Trooperstown, W of a line between the bridge and Harding's house, and about 150yds or so (at a guess) from the bridge. The position or site can still be seen where the earth was dug out of the slope of the field to make a small flat place as a foundation. Harding cleared away the raheen about 14 or 16 years ago (he said). It just consisted of old ruined banks, the one towards the river a bit built up but the others not — with old skeogh bushes on them, some as thick as a man. There were

no walls. The site measures 15 or 16 paces by 26 to 30 paces. There was a gap in the E end of it, and one stone standing by it — he showed [me] the stone where he rolled it into the ditch, an ordinary unshaped granite boulder about 2½ft long. There was also a small font since taken away by Father Geraghty of Roundwood. Between the raheen and the bridge are two large field boulders of granite with flat surfaces: on one are two large cup-markings, the larger [is] 13in. [in] diameter by 7in. deep. The other which is now covered by the grass and which is just beside the road fence above the bridge, had, according to R. Barton and Harding, five or six cup-markings not so large as those on the other stone and close together. I did not see this stone. Water runs out from under the fence (below the raheen) at the lower side of the field, and Harding has it piped — he said people sometimes used this water for a cure, but he knew no more than that. He said one place in the raheen was hollow, and stamped, and it seemed to us all that the sound was hollow, and different from the sound of the earth nearby. Harding said the soil was all sand. He ploughed the field after destroying the raheen, but found nothing more.

I forgot to take the cardinal points, but as far as I recollect the long sides ran from E to W, and the gap was in the short side on the W.

Verified this on 6th April 1931. The orientation may have been very slightly to the N of E and to the S of W, but as far as it is possible to tell from the remains and Harding's description, the long sides ran roughly E and W.

25th March 1931

Information from Mr E. O'Toole of Rathvilly.

On the farm of Mr Pat Reynolds of Killalish there is a field called 'the Church Field'. It is adjoining, and on the W side of, the Killalish road, about ¾ mile S of the crossroad on the Baltinglass–Kiltegan road. The field used to be divided into two by a fence, but the Reynolds removed the fence, and made a small ditch instead along which the water now runs to the house. The northern of the two fields was the Church Field. Pat Reynolds said that his father who died about 20 years ago, aged 76, remembered seeing in this part of the field a portion of a tombstone on which there was an inscription. Timothy O'Toole of Knocklishen aged about 73 told E. O'Toole that Pat Reynolds' mother told him that this piece of tombstone

was built into the inside of the road fence. Robert Brown of Knockevagh told E. O'Toole that Martin Brien of Mount Kelly who was rent-warner and gamekeeper for Lord Rathdonnell, and who died 25 or 30 years ago aged about 70, told him (Brown) that he often saw the marks of graves in this field on a summer's morning when there would be a heavy dew.

At the E side of the road, opposite Reynolds', on the farm of Mr P. Murphy, is a small-sized 'lis' or rath, ringed round with very old whitethorns.

Mr E. O'Toole also gave me some further information as to Killaduff neighbourhood. Eugene Byrne (already mentioned, of Phillipstown) told E. O'Toole that there was a tradition that there was a castle in Ballymanus a little W of Ballymanus House; it was on the brow of the hill, in the field under Brady's house. It was called 'Castle Esmond' (evidently that called 'Castle Laurence' on the OS map). On the opposite side of the road to the castle on Mr Lynch's land there was a small chapel.

'Drumcath' or 'Drumkitt', 'Catgut Cave'.

If we stand in Manning's Bog in a parallel line with Manning's old house we can see on the opposite side of the river adjacent to the birch tree the mouth of Catgut Cave which fell in a few years ago.

This must be the cave referred to as local tradition tells us that Fiach was slain in Manning's Bog.

Manning's Bog (Ballintombay Lower?) is on the left-hand side of the road from Kirikee School to Greenan, more than a mile from the school. It is near Mr Snell's house.

Somewhere in Ballinatone, further down the river than Greenan, and in the bank on the S side of the river, is a place called 'the Cave' — a man could go a long way up in it. The old road labourer who told me this said he thought it wasn't a cave but an old 'shore' (sewer or drain).

13th May 1931

Tobergorey in Monatore near Baltinglass. It is a spring (or well) in a circular hollow in the field, just W of the stream, into which the trickle from the well runs — the well is disused, and all filled with watercress and weeds. It is about 150yds W of Tinoranhill crossroads. An old man from the house near it said it was an old well, that the water in it had been very good, always boiling up all through the summer — that it was not used now — he said it was called 'Tubber go-an or something like that'. Also that the water used to leave a white dust deposit like lime on the pots or kettles that it was used in. There is another well a couple of hundred yards to the W, railed roughly round, it is opposite the house. This he said is a new well, made recently and not as good as the old one. He said he knew nothing about Tobergorey being used for cures.

Raheens Mound (Donard Demesne East). Consists of a slightly elliptical central space surrounded by a bank with a deep ditch contained by another bank: then a more elliptical open space, again surrounded by a bank, ditch and bank. All four banks are made of stones and earth: the outermost shows the stones most clearly as it is evidently partly kept in repair being used on the W side as a field fence. The central space is about 27 paces N and S, and 23 paces E and W. [Inner] ditch is 6yds wide, and contains water. The space between the [inner and outer] ditches is about 6 paces wide on the E, W and S, but on the N side widens out to about 17 paces. The outer ditch is about 3 paces wide, and contains water. The *Namebook* calls this 'a raheen nearly defaced', but this is not accurate: the banks are evidently much worn down, but the outlines of all four are quite clear, and the two ditches are very well preserved and deep. The ground inside the central space is uneven, with three or four long raised mounds: whether these are foundations of buildings or not I cannot say: they do not form the plan of a building. The entrance through both ditches is slightly E of N.

16th May 1931

Parkmore. On the opposite side of the road from the Giant's Grave about 150yds away, about SSE of it, in the angle of the Ballycullen and Sleanaglogh roads, is a circle of stones, with the remains of a central chamber. It has the appearance of a ruined burial cairn.

The circle is 30ft in diameter, all the stones are small, the highest standing about 2ft 8in. above ground level. The chamber is roughly in the centre of it. It has ten stones in place, all small. No sign of a capstone.

The [outlying] stones *A* and *B* are two small pillar stones which give the appearance of having formed part of a passage — 3ft apart. They are on the N side of the chamber and about 5ft 6in. from the outer circle.

There are traces possibly indicating that there was a second circle 2 or 3ft outside the existing circle — two stones of it are in place on the S side and one on the W, and the surface of the ground is slightly raised so as to

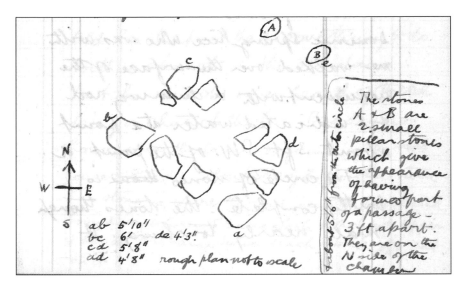

The stones A & B are 2 small pillar stones which give the appearance of having formed part of a passage – 3ft apart. They are on the N side of the chamber

about 5/6 from the outer circle

ab 5'10''
bc 6'
cd 5'8''
ad 4'8''   de 4'3''   rough plan not to scale

Fig. 31—Sketch-plan of central chamber at Parkmore.

form an arc of the circle connecting these stones round almost half the monument on the S and W sides.

All the surface of the monument (including this additional outer circle) is covered with small stones: this seems to me to indicate that it was originally covered by a cairn of stones.

Dominic Spring-Rice who was with me walked over the surface of the monument with a divining rod and it indicated water at a point about 3ft SW of the point *A* [at the S end of the circle].

The circle of stones is pretty complete: the stones though small [are] nearly touching. It looks to me like a circle of containing stones, similar to, though much smaller than, those on the Seechon and Seefinn cairns.

(Compare this with the Lackan monument, *JRSAI* lix, 68, and with the mote on Chaney Hill.)

Sleanaglogh. The bullaun stone is locally called 'the Wart Stone'. If a person washes his hands in it it cures his warts. The old woman who lives in the house nearest to it (about 200yds SW of the stone) told me this, she also said that people had told her that it had something to do with a church in the old days: but she said she never heard of there being a church there. Bradshaw's house where the lamp was found is the next house to the SW about 500yds from the stone. The stone is where the road meets the townland boundary between Sleanaglogh and Aghowle Upper: it has an Ordnance Survey benchmark cut on it.

Stump of the Castle. The 'castle' stands at the SW corner of a square enclosure, of which the N and S sides measure about 41 paces, the W side 45 paces and the E 46 [paces]; outside this on the N side is a wide ditch, and a high second bank: on the E and W sides it can be seen that there was a similar bank and ditch which have been levelled to make roadways: on the S side no trace of either an outer bank or a ditch remains.

The inner enclosure consists of a bank of stones and earth (mostly earth) about 4½ft high: inside it is a flat field with some apple trees planted in it. The outer bank on the N side must be 9 or 10ft above the level of the ditch — the bottom of the ditch would be about 2½ft below the level of the inner enclosure.

The castle is a circular tower, walls 3ft thick, inner diameter about 5ft (or perhaps 6ft). The doorway is on the E side — the chamber is roofed by slabs laid projecting inwards over one another, closed at the top with a single slab, like a beehive hut, or the centre chamber of Newgrange. There is another chamber above it, but it is almost entirely ruined. Two straight walls project from the tower for a couple of feet one to the E, just S of the door, the other to the S. The N and W sides of the tower are round without any sign of projecting walls from them. Greatest height at present, 14 to 15ft. The masonry of the round tower is of rough stones, small and oblong in shape, set in courses rather roughly, with mortar.

No one is living in the house at present. The labourer in charge said it was supposed to be a watch tower, and that he had heard there were other buildings underground, but had never seen them: also that there was supposed to be a passage going from it to an old castle at Laragh, and another to a castle near Avondale.

There is no trace that I could see of any other tower or part of a castle. The house is quite close to this tower, and it was built, according to the labourer, in 1870: so the traces which O'Curry saw in 1839 may have been destroyed when it was built.

20th May 1931

Ballyvolan Fort. The whole fort is overgrown with brambles, nettles, bushes etc., so that it is even impossible to pace the sides accurately. The above [Fig. 32] is a rough plan drawn freehand on the spot, and not all perfectly accurate. As well as I could pace them, the sides are:

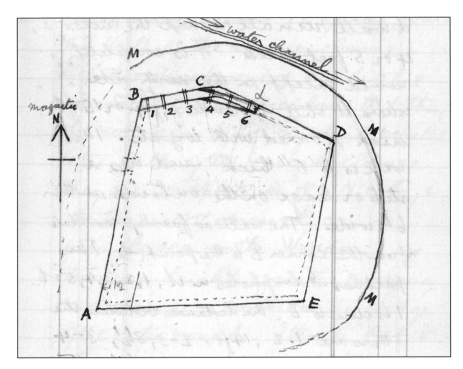

Fig. 32—Sketch-plan of Ballyvolan Fort.

A–B [W side] 55 paces
B–C [WSW–ENE side] 13 paces [part of N side]
C–D [WNW–ESE side] 34 paces [part of N side]
D–E [N–S] 31 paces [E side]
A–E [E–W] 40 paces [S side]

At the SW corner (*A*) there are the foundations of another wall, 12ft from the outside edge.

A wall ran all round the enclosure, 4 or 5ft thick. It is completely ruined except on the N side, where it is still standing, part being 14 or 15ft high, covered with ivy etc. This wall is 4ft 6in. thick, and has a step or ledge on the outside another 6in. wide. The wall is fairly complete from the corner *B* to the point *D*. This part has six loopholes in it: *1, 2, 3, 4, 5* and *6 — 1* is close to *B*. The distances between the others are:

1–2 14ft
2–3 8½ft
3–4 9½ft

4–5 10½ft
5–6 9½ft

1 is stopped up by debris. These loopholes are 9in. square, they are level, not sloping, and are 45in. from the ground level on the inside. The 6in. step is level with the lower edge of the loopholes on the outside. The traces of foundations at the corner *A* suggest that there was a square tower at this corner.

Outside the wall was a slope down to a ditch some 12 or 15ft deep — and outside this a high bank or mound, the top being about 20yds from the wall of the inner enclosure. I could not make out if this ditch and mound were once circular, but they do not seem to be regularly parallel to the walls of the inner enclosure. They are complete on the N and E, and the trace of the mound can be faintly seen on the W side.

There is a trickle of water running in a channel outside the N edge of the outer mound. I think that the stream now running on the S side of the road just S of the fort could have been deflected so as to fill the moat.

The stones of the wall are uneven in size and laid in courses with mortar, which seemed to me to be very soft.

Among Mr S. Lane-Poole's papers is a letter or memorandum written by the Reverend H.R. Huband of Ipsley Lodge, near Farnham, Surrey, who appears at one time to have been familiar with the Ashford–Newrath Bridge district. The following is copied from it:

'Ballyvolan

An old Celtic fortification — multangular [*sic*] and so the English built a multangular [*sic*] castle on it. Old Celtic brooch (10th century) found in the ruins of which I have a photograph. Mr Keane sold it to Lord Carysfort having bought it for 5/– at a sale of Dr Hughes … . Walls 4½ft thick. The old road from Ballyvolan ran past Kilmartin Church and joined the Rathnew Road at Blackbull.'

and on another page:

'There was a tradition which I heard (very often) of an underground passage running from Dunran to Ballyvolan.'

September 1931

Mr Willie Cullen of Rathmore showed me what he said was called a rath or raheen on his land at Rathmore: it was the highest part of the field, but I believe it is only an outcrop of rock with field stones scattered about on it. It is a space perhaps 30yds long by 20yds wide covered with furze and brambles and stones — no banks or blocks of stone, but in three or four places large pieces of rock are exposed, which I am almost sure are the underlying rock outcropping. The remains of the rath are in the next field to the S; only a small portion remains on the N or NE side, where there is an outer bank apparently of earth now part of the field fence, a ditch perhaps 5 or 6ft deep and about 3yds wide, and the trace of an inner bank. The circle of the rath can be very indistinctly seen in the field, which has been constantly tilled. It was a large rath, I should guess 50yds or more in diameter.

27th May 1931

Rathnagree near Baltinglass. A large circular earthwork, consisting of an outer ditch and two banks, enclosing part of the hill. There is no central mound, or anything artificial except the ditch and banks; the rock outcrops in several places inside the rath. (The *Namebook* is wrong in saying it is 'much elevated in the centre'; it is not so now, and I do not think from its appearance that it ever was.) The outer ditch is dug in the surface of the hill; there is no bank outside it, except for a very low piece in one or two places, which looks like an old field fence. Next [to] the ditch on the inside is a large bank of stones and earth. The ditch and bank together are 7 or 8yds wide: the bottom of the ditch is in places 10 or 12ft, in other places about 6ft below the level of the top of the bank. The present average depth of the ditch below the surface of the ground is about 3 or 4ft. Inside this, about 40 paces away on the S and about 50 paces away on the N is an inner bank, smaller and more ruined than the other: it is also of stones and earth, and is complete all the way round — more like a continuous low heap of stones than a bank. This inner ring is about 95yds in diameter. The diameter of the whole earthwork is about 200yds, and its circumference about 700yds. It is shut off from the S by the top of Baltinglass Hill, on which the monument called 'Rathcoran' is situated, but the view to E, N and W is very wide and commanding, Kilranelagh Hill, Carrig and Keadeen —

Brusselstown and Spinans, Ballinacrow, the Slaney, Ballyhook Hill, all the low country towards Colbinstown and Co. Kildare, Tinoranhill.

One man I asked said it was called 'the Ra'; another older man, Brennan of Tuckmill Hill, said it had a name but he could not think of it for the minute, then he thought for a few moments, and said it was called 'the Daheen Ra' and that it was one of four (of which one was the small ring in Ballinacrow Lower, another in Ballinacrow Lower had been levelled and the fourth one, to which he pointed in the direction of Coolinarrig, had also been levelled). (I rather suspect this name 'Daheen' is not a real name at all.) This man said he had seen 'them' one evening riding on grey horses from Ballinacrow up to this rath, as if 'they' were at a burial ('they' = the fairies). He also told me a story of two men called Keogh who with a third man were carting lime one evening past the mote of Rathvilly and the third man heard music, and got over the bank onto the mote, and wasn't seen again, until about ten weeks after — they went every night to the mote to look for him, and the last night he came back, and said he'd been dancing and had just finished his 'hate' (I don't know what this meant, and I couldn't hear him distinctly; obviously 'heat' or 'turn'). And another story about a tailor named Connor whose child was changed, and one day Connor who was a great whistler said to the child 'Could you dance to that' and the child said 'Begob I could if you don't tell the ould one' — so they took the child to the river and tied ropes round it to choke it, and so he got his own child back. (His stories were the typical stories of fairies, but not very detailed, and not particularly relating to any special place, except the one about the mote at Rathvilly.)

Query, could this rath, Rathnagree, be 'Brandubh's House'? It would suit the description of Chanaseach's escape very well (*Silva Gad.* ii, p.410).

A hollow in the hill just under Carsrock is called 'Madam Dunkey's Hole' and it is there that the underground passage or 'escape' from Baltinglass Abbey is supposed to come out.

4th June 1931

Rathdrum Court. 'Barndarrig' is the name of a place on the road from Macreddin to Greenan about 1½ or 2 miles from Macreddin where there is a quarry belonging to a man named Newsome, of Macreddin.

16th June 1931

At Dunran Demesne. The castle faces about SSW or so. I paced the walls roughly, W wall about 13 paces, N wall about 10 [paces]. The stairway is in the S wall — at the SE end of the S wall, inside, is an opening, one goes in and turns to the right and the stairs go straight up very steeply: you reach a landing with two pointed windows. At the SE end of this landing the stairway continued, but the doorway is now blocked up. The stone steps of the stairs can be seen from the landing above one's head. They must have led to the parapet. The N gable is standing inside the parapet. It was not steeply sloping. The castle merely consists of the four walls, there is no trace of a vault in it at any height. The masonry of the opening where one starts up the stairs does not look original or old to me. The S wall is about 7ft thick, I think the others are the same.

See O'Curry's description of this castle in 1839 (*Wicklow OS Letters* pp 210–11). It seems then to have been exactly the same as it is now, with the one exception that there is now no sign of glazing or even of window frames in the windows. The stairway was then blocked up as it is now.

The 'warders' at each corner look like a feature of an old castle — there is no access to them now, but the gardener who got up there by ladder told me there are loopholes in them which command the adjoining angles of the castle.

The foundation of the W wall for about 3ft from the ground looked to me as if it might be old, i.e. pre-16th century. I cannot guess when this castle was built. If the sketch on Petty's barony map is intended as an accurate representation, it can hardly be the same building.

The castle is now surrounded by a wall, enclosing a circular garden: the castle is not in the middle of the enclosure. The wall is not more than 100 or 150 years old I should say.

On the barony map 'Killoge' appears to include the present Dunran Hill as well as the present Keeloge, while 'Killteman' includes the present Dunran Demesne, and the castle shown by Petty is in much the same position as the present castle.

Taylor and Skinner's road map (1777) shows 'Dunran, Gen. Cunninghame'. This was probably General Robert Cunninghame, created Lord Rossmore in 1796: Nevill's map (1761) shows Dunran Hill but not Dunran Demesne. O'Curry says the castle was 'in full habitable order' when Lord Cornwallis was viceroy, i.e. 1798 to 1801, but does not give his authority — perhaps it was local information.

Could the castle possibly have been an 18th-century antique, rebuilt on old foundations by this General Cunninghame?

The demesne has several roadways through it laid out for scenic effect, in the 18th-century style, rather like Synge's (Glanmore) or Tottenham's (the Devil's Glen).

'The Bishop's Rock' is the name given to a rock on a roadway through the demesne, N of the castle — so called because it is the shape of a bishop's hat.

'Aghatore' or 'Aughatore' is the farmhouse on the opposite side of the road and just S of Kiltimon or Dunran Castle. It adjoins Courtfoyle.

24th June 1931

Crossoona Rath, in Boleycarrigeen. A stone about 3ft high standing in what looks like the remains of a wall inside the rath has an ogham inscription on it: 'V (or F) OTI'.

The last dot of the 'I' is at the top angle of the stone, and is not very distinct, but I believe it to be a dot or stroke of the vowel.

I visited Crossoona Rath previously (I think about the year 1924) and did not notice this ogham at that time.

Fig. 33—Ogham stone at Crossoona Rath (courtesy of the Royal Society of Antiquaries of Ireland ©).

114

The circular structure just outside the bank on the NW side suggests to me some kind of sweathouse or Turkish bath; but it seems very curious.

It is a conical mound, with the top cut off. At one side (SE) the base of the mound is cut away, and three or four large and long blocks of stone can be seen lying one on top of the other like the underneath part of the steps of stairs, similar to the appearance one gets in a limekiln. The centre of the mound is hollow — a circular hollow like a well about 4½ft or so in diameter and about 3 to 4ft deep. It is all built of rough stones, I think granite, but they are presumably roughly shaped like a drystone wall, as the surface of the well inside is fairly even. It is built just about where the outer bank of the rath would have run — perhaps with the stones of which the bank was made. The rath is circular surrounded by a bank, a ditch about 8ft in depth and a second bank which only remains in places mostly on the SW.

The 'druidical circle' is about 400yds NE of Crossoona Rath. There are eleven stones standing, mostly about 3 to 4ft high. The highest is about 6ft or 6¼ft. It stands about NE by E of the centre of the circle and [has a pointed shape] with some weathered natural markings on the inner face. These stones are not granite. The circle is 45 paces in circumference, 46ft in diameter. The stones remaining stand about 4ft from one another and are about 3ft wide, and these measurements suggest there were originally nineteen stones in the circle — this is only conjecture.

The dotted [circles are] where there seems to be the base of a stone remaining; the [dotted] lines are where I conjecture stones once stood.

About 110 paces W by N of the centre is a boulder which looks like a standing stone about 5ft high, and 6 paces SW of this stone is a small pool of water that seems to be a well; the field is otherwise dry. E of the circle

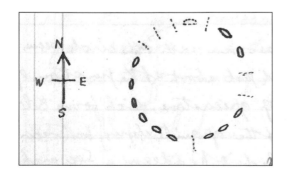

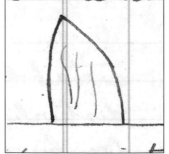

Fig. 34—Sketch-plan of Boleycarrigeen stone circle and profile of the tallest stone in the circle.

115

are at least two cairns, much disturbed, which seem to have been burial mounds, of small stones with large blocks of stone in the centre. They are too broken up to have any shape or measurements that could be noted.

Boleycarrigeen appears to be included in the denomination 'Dooneing' on the Down Survey map.

Both Crossoona Rath and the circle seem to be situated just about at the junction of a patch of greenstone, which forms Kilranelagh Hill, and the granite, lying between Kilranelagh and Keadeen. See map in Farrington's 'Granite schist junction', *PRIA* xxxvii B, p.20.

15th September 1931

A large stone in Moorstown townland. It is 7½ft high, 5½ft broad at the base — it bends over towards the S. It stands in the NE corner of the townland, about 100yds E of the road. I do not know if it is artificially placed or not.

Courtfoyle. 'The Fort Field'. This is the enclosure described by O'Curry. It shows traces of an outer masonry wall especially on the S side. The NE and NW corners seem to have fallen in — at the NE there is a recessed angle instead of the corner, and the slope of it consists of a mass of small stones, like a heap of field stones — the stream still flows along this side and on the far or outer side of the stream the angle is preserved. The [nearby] house is I think the property of a Mr Short. Most of the rest of the townland belongs to people called Evans.

20th September 1931

Kilbeg, near Blessington. 'St Boodin's Well'. The well is just E of a stream which runs down from the Gap road into the valley. Coming down from the Gap, just where the road leaving the open mountain commences to run between walls, one goes down E of the little stream, and the well is about four fields down; it is overgrown with bracken, and old trees, and there are at least three heaps of stones round it, also hidden by the trees etc. These seem to be only field stones. It is called locally 'Boden's Well' and is supposed to be holy. I saw some rags tied on a branch just above the well. Another man called it 'Jin's Well' — perhaps a corruption of 'Boodin' (slender 'd'). It is also called 'Mac's Well', after the man who owns the land it is on.

The well to which the new pattern goes is E of Templeboodin Graveyard in Lackan townland.

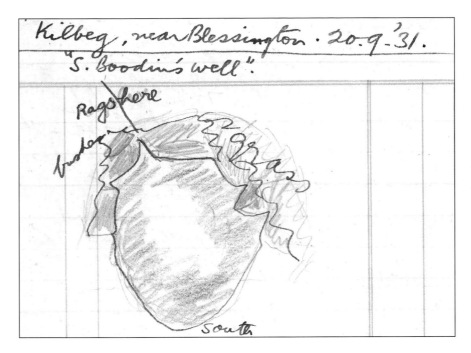

Fig. 35—Sketch of St Boodin's Well, Kilbeg.

The man who is supposed to look after Templeboodin said a bishop was buried there, and you could see his tombstone — Bishop Boden. The graveyard does not seem to have much of interest in it. There are a couple of old quernstones thrown loose on the old wall which seems to be part of the foundation of an old church.

Whelp Rock is not precisely the NW portion of Black Hill, but rather the W part, towards the Ballynastockan Brook. A man told C.G. Thompson this place was called 'Cloch na gulyccn'.

28th September 1931

Visited Hollywood Church after the Dunlavin Court.

Mrs Toomey of Hollywood who has known the church all her life states that it has a stone roof. The roof is, on the interior, in the shape of a Gothic arch, plastered evenly, so that one cannot see what is above the plaster: on the exterior it is an ordinary gable roof, slated. The walls of the church are quite 3ft thick, and slope inwards: height from ground to top of side wall, about 15ft. At the top of the side wall is a wide eave, apparently of stone, from which the roof springs. Height from top of wall to ridge of roof, about 8 or 9ft (measurements are by estimation).

117

Apparently this church is not old: ... 'In 1630 church and chancel fallen down to the ground' — 'In 1718 a church lately built.' [No references are given here.]

There is now no chancel, the church is a simple oblong room. Chimney of stove, N side.

1st October 1931
Rathdrum Court. Mr D.M. Doyle showed me a fine stone axe nearly 12in. long which he got in a field belonging to Pat Hanlon of Rathnabo near Blessington. It was found a number of years ago in Rathnabo Bog, and thrown into the fence in the field, where Mr Doyle found it.

11th October 1931
Tipper Parish, Co. Kildare. Newtown Cross: 10ft high. Perhaps worked on E side.

14th October 1931
Tuckmill. Stone 5ft 3in. high (about), leans a little towards S, there is a flat flag on the W side. (This [stone] was removed in 1954 to clear the field for ploughing with a tractor.)

This stone is in 'Dempsey's Field'. The house of E. Hanlon is just S of this field. Mrs Hanlon (I suppose she was) said she wasn't quite sure where the stones they dug up out of the field were, but she thought it was in a ditch to which she pointed, and which is the E fence of Dempsey's Field. She said they were ploughing the field on the hillside, and cleared these stones. I believe these are only field stones cleared off the field, I don't think I saw the flags D.M. Doyle refers to [in a letter of 14th January 1930].

Boleycarrigeen. Photographed the stone circle. It is called 'the Griddle Stones' but I heard no story about it. The old man who lives in the house just at the bottom of the old lane coming down from Crossoona Rath said that there was a mound near it, down towards the house (that is the E side) and that there was a cave in it, but it has been filled up, before his time — his father told him he had gone down into it, but his candle had gone out, and would not light — but he got in some way, and saw a long hall with little chambers off it. Other people had gone down into the cave too. It was filled in because sheep used to fall into it.

I photographed this mound. (These photos were failures.)

The Griddle Stones are on Byrne's farm: it used to belong to Trinity College [Dublin]: so did Keadeen. The old man I spoke to, who also lives in Boleycarrigeen, said his farm was on Mr Greene's estate.

He also said that there were four letters on a stone on St Bridget's Chair, and also a cross. No one could read the letters. He had looked for St Bridget's Well but couldn't find it; it's buried and you'd have to dig for it. He found a stone near it with the mark of St Bridget's elbow on it where she leaned on the stone to drink out of the well.

Castlequarter. Jackson's of Castlequarter — the Church Field. Oblong enclosure about 24ft x 18ft or 20ft, foundations of a stone wall, 2ft thick. On the S wall of this enclosure is a stone 1ft 8in. long or so. It has a flat surface, in which is cut a channel expanded into a bulb at one end ... . The bottom of this figure is flat — it is 1½in. deep. An elderly farmer up Killybeg, who pointed out the trees on Jackson's farm which mark the church, said he had heard that the young Jacksons had taken this stone away to their house, but that there was so much noise made in the house at night that they had to take it back. He did not know what the stone was for.

Between the house and the church enclosure is a field enclosed on three sides by a high bank 5 or 6ft high and about 4ft wide with a wet ditch outside it with little streams running into the ditch. On the fourth side towards the house is a high bank 6ft high almost vertical: this has been levelled out into a slope at each side so that it does not now enclose the field on the S side. This looks like a square fortified enclosure protected by a bank and a wet moat. There is no sign of building in it that I could see. Query, its date: 17th century? (see *JKAS* iv, p.149).

7th October 1931

Notes got from Mr Norse of Kilmartin:

Mr Norse has been at Kilmartin since 1908. The house was greatly added to by a Dr Hughes who lived there in the [18]50s; he built the front part of it: he also made the small artificial lake in front of the house. The old kitchen is now the dairy. The Misses Wrench, who have the house from Norse, showed it to me. It is paved with grey stone slabs carefully cut at right angles and carefully fitted together — they are all of different sizes. I saw no mark on any except one small indented square (2in. square) about

¼in. deep. It was the Reverend H.R. Huband who said the kitchen was paved with gravestones from the churchyard — I don't know what his authority was.

Mr Norse said the stone lintel was in place when he came there: it is as I thought the large stone lying inside the church. The lamp or vessel drawn by O'Curry is still preserved there. The head of the window in the N wall is broken; it could have been round or pointed; I think there may have been some cut stone round the window which has been removed. The form of the doorway is the only indication for a date: it seems old.

The well of drinking water just on the NE side of the house Mr Norse called 'Martin's Well'. There are other spring wells on the lands. There is a well called 'Nicholas' Well' in Ballyvolan. 'St Patrick's Well' at the Brewery is well known.

The field names on Kilmartin (of which Mr Norse holds all except about 25 acres) include 'Smith's Field', 'Higgins' Field', 'Dowd's Field', 'Church Field', 'Barnavay' ('bearna féithe') which is next to Wickham's of Barnacoyle (i.e. the E side of Kilmartin), and 'Mōneyaneel' (perhaps 'muine-', three syllables, long 'o') which adjoins Cullen's of Rathmore (i.e. SW of Kilmartin), and 'Blue Field'.

The farm called 'Sutton's of Blackditch' where the cist was excavated by G. Coffey is now Smith's farm, it adjoins the road leading to Newcastle station.

19th October 1931

Ticlash, Kilcommon parish. Large block of stone, flat top, flat face on E side. [There is] one cup[mark] on the top and several on the E face. [Measurements are:]

A–B 61in. [height of stone]
C–D 33in. [minimum width]
[There is a channel leading from the cupmark on the top of the stone.]
The channel is very small and slightly marked; runs downwards towards W. Length of channel 11½in.
Diameter of large cup 5in.
Depth of large cup 1½in.
Diameter of [smaller] cups [α and β] 3½in.
Depth of [smaller] cups [α and β] ¾in.

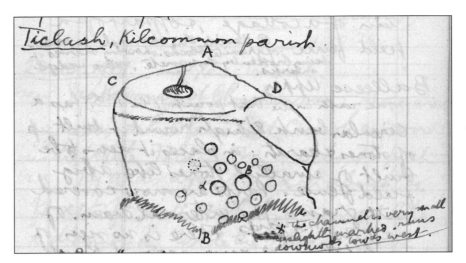

Fig. 36—Sketch of cup-marked stone at Ticlash.

It is 40yds S of well. Between it and the well are the ruins of a cottage or barn (not old), and just E of these ruins are the ruins of a fair-sized, perhaps early 19th-century, farmhouse. The rock outcrops just W of the large stone. There is an artificial channel running W, down the hill, from the well. Beside this channel are pieces of granite blocks, showing marks of being broken by dynamite, and also wedge marks. On the S side of the stone are the remains of old walls, perhaps the ruin of a cottage, and of part of a field fence.

(Note the name 'Tigh Claise', local pronunciation is 'Teeclash'.)

Balleese Upper. The rath in the W point of the townland has a circular bank 8ft high round it built up of stones and earth: in places it seems to be built of smallish stones like a big field fence. Parts are now covered with grass. The internal diameter of rath is 32yds. There is no sign of a ditch or of any second bank. The entrance was toward the NE. The inner level is higher than that of the field outside, and the centre seems to be a little bit higher than the circumference. An outcrop of rock has been made use of on the W to form the bank. It looks to me like a fortified, probably palisaded, wall, round a dwelling. Perhaps it was intended to guard the river crossing, ½ mile to the W.

Was it Hugh Keogh's/Parson's house? I should not say it was a very old construction.

I examined the top of Kilmacoo Hill for O'Curry's 'broken cahir' but could not see it (*OS Letters* 403).

23rd October 1931

In Glen Imaal. Saw James Kavanagh of Clonshannon. There are two graves on his farm at Clonshannon in the White Field. They are about a perch, i.e. 7yds apart. Each about 2ft x 1½ft, with four slabs arranged like a diamond, inside the square grave. Each has a big round stone on top of it. His father found one about 40 years ago, and a workman found the other about 2 years ago, there was a 'crock' in each, but it is broken. The pieces are there. The workman put a 'fack' through the crock in the one he found, thinking it was a crock of gold.

11th November 1931

Photographed the 'cave' on the top of Pinnacle (Baltinglass Hill).

On the top of the hill is a big cairn of stones, partly covered with grass, and with three boundary walls of dry stones built over it. I estimated the cairn as being 26yds in diameter. It has kerbstones round the base in a few places, as at Seechon, Seefin, and on other smaller cairns (see plan annexed).

Lord Walter Fitzgerald gives a short description of it in *JKAS* for 1907, vol. v, p.353, with two photos. It does not appear to have changed at all since then.

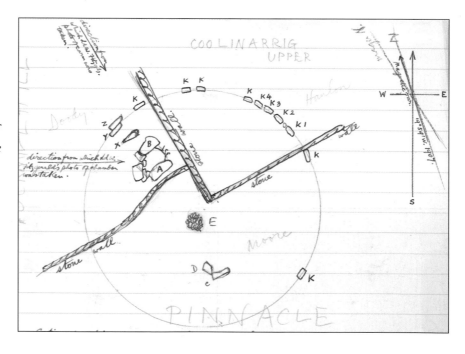

Fig. 37—Sketch-plan of passage tomb at Pinnacle (Baltinglass Hill) before excavations by Patrick Walshe in 1934–6.

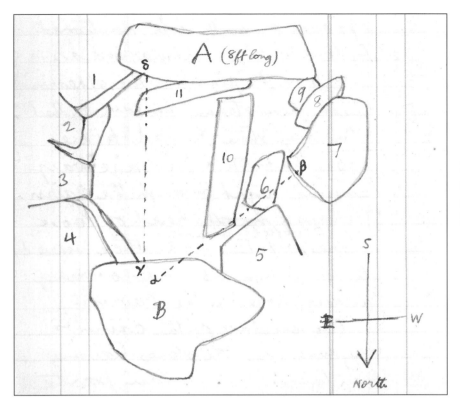

Fig. 38—Sketch-plan of chamber of passage tomb at Pinnacle (Baltinglass Hill).

Fig. 39—Passage tomb at Pinnacle (Baltinglass Hill) after excavations by Patrick Walshe in 1934–6 (courtesy of the Royal Society of Antiquaries of Ireland ©).

123

Fig. 40—Decorated orthostat of passage tomb at Pinnacle (Baltinglass Hill) after excavations by Patrick Walshe in 1934–6 (courtesy of the Royal Society of Antiquaries of Ireland ©).

Fig. 41—Chamber of passage tomb at Pinnacle (Baltinglass Hill) before excavations by Patrick Walshe in 1934–6 (courtesy of the Royal Society of Antiquaries of Ireland ©).

The chamber or cave is almost directly in the direction of magnetic N from the centre of the cairn, perhaps slightly E of magnetic N. I measured it as well as I could with the compass. (Note the plan is not quite correctly orientated, the N–S line is turned with N too much to the right. The red pencil lines are more correct.) The 'large flag or two' on the opposite or S side mentioned by Lord W. Fitzgerald are marked as *C* and *D* on the plan. The appearance which these stones, the cave on the N, and the large stone *X* had to me was that of a passageway running right through the cairn. There is a heap of loose stones 5 or 6ft in diameter at E, and these seemed to be filling up and covering a large hole in the cairn.

The surface of the cairn is very uneven, the stones having been taken from certain parts to such an extent as to leave large hollows. I cannot say whether this was done merely to build the stone walls, or whether the chambers or passage in the cairn have been searched and broken down by treasure-seekers.

The drawing [Fig. 38] is of the N chamber and was made roughly by view. The floor of it is about 4ft below the surface level.

There are four stones on the E side and five on the W. There are two large flat stones lying on the floor; *10* is 5ft 5in. long, and *11* is 4ft 10in. long. The dotted line α–β is 6ft long and the dotted line γ–δ is 8½ft long. The stones *A* and *B* are those shown on the plan.

The bank and ditch surrounding the whole enclosure is now so broken down as to be hardly recognisable. It can be seen still on the SE side of the cairn, a good way down the hill.

15th November 1931

Parkmore, near Moneystown. The Giant's Grave is on John Mernagh's land, the field is called 'the Giant's Grave Field'. The small stone circle is called 'the raheen'; it is on the land of a man named Timmons. There is a place called 'the churchyard' on the lands of a man named Moore, close to his house; it is SW of the Chapel of Ease, three fields from the road: there were stones in it but they were taken away 'as they were no use'. My informant was a young man who was standing near the little shop, he pointed out the 'churchyard' to me.

R.C. Barton told me that a house on the S side of Lough Dan is still called 'Byrne's of Saggart'; he thought it was in Carrigeenshinnagh, but will find out the exact place for me (cf. 'Bolensaggart' of the *Hearth Money Roll*).

It is pronounced 'Seggart', and there are two houses in it, Mick Gaffney's, and Byrne's. It is to the left from Keegan's house in Carrigeenshinnagh. (Evidently somewhere close to the boundary between Carrigeenduff and Carrigeenshinnagh, in Carrigeenduff.)

In the order dated 30th October 1931 (*Iris Oifigúil* of 27th November 1931) closing Glendalough Graveyard, three of the people to whom rights of burial are reserved are Hugh Devitt, Michael Farrington, and Lucy Healy, all of Killalane. The postmaster at Roundwood tells me this place is near Brockagh Chapel.

'Ballinacarbey' in the same order is a misprint for 'Ballinacorbeg'. Killalane is pronounced 'Cilla-léin' at present.

Compare 'Killelane', *Hearth Money Roll*. Devitt's, Farrington's and Healy's houses are in Laragh East, about two miles N of Laragh Bridge, on the right-hand side of the Glenmacnass road.

7th December 1931

Tullylusk. The raheen is a single circular bank, the enclosed space being slightly higher than the surrounding field. Ring 32yds (paced) in diameter. There seems to have been a second bank, of which the road fence may have been a part. It is gone all the rest of the way round. The bank is made of small stones and earth, and stands up very straight in places. Height (estimated) 7 or 8ft. Altogether this is rather like the raheen in Balleese.

9th December 1931

Information given to Mr E. O'Toole of Rathvilly by James Donegan of Barraderry crossroads aged over 60. Bigstone (SW of Baltinglass) is called 'Finn McCool's Jackstone'. The name Mr O'Toole knows is 'Killoura Bigstone', and he has seen it written 'Cloghloura' on a map.

At Moatamoy there used to be wrestling matches, dog fights, badger fights and cock fights when James Donegan was young. He says there is a cave underneath it; and that there is a rock near it called 'the Cat Rock'.

26th December 1931

Fassaroe and Monastery. Followed the old road which leads from Barnaslingan and Annaghaskin to the Ballyman road. It went straight on,

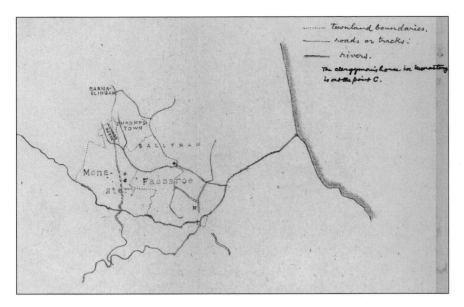

Fig. 42—Sketch-map of Monastery and Fassaroe.

where there is now a gate. Just where it bends round to the left, the remnant of Annahasky Church is on the left: nothing but a very broken piece of a wall, and a lot of loose stones. (The traces of walls measure about 7 x 17 paces; this is intended to be an external measurement, but they are so ruined, it is a mere approximation (23rd December 1934).) Just across the old roadway, on the right is another heap of stones: two local men who pointed out the old church said it was supposed to be 'the clergyman's house'. It is only a heap of stones covered with brambles. The road formerly led straight on to Enniskerry, and the track of it is still clear almost all the way, and is used as a right-of-way, with stiles at the fences. The large house beside it is known locally as 'Rannock House'; it is also called 'Berryfield' which is evidently a name for this part of Monastery townland, as the next house is also called 'Berryfield'. Went on round into Fassaroe townland, and followed the old track down to Ballyman. It is still clear, leading down to the river, across by a bridge of which one masonry support (on the S side) still remains, just near the old church ruin, and on up the hill to the Ballyman road, opposite the old roadway up to Carrickollogan. (There is still a small bridge crossing the river, more to the E of the old church, but this I should say is more recently made.) The well is a little W of the church, there were some rags and medals at it. The inscribed stone is now lying loose inside the ruins of the church (see *JRSAI* xxxi, p.145).

3rd January 1932

Butter Mountain and Ballyfolan, Kilbride Parish.

No. 1. Circle of eight stones, 14 paces in diameter. A large gap of about 15 paces between the stones on the W side of the circle, the stone at the S end of this gap is the biggest, about 4ft high. Inner face 2ft wide — and stone about 2ft deep from inner to outer surface. It and three other stones have a flat surface turned towards the inside of the circle. The inside of the circle is occupied by a raised broken mound, hollow in the centre — the stones are from 3 to 4 paces outside this mound. The mound is deeply covered with heather, grass and moss, and the ground is wet. No signs of stones to be observed. N of it and on W side of road is a small circular enclosure the bank of which has some stones in it. This is near the ruins of a farmhouse. [Later remarked:] It is nothing.

No. 2. In the field E of the road is another raised mound, hollow in the centre, and very much broken. It seems to be formed of large and small stones, but is very much overgrown. Two stones of what might have been an outer circle remain. The rest of the field is tilled.

No. 3. Near the next house to the S and in the field next but one S is another rath on W side of road. It is a large heap of stones, possibly some of the larger stones at the base formed part of a containing circle, but they are not laid longways end to end, and they may be only large stones thrown in from elsewhere on the heap. The circumference of the heap is approximately 55 paces, but its edge is rather scattered. James Ennis of Ballyfolan owns the land on which this and No. 2 are situated. They and No. 1 are the only raths he knows of nearby. They are just called 'raths', and he knows no story about them.

No. 1 and No. 2 are on the boundary between Ballyfolan and Butter Mountain, and just on the N side of it, i.e. in Butter Mountain. No. 3 is in Ballyfolan.

He (Ennis) said there was another rath near the 'Mine of Clochclea' (his pronunciation); the mine is the old iron mineworking.

Dowery, according to the houses which he pointed out to me, is the NE part of Kilbride townland, 'the Dowry Hill'. 'Carrick' (i.e. Carrignagower) is W or NW of the houses that are in Dowery.

4th January 1932

Kilmurry, Redcross Parish. There is no old church or old graveyard now in Kilmurry. There is a field called 'the Church Field' immediately in front of the house of Mr Vickers of Kilmurry, just across the old roadway: this is where the map marks the ruin of Kilmurry Church. There is a fair-sized drinking pool for cattle in this field and near it are several banks of earth, in straight lines, and in a couple of cases at right angles to one another. They have furze bushes growing on them. They seem to be stony banks, and this may be the reason they have not been cleared away as the rest of the field has been cleared. There are no signs of masonry. There is one large boulder in the field not far from the banks of earth: it is about 5ft x 3ft x 2ft: I could see no marks on it. In the same field but at a distance from the boulder and from one another are a couple of large stones: again no markings on them.

If these banks are the remains of the foundations of a building, it must have been a large building or a number of buildings. The banks do not suggest the shape of a small oblong church of Celtic or medieval period at all.

Lady's Well, Kilmurry. The well is still pointed out by old people, and called 'Lady's Well': it is said to be a blessed well. It is in the field E of Mr Vickers' house — surrounded by a wall of large stones and earth, 6ft or so above its surface level. There are two thorn trees growing out of this bank. A stream flows out of it to the E, under a large stone set so as to make a door-like opening. It is a fine well, full of watercress, very clean — seems to be used for getting drinking water — I saw no rags or anything of the sort about.

11th January 1932

John Eustace of Shankill aged about 55 or 60 told me he knows of no old church or church site or place called 'the Church Field' in Shankill. His father owned the whole townland and sold the present rifle range to the government about 50 years ago for £600. John Eustace's is the only house in Shankill, it is just below the road, N of where the road from Brittas comes in. He says the three mountains are called 'Seefing', 'Shankill Mountain' and 'Seechaun', and the flat slope between Shankill Mountain and Seechon is called 'Barnacreel'. (N.B. 'Shankill Mountain' is Seefingan).

(Some miscellaneous notes taken down at different times:)

Roundwood Park. A landed estates court rental gave the title. It was held under a fee farm grant dated 16th February 1911, in lieu of a lease for lives renewable forever dated 13th May 1828, subject to an annual tithe rent charge of £6/7/10. It was described as 'part of the demesne lands of Roundwood, containing 247 acres'.

Russborough. The owner was Sir E. Russborough-Turton M.P., D.L., J.P., of Upsall Castle, Thirsk, Yorks, who was born in 1857 and died in 1929. He was the eldest son of Cecilia, daughter and heiress of the 4th Earl of Milltown, and succeeded to Russborough on her death in 1914.

Rathdrum. 'Brewery Corner' is the corner on the main road ¼ mile W of the crossroad between Rathdrum and Avondale, and ¼ mile due S of Rathdrum Courthouse.

Blessington is pronounced 'Blessing-town' by the old local Wicklow people. I have frequently heard it, e.g. from Mrs Elizabeth Lawless of Rathnew on 15th May 1929.

There is a path leading from the Glenealy direction off the road at Ballymacsimon to Ballylusk School which is used by the children going to school. (I doubt if this represents an old road.)

Glasnamullen. The house belonging to Sutton who lives near the half-excavated mound of sand and gravel near Calary Church is known locally as 'Sutton's of the Moat'.

13th January 1932

Knocknagilky. The rath is flat in centre [and] enclosed by a circular bank of earth with some stones as foundation: outside this bank is a ditch about 7ft in depth below the top of this bank. Outside this ditch which is 3 or 4yds wide is a second bank similar to the first but slightly lower. The double bank and ditch are almost complete. Diameter of space enclosed by the inner bank, about 35yds. I saw nothing I would call an entrance, and no special features. The labourer who showed it to me said it had no special name and there was no story about it. He had been there for 40 years.

Cranareen Graveyard. It is situated in Slievereagh Lower (pronounced 'Slieve ray') but is called 'Cranareen Graveyard' — (pronounced 'Craneerin'). Surrounded by a fairly new iron railing — the gravestones are comparatively modern. I don't think there was any one that was pre-19th-century. The shape of the graveyard is irregular, something like a square with the corners very much rounded off. There are what may be foundations of walls in one place, but they are only loose stones heaped in a line: they enclose a small oblong space, estimated at 10ft x 15ft (see Comerford III, p.237).

Tobernashankill. The well seems to be just beside the brook, on the S side, within 10yds of the bridge, where some stones have been set so as to form rough steps. It seems to have no features of interest, just a spring well, running out at the bottom of a recess in what was the river bank. No rags tied on bushes. I don't think the well is used, to judge by its appearance.

Some local pronunciations:

Knocknagilky	'Knock·a geelky'
Slieveboy	'Sleebee'
Slievenamough	'Slĭnamōg'
Toorboy	'Toolboy'
Cornan	'Cornyawn'
Mullan	'the Mullyawns'
Rathcoyle	'Rathkyle'
Muckduff	'Mungduff'

Field names, Mr James Kavanagh, age about 40, on his farm at Clonshannon:

'The Reesk'
'The Rampark'
'The Inch'
'The Limekiln'
'The Upper and the Lower Park'
'The Far and the Near White Field'
'The Coarse Meadow'

The mill at Knocknamunnion was gone before his father's time.

24th January 1932

At Knockrath with E.M. Stephens ... . I should estimate the whole enclosure at 150yds long by 50yds wide. The tower or castle proper is 28ft square, internal measurement. I estimate its walls to be 6ft thick, they are almost completely ruined. The circular tower is 10ft in diameter, the circle being not quite regular — its walls are 4 to 4½ft thick.

We met a man named James Toomey of Knockrath, aged 50 or more. He said the cottage belonged to people called Lawless (he sometimes pronounced it 'Lyless', which seems like a pronunciation of the Irish form 'Laigheles'). It (cottage) was always that way (in ruins) as long as he remembers, that is 40 years. He thinks some of the family may have gone to Australia. He said the castle was a little higher up the bank than the 28ft square enclosure, Mr MacIntosh the estate agent told him so. He also said that Mr Thomas Edge cleared out the round tower, that it was all flat before he dug it. He pointed out what he said was an old road just beside the stream which is on the E side of the castle, it joins the Clara road, and he said it goes up the hill to the SW and over to Ballintombay.

The bank over this stream is clearly faced, probably as part of the outer fortification of the castle enclosure, so that all the high ground beside the castle was enclosed.

Toomey called it 'King O'Toole's Castle'. Toomey said the terraces were for putting cannon on for defence of the castle.

Neither Ned Stephens nor I could think what was the purpose of this terracing. The three terraces are quite clear — we could not be sure whether they were originally faced with masonry or not.

Toomey said that on the old road from Clara to Moneystown there is a

Fig. 43—Sketch of tower at Knockrath Castle.

stone called 'the Bread and Butter Stone', because the people used to stop there to give their horses something to eat, and eat something themselves.

Opposite Ned's cottage, in Laragh East and on the Laragh–Glendalough road, S side, near Doyle's house is a field with bushes and stones in it: it is called 'the Raheens'. Someone told him they heard a great rushing noise coming out of it one night.

Ned told me there is a large hole in it lined with loose stones which he thinks is a ruined souterrain.

Killafeen [see pp103–4]. The second bullaun stone which was buried has been cleared — Harding got an old man who knew where it was to clear it — we saw this man, he is over 70, I did not get his name. He said the raheen (which was what he called it) was all old blackthorn bushes, and sloes, the biggest sloes he ever saw: there were some banks in it, and they rolled the stones down to the hedge. He said there were stones of white quartz in it like duck eggs. Ned Stephens also had heard this from Miss Harding. The stone has four cavities in it, one 4in., two of 5in., and one 6 or 7in. in depth, the last being hollowed out not quite straight down, but on a slant. Ned found a large egg-shaped granite stone in the fence, which more or less fitted one of the cavities, and might possibly have been used in it for grinding.

This man said the top of Trooperstown Hill is called 'Meeleen', and that 'Glenacawrya' is on the far side of it adjoining Glenwood. The stream S of Killafeen on the other side of the river (the boundary between Ballard and Trooperstown) is called 'the Eskin Brook'.

Killafeen goes as far as Laragh Bridge. There are seven houses in it.

On the NW side of the road, just opposite the lane which leads down to Killafeen and the bridge, and about 200yds above the road, in the furze bushes Ned showed me a small circular place which Harding had shown him. Harding called it 'the rath', and said he had dug there recently and had found some 'marra' there, (i.e. marrow) — 'white stuff like bone manure'. The rath has no feature. There is the slight trace of ⅔ of a circular bank a few inches high — the circle would only be about 10yds in diameter. One would not see anything at all if it was not pointed out.

2nd February 1932

Liscolman. The rath is on Mr Fenton's land just on the N bank of the stream and in the corner of the second field E of the house. It is called 'the rath': the workman to whom I spoke a man of 50 or so said it had always been the same as it is now as long as he remembered; he had often cut rushes on it. He said he never heard any stories about it. It consists of a flat inner surface about 25yds diameter, some feet higher than the surface of the surrounding field, surrounded by three concentric banks or mounds. The first (inner) bank is 10ft in height (almost complete) above the level of the surrounding ditch. This ditch is 10yds wide, and wet: after a week's dry weather the day I was there I had to step through the water on lumps of rushes to get to the inner ring. The second bank is 50–60yds in diameter, practically complete in places 5–6ft in height above the ditch between it and the first bank. The second ditch is dry in most places — it is a good deal filled up I should say, not so wide as first. The third bank must be nearly 100yds in diameter. The field fence on the E cuts through it, and coincides in part with the second bank. This third bank is partly levelled, but can be traced all round. I saw no stones, or signs of a souterrain, or special features. Perhaps the rath is not so very old: query, was it used in medieval times? Water must always have formed one of the defences. I should guess that the builders of it were imitating the plan of the Ring of the Rath.

Miscellaneous notes (no date)

James 6th Earl of Desmond died 1462.

Thomas, his son, 7th Earl continued the exactions of coign and livery begun by his father (Curtis), executed 1468.

James, his son, 8th Earl, murdered 1487.

Maurice, son of Thomas, 9th Earl died 1520.

James, his son, 10th Earl died 1529.

Thomas, son of Thomas, 11th Earl died 1534.

Ballyfolan stone circle … . Diameter of mound of stones and earth 31ft 10in. Diameter of stone circle 53ft 10in.
Stone *A* [at W] height 3ft 8in. Compass bearing *B* to *H* [from stone at SW anticlockwise to N] 12° E of N.
Mound about 4ft high.
Distances between the stones [from stone at W anticlockwise to N]:

A [at W] to B [at SSW]   26ft

B to C [at SSE]	14ft
C to D[at SE]	14ft
D to E [at E]	18ft
E to F [at NE]	21ft
F to G [at NNE]	8ft
G to H [at N]	10ft
H to A	45ft
A to K [outlier at W]	15ft

H is a greenstone.

3rd January 1937

Story written down from recollection by Miss Praeger, and sent me by Dr R.Ll. Praeger, asking if dialect was correct. [This contains phonetically spelt words.]

'A story of Loch Nahanagan as told by an old man in Glenmacnass 25 years ago.

In ould days there was livin' in the County of Down a poor woman that was a cripple. The power of her legs was gone from her entirely, and she could har'ly put a foot down under her. Well, there come to them parts a wise man that was a doctor, and he give out that he could cure all manner of disaises. So the woman sent for him and asked could he cure her lame legs. "There's no cure for you", sez he, "but wan, and I doubt it's too hard for you". "Tell me what it is", sez she, "whether or no". "Well", sez he, "away in County Wicklow there's a lake among the hills — Loch Nahanagan is the name on it. If you can get there and bathe your legs in the waters of that lake, you'll be cured". At first the poor soul thought this was clear impossible. "But still and all", sez she, "I'd be better dead than livin' this way so with the help of God I'll try it". And she set out. Sometimes in a horse cart, or maybe in a boat, wan way and another she travelled south, and after a long long while she found herself among the wild mountains of County Wicklow. And the people there was good to her, and two strong lads put her in a chair, and they carried her up over the heather to Loch Nahanagan. And there they set the chair down in the lake a short piece off the bank so she could bathe her legs quite handy, and there they left her — quarely contented to be at her journey's end.

Now at the bottom of this Loch there was livin' a terrible monster called a waterhorse. And when the waterhorse heard a splashin' and dashin' goin' on overhead, he gets in a towerin' rage, and up he comes to see who dar make free with his property. The poor woman was sittin' as aisy as you plaze, washin' her legs, and watchin' to see them growin' straight and strong, when she heard a noise, and lookin' round her, here she sees the frightful monster, risin' out of the middle of the lake with his eyes rowlin' and his tail lashin' out behind. When he saw the woman he let a roar like a bull and made wan rush at her. But my dear! did she wait for him? In wan minute she was out of the chair, and through the water, and up the bank and over the heather like a hare, and she never stopped nor stayed till she sat down by her own fireside in the County of Down. And the legs of her were cured from that out.'

FIELD NOTEBOOK 11:
February–October 1932

10th February 1932

Casey's Well, Talbotstown Lower. Seems to be merely a large pool, beside the road, quite overgrown with bushes — it is some 4 or 5ft below the level of the road.

Tobernachristhamaun. Talbotstown Lower. About 10yds S of the road. A spring well coming from below some large stones which are arranged in a kind of semicircular manner to form a back to the spring, about 5ft high; but there are also large stones lying in front, over the stream which comes from the well. There are trees standing about the spring and the stream, and on one in front of the spring I saw some rags tied. It is locally called 'the Bless'd Well', and a boy named Lennon who works for Mr Doyle of Talbotstown House says he heard it was St Christopher's Well.

Talbotstown Fort, Talbotstown Upper. An oblong structure, or space, surrounded by a bank and wall and a deep wet ditch. The interior space is about 55 or 60yds long and about 35yds wide. There was originally a stone wall all round going right down into the ditch. The angle remains uninjured at NW corner. About 4ft of the wall stands in the middle of the N side about 7ft above the inside ground level — otherwise the remains of the wall look like a bank, but the facing towards the ditch remains all round, a good deal broken away in places. The water in the ditch is 9 or 10ft below the inside level, and the boy who showed me the place said it was 'very deep'. The ditch is about 12yds wide, it goes all round, no masonry on its outer edge. On the N side, near E corner, two little pieces of wall jut out from the wall of the enclosure, and a slope between them goes down to the ditch. Was this a flight of steps? In the middle of the W side is a small projection or embrasure, and beneath it the boy said there was a hole, which he got into when the water was low in summer, but he was afraid to go in further, it was too dark. At present the place is used for a park or enclosure for calves or ewes and lambs: an entrance has been made into it from the E, across the ditch.

The boy said he heard two old men had dug in it and found a hole or passage, and went in till they came to an iron gate: then they could go no further. They were looking for money. He also said there was a story that a

Fig. 44—Ballyhubbock Bridge (courtesy of Dúchas The Heritage Service ©).

Fig. 45—Motte at Castleruddery Lower (courtesy of Dúchas The Heritage Service ©).

battle was fought somewhere to the W of it between the O'Tooles and the Danes, and O'Toole was killed and buried on Kilranelagh Hill.

The house used to be Mr Fenton's, Mr Joe Doyle has been there 12 years.

Castlesallagh. Examined the site of the castle. No traces of a castle remain, but the haggard of the farm is bounded on the NE by a very wide bank, 7 or 8ft wide, which was built up with masonry on top of which there are now trees growing. Perhaps it was part of the outer embankment — it is too wide to be an ordinary farm fence.

Castleruddery Lower. The mote or mound just N of Ballyhubbock Bridge and W of the road, is a circular flat-topped mound of the truncated cone type. It is surrounded by the remains of a ditch 6 or 8ft wide and an outer bank, now only a couple of feet above the field level — the ditch is not more than 3 or 4ft deep anywhere. The flat top of the mound is approximately 20yds in diameter. No features. I think a Norman mote built to command the river crossing.

15th February 1932

Ballymoney, parish of Ballykine. Tobermurry. The well is locally called 'the Lady Well', and a pattern is held there on 15th August. It is a couple of hundred yards S of the road on the W bank of the stream on Doyle's land. Its appearance is, an oblong pit, each side carefully built up of stones, the grass being level all around it: as though it had been dug out of the ground: but I think more probably it was built up carefully. Two gaps in the stones have been left on the E side, and a little stream runs out down to the main stream. The pit is about 2ft x 1¾ft, and about 2 or 2½ft deep. A little pile of stones has been placed behind (i.e. W of) the well, and there are two small religious statues on these stones. The field behind has been cleared of field stones for tillage, and the stones rolled down towards the stream, and some of these make a bank W of the well — some of these stones were dynamited and show the boring marks. Two large boulders lie E of the well by the little stream out of it: one has a curious curved groove on it, also a flat band in low relief on the front: but I think these are natural weather marks on the stone. [Height] about 2ft.

Information from the postman at Ballinaclash. There is a raheen in Clonerkin, which is supposed to be a graveyard — and a man named Mick Kenny cut holly trees on it, and he has since lost the use of himself. There

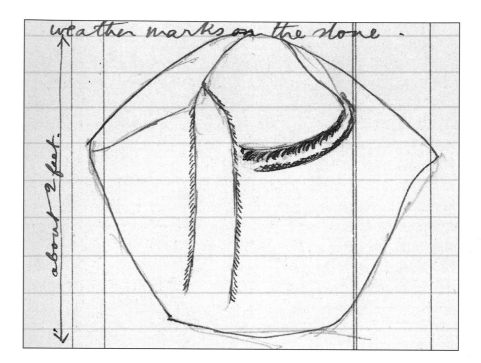

weather marks on the stone.

about 2 feet.

Fig. 46—Sketch of grooved boulder at Ballymoney.

was supposed to be a well near the Lower St. in Rathdrum, called 'St Michael's Well', behind Kelly's forge. The parish priest Father O'Callaghan searched for it, and found the well, but the water was not in it — it has flowed out some other way. A man stopped it up years ago, and was afterwards killed by a kick of a horse.

There is a water font in the field beside the old graveyard at Whaley Abbey, or 'Ballykine', which he said was the right name. It cannot be taken away. I asked why, but he couldn't say.

He said there is a well somewhere near the (old) road leading from Ballinaclash to Meetings. He never heard of St Kevin's Cup, but said an old labouring man, Owen Kavanagh of Knockanode, who works at Castlehoward might know about it. There is a stone called 'the Wishing Stone' near Moore's tree, just beside the Meeting of the Waters.

Bullaun stone at Rathdrum (*JRSAI* vol. 43, p.170; *JRSAI* vol. 42, p.340). The stone is in Ballintombay Lower, about 600yds W of the crossroads (Map 29, 12).

The crossroads at the boundary between Ballyshane and Moneymeen (pronounced 'Monyameen') is called 'Barndarrig crossroads'.

140

The mill in Ballinacarrig is still working: it is called 'Greany's Mill': a new wheel was put in recently.

21st February 1932

The old road leading from Delgany through Stilebawn and Drummin East to Killickabawn is still quite passable: there are some cottages on it, and three or four farms use it. The hill (471ft) at the head of Stilebawn has a view over all the surrounding country up to the mountains. I think it may have had a tumulus surrounded by a ditch on top at one time, as the fence which runs across the top now makes a semicircle just on the top. If I am right the whole tumulus has been removed for top dressing except the S edge which now makes the fence, and has a ditch outside it. All the fences here look old: it is land which has been cultivated for six centuries or more. There is a well in Drummin East, N of this old road: built up with stones: seems to be just a drinking well.

Looked for traces of an old road to Kindlestown Castle in the surrounding fields but could find none.

22nd February 1932

There is a ruined tumulus or cairn in the E part of Moorhill townland, Co. Kildare, at the top of the hill marked on OS map. It is flattened out, and eleven oak trees are growing on it — at a guess, the oldest is about 100 years old (?). The stones of the cairn are now almost entirely covered with grass — there are no very large stones visible, and no curbing round the edge. Diameter about 29yds.

For burials in this locality see an unpublished paper of G.H. Kinahan's read February 1901 and preserved in the Royal Irish Academy (see *JRSAI* vol. 34, p.321, note 1).

24th February 1932

Tobernagoagh, Lowtown, near Baltinglass. This is at present a large hollow place in the field, with bushes growing round it — the bottom is muddy and trampled by cattle, and water comes up out of it about the middle, and collects and runs E down to the main stream. There is no well in the ordinary sense, and no sign of stones having been built up to make a clean protected place for the spring water to collect. It is merely a drinking place for cattle.

Kilmacough, Knockarigg. The local pronunciation is 'Kyle-mahook' (as Lord Walter Fitzgerald says, *JKAS* iv, p.249). In a field called 'the Churchyard Field' on the townland of Knockarigg, just N of an old roadway, is a small square enclosure, 8 or 10yds square, with an iron railing round it; inside the railing is a thick growth of very old box hedge, and inside this are three headstones — one has no inscription on it that I could see, one is early 19th century in memory of 'James Wall', and the third is dated 1889 in memory of 'James A. Wall, Q.C.' I should say the surrounding railing dates from the time of this burial. The local people say it is a private burial ground belonging to the Wall family of Knockarigg House, and that there never was a church there. They call it 'the Churchyard Field' however.

1st March 1932

Tinahely. 'St Ann's Well' is in Glenphilipeen. It seems to be an old well; the back is built up of small stones in a sort of cylinder; about ⅔ of the circle remain and the top is roofed over at a height of 3 or 4ft with stone slabs. But within the past few months Mr Pierce the owner has 'improved' it by hollowing out the rock in front of the bottom of the well to form an oblong basin, and putting a concrete bar in front of it to make one side of the basin. I don't think the name 'St Ann's Well' is at all old; but Michael Byrne said that he used to hear up to 30 years ago (meaning at least 30 years ago) of people going and bathing their eyes in it. This suggests it is a holy well — perhaps 'St Ann's Well' is a corruption of some older name? It is on the side of the hill, not near any existing house.

The hill where it is, is called 'the Dandies' Rock' because the boys and girls all used to go out there on a fine day. 'Dandy' must I think have some such meaning as 'sweetheart' in it.

There is no particular rock, only a hillside covered with furze etc., with some rocks on it.

Cross. Nothing I could see to indicate the age of Cross Bridge — it is three arch with angular projections between. Those on the S side come up to the top of the bridge and are flat, on the N side they are only a few feet out of the water and are rounded off. Probably an 18th-century bridge? At the top of the hill on the left-hand or S side of the road (Cross townland) there is a house, standing back from the road. It has two short avenues or roadways up to it, and they and the road enclose a roughly circular space which is raised 10 or 12ft above them. There seems to be the trace of a circular bank at the top of this space which is 40yds across or more in places. I think it was a rath with a bank and a deep ditch, and that the road runs along part of the ditch and the two avenues in two other parts. The avenues however make angles with the road, and these angular spaces are as high or nearly as high as the rest of the enclosure. The space at the top is flat and covered with grass. (Find out what this house is called locally — it seems to have no local name.)

The S end of the old road from Coolafunshoge to Rathshanmore is still open, crossing the river by a ford. The N end where it joins the present road, at Rathshanmore South, is closed by a gate, and the road is only a very rough track.

From the road, I could not be sure of the 'raheen' or 'graveyard' at Kyle, but I thought it was a small oblong field, full of small bushes.

St Columbkill's Well, Slieveroe. An open pool in the fence beside the road, where a spring rises up at the bottom of the bank. I thought it was quite featureless, but on poking about looking at the stones beside and above it, I found hidden under some heather or grass stalks a piece of cotton and a lump of butter-like stuff which I think was ointment. So evidently there is some tradition about cures still existing in connection with this well.

No marks that I could see on any of the stones.

3rd March 1932

Kilcommon Church, Bahana — near Rathdrum. [There are] carved stones in window in E wall from outside.

From sillstone to top stone over original head of window 40in.

a, b, c and d [on Fig. 47] are the holes in which the bars of the window were set. From the shape of the holes I should guess they were iron bars.

a. 6¼in. above sillstone
b. 15in. above sillstone
c. 25½in. above sillstone
d. centre is 4in. from either side, the hole is 1in. wide.

The inside splay of the window where level with wall is 46in. wide.

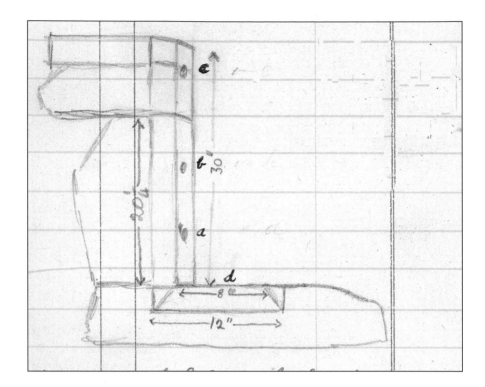

Fig. 47—Sketch of window at Kilcommon Church.

Inside of church 12 paces x 6 [paces].

The graveyard is oblong in shape enclosed by a bank and ditch, which seem to be just the ordinary field fence (see O'Curry's description, *OS Letters* p.373 — the ruin is the same now as it was then).

Newtownboswell, Trinity Graveyard. A tablet let into the wall says:

'THE WALL ENCLOSING THIS
CHURCH YARD WAS BUILT
AT THE DESIRE AND EXPENSE
OF ROBERT H. TRUELL ESQ[R]
CLONMANNEN AD 1845
THE FRIENDS OF ALL INTERRED
HERE MUST CONSEQUENTLY FEEL
EVER GRATEFUL AND THANKFUL
FOR THIS GENEROUS ACT OF
KINDNESS.'

Could not trace a church at all in the graveyard, but the surface is very irregular, as well as being full of graves.

Perhaps Mr Truell's wall was built of the ruins of the church?

4th March 1932

Deerpark, Powerscourt. The 'Praying Stone'.

A stone about 4ft long and 2ft wide, buried in sand and earth. It seems to have been rubbed away, the top surface of the stone only remaining at the end marked *B* [on Fig. 48]. Two circular depressions are at that end of the stone with a ridge between them, the one nearest *B* being about 5in. deep, the other only shallow, then there is a much deeper depression below

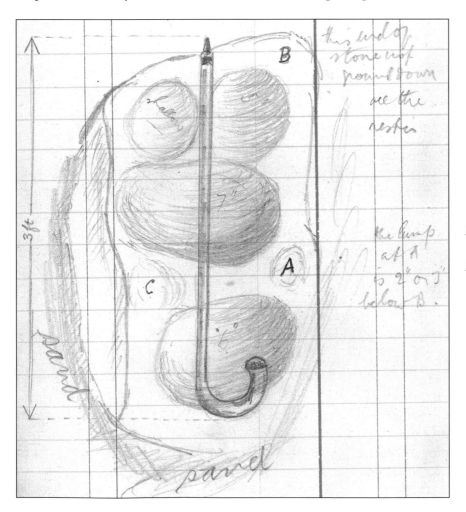

Fig. 48—Sketch of the 'Praying Stone', Deerpark, Powerscourt.

the level of the last two, and 7in. deep below the edge near *A*. It is not round but oval. At *A* and *C* there are two roundish lumps on the stone, as though the surface had been rubbed down around them. The last depression is like the middle one but not quite so deep, about 6in. deep. It is oval. The stone is granite. I don't know if these are natural or artificial. The stone is on the bank of the stream [near the footbridge].

The map shows 'Site of Church' where marked, and O'Curry visited it and describes it (*OS Letters* p.20), but there is absolutely no trace of it there now. It may quite well have been washed away by the river. (Kilcornan?)

6th March 1932

Glanmore, Ballymaghroe. Tried to trace the old road through the demesne, up from Clora Bridge; the bridge pier on Ballymaghroe side is the same as that in Clora. The old road can be traced for a little way up, but then disappears — the field stretches from the wood to the avenue, then there is the very carefully made avenue, and then another field stretching to the road. There is a bend on the road at Mullins' cottage, that is the cottage next E of the farm buildings, and I think the road ran straight from the bridge to this bend.

There is a watering place for cattle near the avenue which is on this line — perhaps the stones which surround this built up a ford on the old road — the stream is a very small one … .

Kilfea Church. The walls are only a foot or so high, and covered with ivy or elder bushes. There is no feature, either in the church or the graveyard, and no indication where the door was. I think the stones are not those of a built wall, but only loose. The graveyard is surrounded by a railing: perhaps there was a bank round it, but it is difficult to see it — the graveyard is higher than the field, but this is merely the natural result of burials (see O'Curry's description, *OS Letters* p.247).

7th March 1932

Castlemacadam. The mote. About ¼ mile SW of the old graveyard, on the brow of a steep hill. About 10yds in diameter and 6 or 7ft high, composed of small stones laid flat, as though part of a building. Trees on it were recently cut down, and their roots are exposed on the outside of the mound, suggesting that it was originally larger. About 40yds N of the mote at the edge of the field is the trace of a masonry wall, about 5ft high for some 15yds. There are great quantities of stones on the edge of this field, some of them built into fences. A lot of these stones are white quartz, both big and small stones. I looked at the other walls and fences about, and they all seem to be built of the small, flat, slaty stones, but I didn't see white quartz except round this field.

The old graveyard is just beside the main road where marked on the map. Catholics and Protestants are both buried there but it is not much used now. The church now standing in it is I suppose the church built in 1817. An old road runs down by it from the village to the main road, but the old main road is now represented by some stepping stones and a track which runs along the side of the hill under the mote, and must have joined the existing main road at Captain Robinson's place. There is a bullaun stone lying in the yard of the house next to the graveyard, a block of granite with a circular depression 14in. across and 8in. deep. I spoke to a middle-aged labourer who said it was there as long as he could remember and that he didn't know where it came from.

The place where the mote is seems just the sort of site that would be chosen for a medieval castle, the field slopes steeply away on three sides. But I could see no trace of ditches round it.

(The oldest tombstone recorded in the old churchyard is of the year 1741.)

9th March 1932
Tobersool, in Knockanreagh near Baltinglass, is just a spring rising on a little slope, and spreading out a good deal among bushes before running down to the little stream of which it is one of the sources. The water is clear and full of cress. It is a big spreading spring, not a small one like a well. There are no rags on the bushes, and no stones built up anywhere near it. There seems to be the track of an old roadway in [the] field near it, running down the slope, and pointing NE towards Tinoranhill. (I believe there is a well which I missed seeing.)

18 March 1932
Three Wells, Aughrim (see plan) [Fig. 49].

A. 'Larry's Meadow'. A small field, with low banks or mounds in it. One at

147

the SW end is called by some of the local people 'the Giant's Grave'. It seems to be composed of small stones, and looks like the foundation of a wall. A small thorn bush is growing on it. Michael Byrne who owns the field says it was the old graveyard.

C. 'Paddy's Meadow'. Belongs to John Byrne. The wall just at the W side of the gate, facing the square or street, is said to be the wall of a chapel. It is the end wall of a building, and at its highest is 9 or 10ft high. The bottom course of the other walls remains, the stones in them are very large. The building is about 15ft x 9ft (estimated) — walls about 18in. thick — it looks like the ruin of a cottage.

The three wells are at the E side of the 'street'. A hollowed-out stone stands loose on one of the walls. It is broken. It is said to have been a Christening font. From *a* to *b* [i.e. width; see Fig. 50] is 25in. There are four not very well marked cup-markings in it, and another smaller one.

The place between the four crossroads is called 'the slibbery' by the young people or 'the street' by the older people. Michael Byrne called it 'the square'.

Michael Byrne's house is the one W of it. Joseph Byrne's is the house E

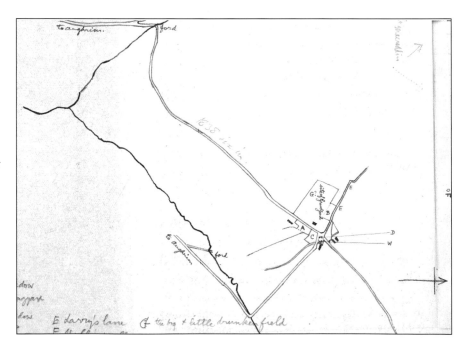

Fig. 49—Sketch-map of Three Wells.

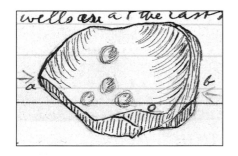

Fig. 50—Sketch of cup-marked stone at Three Wells.

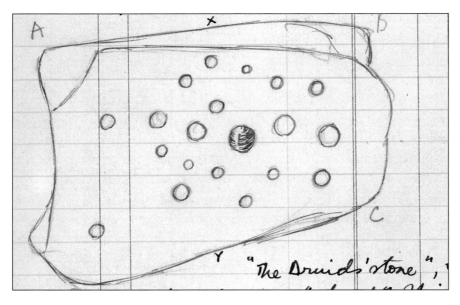

Fig. 51—Sketch of the 'Druid's Stone', Three Wells.

of it, and the three wells are on the W side of his house. The well is all from one spring, but low walls have been built enclosing it into three oblong spaces.

'The Druid's Stone' lies on the edge of the 'street'. It is covered on one side with cup-markings, an inch deep, some rather less, of different sizes. The largest E is 5in. across. [Other measurements, see Fig. 51:] *B–D* 38in. [i.e. length]. *A–B* 29in. [i.e. width]. Depth from *X–Y* about 24in. [i.e. thickness].

Larry's Lane is the old road to Macreddin. N of it the townland slopes up the hill to Cushbawn (or 'Cushlawn' Michael Byrne called it). Some distance up the hill about at 'F' on the map [Fig. 49] is a spring called 'Nelly's Well'. It is where the fields border the mountain — there are two white posts at it now. Keenan could not say why it is called that. He said there were no houses there. A pathway leads from Macreddin to Larry's Lane, and a pathway branches off to Tinnakilly (past Nelly's Well) and on down to Ballymorris: it is marked by stiles. The postman goes by it from the last house in Three Wells to Macreddin. Possibly this is an old road, but the hills here are covered with tracks.

There is a passway from Macreddin through Cronawinnia Gap, to Ballard gate and Ballinaclash. A cart can be taken over it.

Another old road called 'Reilly's Lane' leads from the Fair Green at Macreddin, beside the old Catholic chapel, and down through the river by a ford on to Rosahane. The Fair Green is beside the chapel. The old burial ground is a little to the S; it used to be a mixed graveyard. Keenan pointed out what he called 'Mooreshill' townland on the slope SW of Sheeana, about at Coolgarrow Hill. (Moneymeen pronounced 'Mooniameen'.)

Beside Larry's Lane just behind Michael Byrne's house, Dan Keenan said was the old graveyard. He saw it on an old map. (It is on the 1840 6-inch map.) There is a gravestone used as a window sill in one of Michael Byrne's outhouses — Keenan saw it some years ago, and read the words 'BRIDGET BYRNE' on it. It is set in cement now and the face turned down. Byrne showed it to me, and said it was a stone that was cut and never used.

One of Michael Byrne's fields is called 'the Tullawn'. There is a lump of rock in it, and underneath a tunnel or shore, which he filled in.

He said there was supposed to be an underground passage from somewhere in Macreddin to the castle in Ballinacor. Keenan said 'the big drumken field' and 'the little drumken field' are two other fields of Michael Byrne's.

Byrne said there were 32 'smokes' in the townland once. Keenan says the people say that there was a monastery in Three Wells once. He says the road past his house (the house SW of Larry's Meadow) was the old coach road. He is Dan Keenan, aged about 45, a farmer.

There is no sign of a graveyard or anything in the fields behind Michael Byrne's house. All the fences round the village are very large and thick — I think there were certainly a number of houses there in former times.

20th March 1932
Derrylossary Church. Three 'bullaun' stones — one is at the W end of the graveyard, inside the wall. The hole is 15in. in diameter, and about 12in.

150

deep: it is pointed at the bottom. There is a small depression about 2in. deep and 7 or 8in. in diameter beside it.

In the graveyard, on the S side of the church there are five Catholic headstones close together, dated 1740 to 1778.

Outside the graveyard on the W side of the church is a [triple] bullaun [Fig. 52]: this stone is rather like the one at Ballintombay (*JRSAI* vol. 43, p.170).

A diameter 11 or 12in., 6½in. deep
B diameter 12 or 13in., 7in. deep
The space between *A* and *B* is 2in. wide
C diameter about 7 or 9in., 1in. deep

The third stone is slightly NE of and outside the graveyard. It has a hole 6½in. deep and 10–11in. or 11½–12in. in diameter with a depression beside it about ½in. deep and 6in. wide. The stones are all granite boulders. (Townland Ballinacorbeg.)

Townland of Raheen in a field now owned by Christy Byrne of Raheen.

An oblong [area about 5yds x 2½yds; Fig. 53] composed of large blocks of stone [3½ft to 4ft high], filled in with small stones, and covered with grass and some bushes growing on it. About 400yds W of Derrylossary Church.

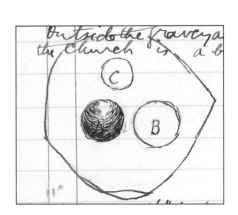

Fig. 52—Sketch of triple bullaun stone at Derrylossary.

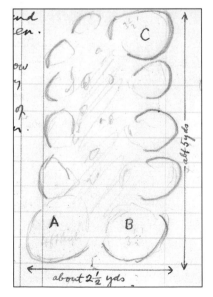

Fig. 53—Sketch of an oblong stone at Raheen.

Visited Mr John Malone of Baltynanima. There is a bullaun stone on his land [Fig. 54].

Some distance SE of his house, in the bog, is what looks like the remains of a raheen, some large stones forming a roughly circular bank with a ditch around it. About 20yds diameter. There are a lot of large boulders inside it also. The field belongs to Healy. Malone said it was *not* a raheen: and it may not be.

Malone is aged about 70, his father lived in Roundwood, his house is now covered by the reservoir. He is 56 years in Baltynanima.

The bullaun is in a field which he called 'the nine acres field' or 'the big meadow'. It is a block of granite with two holes in it. He calls it 'the hole stone'. It is in the townland of Baltynanima.

[One of the holes is] 7–7½in. deep, 15in. in diameter; [the other is] 5½in. deep, 12½–13in. long x 10½–11in. wide — slightly oval in shape. The space between the two holes is about 7½in. The field is about ½ mile W of Derrylossary Church.

Malone says there was a mill once at his house and the mill-race led from Lake Dan.

There is a round font of oolite (a yellowish shell limestone) in the garden of Iver's house at Castlekevin — about 2 or 3ft in diameter — said to have come from Derrylossary Church. Authority, R. Barton.

Fig. 54—Bullaun stone at Malone's, Baltynanima.

Fig. 55—Malone's outhouse, Baltynanima.

[Local names:]

'Brady's of the Big Stone' (in Baltynanima?)
'Kane's of the Charter' (i.e. Charter School lands).

7th April 1932

Visited Mr James Farrell of Carrasillagh (or Kellystown) in Glenmalure. He is an old man aged 84: Gus Cullen, State Solicitor, Wicklow, who is a distant relative of his, and does business for him, gave me a letter of introduction. He was in bed, supposed to have influenza, but I think just feeble through old age. The following notes I jotted down while talking to him. His voice was rather indistinct at times, and I couldn't hear all he said.

He says when he was a boy of 9 he was out with the servant girl, and suddenly he saw the battle going on on the mountain — muskets firing, and men falling — he heard the shots, and saw the smoke — he saw the soldiers in their red coats — that was the battle Feagh McHugh fought. He was so frightened he spilled the can of milk and ran back to the house. The girl saw it too.

His tradition of where the battle was fought is very vivid — it was at the Raheen Bank (Cullentragh Park) and on the side of the mountain (Ballinafunshoge) which is straight before you if you go out of his door and turn left.

[The following is a disjointed list of comments and pronunciations, by James Farrell, written into this notebook.]

Feagh McHugh had three castles, a castle in Clornagh and in Ballinacor and in Castlecavan [Castlekevin?].

The battle was fought at 'Rodarrig' (or 'Lo-darrig') (note — his pronunciation of this was very hard to get exactly — he was indistinct), a mile up from his house, on the right as you go up.

'Drumkitt' is another name for Ballinacor near Cawrawn Bank. There is a 'spaw well' in it, it cured a girl no doctor could cure.

'Russacoose' to the left beyond Farmer's.

'Coolnahoorey' where Miss Farrell was killed [Coolnahorey?].

'Coolalinga' is where Farmer lives [Coolalingo?].

'Jack Cullinan's Big Stone' (it is the big stone beside the road W of the crossroads at Ballyboy). In [17]98 — he lived Clornagh side, he met the yeos and he kept going round it and escaped!

Four 'Waxford' [Wexford] boys shot at Crutchley's — a little cross is there.

'Keerakee'

'Big Mick Farrell'

'The Three Loughs'

Matt Farrell was shot on Dunlavin Green, my grandfather's first cousin — Mick Dwyer was a cousin. Hugo used to go and bathe in Lough Dan, [and] left Thomas outside with the gun; [the] gun was called 'Roarin' Bess'. Thomas fired at the bull, and the water splashed up on Hugo — Thomas went off then with the gun.

There were 30 children when he (Farrell) went to school, in Glenmalure.

Fiach was beheaded in Dublin and his head sent to Queen Elizabeth.

I asked him did he know 'Catgut Cave': he didn't — he said there were a lot of caves. 'Jack Tobery's Cave' and 'Harmon's Cave'.

This house was a woollen factory. Neddie Kelly had a woollen factory. His 'missus' in her house at Aghavannagh heard thousands and thousands of horsemen passing with music and bugles sounding. They came in the air — horseshoes rattling as if they were on a road — went on for Baltinglass — at about 12 o'clock in the day — that was the American War.

Finished up the battle at the head of the Slash of Rathdrum.

Case of Seskin in Imaal is a relative of Farrell's.

Old Jim Farrell's son pointed me out the places: his pronunciation of this was more distinct, but varied slightly: he did *not* say 'Ro-darrig'.

'Lo-darrig' or '(Ch)lo-darrig', the slope (in Ballinafunshoge) up to the Black Knobs — they are at the head of the N side of the glen in W of Ballinafunshoge. That's where the two graves are — Cosby's. The battle was fought from the top downwards. It was fought at the Raheen Bank. Jim Byrnes of 'Cullinagh Park' [Cullentragh Park]. Farrell picked up flints there when ploughing.

'Mullacoor', 'Clonakeen' and 'Cainamuloge'.

'The Spaw Well' at Drumkitt — turn to the right (S) over the Strand Bridge. Up in the wood 25mins from the bridge. It is a little spring.

13th April 1932

At Rathcot with Mr Edward O'Toole, Mr Delany retired National Teacher Hacketstown and Mr Patrick O'Toole of Rathmeague School, National Teacher.

'Racot'. The rath is about 50 paces in diameter, broken-down bank round central space, ditch 9 to 10ft deep on E side, and bank outside it 8 or 9ft high. The ditch and bank are much broken down on the W, where a modern fence has been built. Potato ridges in centre.

'Lurgan shore' — the drain between Kyle and Rathshanmore. Leacy hid in the shore. Mr Edward O'Toole's grandmother was a relative of the Leacys, who are buried in Preban; their tombstone is inscribed:

'HERE LIETH THE BODY OF PHILIP LEACY, WHO DIED 21ST JUNE 1798: AGED 22 YEARS. ALSO PATRICK LEACY, DEPARTED LIFE 21ST JUNE 1798, AGED 20 YEARS. R.I.P.'

His mother often told him that they were trying to get home after Vinegar Hill, and hid under a bridge near Ballinglen from a party of Yeomen, and when the Yeomen had passed Patrick Leacy was sent to reconnoitre, and saw one of the yeomen, a Catholic named Byrne of Coolalug whom he knew: he spoke to him and was told to remain hiding. Byrne went to his Captain and said 'There are weasels under the bridge': the Yeomen then surrounded the bridge, and took the Leacys and shot them.

John Maher told us this story, but placed it at Lurgan shore, saying that Leacy put his head out of the shore and saw this Yeoman and spoke to him.

'The Pattern Green', the old road up from the well in Slieveroe (St Columcille's). Lawrences of Sandyford cut down the old skeogh bush because they said it was superstitious. Lawrence's head was twisted sideways afterwards. John Maher of Rathcot said his father remembered the bush white with rags. The well was closed up and only opened again about 20 years ago.

The Carlow men used to meet the Wicklow men at the Pattern Green, and there was many a fight with sticks.

A fairy funeral: two men saw a funeral pass through 'Ballemurraroe' (behind Moyne) and on for Sheilstown — saw the horses running wild about the field; the procession was carrying something.

We went to Rathcot because Mr Patrick O'Toole had heard that a grave with an urn in it had been found there about 40 years ago, and that a man had dug in it at night looking for gold.

We found two old men who had seen it. One Gahan of Rathcot (name pronounced 'Gayhen') said he saw the top of the crock showing in the lane where the cattle had worn it down — the top was flat, and red-coloured. He said he went and dug it up at night but found nothing but bones in it, and threw them and the pieces of the crock away. He showed us on his stick the height of the crock, about 9 or 10in.

The other old man, Maher of Rathcot (a different family from John Maher's) said one of the cattle put its leg down into a hole, and then they saw the crock — it was like a flower pot, and was about 2ft down in the ground. He said it wasn't touched. Both of them said there was no stone on top of it.

They showed the place as being on the N side of the lane which runs W of their houses. Rathcot is a small townland, and the three or four houses are all together in the E end of it. Neither Gahan nor Maher knew the exact spot, but they agreed it was in a stretch of about 10yds, 50 or 60yds W of the last house. The rath is close to or on the N boundary of the townland.

In the N part of the townland of Castleruddery Lower, and just beside and on the W edge of the main road is a large round boulder of granite, in the top of which is cut a rectangular hollow — 22in. long, 13½in. broad and

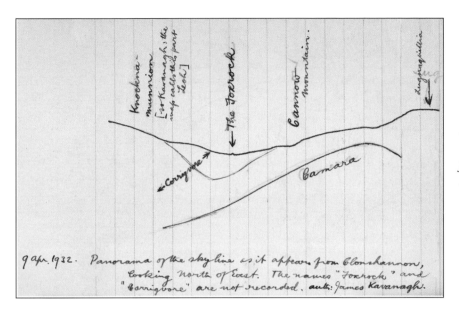

Fig. 56—Panorama of the skyline as it appears from Clonshannon, looking north of east.

7in. deep. I don't know what it is, but the local people say it was a trough for watering horses and that water was brought up to it from the river close by. The shape of the rectangle is regular, but the edges are rounded off or worn, as if by weathering: they are not sharp edges.

(25th September 1946)

Rough drawing of the 'trough' (query, a cross base?) on the W side of the main road in Castleruddery Lower, 250yds S of Whitestown crossroads [Fig. 57]. The rectangle, filled with water, is 21in. long by 12in. broad by 6in. deep. Note that it is impossible to make accurate measurements of these hollows which have rounded edges. The stone is about 250–300yds S of Whitestown crossroads, and therefore some distance, a few hundred yards, outside Rathbran parish.

17th April 1932

Examined Kiltimon Castle. I am satisfied that it is all of the same date of building, and that it is all an imitation antique. Mr Wingfield proprietor of Dunran Demesne says that Lord Rossmore repaired the battlements and corner towers, and put in the arched doors and windows — but there is no difference between the style of building of the battlements and the walls below them, nor is there any line to indicate insertion around the doors and

Fig. 57—Sketch of cross base at Castleruddery Lower.

windows. Lord Rossmore would have enough experience of such buildings to know that the walls would show a batter, as these do.

The original site may have been in the rocky field E of the road, opposite Wingfield's gatelodge. Lord Rossmore acquired Dunran about 1785.

Ballyvolan — examined and photographed the fort. The earthen rampart on the N and E sides is not now continuous, and as the break comes just at the NE corner, it is hard to say if it was originally circular, or whether it ran parallel to the wall and formed an angle. The bushes have been cleared off the SW corner and show the foundations of a building quite clearly, presumably a corner tower.

The road running along the top of Ballyvolan Glen is called 'the Virgin's Road', at least so Mrs Hackett said. 'Virgins' Row' according to George Trim of Ballyvolan, and Daniel Norse of Kilmartin. Norse thought it was a name which was intended to be sarcastic. I asked Trim had the well below it any name, and he said 'No'.

20th April 1932

Went with James Doyle of Rathnew to Ballynagran (pronounced 'Ballinegraan'). Mr Henry McCall who owns the farm of Ballynagran and who lives at Glenealy, showed us the site of the old graveyard at Kilcandra. There is nothing left of it — it lay on the SW side of the boundary

Fig. 58—Kiltimon Castle (courtesy of the Royal Society of Antiquaries of Ireland ©).

between Ballynagran and Kilcandra, where it is marked on the map. McCall pointed out a mark in the field which he said showed in places where the bank was that surrounded it, but it would not be noticeable unless pointed out to one. He had never heard of people being buried in it, but said the old people used to say it was a graveyard. He also said that Mr Davidson of Kilcandra who owns the land had carted away a quantity of stones from that part of the field about six or seven years ago.

The old road from Red Peg's crossroads up by Ballykillavane and Ballymanus is called 'the Black Hill'.

We then visited Mr Webster's farm in Ballyknockan Beg, which adjoins Coolnakilly. In Webster's yard is a 'ballán' stone (diameter 12in., depth 7in.) — a workman digging in a field adjoining the boundary of Coolnakilly found it buried in the field and brought it in. A hole was bored in it by the farmer to enable a plug to be put in and taken out so that it could be drained, and he used it for feeding young pigs. After it was found the field was called 'the Church Field'.

The workman did not know where 'the Holy Stone' is or was. The brook which runs down from Ballymacsimon and forms the boundary between Ballyknockan Beg and Coolnakilly is called 'Coffey's Brook'.

159

There is a well near Bradshaw's house in Ballymacsimon but the man did not know of any name for it.

There are old walls in the grove N of Bradshaw's house. He thought the Holy Stone might be in a field of Bradshaw's called 'the Crow Bank': but I think this was only some suggestion made by a visitor, not local information.

Percival Sheane's, of Coolnakilly: formerly Ward's farm. Query, where the food vessel came from?

30th April 1932
Photographed the newly discovered N doorway in Baltinglass Abbey.

1st May 1932
At Francis Hackett's, Killadreenan House — it is in the SW corner of Killadreenan townland. The road from Newtownmountkennedy to Timmore originally ran straight from the front gate of Newcastle Sanatorium through the grounds of this house and on by Timmore Lane: it is quite clearly traceable still, and the bridge where it crossed Chapel River is still standing: this bridge is about 50yds W of the present Chapel River bridge. It is a single-arch bridge, the arch formed of long stones set on edge — the bridge is about 4½ft wide, and has a parapet on each side about a foot thick. The local people say it was for foot passengers and that vehicles drove through the water — this must be correct, but it is not easy to see now just where they crossed, as the banks are rough and stony and rather steep. The present road has been built since A.R. Nevill's early 19th-century map, and since the road down through Kiltimon Glen was made.

4th May 1932
H.G. Leask accompanied me to Wicklow and examined and sketched the old S doorway in the Protestant church. He also looked at the remains of the Franciscan abbey. The portion remaining with a three-light window was the S transept, with two chapels on the E. The small doorway from the tower or aisle into the transept is he thinks an insertion, and indicates that the transept was added after the aisle was built — the tower in a Franciscan abbey he says was almost always a later addition. The portion of wall running N from the N wall of the aisle is the remains of the walls of the monastic buildings. The graveyard would have lain E of the chancel and

Fig. 59—Romanesque doorway at Wicklow, 1932 (courtesy of the Royal Society of Antiquaries of Ireland ©).

transept. There is not enough to date it by, but he seemed to think it an abbey of normal Anglo-Norman type, perhaps 14th century. The earliest Franciscan abbey, he says, in Ireland was towards the end of the 13th century.

Kilmartin. He also examined this, and made some suggestions as to small repairs, replacing the fallen lintel, removing ivy and elder trees etc. He came to the conclusion that the church was an Anglo-Norman building, not earlier.

Ballyvolan Fort. Leask said that the wall of this is built with mud containing a very little lime, instead of mortar; this suggested to him that it was hastily built. The wall is well coursed. He is inclined to the opinion that the ditch and bank were formed at the time the wall was built, the earth being taken out of the ditch and thrown up partly to form the foundation for the wall and partly to form the bank. He agrees with me that there was probably a tower at the SW corner. He cannot date the structure, which he says is of an unusual type.

Mr George Trim on whose land the fort is said there was a tunnel to this ditch to carry water into it, leading from near the bungalow on the present main road through the ridge of high ground to a point which he showed us, near the SW angle; he said the tunnel was arched with stone. He calls it a Danish fort. He said the brooch which Mr Huband referred to was found in the wall of the fort on the N side, and that it was given to Dr Hughes of Kilmartin House, and that Mr Parker Keane of the Grange bought it with an old box of scrap metal at Hughes' auction.

I don't think George Trim's statements are accurate enough to be accepted without verification.

The river running by Kilmartin is called 'the Black River'. The brewery was Gormley's Brewery.

Goldenhill, Kilbride. The field containing the rath is owned by Mr John Eustace of Shankill. There are only two houses in the townland, occupied by Richard Hanlon, farmer (small and struggling), and Michael Meade, labourer.

Ballyfolan. The small farm W of the road is owned by James Ennis, who told me he owned the field the rath is in. Poor, honest. One son at home. The farm E of the road, nearest the field, owned by Thomas Eustace, poor.

Mr Laffan of the Hibernian Bank Wicklow showed me a printed copy of the County Tipperary *Hearth Money Roll*; some names from it are:

'Athloman'	OS map 'Athlummon'
'Dromlomane'	OS map 'Drumlummin'
'Skartt'	OS map 'Scart'
'Gragepadyne'	OS map 'Graiguepadeen'
'Lieghmokenoge'	OS map 'Leamakevoge'
	Liath mór mochaemhog (*Onom. Goed.*)
'Kyllmokenoge'	can't find the modern equivalent

28th May 1932

Glasnamullen. St Kevin's Well is at the spot marked on the ordnance map, on the N bank of the stream, and just E of the road, with some steps leading down from the road towards it. It is a spring of clear water coming out from the bottom of a fence which is built up to some 6 or 7ft with stones. There are laurel bushes and thorn bushes growing near it, and some rags on their branches: the rags don't look old. The back of the spring has been made to look like a little grotto of a simple kind, decorated with primroses.

Note that O'Curry (*OS Letters* p.202) says the well is ¼ mile *NW* of St Kevin's Church. As he describes it it seems very like the one I saw. Perhaps he wrote 'north' by mistake for 'south'.

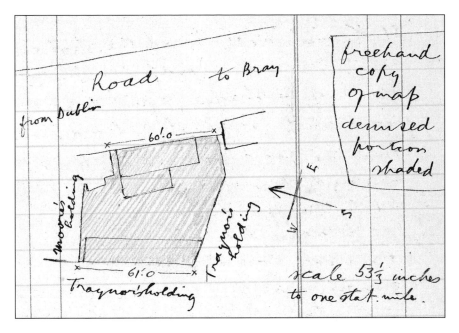

Fig. 60—Freehand copy of 19th-century lease map of a holding on Dublin Road, Little Bray (demised portion shaded).

27th May 1932

Notes from a lease, Bray Court. Lease Robert Maunsell to Denis Carr dated 31st March 1860 of 'The dwelling house with the garden or plot of ground thereunto belonging being part of the lands of Gortinisky situate at Little Bray in the barony of Rathdown and County of Dublin.' Map endorsed.

11th June 1932

Visited the cairns on Seefinn, Seefingan and Seechon with Dr Macalister. He thinks that [the cairn] on Seefinn contains a cruciform chamber with a passageway running N and S, entrance perhaps to the N. One of the kerbstones at W side he thinks shows scribings — an oblong, a circle, and perhaps some cupmarks. He said the ring of kerbstones was the best he had seen.

The cairn on Seefingan he thinks also contains a chamber, probably rifled and considerably ruined. The exposed burial on Seechon he says was a cist, surrounded by a ring of stones and covered by a cairn. The grass-covered mound just W of it is he thinks another cairn — and he pointed out another small cist just NE of the exposed one, and another SW of the cairn.

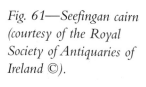

Fig. 61—Seefingan cairn (courtesy of the Royal Society of Antiquaries of Ireland ©).

2nd July 1932

Dr Macalister, Dr Bayly-Butler, P.T. Walshe, F.E. Stephens, Dougherty and myself visited the cairn on Seefinn, and started to clear out the loose stones through the hole in the top. After about four hours work, we got to a floor level about 10ft below the opening, and stopped there as it appeared to be dangerous to go further in case some of the stones of the roof or sides should collapse. We had revealed the lintels of three recesses, one S, one E and one W of the central chamber, the latter being immediately below the opening. The actual floor of these chambers was probably 3 or 4ft further down. The entrance passage appeared to run towards the N. The S recess: 4ft deep, from front of lintel to back of recess: lintel-stone (cracked near E end) 5ft long, about 4ft wide, 13in. deep: the second covering-stone or lintel is under the first, and is also cracked: mouth of recess, 40in. wide.

E recess (only just barely revealed): 5ft deep, lintel over 4ft long, mouth of recess 43in. wide, a support stone at its S side, and the S side of the recess formed by a large perpendicular flat slab.

W recess: 38in. deep: lintel-stone over 5ft long, 26in. wide, 12in. deep, behind and below it is another lintel-stone (or covering-stone) and behind and below it a third.

Dr Macalister drew out a rectangle to enclose the cairn, and plotted on this the kerbstones.

The deepest point to which we got down in the chamber was in the S recess: we estimated that we reached a point about 10ft below the top of the opening at the S end.

The distance between the mouth of the E and the mouth of the W recess was 8ft.

Fig. 62—Seefinn passage tomb before excavation (courtesy of the Royal Society of Antiquaries of Ireland ©).

On the large roofing-stone at the N end of the opening and at the highest point there is a cross incised in the stone [the rubbing taken of the cross is in this notebook] .... The arms are sunk down into the stone like little bowls. It measures 10cm (3¹⁵/₁₆in.) from N to S and 9.5cm (3¾in.) from E to W .... It was Dr Macalister who observed this.

As there seemed to be a possibility of collapse if the chamber walls were not shored, and as it was clearly impossible to complete the work under two or three days, we left it until September: and on Sunday 3rd July, F.E. Stephens, P.T. Walshe, Seamas ua Duilearga and I filled it in again to preserve it from injury in the meantime.

October 1932

P. Noonan of Wicklow told me that on Mr Woodroffe's land in Raheenmore there is a field called 'the Danes Field': at the top there is a ditch very deep and with a high bank. It was higher but has been dug away for top dressing for the field.

Information given to me by Dr William Dargan, of St Stephen's Green, who used to live near Avoca.

On the left-hand side of the Avoca–Redcross road there is a rath in Kieran's Bog and further up on the right-hand side is a smaller one, which is looked on with superstition. Unbaptised children used to be buried there. It was never known to have been a churchyard.

He has fragments of the urn in his house which he got from John Murphy of Knockanree (*JRSAI* x/vi, p.77).

13th July 1932

Visited Humewood (near Kiltegan). The stone referred to by Mr O'Toole (*JKAHS* xi, p.93 (1932)) lies to the E of the house (Humewood Castle); it has been placed beside the avenue. It has several cup-markings on it, some of the cups being surrounded by circles. Below is a freehand drawing made from a rubbing and photograph [Fig. 63].

The stone [4ft long x 2ft wide] is said to have been brought from somewhere in the woods and placed in its present position.

(28th September 1932)

Mr Hume told me that it was found between 1864 and 1870 buried in the ground when the men were digging the Barraderry Lake. As far as he knows nothing was found with it.

The three lakes at Humewood are 'the Fairy Lake' which is an old one, it is to the N: 'the Middle Lake', and 'the Barraderry Lake', which is in Barraderry East.

17th July 1932

Knockatemple. Bullaun stone. Hole 16in. long and 14in. wide (oval in shape), 6in. deep. The boulder does not lie flat, it has been left in a sloping position. The long axis of the hole is about E and W. The boulder lies 44 paces NW of the old graveyard enclosure.

25th July 1932

Friarhill, Dunlavin. The mote. Mr Bond's grandfather saw the stones and put them back and built up the mound. The stones fell when he was taking gravel.

The Fairy Knock. It was two fields and his grandfather was taking up the fence which ran along the hollow that still is in the field and the two workmen took up a crock, and they disappeared, and were never heard of after. His grandfather was 90 when he died in 1908.

The Money Hole — name of a field in Forristeen on Neill's farm. Heard money was found there.

Protestant dioceses and parishes:

Ferns diocese: Carnew, Crosspatrick and Kilcommon, Kilnahue and

Fig. 63—Sketch of rock art at Humewood.

Fig. 64—Humewood rock art.

Kilpipe, Preban and Moyne, Shillelagh.
Leighlin diocese: Baltinglass, Kiltegan, Ardoyne, Aghold, Ballynure.

Catholic dioceses and parishes:
Ferns diocese: Annacurragh and Killaveny, Tomacork, Tinahely, Carnew.

Fig. 65—Sketch of two bullaun stones brought to Glendalough House from Ashtown and Scarr.

Leighlin diocese: Baltinglass and Kiltegan. ([These] should be checked.)

Rathcot. Bronze axe found near the rath in the townland. So were two long stone axes. Another stone axe was found in Moyne on the top of the hill. Two others were found in Rathcot and one in Carrignamuck.

There were five stone axes found a good many years ago in Knocknaskeagh Bog, and a boat: they have disappeared. Some gold rings were found in Knocknashamroge: they were sold in Hacketstown for a couple of pounds. An oaken house was found in the bog in Knocknaskeagh; it was burned by the man who found it. In Knocknagilky Bog there was found a circular structure made of sticks driven down into the bog, and red clay thrown into the centre of it to make a platform.

3rd August 1932

Ballintemple, Arklow. The foundations of the church are 8 paces x 13 paces, seems to be a mixed graveyard, no features. Could not find 'Bride's Well'.

Templelusk graveyard is only a stony space in the corner of the field, entirely overgrown with brambles, holly trees and sloe bushes. In one place towards the W edge, I thought I could see the foundation of a wall. I was told that the land belonged to a Mr Goss, from the mountains. The track which leads down to the graveyard from the Knocknamohill road once joined up with the track which leads up from the river through Ballymorris.

7th August 1932

Near Wicklow Gap:

    1. Teámpall tSíonáin or Tíonáin.
    2. Cor na gCros
    3. The King's Diamond (?)

Names given to J.H. Delargy by an old man named Maguire of Knocknadroose.

    1. is 'Templefynan' on the map.
    2. I got from W. Kavanagh: I have now marked it on the map.
    3. is somewhere at the head of Glenreemore.

17th August 1932

Black Castle, Wicklow. A walled enclosure on a rock, triangular in shape, the base of the triangle being to the S, point to N. Except on S, only the foundations of the wall remains, between 3 and 4ft thick. They look more like the walls of an enclosure than of a building. At the SW corner there are the remains of an oblong tower, interior measurements 12ft x 7ft, with two small windows or large loopholes in the piece of wall still standing. The walls are about 4ft thick, reaching 5 or 6ft in places, and there is what appears to be a buttress outside the W side of this tower. The batter on the outside wall of this tower is very considerable. At the E corner are the remains of another tower: it was perhaps a small round one, but it is difficult to say (Beranger's drawing bears this out). There is what appears to be a garderobe in the wall of this tower, and another long aperture about 1ft square sloping downwards through the wall — possibly for rolling down stones for defence? At the NE side there is a flight of 32 steps cut in the rock down to high-water mark. In places the rock has been cut 18in. deep. There is now a gap in the wall at the head of this flight.

All the walls standing appear to me to be medieval in date — 14th or 15th century?

The deep channel in the rock between the castle and the rock of the mainland is natural, but it has been made steeper by cutting on the side of the castle.

Still further in towards the town is a bank with a deep ditch on the town side of it which may be the remains of an old defence work.

21st September 1932

The Round Mount in Wicklow is a little N of the Protestant church in a field belonging to Mrs Nuzum or Newsom. It is now very much overgrown with brambles. The top is flat, about 17 paces in diameter, but the edges are I think somewhat broken away. A shallow ditch still surrounds it on the S, W and N sides, and on the NE a channel and bank seem to run down to the river.

I believe it is the site of the old Danish fort above their harbour in the river.

'Potash Lane' is the old road to the right off the Marlton Road between Ballynerrin Lower and Ballynerrin Upper. The name appears as 'Potach' in a terrier of Wicklow parishes, dated 1781. (Mason, S. Patrick's p.56.)

2nd October 1932

The Downs. The fort is on the boundary between the townlands of Woodlands and Bellevue Demesne, being locally reckoned as in Bellevue. It overhangs the Glen of the Downs which is on its E side and just below it, and it commands the S entrance of the Glen. It is called 'the Forth', i.e. 'Fort', and the field is called 'the Forth Field'. Its internal diameter is 41yds. There are remains or traces of a ditch and bank on the W and N side, the ditch being 5½yds wide; there is some slight sign of the continuation of this bank round to the NE. The bank of the fort itself seems to have been either built of or faced with stones — query are these old or modern? I think they look old, say medieval.

[The bank at SE is] 6ft above ground level.

[Bank at SW is] 14ft above ditch.

[Outer] bank [at SW] 5ft above ditch, and 6ft wide.

The Fort Field is on Mr Spence's land (that was Mr Stoney's).

5th October 1932

At Tinnakilly. George Woodburn gave me an iron pike or spearhead found at Macreddin in the Castle Field by Mick 'the Rattler' Byrne [he was making a fence], 94 years old when he died six years ago.

[A] 1798 pike — found by George Woodburn at Tinnakilly in a fence near his house.

12th October 1932

Knockshee Moat, Broadleas Commons, Co. Kildare. Seems to have been excavated a long time ago and is now very much overgrown with bushes and weeds. It seems to have been a mound of earth with a passage of large stones in the centre, and perhaps large stones round it [Fig. 66].

A and *B* are large upright slabs about 3½ft high.

C is a large boulder the same height.

D is a flat slab lying on the ground, and the other two are slabs fixed in the ground, almost covered.

At a distance of 20 or 25ft W of *A* are two large boulders which seem to be at the edge of the mound: but they may be part of an old fence of which some traces remain. (*JKAS* iii, p.356 has a note by Lord Walter Fitzgerald, but very little information in it.)

Templeboodin. A new entrance to the graveyard is being made, but the graveyard is not being interfered with. 'Bishop Boden's Grave' as the local people call it is a flat granite slab about 5ft long lying flat in the S part of the graveyard. It does not show any marks, and is probably of no significance. There is a 'bullán stone' just N of the graveyard, on the S bank of the little stream: it is a single hollow in a large granite boulder, 6½in. deep, and 13in. in diameter: not hemispherical, more cup-shaped.

(Miscellaneous notes collected at different times on papers, and now copied.)

A lease dated 20th November 1894 by the Trustees [of the] Duke of Leinster's estate to Henry Owens of the Hotel in Castledermot included 'part of the lands of Woodlands East called "Luggers Garden" containing 1 acre, 2 roods, 25 perches statute measure.'

Mr Kavanagh of Clonshannon, pronounced Knocknamunnion as 'Knocknaminnion'. He said there used to be a Loan Fund Society in Knockanarrigan, and a path leading across the hills from Granamore across Stranahely was called 'the Fund Path'.

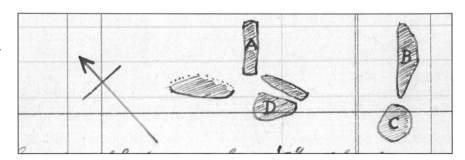

Fig. 66—Sketch-plan of large stones at centre of Knockshee Moat, Broadleas Commons.

'Eyeltyagh' (Oiltiagh) (Adhaltiach) is middleway up the hill in Stranahely. 'Glenmalure' is sometimes pronounced 'Glenmuller' or 'Glanmullard'.

Dr Walshe has heard the ford on the path leading from Tornant to Dunlavin called 'Kill-an-hide-em' or 'Kill-em-and-hide-em'. But which ford? There are three, close together. The middle one is the townland boundary.

Major Con McSweeney, National Teacher of Aughrim in a letter to me on receipt of my paper on Feagh McHugh says: 'Glenlorkin is the whole valley of Aghavannagh', and he suggests Fananierin (or 'Farrenerin') is 'Fearan an thiarna', Fiach's mensal land.

Professor Eamonn O'Toole, Trinity College Dublin, wrote me the following note on the name 'Dervorgil':

' "Dearbhorgaill". There are really two words in the name, viz., *Dearbh* and *Fhorgaill*. The latter is itself a personal name. *Dearbh* = "own". Hence *Dearbhorgaill* means "own (daughter) of Forgall". Cf *dearbh(bh)ráthair* and *deirbhshiúr*. Meyer seems to prefer another explanation, i.e. that the first element is *Dear* which is said to mean "daughter". Bergin has a note on the name in his *Stories from Keating* p.102.'

In *Prehistoric Faith and Worship* by Reverend Canon Ffrench, rector of Clonegal, p.130, it is said 'On the side of Newry Hill there is a pillar stone ... a little beneath it there is the remains of an ancient Irish residence, still called "Rath na Doran".'

Some suggestions about Wicklow placenames made to me by Nioclás Toibín of Carlow (native speaker from Co. Waterford):

'Annacrivey'   'Ath na craoibhe'

'Ballylerane'	'Baile an luaireain' ('ashes'?)
'Ballynerrin'	'Baile an fhearthainn' ('farm')
'Cooldross'	'Cúil dreas' ('bramble')
'Knockaquirk'	'Cnoc an coirce' ('oats')
'Knockrobin'	'Cnoc Ribín' (?) (the crossbar that supports the 'sceacóg' or hawthorn bush)
'Ballykillavane'	'Baile cille abhann' (?) (this is wrong, it is 'giolla': see the old forms)
'Ballinameesda'	'Baile na smísde' (?) ('big' or 'strong')
'Aghavourk'	'Ath an bhuairc' (a sort of spancel)
'Carriglinneen'	'Carraig an gleainnín'
'Kirikee'	'Cior an chíche' ('the crest of the pap'? cf 'an dá chíche', 'the Paps', a mountain in Kerry)
'Clonerkin'	'Cluain an fheircín ('firkin of butter' or 'seire' = 'peak of a hat', 'a tilt', 'a quirk')
'Knockandort'	'Cnoc an dortadh' ('spilling' or 'flowing out'?)
'Bowery'	'Bodhra' ('deafness' or 'a hollow sound'?)
'Achrabowra'	'Acra bodhra'?

The name and address of the man who told Mr Edward O'Toole the stories about the Ring of the Rath is Patrick Travers, Askanagap. *Béaloideas* 1928, vol. 1, p.322.

When we were working at Seefinn in September, we got the following information from young Eustace of Shankill:

1. Mrs Mary Rafter, aged over 50, of Butter Mountain, says the ferns are never cut on the mote of Ballyfolan; if they were ever cut, the cattle or stock belonging to them used to die. She said there was a trunk in it, and three locks on it, and the trunk couldn't be opened.
2. John Doyle of Ballinascorney Upper, aged 90, says he saw steps down (in the cairn at Seefingan) and a well in the bottom, and he remembered seeing a delph mug or some class of mug for drinking out of in it beside the well. There was a tunnel going down towards Seefinn and he believed it came to the cairn there.

John Eustace calls these cairns 'the Chapel of Shangill' (= Seefingan) and 'Chapel Seefinn'.

There are three notebooks of drawings by Gabriel Beranger made about 1780 preserved in the Royal Irish Academy. In 3/C/32 no. 20 is the Black Castle Wicklow (done from the S). He describes it as 'a heap of ruins', and says 'there is a stone bridge by which one has access to the castle' on the other side.

There is also, in the large notebook, a drawing of 'Killpipe Church, Co. Wicklow' (no. 62).

Tipper North, Co. Kildare. Two pottery vessels found at, by L.S. Gogan (1928?) — perhaps Iron Age. Cist burial, cremation, no bones.

The Tryal of William Byrne, Dublin, printed by William McKenzie, College Green. (Billy Byrne of Ballymanus.)

FIELD NOTEBOOK 12:
December 1932–January 1934

No date

[Taken from] notes in pencil on inside of original front cover.

Gone, the rath in Rathdangan. On the hill SE of the village ¼ mile and another W of it ½ mile. Rathcoyle (Dunleary?).

Is there a rath about ¾ mile S of crossroads, just W of the road? The rath in the S point of Toorboy townland, S of the ford and another opposite to Cranareen, near the river.

18th December 1932

Walked from Barnamire up the old road above Curtlestown towards Kilmalin — the track is still quite clear, and it turns to the right towards the Black House in Kilmalin, at a cottage. Instead of turning to the right we went through the gate of the cottage on the left, and the track goes straight on, though it is quite disused and swampy. In Ballybrew at the top of the hill it turns to the right, and joins the modern road just at the top of the hill running down to Glencullen Bridge. The house in Kilmalin is still called 'the Black House'.

This is the road shown on Jacob Nevill's map, 1760.

26th December 1932

St Patrick's Well, Kilquade. A large pool in the corner of a field belonging to Mr Hudson of Kilquade House; it is fed by two drains running into it from the field. These drains were made in the field by Mr Hudson, as the spring was originally in the middle of the field. The stream from the pool runs into the river which flows through Kilcoole village. The local name was given to me as 'St Patrick's River', not 'Well'.

11th January 1933

Rathmoon. The tumulus or mote in the NW corner of the townland is in a field called 'the Mote Field' belonging to a farmer named William Brien. It is circular, about 85yds in circumference.

Height above field at centre 13ft. The outer edge rises straight from the field forming a bank 4 to 5ft high with bushes on it. Then there is a flat

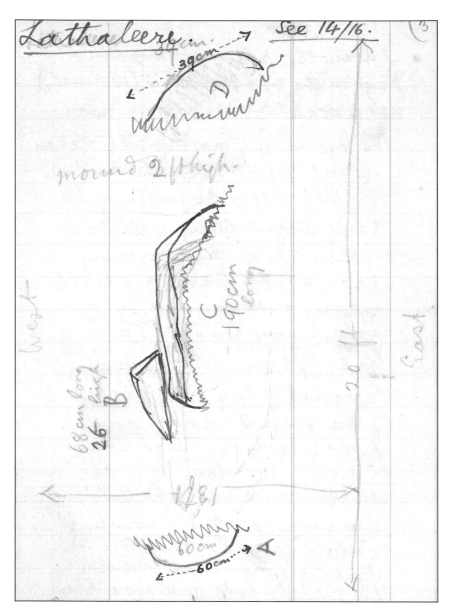

Fig. 67—Sketch-plan of the Long Stone, Lathaleere (not to scale).

terrace or plinth 11 to 12ft wide, then the domed part of the tumulus, 14yds in diameter [ext. diameter 22yds]. It is on a ridge and the field slopes up to it. The domed part is circular — it is not flat-topped.

Lathaleere. Cormac's Chair, big stone in field. Tom Abbey, stone cleaver. I drew the plan [Fig. 67] on the spot: it is (obviously) not to scale.

The mound of grass and small stones is about 2ft above the level of the

176

field. It is 20ft long by 13ft wide, oblong: the trees are planted on this covering a space a little longer and a little wider, and surrounded by a barbed-wire fence. The Long Stone [*C* on Fig. 67] (190cm; 6ft 3in.) seems to be a flat flag, it sticks out of the ground at an angle: it may be 4 or 5ft wide or more. [The other] stone [*B* on Fig. 67] is of similar material (shale?), standing upright: about 1ft is above ground. The other two stones are rounded granite boulders: both are more than half covered with grass, earth and stones: I could not measure them. The long axis of the oblong lies N and S.

I saw Tom Doran again: he said most of what he said before, and added that there was also a big stone called 'Cormac's Chair' near the fence on the N side of the field: Tom Abbey also blasted this.

Perhaps this may be correct, I do not know, but Doran has a lot of information got out of books (e.g. 'Beal-tinne-glas' for Baltinglass) and is not reliable. I do not think any support stones were blasted in the monument itself, but it is impossible to be certain without excavation.

He said he planted the trees in 1911. It was a nun from Carlow told him Dr Comerford had described it.

15th January 1933

Mrs La Touche, Branksome Park, Dorset.

Kilmacurra. Above is Mrs La Touche's address in England to which the old map was taken. The house according to Henry Conner is probably George I or George II: the dining room that is the room on the dexter side of the hall door with a semicircular end, he thinks is of much the same date, or not much later; it looks like an addition.

The old withered tree in front of the hall door is a Spanish chestnut: it is said that when it falls the last member of the Acton family will die. It is quite dead, and one or two of its branches are propped up on thick wooden posts. It is said that a soldier is buried beside it. The tennis ground is immediately beside this tree, and it is here that a number of bones and skulls are said to have been dug up. An avenue of oak trees leading due S from the house on to the road, is said to have been the old coach road from Dublin to Arklow — it connected up with a lane running by Kilmacanoge. However corrupt these stories are they are perhaps worth preserving.

16th January 1933

Knockanree Lower, near Avoca. Went to see Mr John Murphy's field where the urn which Dr Dargan has came from. At the W end of the field there is a 'rath' beside the field fence. The field is a large one sloping down towards the W from the high part of the hill: but at the W end it takes a slight slope upwards, so that this end is a few feet higher than the centre of the field: then the next field commences an abrupt slope of 300 or 400ft down to the River Avoca; and there is from the rath a magnificent view of the Ballymurtagh and Ballygahan ochre and copper mines lying right underneath it.

The sketch plan [not reproduced here] shows the shape and size of the rath [D-shaped: straight side at W is 26yds long, chord from N–E–S is 43yds in length]. The semicircular part [i.e. N–E–S] is a heap of large stones covered with grass, on which trees have been planted. The mound is now about 5ft high. On the inner end this raised mound shows no clear boundary, it slopes downwards and all the enclosed space consists of similar large stones covered with grass, but not more than 2ft above the level of the field surface. The two 'sides' [i.e. from N–NE and SE–S] are straight fences of stones and earth built to connect the mound with the field fence [at W] and so enclose the rath and the trees on it: these two fences are 3ft high. The field fence is a thick one of large stones and earth 5 or 6ft high.

The 'rath' appears to be the remains of a mound or cairn of stones some 18 or 20yds in diameter. The urn is said to have been found in the field near it, but as I did not see Mr John Murphy I could not question him about this. See Dr Dargan's report *JRSAI* x/vi, p.77: urn found *in* rath. William Dargan M.D., St Stephen's Green.

Here and there in the mound there are stones of white quartz, but whether or not these would be found in every heap of stones in the district I cannot say.

A labouring boy who brought me to the place was a stranger to the district, but he thought the field was called 'the Sulphur Brook'.

Map reference 1840 6-inch Wicklow sheet 35, distance from S edge of sheet 13cm, distance from E edge of sheet 40.5cm. Note that the rath is shown on this map as considerably larger and enclosing the whole SW corner of the field instead of [the way] I saw it.

18th January 1933

Knocksink Mote is an elliptical mote or mound on the S bank of the river, about 50ft high over the bed of the stream, and I think about 40ft high on the S side. The naked rock is visible halfway up it on the side of the stream. It appears to me to be a large pointed outcrop of rock, against which earth has been piled up naturally either by glacial action or by water. The top is flat, about 18 paces long and 6 paces wide. It is difficult to find as the sides of the gorge here are steep and covered with trees and underwood.

Canon Scott, *Stones of Bray,* p.31, also expresses the opinion that the 'mote' is not artificial.

Parknasilloge. Measured the dolmen. It consists of three large boulders forming three sides of a rectangle, with a large slab on top [Fig. 68]. In the opening or vacant side of the rectangle lies a smaller slab. All slabs are of granite. It stands in a field which slopes down to a little stream running down to the gorge of the Cookstown River. There are small stones collected round the base of the boulders, and covered with grass: they are hardly enough to justify one in calling them the remains of a mound or cairn.

The dolmen itself is exactly the same as when O'Curry saw it in December 1838 (*OS Letters* p.14), but the stones surrounding it are completely gone. I suspect that the roadway on the W side of the field is made of their fragments. From his description there appear to have been ten large stones 'set on edge', i.e. not pillar stones, standing in a circle round it, about 18ft in diameter; outside these on the NW and E sides were ten more stones, which according to his description formed a rectangle 36ft x 18ft.

Possibly the monument was a cairn containing an inhumation burial (the size of the cist or grave is 6ft x 2ft) but what were the ten stones outside the circle? I think the circle is too small for a cairn.

The top stone measures 64in. from E to W, 63in. N to S, 24in. thick, and is 34in. above the floor of the cist.

The small stone [at W end] *X* is 36in. long, 12in. wide and 17in. deep. Other measurements:

A–B	56in.
B–C	20in.
C–D	62in.

A–D	25in.
J–M	56in.
J–K	23in.
K–L	59in.
L–M	17in.
C–J	28in. (width of cist)

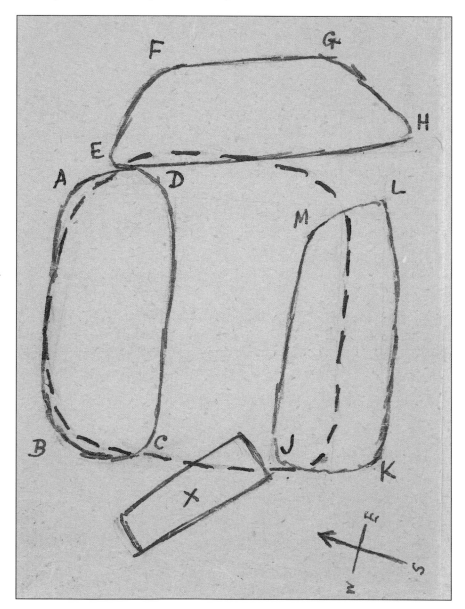

Fig. 68—Sketch-plan of central chamber at Parknasilloge.

E–H	65in.
H–G	29in.
F–G	36in. (this stone is 19in. wide).

21st January 1933

Townland Glencap Commons Upper. There are two piles of stones on the hill below and to the N of the top of Big Sugarloaf. The most northerly (B) looks to me natural, if it is the remains of a cairn it is very badly destroyed. The next (A) is a fair-sized cairn of stones, 44 long paces in circumference and 9ft high on the N and E, but only 5 or 6ft high on the S and W, as the ground slopes from S and W. I could not say if it is a burial cairn containing a cist or not: but it would not take very long to remove enough stones to find out. Going down the slope northwards, there is a bog at the bottom before you reach the next hill: in this there is a hole (C) about 6yds in diameter and 3ft deep, grass-covered, and with a slightly raised lip: it is surrounded by heather. I do not think it marks any antiquarian site. On the top of the next hill, at the S edge, is another pile of stones (D) but it could not now be called a cairn, being only about 2ft high, and perhaps 12yds or so in diameter. Near it are a few stones in a pile, perhaps the remains of another cairn. The one at D must be the one mentioned by O'Curry (*OS Letters* p.44): he says it was then 5ft high. There is no sign of a cist in the centre of it. This is the hill he calls 'Carrick na gCeann'.

Presumably 'Carrignegane' of *Meath doc.* 68 (d. 1622) is the same. I have been unable to trace the place mentioned by Canon Scott, *Stones of Bray*, p.185: 'Karrick Kevan or St Kevin's Rock, which was the old name of one of the townlands in the territory of Glencap'.

23rd January 1933

Knockandarragh. The rath called 'Mulladarragh Rath' on the Ordnance map is a flat circular one.

The diameter of the inner circle is about 39 paces, and the circumference of the inner bank is 124 paces. From the top of the inner [bank] to the top of the outer bank is about 20ft. Inner bank: inner face 5ft high, outer face about 8ft high. Outer bank: inner face 5 to 6ft high, outer face up to 3ft high in places. The outer bank is made of stones and earth. The material dug out to make the ditch seems to have been used to make

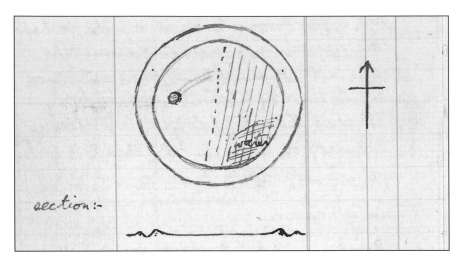

Fig. 69—Sketch-plan of 'Mulladarragh Rath' at Knockandarragh.

the bank. Most of the ditch is full of water, and part of the enclosed space is also full of water. The E half of the rath was cultivated, and the lazy-beds are still there. There is a circular hole about 14ft in circumference and about 3ft deep, with water standing in it, towards the W edge of the circle. The inner bank is rather broad, all grass-covered. The rath stands on the flat ground at the top of a ridge, in a field which looks like cut-away bog, a lot of the field is wet. It is just to the S of an old road running E and W.

In appearance this rath has some resemblance to the Raheens Mound in Donard Demesne East.

29th January 1933
Carrigeenshinnagh. The stone with cup-markings is about 150yds W of the Oldbridge–Lough Dan road, and 600 or 700yds from Oldbridge — you leave the road about 200yds S of Doyle's house. On the S side of the stone the ground looks as if it had been artificially flattened, as though for the site of a building or rath. It is on a rough hillside covered with stones. [Measurements:]

A–B	46cm
B–C	63cm
C–D	73cm
D–E	49cm
E–F	28cm

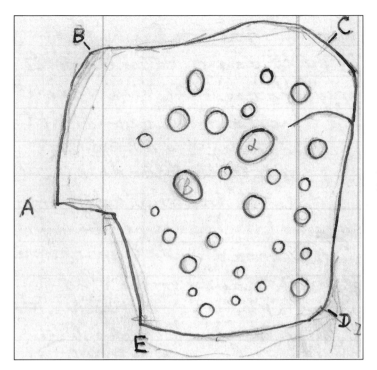

*Fig. 70—Sketch of cup-
marked stone at
Carrigeenshinnagh.*

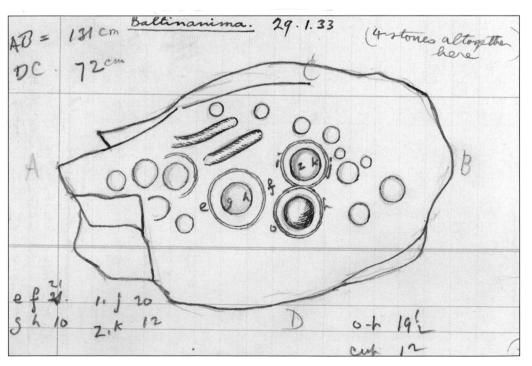

*Fig. 71—Sketch
of rock art at
Baltynanima.*

Fig. 72—Rock art at Baltynanima.

    A–F   16cm

[Cupmark] α 10cm x 8cm, 3cm deep. [Cupmark] ß 9cm x 6½cm, 2½cm deep.

    Baltynanima [cup-marked stone]. ([There are] four stones altogether here.)

[Measurements:]

    A–B   131cm
    D–C   72cm

[Measurements of the three large cupmarks enclosed by a circle:]

    e–f   21cm

g–h	10cm
i–j	20cm
z–k	12cm
o–h	19½cm (cup 12cm)

Baltynanima. A hundred yards or so to SE in next field to cup-and-circle stone [is] a flat flag, with a lot of small cups on it [measures 3ft long x 2½ft wide].

Another, a granite boulder, with six or more small pits, E of cup-and-circle stone, and 150–200yds from it. Another, mica schist, a 'flag' covered with medium-sized and small pits, 200yds or so to S of cup-and-circle stone.

Other stones:

Kilbaylet Lower	[In Notebook 3]
Ticlash	[In Notebook 14]
Three Wells	[In Notebook 16]
Ballykean (fourteen stones)	*JRSAI* xvi, p.224
Glendalough	*JRSAI* xvi, p.229
Merginstown	*JRSAI* xvi, p.229
Mongnacool	*JRSAI* xvi, p.230
Ballinapark	[In Notebook 17] and *JRSAI* xvi, p.232
Ballykillageer	*JRSAI* xvi, p.233

6th February 1933

Killahurler, Arklow. Killahurler Moat is about 70 paces in circumference and 12 to 13ft high with sloping sides. The E part of the centre has been dug away practically down to field level. There is a trace of a trench around the mote. It lies 100yds S of a small house at the crossroads in Killahurler Lower and just on the E side of the road: it is marked on the 1-inch Ordnance map. The mound consists of earth, with a lot of small stones in it (*PRIA* xvi, p.152).

Killahurler Church is in the townland of Mooreshill. A piece of the E wall is standing, about 11 or 12ft wide and 12 to 14ft high (estimated). There is a window in it, sill about 7ft from the ground. The whole is covered with ivy and in a ruinous condition. The outlines of the window are not visible, but I don't think any cut-stone facings remain. The church is a large one: the foundations are visible on the W and N sides, but the ground is so overgrown I could not pace it. From the masonry I should guess it was a medieval building. I was told the most recent headstone in the graveyard (there are only three or four) is about 90 years old. See *JRSAI* vii, p.107: but I don't think Father Ronan visited it.

The field in which the moat is belongs to Mr Daniel Whelan, Killahurler Lower.

7th February 1933

Umrygar [see p.20]. I paced the mote more carefully: its circumference is 96 paces. The top is flat, and not quite circular: the shorter axis is 9 paces across. On the S side the mote is 16ft high. Sloping sides. It is on the land of James Farrell, Umrygar. It is clearly an artificial construction, but is built of the same sand as the ridge it stands on. There is a small depression about 3ft by 2ft in the centre of the top, about 1ft deep. Westropp (*JRSAI* xxxiv, p.343) merely names it: he no doubt got it from Kinahan (*PRIA* xvi, p.158). Carnew village is close by to the E, and seems to stand up on a hill. The young man who brought me to the mote pronounced Tombreen townland (which is just across the Mine River, S of the mote) as 'Tombrane'.

Killabeg. The site which is said to be the old church lies on Mr Griffin's land, just beside Byrne's, about 400yds N of the crossroads at which there is a school, and about 50yds on the W side of the road. It is an enclosure about 25yds long and 10yds broad (estimated) enclosed by low, thick earth banks in which stones can be seen. On the N side a few large stones together have the appearance of the foundation of a wall. It is all overgrown with trees and bushes. The spring on the side of the road is called a Holy Well. On the 6-inch OS map 1887 edition — this is called 'RC Chapel (in ruins)' and the well 'Chapel Well'.

The name 'Killabeg' however as Father Shearman assumes probably represents 'coille beag', 'little wood' (for 'coille' instead of 'coill' see Joyce iii p.417).

19th February 1933

Killamoat. The moat here is just opposite the church to the W. The side is steeply sloped. It is surrounded by a ditch 15 to 18ft in width. It is 14ft high above the bottom of the ditch. The top is about 68 paces in circumference. All the centre of it has been dug away. There was an outer bank round the ditch, but it is quite destroyed in places, and in other places has been made into a field fence. This bank is in places 5ft high above the level of the field: the bottom of the ditch is 3ft below the level of the field. This bank is not immediately on the outer edge of the ditch, but there is a flat terrace first, then the bank. Perhaps this is only part of the ruin of the bank.

Local names in Aghavannagh district from Mr Martin O'Toole of Farbreaga, farmer (age 45?):

1. 'Mullyawnakerim', in Aghavannagh Mountain, 300 or 400yds N of Fallon's house which is just at the E end of Barnameelia. It is just a piece of bog, a bit of a rise in the hillside.
2. 'Crosrahnin' ('Crossrahnyeen Hollow'), E of Carrigatheme, in Aghavannagh Mountain or Aghavannagh Revell.
3. 'Inchafawdrig', at the butt of Lug, in front of the Prison. There is the mark of a house there.
4. 'Lugcoolmeen', the ridge E of Lug, between Aghavannagh Mountain and Ballinaskea.
5. 'Corrigvore' or 'Glanhoolya' ('oo' as 'u' in 'put'), the glen W of Slievemaan in Aghavannagh Ram ('Glan a' chuilleach'?).
6. 'Sleesit', in Aghavannagh Ram. Two houses just N of Aghavannagh River.
7. 'Fleming's Gowlyawn', a river fork near Sleesit.
8. 'Classfortiger'd Hollow' or 'Classfolltiger'd Hollow', E of Carrigatheme, not so far E as Crossrahnyeen Hollow.
9. 'Corriganaffrin', near Inchafawdrig under the South Prison. 'The Big Troch' ('trough') and 'the Three Little Trochs', in the South Prison. Hollows that sheep fall into.
   (I'm not sure whether 2, 3, 8 and 9 are in Aghavannagh Mountain or Aghavannagh Revell. 'Tromawnmacalther' starts between Farbreaga and Ballinguile and runs into the Ow River.)
10. 'Corrigeenafuaras', the ridge E of Lugcoolmeen.
11. 'Doyle's Street', the whole ridge of mountain from the E side of the South Prison to Carrawaystick, or rather the long ridge NE of the Ow River in Aghavannagh Revell.

12. 'Corrigasleggaun', on the side of Doyle's Street (Aghavannagh Revell).
13. 'Corriganarrig', on the side of Doyle's Street (Aghavannagh Revell).
14. 'Corrigahahny', E of Corrigasleggaun. 'Corrigagoppul' [is] further E.

Farbreaga. A stone over the doorway of Mr O'Toole's stable as a lintel is said to have been brought there from a field about 100 years ago. It is 70in. long and averages 12in. wide. The story is that in 1798 the cavalry were coming over Mucklagh and they saw this stone in a field with clothes on it and arms sticking out. They fired on it and wondered that it didn't fall, and went on firing till they came up to it and found it was only a stone. That is how the place got its name. O'Toole showed me the field where the stone is said to have stood, it is called 'the Elder Meadow'. It belongs to Martin Byrne. Field names in Farbreaga are English: 'the Big Park', 'Luke's Hill' — and called after people: 'Dick's Field' etc. Old Mrs O'Toole age about 70 pronounced the name 'Farbraigia', i.e. 'Fear bréige', 'a scarecrow'.

The font from Ballymaghroe Churchyard was brought by Mr P. O'Toole to Knockananna where it stands in front of the chapel. It is of granite; part of the lip or top edge is broken away. It has two Latin crosses in relief on the outside, opposite to one another. There is a hole in it in the bottom leading to a channel sunk in the outside surface of the granite.

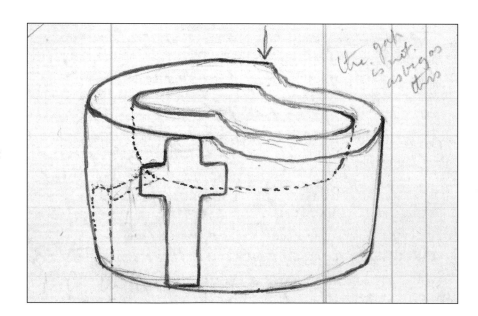

Fig. 73—Sketch of font from Ballymaghroe.

Internal diameter 1ft 8in. to 1ft 10in.

Thickness of lip 5in.

Internal depth 8in.

External depth 1ft 5in.

Cross 1ft 5in. long, 8in. wide.

Width of arms 3in.

The font is circular. The other cross is where [Price has] marked ↓ [on the sketch above]. It is said to have been used as a pig trough.

The large double rath shown on the 1840 6-inch map ¼ mile SE of Rathdangan village has been completely levelled: the field is still called 'the Ra', but there is no trace of the structure left. The other rath, ¼ mile E of the levelled one, is still there: it is called 'the Fort', just beside Keating's house. A roughly circular space surrounded by a bank of stones and earth, with just the trace of a ditch and second bank on the N side. From both 'the Ra' and 'the Fort' the mote at Killamoat is prominent on the skyline to the S about ½ mile away. Perhaps Rathdangan gets its name from the first rath, the mote being 'the Daingean'. The mote which lies about ¾ mile W of the mote at Killamoat is in Deerpark townland, between Highpark and Danesfort.

Co. Carlow *Namebooks*. Tullowfelim parish. Mount Wolseley or Crosslow. O'Donovan's explanation is 'Crois logha', 'Lughaidh or Lewis' Church'.

22nd February 1933

The mote at Deerpark near Highpark. A grass-covered mound which appears to be composed of sand, and small stones, as if from the river. It is on a hill at the end of a ridge, overlooking a small stream, part of the River Douglas. The mote is 108 paces in circumference, sides not very steeply sloping. It is about 18ft high looked at from the SW and about 20ft high from the NE. There is a large depression in the top, NE of the centre: so it may originally have had more of a flat top than it has now. This depression is 4ft below the top. (Sheet 28: 3.2cm S, 6.5cm W.) The surface is pitted with rabbit-holes.

I should say there can be very little doubt that this was the rath at Highpark mentioned by Lewis (ii, p.212) where an urn with bones and ashes was found in the 1830s.

The house at Highpark (Westby's) has been bought by St Patrick's African Mission and is used as a college. The land was bought by a Liverpool man named John Hughes, who has a steward there. Everything in the house was sold by auction. Deerpark is owned by a man named Kearney.

Addresses given me by Mr Ed O'Toole:

Nicholas Byrne National Teacher ... Naas, a native of Rathmeague, says Travers of Askinagap is an authority on folklore.

Mr O'Toole of ... Rathdangan has a story about the 'Farbreaga funeral', a fairy funeral. His son says there are local names in Rathdangan neighbourhood.

14th May 1933

With A. Farrington, P.T. Walshe and D. Coffey investigated the cairn at Big Sugarloaf. We removed the stones so as to make a shallow trench into the cairn from the S, removing the little pinnacle that stood on the cairn. When the level of our trench was 4 or 5ft above ground level, we cleared a circular hole in the centre of the cairn down to what we believed was ground level, about 7ft below the top of the cairn. At the bottom our hole was from 3 to 4ft in circumference, and we found there a flat flag 2ft long, 16in. wide and 6in. thick laid horizontally. On it was black earth about 1in. thick, and there was some black earth on the stones around it: also black earth and stones beneath it, but no sign of a cist or chamber, and no fragments of bone or pottery. Whether the flag was placed there or was merely accidental we could not say. The stones were all of the local Cambrian rock, and were mostly irregularly shaped lumps: flag-shaped stones are rarely found. (We saw two granite boulders among the stones of the cairn.)

It is possible that the flat stone may have had a cremated interment placed on it, which in the course of time has decayed away leaving only traces of black earth: but as the earth which is among the stones of the surface of the mountain is also black, this cannot be more than conjecture. If the cairn was not a burial mound, it is hard to know what it is, as it is quite large.

16th May 1933

Newcastle Upper. Mr Arthur W. Irwin of Prospect,

Newtownmountkennedy, showed me the mound where the burned bones and bronze object were found in 1872, which were deposited in the Royal Irish Academy Museum by his father Reverend H. Irwin, who was then Rector of Newtownmountkennedy. The mound is N of the road: it can be seen marked on the OS map (1-inch) as a small circle just over the 'y' of the word 'Smithy'. It is a grass-covered mound 60yds in circumference, and from 5 to 6ft high. Mr Irwin remembered the excavation (he is 71 years old). He said the cist was not quite at the centre but some feet S of the centre. It was sunk a couple of feet below the level of the field. The mound was surrounded by a bank or wall of loose small stones, 4 or 5ft thick. These are still there covered by the grass. It was Mr Henry Keogh who dug the mound. The owner of the field at present is Mrs McEnnery. It was previously owned by Mr Revell. (*JRSAI* xviii, p.163, description written by Major McEniry of the Museum, in 1887. Mr Irwin says the mound was not 9ft high in 1887, that as long as he remembers it it was not more than 6ft. The find is registered in the Royal Irish Academy Register as 1872/33: it cannot now be traced in the Museum. For Henry Keogh and his digging at Knockatemple see *JRSAI* xiii, p.12. This moate is clearly the one mentioned by O'Curry, *OS Letters* p.216, as near Mr Revell's house. He says it is 50yds in circumference, but I made it 60yds.)

August 1933

The ruin of what was said to be the old mill at Mullinacuff is in Knockatomcoyle, just across the stream from the Moat Field in Stranakelly. There is the foundation of a square building visible. John Maguire of Tinahely, whose people had the farm which Blakes have now, said that his father levelled the walls. The wet patch in the Moat Field was the mill pond.

There is a raheen, nearly destroyed, in Laragh, between Laragh House and the Moat Field. It is 36yds in circumference, a single bank, almost disappeared. It is in the bog, behind the ruin of a house: SSW of the moat, and in the NW angle of the Bog Field. A track into the bog ran near it, leading from the footstick at the bottom of the Moat Field.

18th August 1933

When I visited Mr Edward Byrne of Muskeagh to see his bronze axe, I asked him did he know of any finds on the Coolattin Estate. He said 'No'; but he then said a man came down to Coolattin 10 or 20 years ago, looking for 'the lid of a pot', but he didn't find it. A woman told this man that they used to throw things into the pond at Tomnafinnoge Quarry.

Query, does this mean an old custom?

Baltinglass. In the course of excavations for sewerage in May 1933 Mr Charles Kavanagh of Wicklow the foreman found a piece of limestone inscribed:

'NO DO
MINI
1630'

in the Fair Green, at a depth of 2ft 6in. It is in Baltinglass Schoolhouse. It seems to be a stone from the front of an old house.

3rd October 1933

The rath in Killinure beside the road near Oaks crossroads is nearly destroyed — it had a single bank round it which remains, about 4ft high, on part of the S side. It appears to have been 23 paces in diameter — centre same level as field.

Measured Broomfields dolmen. The owner of the land on which it stands is Mr Laurence O'Reilly of Broomfields. There are some pieces of large granite blocks blasted by dynamite making the fence at the gate of the field — I think it probable that the field was cleared by blasting stones, and probably some stones of the dolmen were destroyed at the time. O'Reilly insisted that the top stone had been pushed off by four men from the Old Mill, who had taken on a bet with Mr Meade the owner of the mill that they could do it.

2nd October 1933

Names from estate maps etc. at Shelton Abbey:

Shelton Estate
Keeloge spelt 'Killoague' and 'Killogue', 1775

Fig. 74—Broomfield dolmen (courtesy of the Royal Society of Antiquaries of Ireland ©).

Imaal Estate, 1773

'The Demesne of Seskin'	'Knockanargon'
'Ballinclay'	'Brittas'
'Straughnahely'	'Knocknamunnion'
'Knocknamunnion Mountain'	'Ballyvoghan'
'Ballyvoghan Mountain'	'Camera'
'Camera Mountain'	'Coane'
'Colliga'	'Killibegs'
'Brusselstown'	

'Bushfield, Moorspark', 1779

Other names shown on 1773 maps, of places not on the estate:

'Kilbruffy', 'Ballenagh' ('Ballinard'), 'Cloonshannon'.

'Tourboy land' is shown on the S boundary of Camara Mountain.

'Lackindarra' is the N part of Knockanarrigan (1773).

'Knocknaneconge' is part of Moorspark. This is called 'Knuckaneconge' on a map of 1766, which gives a survey of Moorspark. On another part of this map of 1766 Colliga is spelt 'Colloger', and on a map of 1820 'Coraga'. 'Knuckaneconge' is the NW end of Moorspark.

'Ballyvohan' is marked on the SW boundary of Moorspark, 1766 and 1773, apparently part of Bushfield, and Ballyreask is called 'Ballyrace'.

The Howards' Imaal Estate was conveyed to Dr Robert Howard, Bishop of Elphin, on 8th March 1734 by the co-heirs of Percy for £12418-1-8.

A map of 1746 of Castleruddery shows that the road from Donard to Ballyhubbock Bridge was the same as in 1760 (Nevill's map) and so was the road from Davidstown to Whitestown.

'Coolcame' or 'Coolcom' (1746) or 'Coolcaume' (1754) was part of Castleruddery Upper, bordering Whitestown — probably 'cúl cam', 'the winding back part', i.e. away from the road and the castle.

Knocknaneconge seems to be 'Cnocán na conga', 'the little hill of the narrow part of the river' ('cung'). See Joyce ii p.409.

16th October 1933

Further examination of the 1773 estate maps shows that the estate included the W part of Donaghmore parish, the boundary including Blane, Brittas, Seskin, Moorspark, Knockanarrigan, Colliga, Coan and Lugnaquillia Mountain.

(Hodgins, Marsh and Waters: several skeletons found ¼ back from front of house to the back of the plots. The fairies supposed to be round it.

Mr Graves owner of farm 50 years ago. It was called 'the Moate'. Mr Michael Sheridan ... two different burials.)

On the 1773 maps Stranahely appears to include Lobawn and Pollaghadoo, though the acreage given (645 Irish acres) is about 200 statute acres less than the three present townlands.

'Knocknamunnion Mountain' is the present Crissadaun and Table Mountain. 'Ballyvaughan' and 'Ballyvaughan Mountain' are Knickeen, Leitrim, Ballyvoghan, Clornagh and Leoh. 'Brittas' includes Blane. 'Camara' includes Cannow, and 'Camara Mountain' = Cannow Mountain and Lugnaquillia.

Ballinclay House is shown in 1773, but the road to Knockanarrigan was not built. 'Snugborough' is marked on the map of 1766: it seems to have included the present Sugarloaf townland.

The name 'Ballyvohan' on the SW boundary of Moorspark is very curious — is it a mistake?

'Coolcam' was the name of the two large fields in the W of Castleruddery Upper, S of the river and W of the road to George's Bridge: its acreage is given as 32 Irish acres. Oldmill in Ballylion near Donard appears as 'Old Mill land' on the map of 1746.

A 'raheen or forth' in the NW of Seskin is marked on a map of 1820. The road came down the E boundary of Seskin, across the river by a ford, and joined the road leading E 'to the Barrick' over the river, where Seskin Bridge is now.

On the 1773 map Castlequarter is called simply 'Part of Brusselstown' (the name 'Castlequarter' does not appear). On the 1773 map the road through Brusselstown running N, which now bends slightly to the W and runs N near the W boundary of Knockaderry, bends to the NE instead, and goes much nearer to the E boundary of Knockaderry.

The Shelton Estate, maps 1785. The old road by Templerainy and Ballyrichard is shown the same as on Nevill's 1810 map, and as I have marked it on my road map. It ran along the W boundary of Oldtown field in Ballyrichard.

The road through Keeloge, branching to Ballinabrannagh and to Templemichael, was the same. Snugborough was then part of Glenteige — Snugborough House is shown in Glenteige, and called 'The Reverend Mogue Dempsey's'.

Sheepwalk townland is shown on this map of 1785; so is 'Poulafooca', on the bounds of Barranisky.

[Note inserted 10th February 1940:] The Synge Hutchinson estate bordered the Howards' Imaal estate on the SW. This property descended to Hely Hutchinson and E.M. Stephens tells me that Miss Hely Hutchinson, an old lady, of ... Co. Dublin has some six tin boxes full of papers relating to the Hely Hutchinson property in an outhouse there.

March 1933

Visited Dr E. Fleury at Oldcourt. Received local names and information from Mr Martin Murphy, of Oldcourt, aged 70, he has a farm of about 20 acres. His grandfather named Brady lived in 'Ballynoulthagh' [Ballynultagh]. Mr Murphy never heard any Irish.

The names are in my placename book (Blessington DED):

'The Cahsheerach', is a flat dirty field, tilled.

'The Glanloss', a small green on the hill.

'Moinyeenroo' [Monyeenroo] joins Cruckaunroo.

'Glanthaun' is a field.

'Askavore' is a 'mashy' bog, joining Corrauncoyle or Kyle.

'Glenavuan' [Glenavooan] is the NW side of Sorrel Hill.

'The Gorraclogh' is 'the other side of Ballinatona [Ballinatone], between it and Ballydonnell'.

'Gorryathochar' is over the village of Ballinatone.

'The Toorbeg' is on the road to Ballysmuttan.

'Corrnahŏlta' is on Ballysmuttan Rock.

'The Cussaun' is on Carrigleitrim, a bit of a hollow in the hill.

'Park' or 'Partyahubbaun' [Parkyahubbaun] is a long field as you cross Ballyknockan Brook, between Lugnagun Upper and Lugnagun Lower.

'Lackinvore' is a stony patch with a couple of bushes on Carrigleitrim.

'The Mullauns' or 'the Mullyawns' is a piece of flat land near the Liffey.

'Bullyaunbawn' is a little round field over the brook between Upper and Lower 'Ballinasculloge' [Ballynasculloge].

There are only four houses in Ballynasculloge. 'Ballyknockan' is the name of Ballynasculloge Lower (he meant Upper: he only used 'Ballinasculloge' as meaning Ballynasculloge Lower): there are two houses in it. The Long Stone (on the side of the road above Oldcourt) there was never any history about it: old Mr Mooney said it was over a man shot in [17]98 (asked about Oldcourt). The old walls at the crossroad in Oldcourt belonged to a farmhouse. People called Kavanaghs lived there. Mr Murphy never remembers it standing.

'Scorlock's' Churchyard is near Liffey Cottage [Scurlock's]. The well is right at the butt of the wall, to the left, leaving the graveyard to the right. There's cures in it. You must rise the water in a certain way, in a bottle, and drink it: it's a cure for diarrhoea or vomiting. Lackan Well is right under the chapel, a little 'bóryeen' in to it, and then go down under a bit of a field. The protection wall was built by the clergy: the well is inside the wall, and outside too. People used to be washing their feet and hands there, and so they built the wall. People used to go to it in droves; Mr Murphy saw crutches and sticks stuck down there: they mouldered away. He knows

'Tample boorin', but he never had any recourse to it. (Asked about Whelp Rock.) He thinks when you are on Black Hill, facing for Blessington, it [Whelp Rock] is on your right. A kind of flat place behind them is called 'the Brishes'. (Asked about the mote of Butterhill.) Mr William Deevy planted the tree on it. Ned Deevy's father owned it; Mr Smith came after him, and Mr McDonnell has it now. (Asked did he ever hear any stories about Cleevaun Lake) — only that there was a girl going to be married, and the fellow left her, and she kept going round the lake till she fell in. If people were up there late, they'd make you no wiser, but they'd get away quick: there might be a noise or something like that.

The baskets for putting across a donkey for drawing turf are called 'a pair of cleeves'. Mrs Murphy saw a pair made. Old Ned Richardson of Lugnagun made them.

Later he [Mr John Murphy] gave Dr Fleury another name: 'Mullanagreagh' — a townland near Valleymount. [He also told] Dr Fleury that Billy Byrne's Gap was between Black Hill and Moanbane.

'Lavarnia Gap' [Lavarney] is next to Stoney Hill. Dr Fleury suggests it is 'Leath barn', 'half a cake' meaning 'an amphitheatre' (Joyce ii, p.56).

26th November 1933

Kilmalin, Powerscourt: St Moling's Well has been piped to make a water supply: to Powerscourt House? It has been built in with concrete, and there is an iron lid or trap. O'Curry (p.16) says the moate 30 perches to the SW was called 'the Fairy Moate', and that on the top was 'the base of an ancient cairn of moderate dimensions'. No sign of this remains there now: I examined the hill and it appears entirely natural. It is planted with trees. If there ever was an artificial structure on it, it has quite disappeared.

10th December 1933

Butter Mountain. I went up the road which leads from the stream which is the county boundary through Aghfarrell in Co. Dublin. It goes for ½ mile up to the house on the left, then continues straight on as a laneway for ¼ mile: the walls are there, covered with bushes, and the track between them at a lower level than the surface of the mountain. The line then goes straight on as a ditch up to the county boundary at the top of the hill, but the track bends to the left, going to the angle made by the county boundary, where there is a small cairn of stones: it then goes on straight towards Kilbride Camp. It is obviously an old track, worn or dug out in the mountain side. A path runs along beside it, still much used. I walked S along the top of the hill and on the top, which is flat, there is another roadway still in Butter Mountain running NW and SE. Tracks of carts are visible on it, but it is not sunk into the mountain, like the other track. It is in Butter Mountain, before you come to the townland boundary between it and Ballyfolan, which is further S.

15th January 1934

Tigroney. Tobernaclo is a well or natural pool of water, underneath a large rock, about 6ft high; it is on the slope of a hill, which has a number of streams running down it; this pool seems to be a spring from which one of these streams starts. A young man named Byrne said it was called 'Tobernacloch': then he said a Father Carroll who used to be in Avoca had that name for it in a book, but the old people (he named an old Mrs Neill) used to call it 'Toberaclone' or 'Tobernaclone'. He said it was a blessed well, the people would drink it to cure headaches or stomach aches.

The Spink is the hill just over 600ft in Tigroney West. The Bell Rock is the rock with trees on it in Ballygahan Lower, and the Red Road runs up behind it, on the boundary between Ballygahan Lower and Upper, then into Ballymurtagh, then it turns at right angles towards the W and runs to the 'ten houses' at the top of the hill. It runs through the mines.

The field names in Tigroney seem to be English.

18th March 1934

Visited Dr Fleury again at Oldcourt, and saw old Mr Murphy again. He gave me some more names:

'The Trudders' is a passway to 'Kilebeg' [Kilbeg or Killabeg?] — it is near Green Flank, out over 'Kilebeg Lodge' on the flat up there, on the bounds between 'Kilebeg' and 'Ballynoultha' [Ballynultagh]. 'The Tórenawn' is joining it, in about the same place.

'Brushy' is in the same place (this is the place he called 'the Brishes' in March 1933).

'Corrigadoun' is at Athdown Mountain: it's a green, and a break of rock

198

across it, going up the mountain, down to the right, not up near Seefinn. 'Druimagar' is a kind of hollow on 'Ballinoultha' [Ballynultagh]: in from the 'Tunnachas', between it and 'Glanacopple' [Glennacapple], under 'Brushy'. The road runs right through the Tunnachas, there is a turf bog at the head of it. (It (the Tunnachas) is not a field, it is the name of a place, a local name.)

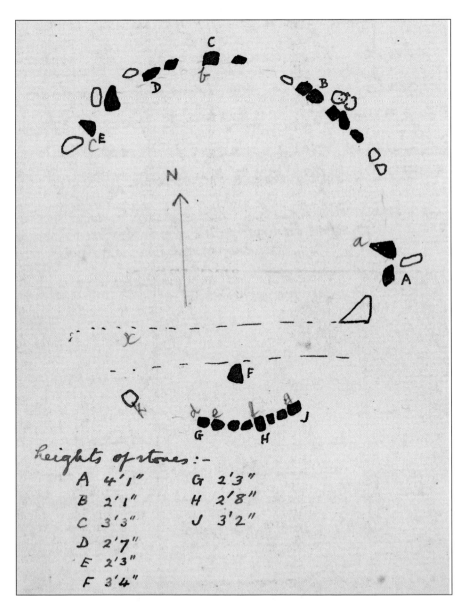

Fig. 75—Unaccompanied sketch-plan of stone enclosure at Rath East.

A young fellow from 'Kilebeg' [Kilbeg or Killabeg] (or Lugnagun?: I forget his name) was in with Mr Murphy and gave me a couple of other names:

'Gornahunniker' in Lugnagun Great, a field.
'Parknahubbawn', a field in Lugnagun Little (this is the name Mr Murphy gave me before).
'Mooneen', a field in Lugnagun Little.

There's a big stone on 'Blackamoor Hill' [Blackmoor Hill], goes by (the name of) 'the Long Stone': it is on the Sorrel Hill side of Blackmoor Hill. There is a mote in Rathnabo, on Osborne's land: there are rings round it. Daniel Lyons or Laurence Hastings of Lugnagun would know the local names.

Asked the young fellow what was the well in Kilbeg called (the one marked 'St Boodin's Well' on the Ordnance map). He said it is called 'the Wart Well': it cures warts: it is in Templeboodin by rights. (I don't know if he was confusing it with the other well lower down.)

Mr Murphy used the word a 'drundle' in speaking of the Trudders — he said it means a passway for water.

FIELD NOTEBOOK 13:
1933

4th July 1933

Aghowle Lower. 'The Churches'. The enclosure is very roughly circular, and appears to have been built up considerably at the N end to make it flat. The wall is very much ruined, about 2ft high in places, and 6 or 7ft high at the N end. It is approximately 80 paces in circumference but is difficult to pace, the ground being very rough. Nearer the N end than the S are some stones which might be the remains of a wall [semicircular shape]. Length W to E 16½ft, width 14½ft.

[There are] two [opposing] slabs of stone standing [at the E end] ... each 3ft high and approximately 4ft long at base — they are in the lines of the two walls of the building, if it was one. They are of even width, about 4in.

The outer circle or ring wall has an entrance about 3ft wide on the S side. There is an outcrop of rock or large stones between the enclosure wall and the 'building' at the N end.

The local story about this place, as given to me by a man named Byrne who was cutting turf, is: 'The saint — what was his name, St Columba, I think — was going to build a church there, and they had brought up all the stones: but the wind took his cape and blew it down to where the church is, and he built the church where the cape lay.'

Joe Myers of Aghowle also knew this story.

Between 'the Churches' and the raheen which is just at the westernmost point of Boley townland, in the heather, there is a mound of stones covered with grass and heather; it is about 24ft in diameter and 5ft high. It has been disturbed, the E side having been pulled down: and the disturbed part has a flat flag lying at the bottom, diamond-shaped, the sides about 2ft long, and about 3in. thick. It is a very even flat slab, I think greenstone, but [I] am not sure. It is loose in the heap, not covering any support stones. The mound has the appearance however of a cairn of stones which was piled over a cist, of which this slab might have been part (and see Money Lower [pp 217–18]).

8th October 1933

Ashtown. Examined the ruin of the old church at Ashtown (Ballinafunshoge) near Roundwood with R. Barton. It is marked as a rath

Fig. 76—Doorway at Ashtown (Ballinafunshoge) Church (courtesy of Dúchas The Heritage Service ©).

on the OS map. There is a circular bank round it about 35 paces in diameter: the bank is about 2ft high, and no doubt enclosed the old graveyard. The walls of the church stand from 2 to 3ft high; the facing of the walls is clear on the inside, but on the outside the stones are lying in a heap, so that it is only with difficulty that one can distinguish where the face of the wall is in one or two places. There was a nave and a chancel connected apparently by an arch.

Internal measurements:

 nave 31ft 6in. long, 18ft 6in. wide
 wall of arch (?) 3ft thick
 chancel 24ft long, 13ft 6in. wide

At the SW angle outside there is a granite block, tooled, and with the corner chamfered; this seems to be the angle stone still in position — the nave walls seem to be 2ft 9in. thick (measured beside the door) or 3ft thick (measured at the W end near the SW angle). There is a doorway, ruined, consisting of five large granite blocks; the two lower ones of the W jamb and the lower one of the E jamb are 2ft 9in. thick, extending the thickness of the wall. The W jamb is 11ft from the SW angle (inside). The doorway is 32in. wide at the bottom, and 31in. wide at a height of 3ft from the ground. The upper stone of each jamb may perhaps have been placed there recently; they have not quite the same original appearance as the others. Including these stones or blocks, the W jamb is now 5ft high and the E jamb 5ft 4in. high. A drawing of it looking from inside of the church [follows] [Fig. 78].

The large stone (*d*) has two angles cut out in like partial rebates, more than halfway up on the outside face and about a quarter-way up on the inside: it is not obvious what these were for.

At the E end of the chancel there is a low stone platform stretching across the whole width of the chancel; it is 54in. from the E end, like an altar platform. Raised up on this is a 'bullaun stone', a granite block, with bowl-shaped bullaun, 14in. in diameter and 6in. deep. This is practically the same size as the one now at Glendalough House, which was brought there from this site. On top of this are some carved stones, of what R. Barton calls 'Bath stone' or 'oolite'.

Three of these stones are of the plan as at [Plan] *1* [Fig. 77], and a fourth, much broken, seems to have been of the same plan; a fifth is of the plan as at [Plan] *2*. They look like window mouldings. They vary from about 4½in. to about 6½in. thick.

About 100yds to the NE of the circular bank is a granite block

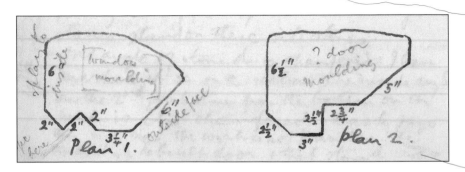

Fig. 77—*Profiles of carved stones at Ashtown (Ballinafunshoge).*

203

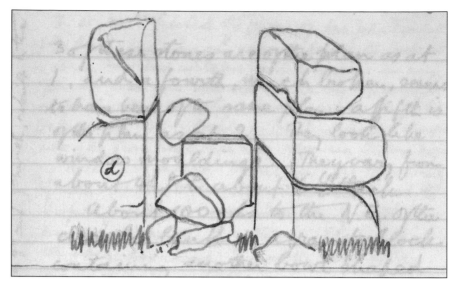

Fig. 78—Sketch of church doorway at Ashtown (Ballinafunshoge).

containing another bowl-shaped bullaun, 13in. x 11in. oval, and 4in. deep. The block is buried in grass and earth: there may be other hollows in it.

There is mortar in the wall of the chancel arch. Was the chancel an addition? The walls of it are not bonded in to the cross-wall.

There is a sill below the doorway — two large stones, 38in. wide, that is, projecting 5in. in front of the door. The jambstones stand on these sillstones.

One angle of stone *d* is chamfered: I have marked it *x* on the section. The inside angle on the second jambstone from the bottom on the W is also chamfered. Leask says this is a sign the work is not primitive. He thinks it is a rebuilt door, and that stone *d* was originally the lintel. A primitive (8th- or 9th-century?) church, rebuilt in the 13th century?

3rd April 1933

Visited the farm of Mr John Tyndall of Ballinabrannagh near Arklow to look at a stone marked with parallel lines — in my opinion these are marks made by a plough or pick while the stone was lying in the field. He told me that a field in Ballinakill, about 200yds E from his house and adjoining the boundary of Ballinabrannagh is called 'the Hurling Green', and that hurling matches used to be played there, and wrestling matches: he said, because it is the only flat field in the neighbourhood. It is on the farm of Mr Ryan of Ballinakill.

I asked him where was Whitsun Hill, and he said somewhere on Lord

Wicklow's lands at Shelton Abbey: he called it 'Whisson's Hill', and said it is called after a family named Whisson (see Wicklow *OS Letters*, p.412).

He said he had heard that some labourers dug in a pile of stones, long ago, either on Ballyrichard Hill or on 'Glantayg' Hill, and found a lot of Danes' pipes, little clay pipes: but he did not know the exact spot.

He called the green hill in Carrycole 'Caracole Rock'.

He said an old road used to lead across the N slope of Caracole Rock and up to Ballinabrannagh and then straight across the hill to Kilmagig Graveyard.

(Lawrence?) Case of Seskin — cist behind his house. Raheen — Mr Mark Fenton's. [He] lifted [a] stone: found it was resting on others. Nothing in it, removed all traces. In a triangular field behind Carriggower Quarry.

26th April 1933

Ballinclea, Glen of Imaal. In a field on the W side of the road about ¼ mile S of Ballinclea House (the large field on the S side of the river) just inside the gate, there is a mound of sand and small stones, almost destroyed. It belongs to Mr Fenton, and he uses it as a sandpit, drawing from it when he wants sand. The piece of the top remaining is a little ridge covered with grass, about 11ft high. On examining the mound, I saw at the SE edge some bones which appeared to have been burned, just at the top under the grass. I removed all I could collect, digging them out with a knife. They were not protected by stones, nor could I see any sign of any pottery. Mr Richard Fenton told me the field is called 'Webb's Height' (*JKAS* iv, p.355). It was he who found the (flint) stone knife which the Museum bought in 1932. He found it on Brittas Mountain, in earth dug out by rabbits on a little mound or hillock on the mountain side.

29th April 1933

(Ballinclea continued.) Mr Stelfox examined the bones in the National Museum, and in his opinion they are burned human bones, and as they are very small, he thinks they are those of a child. I selected any fragments which were at all identifiable and left them in the Museum.

24th March 1934

Ballynerrin, Kilcoole (Kilfernoc?). The old church stands in a field called 'the Church Park'. I made it 12½–13 paces long, and 7 paces wide (external). It has a splayed window in the E wall — the top broken, ope was about 4ft high. Cannot measure external width, it is too much damaged. This wall is, I guess, about 9ft high. Two or 3ft of the N wall adjoining the E end is standing, about the same height, and about 12ft of the S wall, same height. Splayed window 6ft (internal measurement) from E corner in S wall. The ope is 12in. wide on outside, only about 2ft high, top broken. It is difficult to say if there was cut stone facing these windows: the mortar shows that stones have fallen or been broken away, but I think they were only constructional stones. The door was in the W end, only about 2ft of the N side of it is standing. No jambstones. The walls are 3ft thick. Inside in the SE corner, there is a square hole 1ft square, and 1ft deep, the bottom 3ft from the ground. The church was built with mortar. There are no carved stones visible. There is the trace of a square or oblong mound around it, probably a graveyard.

Fig. 79—Plan of church remains at Ballynerrin.

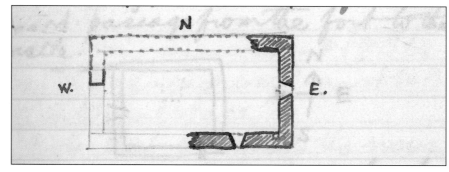

It is in exactly the same condition as when O'Curry saw it in January 1839 (*OS Letters*, p.187). The stone he speaks of with marks on it is lying inside the doorway. They are marks where tools have been sharpened. If it was part of the doorway when he saw it, then the door is more broken now.

A local man said these marks were made by spears — there was a great battle there long ago.

5th September 1933
Ballyraine Middle, near Arklow. The square fort is about a mile W of Arklow Castle; it is on high ground (nearly 200ft), and about ½ mile SW of the old ford called 'the Horse's Ford'. The local story is that there is an underground passage from the fort to the castle.

I paced the top of the inner bank and made it 80 paces. From the top of the inner to the top of the outer bank is 36ft, by the tape. The ditch varies from 10ft deep to nearly 20ft in places, below the top of the bank. It is wet; a stream runs in along a field fence at the NW corner. On the W side there is an entrance causeway through the ditch, perhaps modern. Fifteen paces from the SE corner along the S side is a narrow passage through the inner bank down to the ditch: this looks original. There are no traces of masonry: the banks are made of earth: after the recent dry weather it is very difficult to poke a stick into the clay, but I could find no stone.

Inside the enclosure there are raised banks in the field on the N side, they might be foundations of buildings, but one would have to dig to find out.

O'Curry's measurement (*OS Letters*, p.424) '62yds each way' must be of the internal space.

Note that O'Curry spells the name 'Ballyrane' (1839); this is also the spelling in the 1847 Rate Book. This was no doubt originally 'Baile raithin' referring to this fort; then it was pronounced 'Ballyraan'; then corruptly, 'Ballyrayne': then this was made permanent in the spelling in the Ordnance Survey, 'Ballyraine'.

Compare the fort with Courtfoyle, 56yds square, Ballynagran McDermot 56yds square outside, Stump of the Castle 45yds square inside and Talbotstown 60yds x 35yds inside.

The Horse Ford. Forge on Ballyraine side. The double dale ditch ford 300yds W from the end used to be a bridge for the cattle to come across [...] for drawing wagons along [the] track. Mary's Bog, between ditch and ford.

4th July 1933

Barnacashel. Joe Myers of Aghowle also said that Mr Haskins (who used to live in the Hall, Coolkenna) had opened a place on Whelan's Hill in Barnacashel: there was a flag in it and they blasted it: and there are four or five stone pillars round it. Myers had never seen it. Whelan's Hill is the mountain part of Barnacashel, on the W side, above the enclosed land. Reverend Mr Young had also heard about this, and said he was told that Mr Haskins had first dreamed about the place, and that he found an underground passage in it.

27th March 1934

Brittas, Glen Imaal. The Holy Stone or St Laurence's Stone. A granite boulder 5 or 6ft long in a piece of boggy land on the N side of the road. Four round basins and one elongated hollow, having a circular depression at one end and an oval depression at the other with a ridge between. This was called 'the Joyant's (i.e. "Giant's") Foot' by the old people. Measurements [see Fig. 80]:

A   28in. long, oval 11in. wide, 7in. deep. Circular hollow 10in. wide, 5in. deep. Ridge 3in. deep

B   diameter 11in., depth 6½in.

C   diameter 10in., depth 6in.

D   diameter 8in., depth 4in.

E   diameter 11in., depth 7in.

'Goalya' ('Golier' on OS) is the ridge in the N of Brittas and S of Stranahely.

Another very large rock a little to the W of the last has four basins in it. [Measurements] [see Fig. 81]:

Spaced as shown. From edge of A to edge of B   33in.

A–D   23in.

A–B   33–36in.

A–C   21in.

B–C   15in.

C–D   6in.

A   diameter 12in., depth 5in.

B   diameter 10in., depth 5in.

C   diameter 10½in., depth 5in.

D   diameter 10in., depth 4¼in.

There is a third rock with one basin in it, a little further to the W. Diameter of basin 12in., depth 4in.

I was told there is a granite rock further up towards the mountain, still in Brittas, with the mark of a cow's foot in it — 4in. wide, 1in. deep.

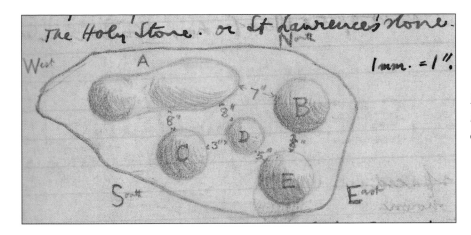

Fig. 80—Sketch of St Laurence's Stone, Glen of Imaal.

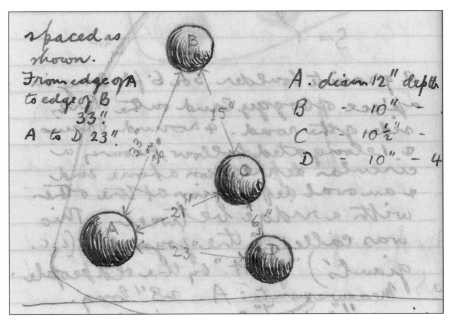

Fig. 81—Sketch of bullaun stone near St Laurence's Stone, Glen of Imaal.

27th November 1933

Cannow. Local names which I got from the farmer who owns 'the Church Field' in Kilbreffy. He pronounced Cannow 'Kinn-ow' ('cinn abh').

At the lowest point of the mountain line, where the townlands of Leoh and Cannow Mountain meet, is 'the Fox Rock' (Mr James Kavanagh of Clonshannon had given me this name). Below it is 'Iletyah' ('Oiltiagh', 'Aill teach') (this must be 'Oildarrig') and below this is 'Assnaglass', on a stream ('Eas na glaise'?), and below this again is 'Shantoor' ('Sean tuair'). He said these were in Cannow: they must be near the boundary between Cannow Mountain and Leoh. 'Brishadarrig'('bruise dearg') is on Cannow, on the side of Lugnaquillia.

27 March 1933

Coolamaddra. There is a local tradition of a 'place where the soldiers are buried', at the NW side of the Brusselstown Ring — you can see the stones in a line making the graves a foot or so above the ground. There was supposed to be a great battle there, from the Ring down to the river. I was told this after coming down from the Ring, having looked for the dolmens Tony Farrington said were there, and having failed to find them. These must be they.

The more I look at the mote above Ballyhubbock Bridge the more I think it is an Anglo-Norman fortification.

Cronroe. Fee farm grant dated 5th March 1862 Wilkinson to Eccles reciting lease dated 22nd December 1716, Richard Viscount Rosse to Sir John Eccles of Mount Eccles in Co. Dublin, of Corranroe Ballygally the moiety of Scheskin and Croneporee, barony of Newcastle and Co. Wicklow containing by survey 335 acres Ir. profitable and 6 acres unprofitable. Renewable forever Conveys said premises to Hugh Eccles of Cronroe. (There was a map on the lease of 1716.)

The estate map shows the following names in Cronroe:

a. 'Ballyknockan Field'
b. 'Fair Green'
c. 'Coshel Hill'
d. 'Middle Hill'
e. 'Sweet Hill'
f. 'Pond Hill'
'Ballyknockan Field' adjoins Ballyknockanbeg townland.

19th March 1933

Delgany. The ruin of a church, that is the foundations of walls in places 3ft or so high, are near the S side of the churchyard, they are all covered with grass, brambles and ivy. The old cross shaft is standing, with the inscribed face towards the S, about the middle of the churchyard, towards the N side.

Mademoiselle F. Henry was with me, and all she could read of the inscription was

'OR ... OCUS... DR... SAIN'

But the light was not good, sun shining directly on this face, and throwing the shadow of a tree on it. She thinks it could be read from a good flashlight photo, or perhaps with the sun shining from the E or W. There does not appear to be any other feature of interest in the graveyard. We thought the cross comparatively modern — 12th or 13th century? See Petrie, 'Christian Inscriptions', in *Irish Language,* vol. 2, p.35. He reads it:

'OR DO DICU OCUS [MAEL]ODRAN SAIR'

Information given to me by R.C. Barton of Glendalough House, Annamoe. A man named Osborne, a rabbit-trapper living between Laragh and Rathdrum, came to him about 20 or 25 years ago with a copper cauldron or pot, three-legged and waisted: he said when he was trapping rabbits he saw a rabbit run into a hole, and going to look at the hole found it was the inside of this pot, and the rabbit was running round and round in it. It was in the ground in Derrybawn or near it. He offered it to R. Barton asking £5 which Barton thought too much, so the man said he would offer it to John Lucas, Lord Meath's gamekeeper, and Barton never heard any more of it.

Is this the pot which the museum purchased for £7 from R. Mackintosh in 1911?

29th October 1933

At Drummin with R.C. Barton. The brook which runs down from the top of Scarr and passes by Glendalough House is called 'Keocha's Brook'. The ridge N of this, which forms the N part of the townland of Drummin, is called 'Drumray' (for Drumreagh?). Barton has been unable to find out from the traditions of any of the old men when this ridge was first tilled; but it has been tilled, by hand, right up to the top, on the S side, and was good land, and is still good pasture. It is full of ruins of old houses. An oblong enclosure near the road, N of the brook, is called 'the Raheen':

nobody knows why. It is about 35yds x 15yds. A little W of this is a flat granite slab covered with small cup-markings, like the one on Carrigeenshinnagh: it is 3ft long by 2ft 3in. wide, and has about 24 pits on it, the largest about 4in. in diameter and 2in. deep.

A little SW of this is what is said to have been a millpond, with traces of a headrace; the oval pond is 6ft deep, sides built up with stones — now broken down in places: an exit to the S where the wheel is said to have been, with [a] tailrace leading to [the] brook.

The top of the hill (1171ft) is called 'the Whistling Bank'. Further W than the pond near Johnny McDonnell's house (which was previously Farrell's) are three 'bullaun' stones, all granite blocks, natural boulders. The first has three bowls: two of them 13in. each in diameter, and 7½in. and 8½in. deep respectively: close together, rather vertical sides: the third is very shallow — 10in. diameter, 1in. deep: like a place where a bowl was started.

The second [stone], 40yds S of this, has two bowls, one 12in. diameter, 7½in. deep, the other 10in. diameter, 3in. deep: close together.

The third, to W, has one bowl, 11½in. diameter, 4½in. deep, sides not so vertical.

Still in Drummin townland, S of Keocha's Brook, 50yds up the lane from the road to the Brusher Gate, on Anne Doyle's land, is a fourth granite

Fig. 82—Cup-marked stone near mill site at Drummin.

boulder with a bullán; one bowl, oval, 18in. x 15in. and 7½in. deep: sloping section on long axis, more vertical sides on short axis. There is a fifth granite boulder with a bullán near Anne Doyle's house, E of the road, near a destroyed raheen: it is 16in. x 15in. in diameter, not so evenly made as the others: 5in. deep.

A house further up on the lane to the Brusher Gate was built on a fairy pass, and two families who lived in it were unlucky: it is now used by Johnny McDonnell as a cow house.

Just beside the road, on the W side of it, at the boundary between Drummin and Laragh West is a field called 'the Church Field': there is said to have been a thatched chapel there.

Souterrain, Grannahbegg in the mountains of Wicklow. (*Exshaw's Magazine* 1788, p.444):

'Wicklow, August 16. Some gentlemen shooting on the lands of Grannahbegg in the mountains of Wicklow, having set down to refresh themselves with cold provision at the foot of a rock, the earth suddenly gave way, and one of them fell into a chasm four feet deep, but received no injury. On removing the rubbish by a countryman to whom a shilling was promised, they discovered a subterranean gallery, which they entered with a lighted candle, and after a space of about twenty yards brought them to a square room or vault in which was a druidical altar of coarse native stone two feet and a half high by a yard and fourteen inches long. In another part of the cave was a stone chest in the form of a hog-trough, seven feet long and two feet wide, which on breaking discovered a large human skeleton near which lay a brazen head-piece and rusty spear, whose staff or handle on touching fell into dust. It is supposed to have been the body of some ancient chief which was there deposited as in a temple for greater honour.

The spear and helmet are now in the custody of a neighbouring gentleman at whose house the sportsmen stopt on their return from the mountain.'

27th November 1933

Kilbreffy. The site of the graveyard is where marked in the OS map, in the large field N of the house. This field is called 'the Church Field'. There is no mark of any piece of ground different from the rest, but the farmer thinks the graveyard may have been at the highest point of the field, as he has turned up more stones there than elsewhere, some like broken pieces of flags. He calls the townland 'Kilbruffy'. His other fields are called 'the Broom Field' because it had a hedge of broom; 'the Orchard Field': there was an old orchard there; 'the Road Field' and 'the Bottom Field'.

He said there were Irish names in Cannow and he gave me some.

12th November 1933

Kilcoagh. At the point marked '1629ft' ('Pinnacle') on the 1-inch OS map

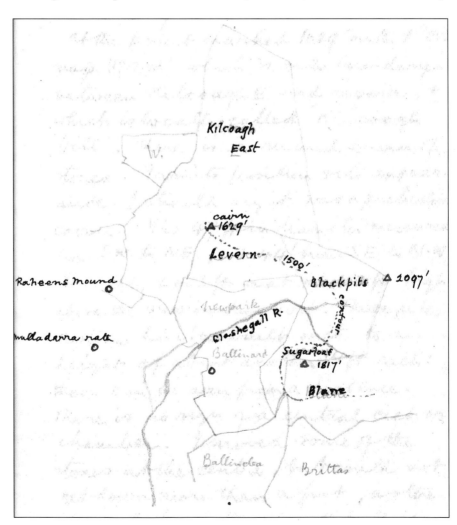

Fig. 83—Sketch-map of Kilcoagh locality.

(1913 ed.) which is on the boundary between Kilcoagh East and Levern, and which is locally called 'Kilcoogh Hill', there is a ruined cairn of stones. From its position and its appearance I should say it was a prehistoric cairn. It is 47ft in diameter (measured) from SW to NE, and 44ft from SE to NW. It is only 2 or 3ft or at most 4ft high above the surrounding turf. Three piles of stones have been built on it to a height of about another 4ft each: these can be seen from a distance. There is no sign of a central cist or chamber. I moved some of the stones at the centre, but could not get down more than a foot, as the space between them is all full of turf mould, and one would need a spade to clear it out. I could see no large stones where I dug.

5th September 1933
Kilcommon Parish Church, Lugduff, near Tinahely. There is a high bank which seems to have been part of a circular enclosure round the graveyard: it has been removed on the N side, and is clearest on the W. The graveyard is mixed, several 18th-century Catholic headstones on the S side, and one or two elsewhere — (Catholics are not buried there now but at Killaveny). Outside the church on the N side, near the path, is a large block of granite, partly buried. It is cylindrical in shape, 2ft high and 3ft in diameter. There is a kind of rim 3 or 4in. wide round the upper surface: this I think marks the place where originally there was a large vessel to hold water, the sides of which have all been broken away, leaving only the cylindrical base. A large granite font?

30th March 1933
With Dr Mahr to Belfast. Met Mr Deane, Mr Stendal at the Museum, and evening with Mr C. Blake Whelan. There do not appear to be any Co. Wicklow localised objects in the museum, but Mr George is going to examine the card index and let me know.

31st March 1933
With Mahr and Blake Whelan to Toome and Newferry where we saw the ford sites and the 'Bann' (diatomaceous) clay. To Ballymena, visited Dr D'Evelyn and saw his collection, which consists chiefly of stone implements of all kinds, but includes bronze (one very fine flat axe from Ballyweeny, Co. Antrim, decorated, about 8 or 9in. long, the cutting edge

injured by an indentation) and at least one small gold penannular ring, and some pottery. Then visited Dr John B. Stewart of Portglenone and saw his collection of stone implements, all local — especially the long axes, or clubs — one about 2½ft long and 24lbs in weight. He has a few bronze implements, and a nice very early copper axe.

1st April 1933
Collected a quantity of flint implements from Mr Shanks of Ballyfounder, Co. Down, near Portaferry.

Placenames:
Killyless, Co. Antrim, pronounced 'Killylesh'.
'Carravanish', Co. Down — not a townland or parish name. Near Strangford. Probably contains the Scandinavian name 'Maghnus' (cf. 'Curravanish').
'Tara Fort', near Portaferry.

21st January 1934
Kilmacrea. The greater part of the townland is a fairly high ridge of a hill. The raheen marked on the map near the stream bounding Springfarm was not to be seen: perhaps it is destroyed. The farmer nearby did not seem to know it, but I don't think he is a native. The stream runs out of a green angle of the hill. Query, could this raheen be the one which O'Conor says was formerly used as a burying ground? It is more likely than the one on the top of the hill. This ('the Round Ball') is 51 paces in diameter; a single wall of stones and earth, mostly destroyed, the stones being used to make fences. About ⅓ of it (S side) is built as a drystone wall to make a field fence. The NE quadrant is marked off by a low grass bank, like the foundation of a wall. The rock outcrops inside the rath, on the W side.

The Cat Rock is only an outcrop of the natural rock.

22nd March 1933
Kiltegan. Mr E. O'Toole of Rathvilly wrote to me saying there was a place called 'the Norman Moat' at Kiltegan, on the farm of Mr William Murphy. I went to look at this today. Mr Murphy showed it to me: he calls it simply 'the mote'. He said there was a story that a passage led to it from

Humewood, also that lights had been seen on it at night. It is a low mound, grass-covered, and the lower edge is sloped off sharply down to the field ... with a very small bank at the top of this slope. This steep slope, which looks like the side of an earth fence, goes unevenly all round, not always keeping the same height: it is not circular. The mound seems to consist of sand: Mr Murphy is digging sand out of it in one place: he says it is too fine to be good sand. I believe this is a natural mound of sand (glacially deposited?), and that the bank round was made for some purpose, perhaps when the field was ploughed; or, as the field is now very boggy, and perhaps was never suitable for ploughing, it was perhaps banked to make an edge to the mound: Mr Murphy said the water once went all round it; so perhaps a sort of fence was made on the mound.

Kiltegan old graveyard is also on Mr Murphy's land: it is about 500yds E of the Protestant church. There is no trace of a church in it. A few old people are still [asking to be] buried in it. The font which was in it has been moved to the 'Oratory' in Kiltegan village. There are no gravestones in it of much interest. One which looks like 18th century, of granite, the face much weathered away, has one side of the back covered with horizontal grooves which look at first sight something like ogham: but I think they are only decoration. The scores or grooves are certainly artificial.

22nd October 1933
At Kindlestown Castle with H.G. Leask. The N wall is standing and a bit of the E wall. At the NE and NW corners are the remains of towers. Internal measurement was 55ft x 20ft. The underside of the vaulting can be seen all along the inside of the N wall, the plaster was laid on 7in. planks, which Leask says is a mark of more recent work: old plastering was laid on wicker. The E wall is 9ft thick, with a small vaulted chamber 3ft wide in the middle of it. That vault was laid on wicker. The W and S walls have disappeared to the foundations.

4th July 1933
Money Lower. With Reverend T.B. Young. There is a mote in Money Lower, some 500yds S of Money Bridge, and on the W side of the road, in a field. It is called 'the Hulk', we did not visit it, but saw it from Aghowle Mountain.

Fig. 84—Bullaun stone at Aghowle Lower (courtesy of the Royal Society of Antiquaries of Ireland ©).

Aghowle Lower. In the field SE of the old church there is a boulder containing 'bullauns'. It is in the middle of the field.

In a large field W of the church there is a large rock. Joe Myers of Aghowle said a wizard threw it there and the marks of a foot and of fingers are on it.

4th April 1933

Money Upper townland, Rockview Lower. A place on the boundary of Moylisha and Money Upper, 600yds N of Labbanasigha, on the farm of a man named Loughnan there is the remains of a cist and a cairn. Between 30 and 40 years ago old Loughnan carted away the stones of the cairn: he found three slabs standing up, and one on top, and a flat flag beneath with what he called 'red bog clay' on it. Apparently when he came to this he left the remaining stones: they are now covered with earth, but some of the stones can still be seen in the field. It is on the N side of the road. (See also Newry, below.)

20th March 1933

Moorstown. The field in which the standing stone is was being ploughed, and a big slab of rock, 8 or 10ft long, was visible lying immediately on the E side of it. This rock also crops out some distance to the N in the same field.

I doubt if this stone is an artificially erected stone, though I am told Mr Haslam of Newtownmountkennedy calls it 'the Druid's Altar'.

1st August 1933

Mullinacuff Church. The outline of the E window is undoubtedly pointed, but the point of the arch is not clear cut, it is rounded. It is however not a round-headed window. Perhaps it is early Gothic. The window is larger than in the usual Romanesque church. It is deeply splayed inside. The outer angle is chamfered, then there is a groove round the stones. There is a hole at the bottom for a mullion. The granite facing is much worn.

In a niche in the NE angle of the wall, inside, there is a granite basin, broken into four pieces. It is about 18in. across. Mr Bishop said there is another, buried in the ground, near his family grave. It is rather bigger, also of granite, not broken. He has seen it when a grave was dug there.

Bishop's house is in Stranakelly, ¼ mile SE of the old churchyard: between the churchyard and his house is a field called 'the Racecourse'.

In the Mote Field, N of the mote, beside the stream, is a mound showing some foundations of a building. This is said to have been a mill belonging to a man named Cuff. I don't know if this is genuine tradition or if it is merely a guess suggested by the name 'Mullinacuff'.

Bishop told me a curious story of an herb cure. His son Eric, a boy now about 4 years old, was ill, and was sent by Dr Clements of Tinahely to the Adelaide Hospital in June 1932. He was very wasted, his bones without flesh on them, legs were sticks, his stomach very swollen. The hospital people said he had tubercular peritonitis and sent him home as incurable.

Dr Clements who had practised in Rathangan, Co. Kildare (his wife comes from there) said to send the child to a man named Peter Behan of (Mr Bishop said 'Killanty' a couple of miles the far side of Rathangan: is it 'Killahan' in King's County?). Mr Bishop brought him [the child]; and Behan gave him a bottle, with instructions; to take a spoonful and throw it in the fire in the name of the Father, Son and Holy Ghost, then a spoonful to the child, another in the fire, another to the child, a third in the fire, a third to the child; with the fourth spoonful they were to make the sign of the cross, with the finger, on the child's right hand and left foot, then on the child's left hand and right foot, then on the crown of his head and on his chest; they were to do this three times round these points, to mean the Trinity. This was to be repeated three times every second day. They did this, and with the second bottle the child was cured. When the child was first taken to Behan, it had on its stomach cloths soaked in cod liver oil, put there by Dr Clements: Behan said to take them off and throw them away, as the oil was feeding the disease he was trying to cure.

I saw the child (1st August 1933): he appeared quite well, and fat.

The wall round Mullinacuff Church was built by a Mr Rainsford. A memorial stone in recognition of this was put up: it is now lying near the gate into the graveyard. The date '1853' is legible on it.

Mr Young told me Mr Eddie Byrne J.P. of Muskeagh had had a bronze spearhead in his house which was found in a bog in the neighbourhood. He thinks Mr Byrne gave it to his son. (18th August 1933: it is not a spearhead but a bronze axe; Mr Byrne showed it to us, and I have drawn and measured it.)

4th April 1933

With the Reverend T.E. Young. He showed me, first, a mound in Money Upper in a field called 'the Mote Field' on Mr Lawrenson's land. It is 400yds or so S of Money House on the other side of the road. It is 64 paces in circumference, and about 9ft high. It is composed of large stones, or small boulders, of granite piled together, with yellow clay, which holds them together, and it is covered with grass, and has some old trees planted on it. On the SE side it has been slightly dug away and the boulders apparently used to face the field fence just beside it. I should say this is a prehistoric cairn containing a burial chamber, which is very probably undisturbed.

Newry. The pillar stone mentioned by Canon Ffrench is on the W slope of Newry Hill, near the top; it is about ... [near] the house called 'Ureland's House' on the map, which is occupied by a Mr Wilson. The stone is now fallen, and has fallen quite recently. The boy who showed it to Mr Young about a month ago said that when he had seen it before it was standing; it is now 9½ft long, and the mark of the earth at the base shows that it was sunk 2ft in the ground. It is 6ft 7in. in girth: it is of a slaty kind of stone, quite rough: no marks on it.

It has fallen with the top pointing down the hill, and with the bottom which was in the ground just resting on another stone, a slab 51in. long, 8½in. wide, and about 18in. deep, the top just level with the surface of the ground. This looks as if it was placed in position as a support for the pillar stone. There are other stones beside it on the W side, but I could see nothing like a cist. Loose stones and earth had been thrown into the hole the pillar stone had stood in.

7th April 1934

Newry. Mr Twamley of Ballyhacket, Co. Carlow, who used to live at Newry told me there is a round stone 3ft in diameter and 18in. deep with a hole in the centre, 50yds W of the road and 20yds from the townland boundary, Newry–Moylisha, in a cut-away wood, near a stream, on the land of Mr Wilson of Newry.

20th March 1933

Nunscross. Canon A.D. Moore, Killiskey Rectory, Ashford, told me that the Reverend Mr Huband had given his notes on Killiskey parish to Miss Crofton of Broomfield. He made some extracts from Huband's notes, as follows:

> 'Dr H.P. Truell told me that his father told him while repairing the bridge at Nun's Cross they came across the remains of an old wall in which was found a skeleton immured. It was said to be an old nunnery wall and the skeleton was supposed to be that of a nun. The cross in the wall of the present bridge marks the spot where the body was said to have been found. On telling this to Mr Deans he said that in the year 1850 a man named Cullen built the present wall in which the slate cross

is. Before that a thorn bush stood there, before which Roman Catholic funerals used to stop and repeat prayers. This thorn bush was looked upon by the Roman Catholics as sacred and called "the Nun's Thorn". Protestant boys were warned that if they touched the thorn they would be visited with "divers kinds of penalties". Cullen (when repairing the wall) cut down the bush, and placed the cross in the wall in its stead. The cross is of slate brought from Glanmore. The site of the old nunnery is said by some to be near Tubber, and just beyond Toole's house there is a circle of thorns which is said to mark the site of the nunnery. Others say it was near Kilfea Churchyard and that the Tubber thorns marked the limits of the nunnery grounds. On August 27th 1900 I had a conversation with Arthur Robb of Killiskey on the above subject. He told me that in 1855 he was told by Miss Baxter "an educated lady" a relation of Dr Fletcher that the remains of an immured nun was found buried at Nun's Cross (with outstretched hands). He also said she told him that the monks of Kilfea used to meet funerals, coming from Killiskey direction, at a spot near the present Nun's Cross Bridge and funerals coming from Ballinalea at the spot at Tubber mentioned above. He said the spot [at Nun's Cross Bridge] was called "the place of mourning". He remembered the bush being called "the Nun's Bush".'

Canon Moore has heard the story of the nun being immured, with the addition that it was for some misdemeanour, and that the people used to bring her food secretly.

'Tubber' must be 'Tubber Brighde' in Ballymacahara.

Could all these stories be derived from an attempt to explain the name 'Kilfea'as 'ceall feadhbh' in the sense of 'Nun's Church'?

1st May 1933

Parkmore. The Giant's Grave. The two pillar stones are 26ft apart (measured from the inner surfaces). The taller is 131° E of magnetic N of the other, that is they are in a line running WNW and ESE (true bearing). The taller one (to the E) is 5ft 3in. high and 3ft wide (35in.); the other (to the W) is 4ft 3in. high and 2ft square.

I took a bearing from the W side of the stone circle to the more westerly pillar stone: it was 359° E of magnetic N. That is this stone is NNW of the centre of the circle (true bearing allowing for a variation of 17°). I don't think they have any connection.

The stones which may be a chamber in the centre of the circle are only 18in. over the ground, except that to the NW which is 2ft high. There are eight stones, and a smaller one, which may belong to this chamber.

I have plotted them [see below] ... somewhat more accurately than [before]. If they formed a chamber, it must have been of a square or oval shape, about 4ft long and the same width.

The pillar stones are about 160yds away from the circle.

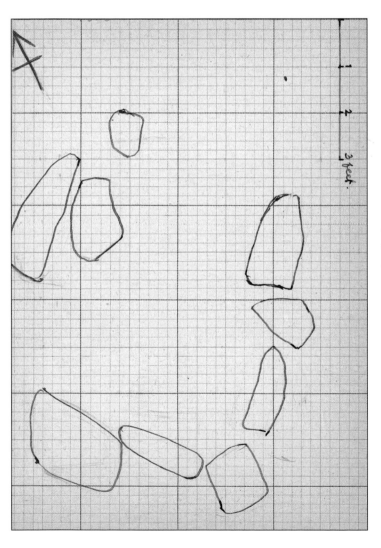

Fig. 85—Sketch-plan of central 'chamber' at Parkmore.

27th September 1933

Raheen, near Baltinglass. The 'raheen' is circular, about 40 paces in diameter, interior measurement from bank to bank: the surrounding ditch is 8yds wide (measured), from inner bank to top of outer bank. The inner bank is about 4ft above the level of the inside enclosure: the ditch is 10 to 12ft deep below top of inner bank: the outer bank is 3 to 4ft above the level of the surrounding fields. It is all greatly overgrown with ferns and brambles, but I could see no sign of foundations of buildings, and no stones. There are a few thorn trees in it, not very old. From the rabbit-holes, the walls seem to be made of earth: they are probably piled up with the earth taken out of the ditch. (This is the one I described [before].) (Sheet 27: 5.5cm W, 5.4cm N.)

2nd October 1933

Shelton Abbey, Arklow. There is a bullaun stone in the garden, near one of the concrete bridges over the stream. It is in a rough block of granite. The cavity is almost circular, the diameter varying from 15 to 16½in. and the depth from what was the original sloping surface of the stone is 5in. Mr Myers the agent who has been there 30 years said some old men had told him it had been dug up in the old graveyard on Whitsun Hill (now called 'Whisson's Hill') and brought down to the garden.

I found the name 'Whitson Hill' on an estate map of 1823. The place is in the N of Shelton Abbey townland, where 'Site of Graveyard' is marked [on the map].

Lord Wicklow said that the old road to Arklow used to pass Shelton Abbey House, and cross the river by a ford just below it.

Sir Neville Wilkinson who is living there at present said he thought the house was built about 1648 (actually it was probably a few years later), and that the name was probably taken from the name of the then owner's family place in Cheshire.

The Howard family (Lord Wicklow's) also acquired an estate including Castleruddery, Seskin, and other lands in Imaal, and an estate including Crone, Ballydonnell and Kilmagig, and other lands; I think they were purchased. The original grant of each of these, temp. Charles II, under the Acts of Settlement, is in a deed box in the Estate Office.

FIELD NOTEBOOK 14:
February–September 1934

[There are also several entries in this notebook dating from November and December 1934 and from 1935.]

February 1934

Kilmacoo. The base of the walls of the old church are still remaining, stones covered with grass, and some brambles, about 2ft high. Internal size 13 paces by 5½ paces. Walls about 3ft thick, doorway in S side close to W end. In the grass just outside the doorway lies one of the stones from one jamb of the door, about 3ft long. Also two cut stones: cut to form part of a circular opening, one edge of the circle chamfered. They may have gone together to form the top of a window opening — if so the opening was nearly 3ft wide which seems too big for a window. Were they over the door? They have been put lying together in the grass, like this:

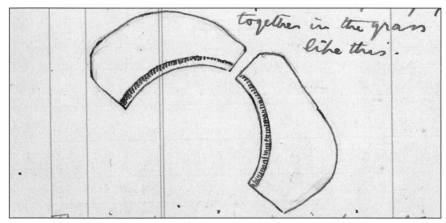

Fig. 86—Sketch of cut stone fragments at Kilmacoo.

There is a piscina 8in. in diameter and 2in. deep cut in a granite stone which is lying inside the church about 6ft from the E wall of the church.

14th April 1934

Visited Ballyknockan in Kiltegan parish (near Rathgorragh) with P.T. Walshe and a Miss R. Walsh, National Teacher of Donard. There is a stone on a lane on the land of Mr Charles Reilly — his uncle and a man named Byrne turned it up about 50 years ago, and found what they called a stone box under it, with bones in it. They put everything back and left the stone there. It is about 4ft x 2ft.

Visited Mr John Metcalfe's house, Old Mill, Ballylion, near Donard. It is the only house which is called 'Old Mill'. The large field S of his house is called 'the Pipers' Field', and on the scrubby land beyond the S fence of this field is the place where Father Kavanagh took the Donard ogham stone from. The 'comrade stone' of the one Father Kavanagh took is there still — a pillar stone about 4ft high — no markings on it (of schist or slate?).

The site of the old mill is shown at the end of the pathway leading E from Metcalfe's house to the river — a raised grassy bank just on the edge of the river.

Mr James Donohoe Police Constable of Donard told me that when Father Kavanagh was in Donard, he got a pot which was found in Kelshamore, near Kelly's cottage, when the man was ploughing on Jones' land. A reddish earthen pot. Father Kavanagh took it away with him. (It is a kitchen mortar. I have it.)

Miss Walsh is trying to collect local names in Glen Imaal. She heard the name 'Levern' only once: it was pronounced 'Leverthen'.

22nd April 1934

At Whaley Abbey (Bahana Whaley) with R.C. Barton. The church is a complete ruin. The base of the W, N and E walls remain, stones and grass, 1 to 2ft high — the S wall is mostly gone, graves being dug there. It is 17 paces long, external, and about 7½ paces wide, external. No sign of the doorway — if it had been in the W wall it should be visible. There is a granite slab lying near the E end of the church, inside. It has a cross incised on it with a circle joining the arms. Dimensions: length 60in., width 19in., diameter of circle 15½in., arms of cross 2½in. wide (double line). From the end of the head of the cross to the lower edge of the circle is 24½in. There are traces of a raised centre.

Fig. 87—Sketch of cross-inscribed slab at Whaley Abbey.

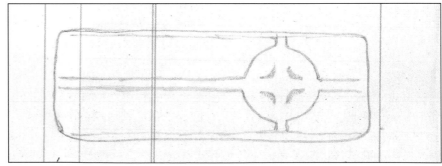

In the field N of the church is a granite boulder with a single bullán in it 13½in. in diameter and 6in. deep.

For the stone with the inscribed cross from this graveyard see [one of my earlier notebooks].

January 1934

Castleruddery Stone Circle. I took some preliminary measurements for a plan.

Internal diameters 97ft and 94ft (97ft opposite entrance, 94ft at right angles to entrance).

Approximate external circumference 121 paces.

One would need a slash hook to clear the internal space, 200ft of strong twine, and 22 pegs.

The owner of the field, Mr Doody, lives at Templeogue. The herd lives in the house near Ballyhubbock Bridge.

28th April 1934

Fassaroe Castle. Part of the S and W walls of a tower now roughly square but probably originally oblong is all that is standing. It is at the back of some houses W of the old road, and is used as part of the outbuildings. The wall is 6ft thick. The interior measurement of the S wall is 25ft and of the W wall 18ft, as far as they remain. There is a large embrasure in the S wall, it looks like a fireplace, but it has a loophole at the back, with a short horizontal aperture halfway up it. It is cracked through, and is built up on the outside. The base of the W wall remains complete outside: it is 30ft wide, battered, and at the S corner stands some 25ft or 30ft high. The castle was vaulted, the vault running E and W at a height of about 18ft. There is no sign of a door. There are four square embrasures in the S wall — not through.

There is a stable built against the S wall outside, and a modern wall built to the N of the W wall.

29th April 1934

Balally, Dundrum. In the wood at the back of Moreen House, Frank Aiken showed me a curious stone building, which a local man named Keane or Keans called 'the Round Churn'. A boy called it 'the Druid's Altar'. It is a pile of granite stones, oblong with rounded corners, 10ft high: sides sloping

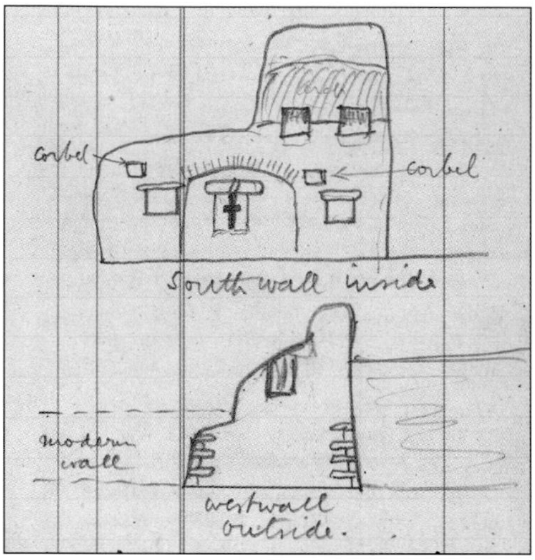

Fig. 88—Sketch of elevations of Fassaroe Castle.

Fig. 89—Fassaroe Castle, 1942 (courtesy of Dúchas The Heritage Service ©).

228

inwards. It is about 22ft across at base, and 18ft across at top. It has an entrance at the N, 3ft wide, open up to the top. Steps go up to the top, they are granite slabs, 10in. wide and 9in. high (approximately). At the top there is a flat platform 6ft 9in. long, and with a triangular wall at the back, sides 3ft long. The entrance seems originally to have been roofed with slabs: the top is ruined, but there are two slabs, now out of place 5ft 9in. long. The slabs were all cut with big wedges, Keane says old wooden wedges, which have been out of use a very long time.

Difficult to say what this building is. I do not think it is a prehistoric monument. The stones are shaped so that the walls and the rounded angles are flat. This could be done by breaking them, as in building drystone fences. The top is ruined: so is the S side.

Moreen grounds were laid out in the late 18th century (Ball ii, p.75).

There is a well with two or three steps down into it just under the E side, and another about 20yds to the NE.

1st May 1934

Crossoona Rath. Stone on S side, with [circular] groove in it. Granite block. Internal diameter 32in. Covered ... by earth etc.

7th May 1934

Kilmagig Graveyard. A very ruined church, length, external, about 12 paces, internal width, about 17ft. The walls are very badly ruined and overgrown with grass and bushes: they are about 2ft high, and 3 or 4ft wide. No sign of any doorway. There are a few squared blocks of granite lying in the graveyard. A modern wall built round graveyard. It seems to be exclusively Catholic. A good view of the Ballymurtagh mines from it.

(O'Curry (*OS Letters,* p.404) says '27ft long, 15ft wide'. This must be internal.)

21st May 1934

Ballyknockan, near Rathdangan. Excavated Bronze Age cist. A local person told Miss Rose Walsh that 50 years ago Mr Charles Reilly's uncle had moved a large stone when making a lane, and found the cist. They put back the stone, and it was not moved since. Mr Charles Reilly and his neighbour Mr Martin Byrne dug it for us. When we moved the capstone, we found it

Fig. 90—Sketch of the 'Round Churn', Moreen House, Balally, Co. Dublin.

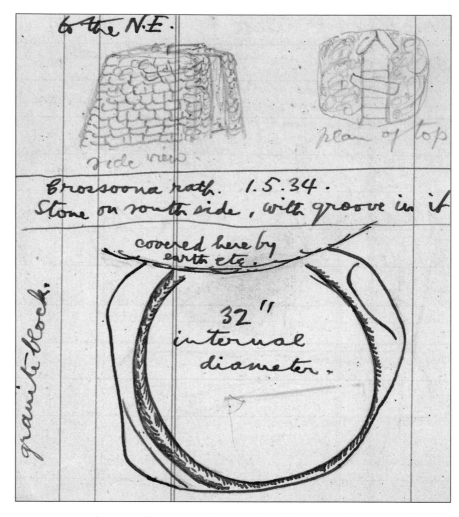

Sketch of carved stone at Crossoona Rath (Boleycarrigeen).

was supported on small stones resting on the sidestones of a rectangular cist 2ft by 13½in. internally. The stones of the cist were undisturbed. We dug the cist to the bottom which was 3ft below the ground level and found that it had been disturbed right to the bottom, the contents evidently dug up and thrown back again. All we found was some small fragments of burnt bones, and three or four minute pieces of a pottery vessel, the walls of which were about 1cm thick. The burial was therefore a cremation burial with a vessel which was probably a food vessel.

Martin Byrne said that there had been a rath in the field W of the lane, just inside the fence. He pointed out where it had been: it appeared to have been about 15yds in diameter, and the cist was on its E edge. The field is

Fig. 91—Ballyknockan cist under excavation.

called 'the Rath Field'. The other fields have English names, 'High Field', 'Cross Lane Field', 'Beech Field', 'Far Fields', 'Bog Meadow Field', 'Furry Field', 'Long Field' — except one, SW of his house, which is called 'the

Lochans' or 'Glochans' (from 'clochán'?). It is divided into two small fields. In the corner of one are two very large blocks of granite: they don't look like cover-stones.

While there, Mr John Connell of Ballinabarny Gap, brought Dr Walshe a stone axe which he had in his house. He said he found it in one of his fields about 15 years ago. 6.9cm long, 4.5cm wide, polished all over. Of a fine-grained igneous stone, diorite?

We then went to Mr Perry's house at Slievereagh Lower. Man of 65 to 70? His father and grandfather had lived at Derrynamuck. The house where McAllister was killed was on their land. There was a field there called 'the old town' where he dug up some quernstones. One was an ordinary kitchen mortar, another a round stone. The other two were shaped pieces of granite, one ... about 10in. high. The other about 9in. high [bell-shaped]. [The latter] has two small holes and an inverted 'T' mark incised on one surface [Fig. 92]. The little holes are I think made by a metal drill or punch.

What is it? There were 'old banks' in the field and the stones were found clearing them away. Are the last two garden ornaments? Mr Perry said he remembered the well in Rostyduff. There was nothing special about it, until fairly recently when Father Hanlon blessed it — it is since then it is called 'St Bridget's Well'.

(But Fr Shearman called it 'St Bridget's Well' in 1862.)

John Connell of Ballinabarny Gap found [a] stone axe about 15 years ago.

Then we went to Mr Lambert's farm at Coolamaddra, and in the field

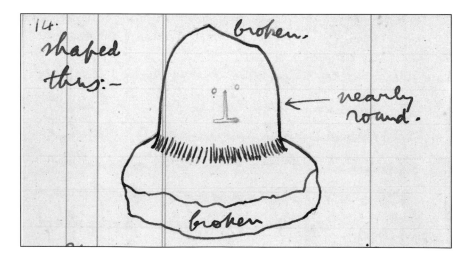

Fig. 92—Sketch of bell-shaped stone.

behind, i.e. NE of his house, we saw a standing stone 5ft 8in. high on one side, 6ft high on the other — 2ft square most of the way up, rounded at the top — granite. Mr Plant had told Miss Walsh that the Briens who owned the farm, dreamed there was gold there, and dug, but only found a pot with bones in it. They replaced it. He said it was in the field that had the big stone in it. The stone marked the place. Mr Lambert said the Briens had died about 20 years ago. He knew the story, but did not know the exact spot.

This was evidently a Bronze Age cist, and probably the stone had some connection with the burial. (Compare Tuckmill.)

Mr Lambert said some men had dreamed three times there was gold in a field in Castleruddery (Mr Bolton's, i.e. Castleruddery Upper?). They went at night to dig, and came to a flag, but it came on to pour rain, and there was thunder and lightning and they ran away.

Mr Donohoe of Donard said he had heard that old Mr Tyrrell of Kilcoagh East had buried a horse, and in digging the hole near a big stone found two pots. He put them back. He is dead but his son John Tyrrell owns the farm. It is where the old church was supposed to be. Old Colonel Heighington was shown where the place was: he is dead now.

10th June 1934

Kilcashel, near Avoca. A very large rath with a double ring wall of stones and earth, which is 14 to 15ft wide, and the ditch between 6ft or in places 8ft deep. The ditch is well preserved on the W side, and a small piece separated from the rest is preserved beside a modern field fence on the E. The church ruin merely consists of grass-covered banks, 3ft high in places; the oblong enclosure is well marked, but difficult to measure; it is about 12½ paces long and 6 [paces] wide, external measurement. It is on the land of James Brady of Kilcashel, an elderly farmer, who showed it to us (65 to 70 years of age?). He said neither he nor his father ever remembered anyone being buried there. His great-grandfather had the same farm. There are two modern walls, built to preserve the enclosure, on the S and E. He said that the part at the SE just outside the modern wall was called 'the School'. Asked where he heard it was a school, he said from the old people. There are stones lying about here and there, some of which he said were old headstones. We saw one stone which was a piece of cut stone from an arch or window or door, 12in. deep … (*OS Letters* p.404, no further particulars).

18th June 1934

Rostygah. Mr Dillon of Arklow whose mother lived in Rostygah, and died recently aged over 80, came out and pointed out 'Bryan's Field'. It is a large field, about 30 acres, at the W corner of the townland, called 'Bryan's Meadow' or 'Frederick's Meadow'. There is a well near the bush in the middle of the field, and close by a heap of stones. Is this the foundation of a house? No foundations or old walls in the field. Only the name is remembered, nothing about the Bryans, except that 'three families used to be buried in Killahurler, Ryans, Bryans and Dobsons'. The Dobsons came from the North 'sheer', i.e. shire, from Ballinacor, near Kilbride (see… *Memorials of the Dead* for Bryans). Bergins owned Rostygah, including Bryan's Meadow: they are gone 50 years.

We saw Kilcarra Graveyard. A fairly new wall round it. It was probably larger than now, as the foundations of the church are near the W wall. Church about 40ft (13 paces) N and S, and 24ft (8 paces) E and W. I could see no carved stones. A lot of white quartz stones about which Dillon called 'bracket stones' (obviously from 'breac', 'speckled', as the quartz is full of holes).

A place in Ballinasilloge, on the mountains above the houses is called 'the Móintyeen' — there are springs in it, a road runs through it.

Above Ballykillageer on the mountain the hill is called 'Barnyavore' ('bearna mhór'). There is a passway through it, which goes up from the old road, W of Ballycoog Chapel. Raheenleagh pronounced 'Ráwhin-lyugh' or '-lyih'. I suppose 'Ráitín liath'. Ballinaheese pronounced 'Ballinaheeze'. Knocknamohill pronounced 'Knocknamóghill'. Mongan pronounced 'Muñgawn'.

The old crossroads in Arklow was at a place called 'Martin's Lane'; S of the present crossroads, where the Coolgreany road goes out. The old road was closed when the railway was built.

18th June 1934

Walked through Raherd. There is no rath in it. The owner, a young farmer not many years there, said he knew of no 'raheen' in it, but that he had sometimes thought there was the trace of one in the big field, a bit S of the groves up at the top of the field. I looked at the place, but could not say I saw the trace of a rath, though there is the track of a piece of an old ditch, filled with rushes.

27th June 1934

Spoke to Mr Luke McDonnell, rate collector, about the cairn on Pinnacle. He said that he had not heard any name for it locally, but that he thought it was called 'Rathcornan'. He lives in and is a native of Coolinarrig Upper. I think he must have heard the name from old people, as if he got it off the map, why should he change 'Rathcoran' to 'Rathcornan'? 'Rathcornan' would also explain the corrupt form 'Rathcormac' (given to me by Mr Matt Byrne ex. National Teacher) better than 'Rathcoran'.

'Rathcornan' probably 'ráth carnáin', 'rath of the little cairn'.

Mr MacDonnell says there is a large flat stone with a round chiselled hole in it, in a field SE of a rath which is on the SW side of the byroad from Tuckmill to Boley: in Coolinarrig Upper. Query, a millstone?

June 1934

Mr Henry Sandys of Dargle Hill, Cookstown, lent me an old rental of the Powerscourt Estate containing the names of the tenants, the townland in which each holding was situated, and the rent, written by some newly appointed agent or subagent, covering the years 1755, 1756 and 1757. Some pages at the beginning are torn out. The first page remaining deals with 'Lackendara'. I have entered all the townland names from this rental in my placename list; the name is shown with the letter 'r' prefixed.

Robert Walker is given as one of the tenants of Coolakay: it was presumably from one of this family that 'Walker's Rock' was named.

One of the townlands given is 'Churchfield', tenant William Bullen, yearly rent £5. This comes next after Ballyman, and next before Cookstown. I do not know where it is, but it may be the land round the old church in Ballyman.

The rental also includes Montagh, William Wilson, tenant, £30 yearly rent. Is this Mount Usher? Castlemacadam, Amadeus Take, tenant, yearly rent £35 and £1: 10 duties. Three tenants in Wicklow — and Ballycullen, Laurence Tool, tenant, yearly rent £50.

11th July 1934

Extract from a letter from Dr Walshe:

'Miss R. Walsh, Donard, secured another stone axe — a fine specimen with a small chip gone at one end of the edge. It was found in Glen

Imaal. She had not the details so I asked her to get me these.'

7in. long, 3½in. [wide] at cutting edge
1¼in. [wide] at haft, 1½in. thick

Acquired by National Museum — 21st July 1934, piece of pottery from Rathdown. 'Piece of a carinated vessel.'

Donation by Abraham Cohen ... Ormond Quay. No information available (probably Bronze Age). 'Found with many other objects formerly belonging to the collection of Dr W. Frazer.'

10th September 1934
Mr Frank Healy, rate collector, handed me a flat bronze axe after Blessington Court. It is 21.1cm long, 7.2cm across cutting edge, and 0.9cm thick.

The edge is ground flat to a depth of about 1cm on each side. It has straight lines down each face, which look more as if they were on the face of the mould than as if they were incised: they may be intended for decoration.

It was found by his brother, Mr Patrick Healy at Ballynasculloge (probably Lower) near Blessington, in June or July 1934, when he was digging turf on a cut-away bog. He did not find it in the turf while he was cutting it, but afterwards when he was 'footing' it, i.e. leaving it set up to dry. It is a very nicely preserved specimen.

8th September 1934
Miss R. Walshe's stone axe. Killamoat Upper. The stone was found in an out-office attached to the house of Mr John Cullen, of Killamoat Upper, by John Cullen and Simon Byrne of Killamoat when they were about to re-roof one of the out-offices. It is now a barn, but was used by the present Mrs Cullen's grandfather as a calf-house. The axe was found lying in a small box-shaped hole, 8in. x 8in., in the wall; there were several other similar holes in the wall.

Mr Henry Sandys also gave me the field names in Tinnapark Demesne townland [see Fig. 95]:

a   'the Grove Field'

Fig. 93—Flat axe from Ballynasculloge.

b   'the Crow Field'
c   'Synnott's Field', with the ruins of Synnott's house; part of the 'Whin Field'
e   'the field between the walls'
f   'the Oak Field'
g   'the Pond Fields'

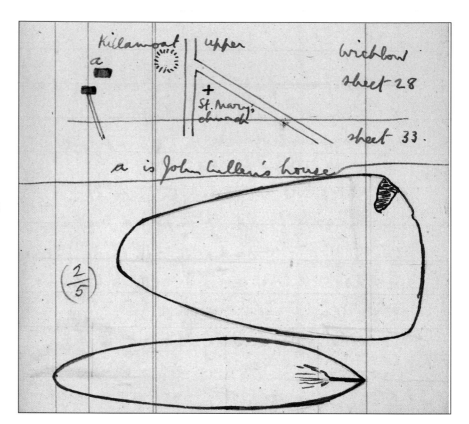

Fig. 94—Stone axe from Killamoat Upper.

On the SE boundary behind the house there is a well with some old yew trees round it.

When Mr Sandys was in the house, there was a bullán stone of granite lying near the house. It was found in the Crow Field (*b*), and was put under a Spanish chestnut tree, in front of the house, to the right of the hall door. The cavity was about 3in. deep and 6in. in diameter, according to Mr Sandys' recollection.

A field behind the house in Cooladoyle was called 'Bullockbawn'. The Killeen Field is in Holywell (or Killickabawn?) between the old laneway and the avenue to Holywell House, just beside the road.

22nd July 1935

Field names in Whiteleas, Co. Kildare. 'Big Tonelegee' and 'Little Tonelegee' — the latter is the lawn at the back of Whiteleas House, the former is near it ([informant] Michael Ó Ceallaigh).

238

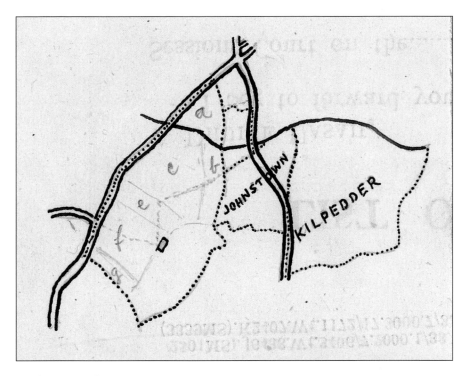

Fig. 95—Map showing location of field names in Tinnapark Demesne.

26th September 1934

Snugborough, Glen Imaal, near the boundary of Knockandarragh. There is a well-preserved rath here on the point of a hill, which has been shaped to make the rath. I had no rule or measure, but paced and guessed distances and heights.

Internal diameter 32 to 33 paces. Ditch on N side for 48 paces — about ⅓ of the circumference here. This ditch may have been faced with stone at its N side. The bank rises very steeply out of it, and is about 20ft high above the bottom of the ditch.

The ditch is 5ft deep below the level of the surface on the N. The bank on the N side for about ¼ of the circumference is much higher than the rest, and is about 25ft wide. Elsewhere the rath is protected by the natural steep slope of the hill.

From the inside the bank is here 9ft high: elsewhere about 3ft. The ground inside the rath is level, and about 5ft above the outside surface on the N. The bank (except on the N side) is about 10–12ft wide. The ditch on the N is 5 or 6 paces wide.

4th November 1934

Walked from the top of Ballinaslaughter Hill to the cairn, which is on the boundary between Ballinahinch Upper and Ballinahinch Middle. It is a very small cairn, just a pile of a few stones. I could not see any sign of the 'ruined cahir' on the top of the hill of which O'Curry speaks (*OS Letters*, fol. 204).

I saw a mound in the low land of Ballinahinch Upper, W of Kilday, which looked from a distance like a burial tumulus. It may be one of the 'three moats in Ballinahinch' which O'Curry mentions (fol. 204).

11th November 1934

Looked at this mound: it is only a natural hillock, an outcrop of the rock, with a flat grassy top. There is another similar hillock near it. James Pharr of Ballinahinch told me he knew no moat in the townland: he is 17 years there. The ruined house S of his is Fleming's: the house S of it, nearer the

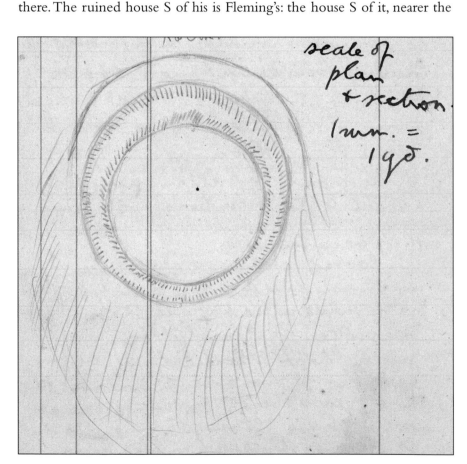

Fig. 96—Sketch-plan of rath at Snugborough.

road is Joe Fisher's. Two of Fisher's fields have Irish names: 'the Skeogh Field', from a big skeogh bush that stood in the middle of it, and 'the Meelyeen', a small field — both these are towards Knockfadda. (If 'maoilín' means 'the little bare place', the reason for giving it the name must be of a long-past date, there does not seem now to be any reason to call it bare in contrast with the barren-looking ground all around.) The other fields are called 'Collin's Field', 'Birch's Field', 'the Heathy Field', 'Taffy's Meadow', 'the field by the wall', etc. It seemed to me there was a piece of an old road leading S from Fisher's house, and there certainly was a lane from Farr's to Fleming's ruins. Perhaps this was the old road here.

Tomdarragh. The rath here (which I always thought was in Annagolan) consists of a big ditch surrounding the top of a low flat hill. A little more than half of the double ditch remains, round the E side. On the W side it has been converted into a big field fence of stones and earth, single wall. Measuring from about NE to SW the internal diameter, wall to inner bank, is 124 paces. The inner bank is very low, nowhere more than 1ft high. The outer bank, which was probably made of the earth from the ditch, has now been made into a field fence, earth and stones, and faced with drystone walling. From the top of the inner bank to the inner face of this outer wall is from about 15ft to about 18 or 20ft. The outer wall is mostly about 6ft thick, and 4 or 5ft high above the bottom of the ditch. The field level outside is of course lower than the level of the rath inside, as the hill slopes down. The bottom of the ditch is mostly 7 or 8ft below the top of the inner bank. In the centre of the rath are some loose stones, and slight lumps in the grass, which are stony: these are perhaps remains of foundations of buildings.

The rath is almost 1 mile S of the footstick over the river between Roundwood and Knockadreet. The ground on the W side of the river before it was drained, and cleared of stones, must have been very marshy: it is still very wet in places. It slopes fairly steeply up on the E side, but it is rather wet there also.

This looks like a fortification to protect a crossing, but there is no crossing there now.

Opposite, in Boleynass, there is a small rath 32 paces in diameter, bank almost defaced. Query — 'the buaile'?

14th November 1934

On Monday, before Blessington Court, Mr James McKenzie brought me in some pieces of a pot which were found in a sand-pit at Dillonsdown. They were pieces of a food vessel. I went and met him there this afternoon. The sand-pit is in a hill of sand and gravel, the end of a spur; and some day last week, when they had worked back to the top of the spur, some big stones were found; when they let them fall down, they found bones among them, and the pieces of the pot. One of the men said the pot was broken by a stone that fell on it. It was quite freshly broken. As far as I could make out from the description there was a small cairn on the top of the hill, with a cist in it. There were three big stones together just under the grass — when

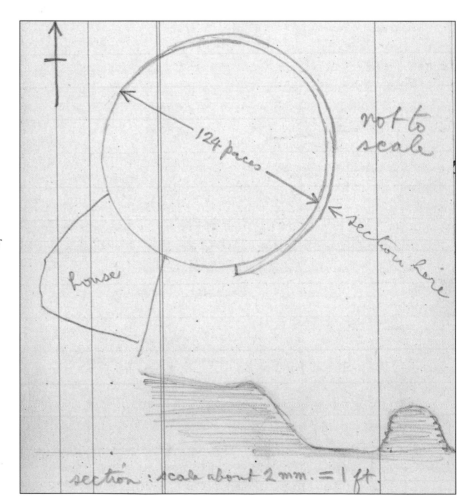

Fig. 97—Sketch-plan of rath at Tomdarragh.

they were taken away, there were smaller stones, boulders not flags, under them, making a passage 3ft wide and 5 or 6ft long. One of the men said the bones and the pot were at the side of these stones, not in the 'passage'. He said 'there were ten horseloads of small stones there'. Everything had been thrown down into the pit, but they had kept the pieces of pot and some of the bones. They said there was no skull, and no long bones. I have the atlas vertebra, five other thoracic vertebrae, two scapulas, part of a humerus, several pieces of rib, a piece of collar bone, and two pieces of skull. Mr McKenzie showed me one of the top stones in the pit, it was 4ft 3in. long, 16in. wide and 16in. deep, also one of the blocks which he said it rested on — a small boulder 2ft high. He said the passage was open at both ends.

The vessel is decorated with herringbone ornament. It has a moulding at the shoulder. It can be completely reconstructed.

18th November 1934

At Lackan [see Fig. 98].

No. 1: the rath near the W boundary of Lackan townland (the most northerly one of the three in Lackan) is completely defaced. What seems to be a small bit of its bank remains on the S side, and it went nearly to the house. Single ditch and inner bank? Diameter 50yds?

No. 2: Ballinahown about 35 paces internal diameter. Ruined bank 3ft high at SW, ditch outside it. No outer bank, internal surface of rath 6ft above field and 12ft above stream — on a natural hillock? The bank and outer circumference is nearly all washed away by the stream. It is of clay — not sand or gravel.

No. 3: in Lackan, bank 6ft high from outside, where ditch is filled up, 8 or 9ft thick. Internal surface higher than field (4 or 5ft?), 55 paces diameter. There was a ditch and a low bank outside it.

No. 4: in Lackan, 35 paces diameter. Flattened bank 8 or 9ft wide at base — now set in a square, wet ditches round it. Cannot say if it ever had a ditch — no trace now. Was in a marsh.

No. 5: Ballyknockan 1, 22 or 23 paces diameter, bank 2ft above inside, 6–7ft above ditch. Bank and ditch 15ft or so wide. Surface inside 4ft above wet field.

No. 6: Ballyknockan 2, 12 paces across, 2 or 3ft high. Thorn bushes growing on it. If this is a rath at all it is more like a tumulus, looks as if it was dug in middle. Much ruined. It is said to be a 'rá'.

Of the above six raths, No. 2 (Ballinahown), Nos 3 and 4 (Lackan) and No. 5 (Ballyknockan) are of the same type — raised central surface and bank.

I did not examine the one in Ballynastockan.

2nd December 1934

Kilbeg. The rath between St Boodin's Well and Templeboodin Graveyard. It is almost levelled. A bit of inner fence at N and a bit at S, about 70–75yds (paces) inner diameter, may have been a ditch round it. Surface same level as fields round.

A man named Molloy who lives up on the road said this field was not the 'raw'. It was called 'the Round Croft' and an old man named Pat Lawlor had told him that all the rent of the country used to be paid in that field long ago. The 'raw', called 'Katty's Raw', is in the corner of the field just SW of this. This is interesting, because 'Katty's Raw' is only a bit of a straight field fence at the corner of the field. Whereas the Round Croft is I think certainly the remains of a rath. It shows that a mere residential or

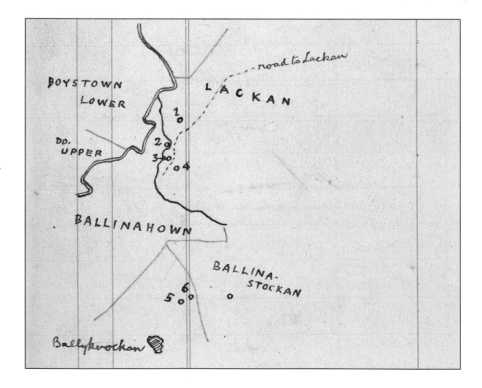

Fig. 98—Sketch-map of raths in Lackan and Ballyknockan.

fortress-type rath has no sacred association. Whereas you must not cut bushes on a true 'raw'. This may indicate that the places locally known to be 'raws' are always old burial places.

Near Molloy's house is another 'raw' with a lot of thorn bushes on it. No features, just a bit of a bank with a fence running across the top of it.

Remains of a cairn on top of hill in Carrig [24 paces x 20 paces in diameter]. ... Eight or nine kerbstones and an uneven patch of stony grass with a few blocks of stone lying in it.

The cairn is on the boundary of Carrig and Sroughan, at the angle, where the boundary touches the old road at the top of the hill (914ft).

The measurements show that it was of about 34yds diameter: the remaining stones show about ⅛ of the circumference of the circle, the rest is gone; but the grassy rough area is where the cairn stood, and it must be still full of stones, or it would have been tilled. All the nine stones are in the line of the circumference, i.e. of the kerb.

The rath shown on the map beside the road in Blackrock near Blessington is a small one, about 23 paces internal diameter, bank 2 to 3ft high — same level as field. On the SW side is a field fence which makes an outer bank to the rath, and a ditch between — but I don't think there was originally a second bank and ditch round the rath. Inside it are some grass-covered mounds or banks which look like foundations of a house or houses — perhaps a fairly modern cottage.

The Dillonsdown vessel reconstructed:

[Measurements of the Dillonsdown vessel:]

4½–4¾in. high
about 6in. diameter at mouth
about 6½in. diameter at shoulder
about 2¾in. diameter at base
moulding at shoulder ½in. wide, 2½in. from base, 1½in. from rim.

Wicklow People, 15th December 1934:

'Bronze Axe
The finder of the bronze axe at Knockanooker some time ago was

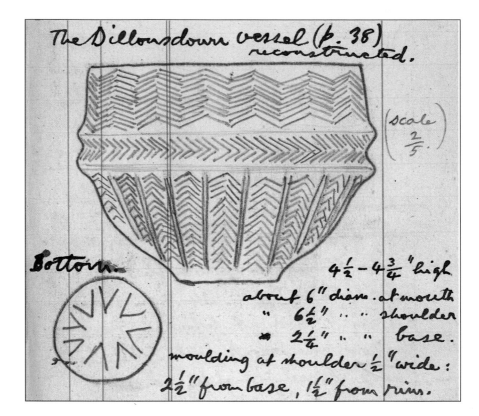

Fig. 99—Food vessel from Dillonsdown.

incorrectly reported as being Mr Wm. Kelly. The actual owner of the axe is Mr Phil Kelly. It has been forwarded to the National Museum, together with a stone spining [*sic*] wheel found by Michael Kavanagh at Shamrock and an artefact found at Kilamoake on Mr Byrne's farm.'

P. O'Toole sent up a grey flint flake labelled 'Rathshanmore' to the Museum. Mahr calls it a 'flint flake with a lateral "encoche"', that is a hollow at the side showing secondary flaking.

The bronze axe (Knockanooker) is a fine one of the palstave type, 14.8cm long, 6½cm broad at blade. The Y-shaped ornament below the stop-ridge is very slightly raised.

23rd December 1934

Monastery. Near Rannock House there is a mound of earth with thorn trees growing on it. It is just above the Enniskerry road and can be seen against the skyline from the lower road from Bray to Enniskerry. It looks

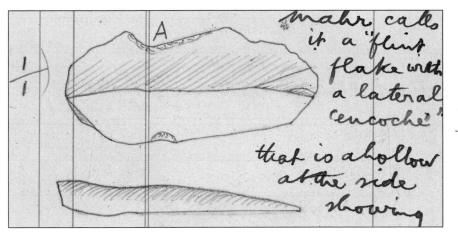

Fig. 100—Flint flake from Rathshanmore.

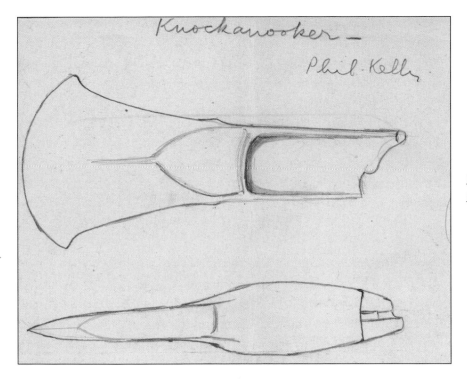

Fig. 101—Palstave from Knockanooker.

like a sepulchral mound. It is on the top of a long ridge running E and W. The circumference at the base is 76 paces — the ground on the W, S and E is flattened, as though the earth had been dug away there, and piled up on the mound. It is 11ft high on the W, 14ft [high] on the S, and 12ft [high] on the E: on the N the slope is continuous with the slope of the hill. The

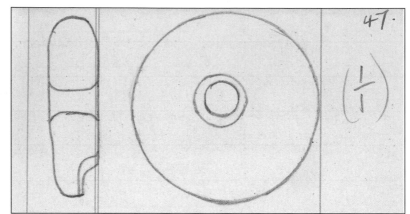

Fig. 102—Spindle whorl from Knocknashamroge.

top is flat, and 8 paces in diameter. On the 1-inch map it is about 1cm very slightly E of S of Berryfield House.

There is a limekiln just below the mound on the NW side. It is built of big stones and slabs of granite, which are cut by the old type wedges. Were they cleared off the slopes?

Perhaps the name 'Rannock' is derived from this mound. It is in the fields belonging to Rannock House. This must be the 'fairy moate' O'Curry refers to ([*OS Letters*] fol. 20) but his measurements are much too large. I do not think there is any trace of 'a mound and trench' surrounding it.

7th January 1935

Kilbride near Arklow. The old church ruin is on a height, whether wholly natural or not I can't tell: it is a low flat mound 6 or 8ft above the field level around it. The W wall is standing, about 13 or 14ft high, with a small window about 8ft up — built up on the outside, by having a flat stone, or perhaps more than one, set into it in mortar. The ope would be 12in. high — and about 3in. wide. It is splayed towards the inside, but not evenly. The splay does not look like original work. The foundations of the S wall and most of the E wall remain. Internal measurements: 9 paces long by about 5 [paces] wide. Walls about 2½ft thick. The N wall is quite gone above ground. I saw no carved stones. There is a wide view from the site over Arklow and the harbour.

Fig. 103—Mound at Monastery (Dúchas The Heritage Service ©).

9th January 1935

Visited Kilkea Castle with Con Curran and Father Moriarty. The prehistoric objects are in a case in the hall — gold torque from Tipper (*PRIA* iii, p.98?), flat bronze axe (*JKAS* vi, p.106), socketed dagger axes etc., food vessel from Gurteen (*ibid.* v, p.119) and urn from Mullachreelan (*ibid.* ii, p.325).

There is a diamond-shaped socketed spearhead in the case, not labelled: is this Aylmer's one from Glen Imaal?

Leask's note 10th December 1935 [note referenced]:

' … given me by a one time resident of Castlekevin. Mound in bog, query a crannog, the supposed site of Cromwell's artillery for the bombardment of Castlekevin. Just E of Annamoe and close to the W angle of the plantation N of the Tomriland–Annamoe Road. … In the 17th century the 6-inch cannon had an extreme range of about 1300yds, and the 7-inch, 1500yds. A 6-inch cannon took fifteen horses to pull it, a mighty load for the bog.'

(This site is in Tomriland, near the W boundary.)

27th January 1935

Killegar, examined four raths.

No. 1: 27 paces diameter, single bank of earth and stones. Almost completely ruined. Centre level with ground outside.

No. 2: about 20 paces diameter, overgrown and almost levelled. Single bank. Centre a little below level of ground outside. The Church Well, only a pool in the field, used by cattle. Evidently a spring about 10ft in diameter. Some small granite boulders at its edges.

No. 3: 18 paces diameter. Single bank, much ruined. Centre a little lower than field outside. A man said it was called 'the raheen': it was never ploughed. 'My mother told me one of the chaps found a little thing made of rubber (!) in it and it was alive, she made him put it back' (a brown lizard?).

No. 4: a piece of a field, which has been left untilled, and is a foot or so above the level of the field. The side which is 20 paces long (N side) might have been a bit of a bank of a rath, but I would not say so for certain. The rest is flat. There are some stones on it.

3rd March 1935

Looked for old river crossings between Powerscourt and Charleville. The piece of a track at the N end of Charleville, leading from the gate lodge to an iron bridge over the river, is old, I should say a piece of an 18th-century road. Tinnehinch Bridge looks early 19th-century. On the Powerscourt side of the river there is now no trace whatever of an old road at the iron bridge. Further S where the back avenue to Charleville leads down to the river, there could have been a ford — but the Powerscourt bank of the river has been built up for the road through the demesne. There is however a track leading up from the river to 'the Churches', a mere footpath up the hill. There is a road then completely overgrown, leading from 'the Churches' into the back avenue that goes to Annacrivey School. Turning to the right at the avenue, one comes up to Powerscourt House. This may all be the track of an old road, from Kilmalin to Churchtown and thence to Kilmacanoge. If so perhaps the crossing place of the river is 'Aghnegarr' of the Civil Survey, 'Áth na gcarr'.

The graveyard called 'the Churches' or 'Churchtown' is in a hopelessly overgrown condition full of trees, brambles and masses of ivy. There are a number of what look like early 19th-century headstones in it. I saw one more modern cross with 'IHS' on it. There is the foundation of an oblong building, seems to be orientated NE and SW (I had no compass), about 21ft long, 14ft wide, and walls about 2ft thick — to the N on the W side is another bit of very ruined wall foundation.

O'Curry was able to see a good deal more in 1838 (*OS Letters*, p.18).

I think my points of the compass must be wrong. The little building I could trace must be what he calls 'the chapel'.

4th March 1935

Johnstown South in Kilbride parish. A young man named Bury of Arklow, a carpenter, told me that when working some years ago, about 1914, at Johnstown House he met an old plasterer named Byrne from Wicklow, then aged about 60. Byrne said that the rath in Johnstown South, near the road was an old graveyard — that he had found human skulls in some sand near Johnstown House, and had asked about them and been told that there had been a doctor living in Johnstown House who had taken bodies out of the old rath where they had been buried.

Bury also said there are chalices in Castlemacadam Church which were made out of silver from the Cronebane lead mines.

13th March 1935

Knockaulin, Co. Kildare. The ditch round the hill is mostly about 11 or 12ft deep, from the top of the outer bank. The earth from the ditch was thrown up on the outer bank — there does not seem to be any inner bank. The ditch is 25 to 30ft wide, from top of inner to top of outer bank. [Width of ditch at top 25–30ft, depth 11–12ft or 15–16ft in places.]

It is an imposing earthwork. At the highest part the outer bank must be 15 or 16ft above the ditch. The ditch I should say is much silted up. The rock is immediately below the grass on the top, and elsewhere on the hill. There is a hollow quarried at the top — on the inside edge of a small semicircular bank, and two large boulders, 3ft high beside the hollow.

15th April 1935

Letter dated 9th April 1935 from D.M. Doyle about a find by a Mr O'Neill at Kilpipe (letter filed).

Visited Mr P. O'Neill. His house is in Killacloran about ¼ mile from Annacurragh crossroads, on the S side of the road leading from Annacurragh crossroads to Killacloran and Clone, just near the boundary of Kilpipe. The find was in a field of his which used to be the Annacurragh football ground; it is 300yds S of Annacurragh crossroads, and about 100yds W of the road. He found a number of stone slabs, 3ft or so long, set on end, leaning against one another and making a line or wall about 10ft long, curving round at the end. He said it was as if they were lining one side of a hole as if those at the other side had been taken away. They were packed at the back with smaller stones. Outside them was a stone with a bowl-shaped hollow in it, broken. It looked artificial. He was removing a fence from the field, and took out the stones. There was no roofing. I could not make out what they were, but I think the structure had been largely mined before he discovered it.

Mr O'Neill said that 30 or 40 years ago he found an urn. The site was in Kilpipe townland, near a raheen, a good way S of the old church. He and a workman were ploughing, and the plough struck a stone in the ground. It was a flat flag 5ft long, they raised it with a crowbar, and under it was a square made of four flags on end, one at each end and one at each side. From the size he showed me it might have been 2ft square, or 2ft x 2½ft. Nothing inside but 'a little urn; it was broke'. It was 'shaped like a bowl', and 'corded all round' with a pattern that was 'like thick corduroy, the old kind of corduroy'. He showed me a biscuit tin about 9in. across and 5 or 6in. deep, and said 'it was like that only bowl-shaped', that is, it curved in towards the bottom. There were no bones in it, 'only fine red ashes like a cremation'. The urn was broken in two pieces. He gave it to some local person, he can't remember who, and he didn't know what happened to it. This was evidently a food vessel. The flag was about 5 perches outside the raheen, towards the S or SE.

Mr O'Neill is elderly, about 65? Seems a fairly small farmer, but of some culture. He said he used to be interested in such things.

28th April 1935

With Ó Ríordáin and Leask. Examined Boleycarrigeen stone circle and the neighbouring mounds. Ó Ríordáin believes the space within the circle is of a lower level because it was dug out to make a bank, of which there are traces immediately outside and touching the standing stones. He thinks there was a fosse outside this bank. The circle is therefore quite possibly undisturbed: there might be burials in it. The small mounds might be the remains of cairns: or of hut circles, but this is not so likely.

Crossoona he believes to be of early date, a settlement site — they saw at least three house sites in it, old. Part of it may have been a graveyard. At any rate it is certainly older than Anglo-Norman. The stone with the circle may be only a stone which people at some period tried to make a millstone out of, but found unsuitable. I do not myself think this is a very convincing explanation of the groove.

Rathmoon tumulus Ó Ríordáin thinks is Bronze Age in date — Leask suggested that the banking up, which the bushes round the edge seem to indicate, may be recent, and have caused the terrace-like appearance.

30th April 1935

Luggala. Drove John MacNeill to see the district. A path leads up from the back of Luggala Lodge to the gamekeeper's house W of Boleyhorrigan Bridge. It is clearly a path made in modern times, the stones being placed in and pounded down to make a track, and the road being graded to take the curves easily. It is very steep, and does not follow an old path — that is, no sign of an old path is visible, and the course of the track is not the kind of course an old natural pathway would have followed. The roadway from the W, after crossing Boleyhorrigan Bridge, went by a path over the mountain, and followed the Stoney Pass River. A young man working at Luggala told me that this path where it goes up the mountain on the W slope, is called 'the Murderin' Steps', or 'the Robber's Path'. He also gave me the name 'Bolaherrim' ('Bólaherrim') for the valley W of the lodge — also 'the Copse', just under Archer's Meadow, near Lough Dan: and 'the Scalls' ('Scál'), on the N side of the Inchavore River, where the green road ends.

MacNeill's identifications of Gravale and Djouce [Douce Mountain]

Fig. 104—Boleycarrigeen stone circle, 1935. The photograph shows Liam Price and Seán Ó Ríordáin, and was presumably taken by Harold Leask (courtesy of Dúchas The Heritage Service ©).

indicate remarkably well the two mountain masses that are landmarks for the old track from Kilbride.

From Charles Dickson — Simon Flood, of Ballydonnell, the second house down from Ballynultagh, a man with good local knowledge and pronunciation.

12th May 1935

Walked up from Boleyhorrigan Bridge to the gap N of White Hill, then along the ridge of White Hill, up Djouce [Douce Mountain], and to the outcrop of rock ¼ mile W of the top. All the rocks on Djouce are definitely outcrops, there are no traces whatever of any cairn there. It is safe to say there never was a cairn there. Came down White Hill to the head of the Stoney Pass River, thence down the Murderin' Steps to the road. The ruin just NE of Boleyhorrigan Bridge is that of a substantial farmhouse, with enclosed fields, and big dykes of stone and drains separating the bog from the enclosed land. There is another ruin further up the stream, no enclosed land near it. There is a well-marked track leading down from the flat gap between Djouce and White Hill, going in the direction of Calary and the Red Lane. The track down the Stoney Pass River, and 'the Murderin' Steps', are the same track. Its general direction is towards Wicklow.

On the road I met a man named Fanning, of Ashtown, a sheep farmer. He gave me some names. The hill SE of Boleyhorrigan Bridge and SW of White Hill (the next rise in the ridge SW of White Hill) is called 'Barr'. He also gave me the name 'the Murderin' Steps' for the track. The house near the bridge he called 'Counsel's (or Council's) old walls'. The other ruin further up he said was a sheep pen. The stream itself he called 'the Piper's Brook'. He pointed up towards the Sallygap (we were about a mile W of the bridge) and said 'just there (in front of us) is Tràmònyuwìggin', 'Tramon (or Tromon) iú wigin'. (This is the name 'Tramonawigna' given to me by Thompson.)

He pointed to the glen of the Annamoe River between us and the Fancy Mountain and said it was called 'Bólyaherim' (same name as was given to me on 30th April, 'Bolaherrim'). 'Glannagannail' he said was the top of Fancy Mountain ('Glanaganáil', second syllable unaccented). 'Foolya' is the next hill S of it. He also said when I asked him about the old track that went by the Murderin' Steps, that he thought the old road divided somewhere up on the hill (that is, on White Hill) and one branch went more N than the other. He said this without my leading him at all.

He also said something like 'Bore a horrigan', rather than Boleyhorrigan. (This was also more like Peter Doyle's pronunciation which was something like 'Borra–horrigan'.)

4th June 1935

T. Fleming of Shillelagh says there is a stone in Carnew at Geraghty's Corner, set in the wall on the street, a long slab with marks on it.

9th June 1935

Lodarrig is a wide almost level green space at about the 1250ft contour between Cullentragh Park and Ballinafunshoge. It is covered with good short grass, and is not boggy, though the rest of the ground at the top of the cliffs is boggy. There is no trace of an old track now existing anywhere on the N side of the glen, but it is probable that an old track came up through Cullentragh Park and Ballinafunshoge across Lodarrig. An old man told me there was an old road along the top of the glen on the N side: it did not come down and join the road through Camenabologue, but came to an end. The raheen is just below the road near the Cullentragh Park–Ballinafunshoge boundary. It is overgrown with whitethorn bushes. This old man called the cliff in Baravore overlooking Ballinaskea 'Billduck' or 'Bellduck'. I do not know what this means — ('biolduc'). He did not know the name 'Borenacrow'. I think he must have been James Nolan, who is not a native of Glenmalure. Probably he meant 'Bendoo'.

2nd July 1935

Information from D.M. Doyle (see his letter of 11th June 1935, filed). At Ballymacsimon, about 50 years ago, on land then in occupation of John Farrell, now Mr John Doyle's, two men (names, James Heffernan and — Laverty) were knocking down a ditch, and found a cist made of flagstones (described as 'a sort of stone box'). There was an urn in it, said to be turned mouth downward on a flag; it contained bones. The urn was broken up and thrown away. (Seems to be a Late Bronze Age burial.)

On the same John Doyle's land there is a mote with a ditch round it, called 'Lugglŏs' ('Lug glas').

The site where the cist was said to have been found is about ³⁄₁₆ of a mile S of the 'n' of 'Ballymacsimon' on the 1-inch OS map (1911/1913 ed.).

Several fields at the N end of Ballymacsimon, between Ballylusk and the rest of Ballymacsimon have a separate name, 'Cróokery ónnory'. All the above on authority of D.M. Doyle.

September 1935

Three field names in Whiteleas, Co. Kildare: 'Big Tonelegee', 'Little Tonelegee', 'the Bracket Stones'. Authority Peter Freeman, herd, of Broadleas. *per* Michael Kelly, of Hollywood, District Court Clerk.

20th October 1935

Courtfoyle. The rath on the E side of the townland is a ring of earth and stones, on the hill, almost defaced, about 45yds diameter (estimated).

The side of the square fort is about 50 paces. There are said to have been battles on the hill to the S of it.

7th September 1935

Glenmalure. Walked from Kemmis' back lodge near Strand Bridge, up a grass road in Fananierin to the fields in the upper valley of the stream. They are called 'the Lime Fields'. Some are now covered by bracken but are fair grazing: others have gone back into mountain, but show wide cultivation ridges under the heather and ferns. There are two or three house ruins in Fananierin, and at least one in Ballinacor. Could see no sign of chimneys or fireplaces in the ruins. The walls are built of stone with mud or clay for mortar. There was a big stretch of fertile land here at one time: 18th century? Part of it is good natural grazing, probably very old inhabited country.

8th September 1935

Walked from Carriglinneen down to Kirikee. The stone cairn up at the top of Carriglinneen is quite a small one — not prehistoric. This was not the true cairn: the cairn is at the top of the ridge, quite obvious beside the old track. It is a very small one, a sort of guide mark? An old track leads down by the houses in Carriglinneen (E side) which I believe is Russacoose, but I could not get the name. Another old track comes down in Kirikee, coming out eventually at the National School. It is called 'Glendurroch'. Just below where 'Kirikee' is printed on the 1-inch OS map is a house which belonged to Grants. It is in Kirikee but is called 'Coolahory' or 'Cóolahoóry'. The old people pronounce Fananierin 'Fananerrun'.

FIELD NOTEBOOK 15:
February–December 1936

[There are some notes in a pocket at the front of this notebook which are not reproduced here.]

17th February 1936

Arklow Castle. The round tower is at the N angle of the castle. The old wall which is beside the courthouse runs towards the SE by S. The ground level inside the enclosure of the wall must be nearly 20ft above the ground level round the courthouse. Loopholes which can be seen from the courthouse grounds on the outside of the wall are below the level of the ground on the inside: the wall on the inside is about 9ft above ground level. Outside the SW by W wall the ground slopes down towards the Coomie in a very level and regular slope. The old barracks, now pulled down, stood a few feet inside this wall. The enclosure in which the barracks stood is now held on lease from the Board of Works by Mr James Kavanagh who has built a couple of houses in it. It is very irregularly shaped. But this SW by W wall looks old, on the outside, so does the SE by S wall, as well as the continuation of the latter at an angle to the S. The round tower is, by estimation, 32 to 35ft high at present. At about 16ft from the ground on the NE (the courthouse) side, there is an aperture, broken into an irregular shape: it was an oblong window or port. Inside it is a wide embrasure arched, which had steps up to the port. I got in from a ladder. Inside is a round chamber 9ft in diameter, on the S side of which is a door, 5ft high and 2ft 8in. wide, with a lintel-stone across — at the back of this, on the left or E side were stairs in the thickness of the wall. They are now blocked up. The walls of the tower are 6ft thick. There seems to be another small broken porthole on the W or NW side, but from the inside it is blocked up, and ivy is growing in.

Above this chamber is another, the floor of which is made of concrete, which has been put there within the last 20 or 30 years. You get to this chamber from inside the barrack enclosure, up some steps in the N angle: the steps lead to an arched door, about 6ft high, lined with cut stone very much worn and weathered. This door is at the S side of the tower, and on its right, the E side are stairs leading to the top of the tower. The diameter

Fig. 105—Copies of picture postcards of Arklow Castle.

of the tower measured here is also about 21ft, but it is hard to tell the thickness of the walls, as the concrete floor covers the inside. But just beside where the stair is the wall is 3ft thick.

At the bottom the tower has a batter, running up to about 6 or 8ft from the ground. The diameter at the base of the tower must be 24ft or so.

Above [left] is copied from an old picture postcard 'Castle Ruins Arklow', Valentine's series, printed in Scotland. It is pasted on to a report dated 1918, which also contains the sketch [above, right], made from inside the yard.

Some work was being done at the R.I.C. barracks in February 1918 and the contractor Denis Kavanagh, who owned the land adjoining the barracks on the NW, complained that the castle was dangerous and that stones were falling from it onto his land. As a result the Board of Works surveyor Mr W.M. Paton recommended that a portion of the masonry at the top should be taken down. This was done in May or June 1918, at a cost of £40.

The barracks site belonged to the War Department, but it was, with several other military barracks, transferred to the Board of Works in perpetuity for conversion into R.I.C. barracks in 1881.

In March 1931 Arklow U.D.C. asked the Board of Works to take over and preserve the castle.

A comparison of the postcard with the drawing made in 1794 shows that the height of the ruin is the same in each but the walls of the upper part had evidently become much more ruinous.

Mr Paton's report dated 26th February 1918 says:

'All that remains of the higher portion of the old castle is a ragged and disintegrated block of masonry which was formerly the winding staircase ... . The modern wicket gate and steps out of the District Inspector's backyard lead up to a concrete floor or platform with a projecting railing, laid over the remains of an old circular tower or bastion ... . This platform projects beyond the high portion still standing and has been damaged by the falling masonry but "per se" is safe ... .'

He notes below the photograph, 'Ivy non-existent'.

Cist at Berryfield, Fassaroe (reported in *JRSAI* lxv, p.325). The owner of the land did not want his name mentioned in the report. He is Alex. Smith, of Berryfield, and the cist was in the townland of Fassaroe just inside the townland boundary between Fassaroe and Monastery, in a field called 'the Mote Field'.

October 1935
Notes made from some recent Museum files:

Fortgranite: Stone axe, 10in. long, found on Mr Dennis' estate. Picked up by a workman with stones in a field. Six-inch map, sheet 27 (37.5cm from left (W) margin, 8.5cm from bottom (S) margin). Presented by John W. Tate.

Ballyknockan, Kiltegan: Stone object (probably a hone) found on the lands of Mr Martin Byrne, under 1ft of turf. Position, NW corner of townland 20yds from road and 10yds from townland boundary, Ballinabarny Gap. It is also noted on this file that an urn which was destroyed is said to have been found in Ballyknockan, close to the road, about ¼ mile S from the townland boundary, Ballinabarny Gap, and ¼ mile W of the cist which Walshe and I excavated.

Ballymanus Upper, Glencaly: A much corroded iron axehead, presented by Mr

261

D.M. Doyle (7th August 1935). Mahr calls it a 'crannoge axe'.

Bray: A cup-shaped stone found in the garden at 'Ballinacurra', Convent Avenue, Bray, 400yds from the sea. House built in 1923 — previously a field used for grazing (30th September 1935).

11th April 1936

Ballyhad. At Knockrath Cottage with the Stephens — Lillo Stephens showed me a bullaun stone which she had found on the top of the hill at Ballyhad. It is a flat granite boulder, in a pasture field now overgrown with furze bushes, but which has ridges showing old cultivation — but I saw no house site. The boulder is about 2ft long.

Two hollows, *A* 9 to 10in. in diameter, and about 3in. deep; *B* 13½in. in diameter, 5in. deep. The two holes are ground just beside one another so that the ridge between also shows slightly the mark of the grinding.

The stone seems to be at the very top of the hill, which is flat. Point '696ft' on the 1-inch OS map, 1904 edn. It is a good way from the raheen, 300yds or so.

12th April 1936

Rosahane. An oblong font or trough of granite, with a slit and groove at one side, is at one side in the graveyard. Internal measurement 17in. by about 13in.

The graveyard is on top of a flat hill N of the Ow River, with a wide view, especially over the Ballymanus valley. The wall round it is I think fairly

Fig. 106—Sketch of bullaun stone at Ballyhad.

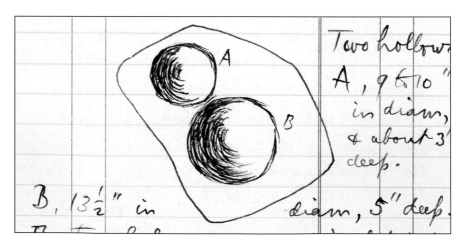

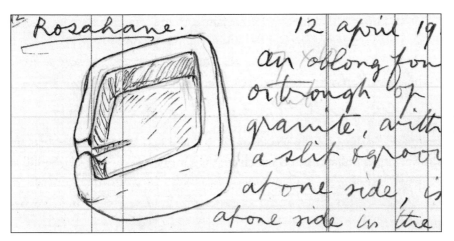

Fig. 107—Sketch of font or trough at Rosahane.

recent. The ruins of the old church are visible as grassy banks — dimensions approximately 20 paces long and 7 or 8 paces wide — seems to have been divided into nave and chancel, as there is a bank across the oblong, about 11 or 12 paces from the W end.

There is a fragment of an arch lying in the grass, E of the church. It has a round moulding on the edge, no other decoration that I could see. It reminded me of the moulding on the carved stones on Church Mountain. Query, was this an 11th- or 12th-century church?

Aughrim. Mr William Fogarty showed me 'the Castle Field' which is on his land. There are no traces of building, and no banks in the field — but his father cleared away old banks there. The field has since been ploughed more than once. It is on the N side of the old road from Aughrim to Macreddin.

Copied from some old notes on bits of paper, taken down the day I saw George Walker at Newcastle. Pronunciation by Walker of some placenames:

'Barəncoyle'
'Teeglin'
'Timmore'
'Ballăvolan'
'Lāymore', 'Lāybeg'
'Kilmŏolin'
'Glaneely'
'Ballaphilip' — 'Old Major Tottenham got three ponds made.'

'Newcastle — that used to be the parish chapel, and the burying ground at Killadreenan used to be the parish church.'

'Wickhams were in "Barəncoyle" — some of them were killed at the "Mú(o͝o)nnybeg".'

Taken down at Castletimon, probably the day I photographed the Brittas dolmen. The ogham stone is on Darcy's land, of Little Limerick (i.e. Darcy's address). The writing means 'the King of Ten Battles'.

It was taken away long ago by the man who owned the forge to use as a hobstone, but he had to bring it back, as he got trouble. Mulhall was the man who was in the forge.

13th April 1936

Went to Captain Kemmis', Ballinacor House. He was away, so the steward, Fitzsimons, allowed me to look round. The house in its present form is 19th-century. It stands on a platform, the flat lawn in front has evidently been banked up, and at the back of the house a considerable amount of solid rock has been cut away, and the house now runs back almost touching this rock. The hill runs straight up behind the house covered with rhododendrons, stony, and clearly never cultivated. The hill called 'Caran' ('Cawrawn') is mostly an oak wood. I did not see the Spa Well, but Drumkitt is either the same place as Caran or some part of it. Where the avenue from the house to Strand Bridge joins the road from Greenan to Strand Bridge there is a wide grass field, stretching towards the river: this is called 'the Rampart'. There are no banks or walls on it or round it now except the field fence which does *not* look like part of an old fortification: all the centre part of the field is flat, and on each side it slopes a little down towards the fences, except on the S. The name 'the Rampart' is therefore probably derived from features which have been removed. I think this is probably the site of Feagh McHugh's house, and 'the fort at Ballinacor'. It is just outside 'the mouth of the glen'.

Some of the tillage land near the house, beside the little stream, may be old, but some I should say is land cleared by the Kemmis's. The name 'the Lime Fields' in Fananierin must date from the Kemmis's time no doubt 18th-century cultivation: but I should say this is old tillage land, probably the site of the old village or town of Fananierin. The man who told me the name of the field 'the Rampart' was a young workman on the place, carting manure. He said the other fields were called 'Farrell's Field', 'Paddy's Field' and 'Tate's Field'.

2nd May 1936

At Crossoona Rath with Dr Macalister; he photographed and took a rubbing of the ogham, which he reads 'VOTI'. He says the stone is not in its original position but has been utilised as building material in the wall. He explains the grooved stone outside the rath as a stone used for heating and expanding the iron tyre of a wheel which had fallen off; being beside an old road this is likely enough.

He also saw a worn ogham stone in Clonmore old graveyard, hitherto unrecorded ... 'RENI'?

6th June 1936

At old James Farrell's of Kellystown, Glenmalure. He was in bed, has been laid up since February, when he got a kind of weakness — he is about 87. He told me the story of the battle again — it was at the 'intrinchments' on Lodarrig — ' "Lo" is a place, isn't it, and "darrig" is blood'.

The soldiers were coming along from the gap that leads up from the Churches — that is on the N side of 'Mullawōr' (i.e. Mullacor). They came right down to the place where the raheen is below the road — 'Borenacrow' — that is the oldest church in the country. He also told me a story of two young fellows from 'Imail' who were up in Co. Dublin cutting corn and heard about the rebellion in 'Waxford' they came from Stepaside across the hills by 'Luggelaw' to the Churches, then asked their way and came on to Ballinabarny. There they asked a farmer named Correll (I think) he brought them to Langrell of Ballinabarny, and they brought them to Critchley — Critchley was rounding up his stock on Ballyboy, for fear the rebels would take them — he made them all help him — next day Critchley brought the two young fellows down to below 'the Big Rock' (Corrigurtna) and had them shot — and afterwards Dwyer and some others brought Langrell and Correll to the same place, and piked them. The little cross was found above the road about 10 years ago by a road worker named McDonnell, and was put up where it is now (in the field below the road under Corrigurtna).

He also told me a story of Dwyer which a woman named Biddy Rafferty told him. She was a young girl living near the raheen in Cullentragh Park. One evening she saw Dwyer and four other men bring a young fellow along. She was behind a fence and was not seen. (He mentioned the names of the four others but I could not catch them.) They stripped the young fellow, and then two of them thrust their pikes into his groins, two into his shoulders and one into the pit of his stomach, and they lifted him up above them to the height of their pikes — she saw his face and it gave her a shock she never forgot. One of them gave him a chew of tobacco to ease the pain. (He also said something about Philip Harvey trying to stop them but I could not quite catch it.) He began this story by saying 'Now I'll tell you a story about Dwyer that I never told you before', and he ended it with 'Now wasn't that a brutal thing to do?'

Note given me by Mr Charles McNeill: 'The White Book of the Exchequer was burnt in Sir Francis Aungier's closet, an. 1610.' *Analecta Hibernica* i, p.136, from Rawlinson B484, i.e. Sir James Ware's MS LXX.

Note from Mr Edward O'Toole of Rathvilly: 'My mother had relatives at Moyne, Co. Wicklow. She always pronounced it "Mween". She pronounced the name Preban as "Pribawn".'

Oswaldstown, Co. Kildare. In a sand-pit at Whitehills near Naas, a skull and a vessel were found by Dennis Byrne in 1933. In November and December 1934 John Connolly of Oswaldstown found four skeletons, which he reburied — and two pieces of pottery. Thomas McCabe, Naas, found a stone axe there. All these finds sent to the Museum 29th December 1935. The urns from Tipper were found in Jones' sand-pit.

Father John Meagher, Kilcullen, showed me a map of County Kildare dated 1752, by Noble and Keenan.

Note from J. Mackenzie of Highfield, Blessington 30th November 1934: '... There is a grave with a flat stone on top between Oakwood and Glanree near the Wicklow Gap, perhaps you have seen it ... .' Heard from Pat Smith of Glenbride — Grave of a man [who] lost his way going across to the Seven Churches and was buried there. Thirty years since Mackenzie heard the story.

20th June 1936

I and Seamas Delargy and Sean O'Sullivan of the Folklore Commission brought down an Ediphone machine and tried to take a record from him [i.e. James Farrell of Kellystown, Glenmalure]. He was up and dressed. But he was too weak for his voice to record and we could not manage it.

His son Brian Farrell showed me where the stone is that he mentions as the place from which he saw the vision of the battle. It is near a bush at the top of the zigzag path, a big block of stone with a flat top, where men used to play cards, sometimes. It is near the 'Bolia Walls' — a new name to me, evidently referring to a time when there was a *buaile* in that valley (Corrasillagh).

From this place Lodarrig is in full view across the valley. Brian Farrell had a story of two parties of yeomen in 1798: one came down Corrasillagh to this place, the other came down Lugduff or Mullacor, dressed in disguise as rebels with green sashes on; and they fired at one another across the valley — he heard that bullets flattened against the stones were picked up in Corrasillagh.

8th July 1936

Goldenfort. The old graveyard is called 'Rabran'. The old woman who lives in the cottage beside it came and showed me 'the Foal's Foot', a flat semicircular stone with a pit cut at the centre — the break across the stone gives this pit something the shape of a small horseshoe. 'The foal jumped across from the top of Kilranelagh Hill there, and made the mark in the stone.' It is a broken circular millstone or quern, I think of granite. Diameter 17in., central pit about 4in. across. The graveyard is still used: a man from Rathdangan was buried there the other day. 'Is it for Protestants and Catholics both?' — 'Oh no all Catholics: one of the others wouldn't be let into it, not if he was known.' The graveyard is much overgrown, very uneven, and the grass very long. I could see no sign of the ruin of the church.

She said there was a monastery over there at the clump of trees in Gibraltar. This is rather N of Goldenfort House. I went to see it: it is a high piece of ground with the ruin of a large rath on it. (Perhaps it is from this fortification on top of a hill that the name 'Gibraltar' was given to it.)

[Internal dimensions: 55 paces; inner bank almost ruined; it is about 14ft above the bottom of the fosse; outer bank 3ft wide; from top of outer bank to top of inner bank (estimated) is about 20yds.]

A couple of big blocks of granite outside to the NE: one shows old wooden wedge-marks for breaking it.

A well outside, 50yds away, to the SW. Walled round, and with a circular stone in front for a stepping stone, 23in. diameter, 7in. thick. Perhaps part of a mill?

Mrs Norah Fleming is the old woman's name who showed me the 'Foal's Foot'.

In the field outside the churchyard railings old foundations of walls have been seen when the field has been ploughed. These are supposed to have been the monastery: not the fort in Gibraltar. But there are terraces below the fort on the E which are supposed to have been 'monks' gardens'. I did not see them.

Cabra is at the S end of Goldenfort where the road turns off to Rampere and Tinoran.

Threecastles. Went and looked at the Holy Well; it is still used, as there were fresh bits of rags tied on the bushes. It comes from under a bank of gravel or boulder clay which was once on the bank of the Liffey. It has a bar across it: outside the bar is used as a watering place for cattle.

There are no ruins of a church, nor foundations, in the graveyard (Scurlock's).

Occasional notes, taken down at different times on scraps of paper: copied here:

Kilcavan graveyard. Has been ploughed up and tilled a long time ago. The headstones were taken up and built into the walls of a house which is still standing. It is built on the site of the graveyard. A man in Carnew knows the site.

Ballylion. Old Mill. About 70yds from the gate leading to Old Mill, on the right, there is a stone 18in. high, and a mound in the hedge to the W, 100yds or so away. A ditch running through. (I don't know if these are ancient or modern.)

Darker's Pit, Blessington. 4th August 1934, date bones found, reported to coroner (Paddy Crowley).

Names of fields in Killinure Lower:

'The Mote Field'

'Ballybrack' ('Ballɔbrack')
'Shaw's Land'
'Woodfield'

There was an open well in Ballybrack. (Got from a man named Redmond.)

J.W. Murphy of Crab Lane, Aghowle Lower has a bronze cauldron inscribed: 'T HA † 1635'. Three-legged, two handles. He says it came from Wexford.

Extract from a letter from Reverend T.E. Young, 28th February 1934:

'A stonecutter named Connolly of Kilquiggin told me how he discovered a lot of bronze spears and pins, on Doolin's farm near Hacketstown. He said the bronze spears were shaped like a tobacco knife used in a Tobacconist's for cutting plug. At the time he set no value on them and gave them to a carter, but he said he enquired afterwards at the Museum and recognised them in the collection as presented by the Dean of Waterford and found beside a big stone near Hacketstown. He also had a piece of copper about the size of a saucer and shaped like the inside of it. He found it in a field near Rath House; but he did not know what became of it. It was about his house for a long time.'

'Raheennagoppul' on the Shillelagh side of Tinahely, on the upper side of the road, on the Shillelagh side of the bungalow. 'The Religeen' in Minmore, two fields from Yew Tree Graveyard.

9th September 1936

Rathsallagh. Walked in to Rathsallagh House. The house is empty at present. It might be an 18th-century house. I did not see the inside. The steward or man in charge, named Fletcher, who has been there 30 years, showed me where Old Town was. It is really part of Oldcourt townland. You go out at the back of the house and along a lane which leads directly to a field called 'the Pond Field': there is a pond in the NE corner of it. In this field not far from the gate is a roughly circular bank, almost levelled; and so obliterated I would not even be certain it was the bank of a rath but it looked like one. I'd guess the diameter at 60yds. Inside it are banks like old walls overgrown. This Fletcher said was the Old Town; an old man had told him it was the old Dunlavin. In this circle are some five stones, two flat, three standing. One of the flat stones is a slab with two crosses in circles joined by a line thus [Fig.108]: the circles and crosses are in relief. Stone granite. The other: cross in relief. Stone about 2½ft long. One of the upright stones has a cross in a circle, like No. 1 above. The others have simple circles.

Fletcher never heard it called a graveyard. But it evidently was one, or else there was one close by. -

Another flat stone beside these is ornamented in the same style as the Tornant slab, now in the Museum: 33in. long, 20in. wide [Figs 108 and 109]. A groove down to the side of the stone: cup-and-circle ornaments,

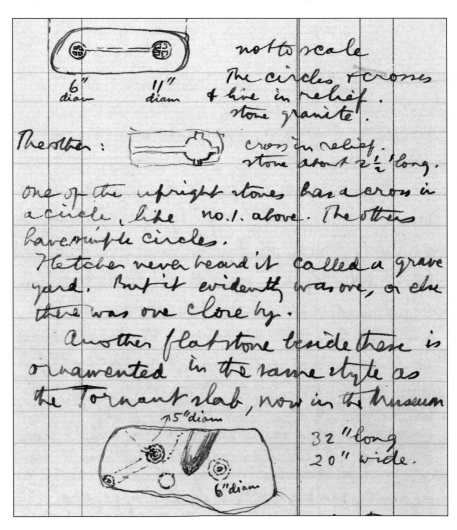

Fig. 108—Sketch of carved stones at Oldcourt, Rathsallagh.

Fig. 109—Rock art at Rathsallagh (courtesy of the Royal Society of Antiquaries of Ireland ©).

pocked; one of them has a channel leading from it. It is a sort of sandstone or grit, I think: Fletcher called it a 'quarry stone', and said it was like the stone you'd get in 'Vinegar' (Griffinstown). This is pre-Christian.

Fletcher said there is a rath in Oldcourt, near the Ballylaffin road (see Wicklow *OS Letters*, p.49).

Postcard received from Charles MacNeill on 6th September 1936 giving me a note made by him on 24th July 1935 in Glenmalure, Co. Wicklow:

'Found out "Art O'Neill's Cairn", a small heap of unmossy stones, not covered with any vegetation. Very recently a small cross has been laid out in white quartz stones. The spot, therefore, is now a "grave", and is being made a place of pilgrimage. From it Ballinacor is clearly seen across the glen, not three miles away. A farmer's wife living nearby and a native of the place did not rise to a cast for the Art O'Neill story. She had not heard it or any other legend about that spot, though otherwise well up in local lore of later times. According to her the heap had always gone by the name of "the Cloran" and nothing else. She had never known of any old graveyard or church ruin in Glenmalure.

C. MacN.'

This is a verification of my opinion that the connection of Art O'Neill with this place is quite modern and due chiefly to C.M. Byrne. See his article in the *Wicklow People* of 31st March 1928. He mentions this 'clogharan', and says 'There has always been a tradition that under this Art O'Neill was buried'. I think it probable that C.M. Byrne got this information from Jim Byrne ('Jim of the Road') of Glenmalure, who writes as 'J.W.B.' He published this tradition in the *Wicklow People* on 1st June 1935, in a collection called 'Here and There through the County' which contains a lot of badly digested information taken from books, mixed with a little local tradition, never given in a pure form. (See his further article of 11th January 1936 in same paper.) The tradition concerning the site in Oakwood seems to be the true one.

6th October 1936

Ardoyne old church is a ruin showing a main building about 14 paces by 8 [paces] and a chancel about 8 paces long at the E end. (Short paces as ground very uneven — say total length about 60ft, width about 20ft.) I saw no carved stones showing any mouldings or characteristic shapes. The few tombstones in the graveyard are Catholic. The wall surrounding the graveyard is not old.

(Note that Dr Comerford, *Diocese of Kildare and Leighlin* vol. III, p.395, says 'One gable is still standing'. This must have been about 1886 or shortly before. There are only grass-covered foundations of walls now.)

The 'moat' in the large field at the opposite side of the road is a curious structure. It is called 'Ardoyne Moat'. The field is very long; at the W it is quite flat, low-lying, looking like a cutaway bog. Then the ground rises steeply, I should guess about 80ft, or more. At the top of this slope or bank is the mote. It has a trace of a ditch and bank on the N side. On the E is a large hollow 15 or 20ft deep. On the S and W the mote rises from the field without any ditch. It is on the S about 12ft high, but on the E, where the hollow is, the top of the mote must be 35ft above the bottom of the hollow. The top of the mote is 30 to 40ft across, flat.

On the whole this does not look much like an Anglo-Norman mote. Could it be a burial mound, the material for which was dug out of the hollow? The field seems to be a bank of boulder clay.

Note from Charles McNeill — there were four orders of friars known in Ireland: Dominicans (black), Franciscans (grey), Carmelites (white) and Augustinians. The Cistercians, Carthusians and other orders were monks, not friars.

9th November 1936

Mr J. McKenzie of Highfield gave me further particulars of how he heard of Art's Grave. A man named Mike Toomey, whose father used to live in Hank's Bog near Valleymount — the father was called Cashoge Toomey — has told McKenzie that it was a place where a man died — one of three men who were imprisoned in the North, and who went across towards Glenmalure — the two got to Glenmalure but this man died here before the men who were sent to rescue him got to him. Toomey says it wasn't Art O'Neill.

(This sounds like a confused recollection of a book story. Pat Smith would be a better authority.) To get to the place, don't go up as far as Oakwood — go to Burke's of Glanree, and follow up the brook: it is at the head of the brook.

There's a graveyard in Ballinagee — it is called 'the Churchyard Park'. It is on the left of the road, past the Glenbride Road, and just beyond the bridge — it is above the ruins of a house called 'the Long House'. (This is Templefinan.)

There is a graveyard in Granabeg. Joseph Plunket the man who led the Irregulars in 1922 is buried in Knocknadroose, near an old house of Norton's. He was shot getting across a wall and is buried beside it, a big stone wall, and there is a cairn of stones on the place.

23rd November 1936

At Rathbran. Mr M. Harrington, National Teacher of Stratford-on-Slaney, heard some stories of old finds and told Mr Edward O'Toole who told me. I went today to see Mr Harrington but he was out. I went on to the farmer he heard them from, Mr Tom Dwyer of Rathbran, who lives on the road leading from Stratford to Rathbran through Gibraltar. Mr Dwyer brought me first down a lane near the NE boundary of Manger, and showed me a spot where he said an old man named Fleming had levelled a mound for Mr Wynne — a small mound 15 or 18yds in diameter and perhaps 6ft high, and under it they found a round hole like a well, not made with stones but in ground hard like concrete. They fastened two plough reins and let them down, that would be 16yds, and didn't get the bottom — and then they threw in earth, and it took them half a day to fill it. It is covered now with grass and bushes. It is on a sloping bank or brow above a hollow — marked on my map in the D.E.D. list. Mr Dwyer spoke of it as a tunnel. His house is in the townland of Gibraltar.

At the place where the road crosses the townland boundary between Manger and Gibraltar, just inside Gibraltar, on the N side of the road, there is an old quarry, and here Mr Dwyer said that urns were found long ago, with dust or ashes in them — they were something like large flower pots and they had lids. He didn't know what happened to the urns. It was his father told him this: his father died in 1900 aged about 80. Mr Dwyer himself is 62.

He then brought me to Goldenfort townland, and we walked up from the direction of Cabra, to a point about 150yds SW of Goldenfort House. This is the highest point of a low hill or rise — there is a circular bank of earth here, like a small rath 25 or 30yds across. Mr Dwyer said this was only an enclosure where trees were planted. On the N side of this, towards Goldenfort House, there is a grassy hollow. Mr Dwyer said it was an old sandpit — there was another a little towards the E. The men digging sand here a number of years ago found skulls and bones — which they reburied — Mr Dwyer saw one of the skulls himself. He said it must have been very old because it was so big. We were looking across at the fort in Rathbran (Gibraltar). I asked him what it was, and he said it was supposed to be the fort of King Brandubh — that there was supposed to have been a castle there, that perhaps General Saunders pulled it down to build Goldenfort House.

Mr Dwyer also told me there used to be a castle in Manger where the Grove House is now. He meant Saundersgrove.

9th December 1936

In the townland of Old Kilcullen, Co. Kildare, about ½ mile SW of the round tower and graveyard, on the top of the hill (594ft) and about 50yds S of the old road which crosses the hill, is a small mound — grass-covered. It is 6ft high, about 28yds in circumference and about 9yds in diameter (paced). The top is flat, 6ft across — in the centre of the top is a small shallow depression, a foot or so across, and a couple of inches deep.

This look as though it was a prehistoric burial mound. Father John Meagher, CC, Kilcullen, who drew my attention to it, thinks it is a burial place of a hero mentioned in the Book of Leinster and said to be 'ós Cill Cuilin', i.e. over Kilcullen. It is certainly the nearest hill which is over the graveyard, and from it one looks down on the graveyard and round tower as well as having a very fine view all round, Dun Aulin, the Hill of Allen, Wicklow Mountains, etc.

27th December 1936

Ballintombay Upper, Rathdrum. On the lands of a farmer named Fitzpatrick (house shown on 1-inch OS map, ½in. S of the word 'Ballinderry' and ⅗in. W of the road, on an old lane), Ned Stephens showed me two more bullaun stones — they are near an old, almost levelled rath, in wet ground on its NE side. Both are granite boulders — one about 3ft, the other about 4ft across.

[Bullaun 1: two hollows]: *A* 13in. wide, 8in. deep; *B* (oval) 16in. wide, 9in. deep.

[Bullaun 2: two hollows]: *C* (oval) 16in. wide, 9in. deep; *D* (round) 10½in. wide, 4½in. deep.

D is quite shallow. Both stones are more or less hidden by furze bushes.

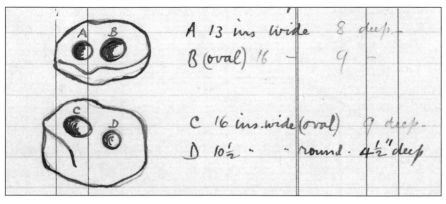

Fig. 110—Sketch of bullaun stones at Ballintombay.

275

Fig. 111—Rathnew village.

28th December 1936

Went with Tony Farrington to Wicklow neighbourhood. Walked in from the main road at Merrymeeting to Tinakelly House (Miss Halpin's) and on through Tinakelly to its NE corner to the house called Tinakelly Lower. Tried to get to the bank of the Vartry River just N of this house, but the tide was coming in and the water from the Broad Lough floods all the flat land, and we'd have required rubber boots as the water was all through the grass. Came back to Tinakelly House and along the farm road to Knockrobin Avenue, which we crossed: we went up the little hill in Knockrobin and down through Glebe on to the main road. There is no sign of a church ruin either at Glebe or on Knockrobin Hill.

The avenue to Tinakelly House is a continuation of an old road from Rathnew. It has been made an avenue out of an old road. Beyond, i.e. NE of Tinakelly House, it is still a road, and clearly old. After ¼ mile it comes down from solid ground to flat fields, with deep ditches into which the tide comes: these fields have evidently been reclaimed, but they are not good: perhaps they are deteriorating, the drains may not be properly cleared. The road runs across this boggy ground for 200yds or so, ditch on each side:

276

Fig. 112—Rathnew village

then it comes to an island of solid ground beside the Broad Lough. It runs on then to the house called Tinakelly Lower (now owned by Mr Besson of the Hibernian Hotel, Dublin). This is a Georgian house nearly 200 years old I should say.

There is no trace of its having crossed the River Vartry behind Tinakelly Lower House. We could not examine the river further W as we could not cross the fields. The road crosses the small river, which comes from Rathnew, by a one-arch bridge — perhaps 18th-century. The straight course this river follows must have been made for it when the country was drained. This road, a stone-built road, must have been made subsequent to the English colonisation of the district in the late 17th or early 18th century. But of course it could have followed the line of an older track.

From a letter of Admiral Boyle-Somerville written to J.R. Wade, 14th November 1931:

Azimuths of *apparent* sunrise, latitude 53°14' at midsummer, equinox, midwinter etc.

Elevated	0°	1°	2°
Summer solstice sunrise	47°16'	49°20'	51°13'
Bealtaine sunrise	60°49'	62°35'	64°13'
Equinox sunrise	89°01'	90°49'	92°16'
Samhain sunrise	117°28'	119°14'	120°56'
Winter solstice sunrise	130°40'	132°45'	134°50'

Bearings, termed Azimuths, reckoned from True North, clockwise right round the circle.

FIELD NOTEBOOK 16:
January 1937–April 1938

[There are some disjointed notes in the front of this notebook which are not reproduced here.]

31st January 1937

Knockraheen. There is a rath just at the E boundary of the townland near Ballinahinch: it is marked on the OS map. It is in Ballinahinch, Calary parish. It is a circular field, 90 paces in diameter; the E side of the bank has been demolished, and straight fences built, but the trace of the circular bank is visible in the field. The bank is only from 3 to 4ft high, stones and earth with bushes on it. On the outside [are] the remains of a ditch, almost completely filled up. I spoke to a young man who came into the field. He said it is called 'the Raheen Field', and has never been ploughed: long ago a man tried to plough it, and he went queer that night and ran over the fields with nothing but his trousers on. The old people said there was a church there long ago. I mentioned other old churches to him: he said there was an old church in Kilmurry: it was N of the ruined church (R.C.) and at the bottom of the hill: there is a blessed well there. (I wonder was he really referring to Holywell?) He also said there was a blessed well in Drumbawn. I did not think this rath looked like an old graveyard.

1st February 1937

Inchanappa. The old graveyard is in Inchanappa South near the boundary of Broomfield. It is in a field called 'Church Hill Field', just beside an old roadway leading to Broomfield House.

It is not fenced; there are some trees growing in it. There is at the S side what looks like the remains of a circular bank of earth and stones, but it is not certain that this was ever part of a wall surrounding the graveyard. There are no headstones, but a few flags of slate without any markings. At the N side there is a big pile of stones stretching for about 15 or 18ft, grass-grown, and at the W end of this another pile comes out at right angles. (As O'Curry speaks of the foundation of the church I suppose there was more remaining in his time.)

Set up at a slant on some other stones there is an oblong trough of

279

granite, the internal measurement being 18½in. x 16in. and 4 to 5in. deep. One side is broken. It is shaped in a rough boulder of granite 2ft long — and the rim is outlined by a wide groove, but this does not go all the way round. This looks like a primitive font.

Extract from a letter written by Father Shearman to Mr John G.A. Prim (the co-founder of the Kilkenny Archaeological Society): preserved among other papers by Mr Prim's grandson, and shown me by E. Curtis, October 1936:

'Dunlavin January 2nd 1864

...I have all the rubbings taken of the bilingual ogham and yesterday I gave the model the last touch so that I will begin, after the holidays, to write on the subject. ... Since I saw you I got some stone and brass celts and most magnificent bronze spearhead 22 inches long with precise history etc. An old clergyman near here had it was found on his father's land. He prized it very much. At his decease I got it with many other curiosities etc. ...

Yours very sincerely
John Francis Shearman.'

7th February 1937

Rathturtle Moat, Blessington. Measurements (approximate) diameter of internal space 38yds. Width of ditch from inner [bank] to top of outer bank about 9 or 10yds (estimated). Height of inner bank varies very much, but approximately 4ft. Height of inner bank above bottom of surrounding ditch 10ft (varying). Height of outer bank above ditch 6ft. The rath has been made at the top of a steep hill, and the centre of the internal space rises and is as high as the inner bank, or higher.

The rath has been planted with trees (Scotch pine), now 4ft high or so.

21st February 1937

Sleanaglogh. The bullán stone is on the E side of the road at the angle of the boundary between Sleanaglogh and Aghowle Upper, and on the boundary between Derrylossary and Killiskey parishes, i.e. between the territory of Glendalough and that of Wicklow. It is 12½in. in diameter, circular, and 6in. deep, bowl-shaped.

The well called 'Ladyswell', must according to Nevill's map be a little S of the SE corner of Sleanaglogh: about ½ mile SE from this bullaun stone.

We went up Carrick Mountain from the deserted farmhouse which is in the neighbourhood of where Ladyswell must have been — and A. Farrington showed me where the ruined cairn is. It is on the peak which is on the boundary between Aghowle Upper, Ballymanus Upper and Ballyknockan More — at the angle. This is the boundary between Killiskey and Glenealy parishes. This peak is about ¼ mile S of the highest peak marked '1252ft' on the map. This peak is very little lower. The cairn is almost entirely ruined and in fact might not be noticed, but the stones as Farrington pointed out could not be there naturally as all the peaks are naturally scraped clean by glacial action. The ruin of the cairn is about 12yds in diameter, approximately circular: it appears to be of 2 to 3ft in depth.

This looks like a ruined burial cairn: but any human or pottery remains must have disappeared long ago, completely disintegrated by moisture and air.

11th April 1937

Athgarrett, Co. Kildare (parish of Rathmore). At the point marked '890ft' between Eadestown and Glen Ding, there is a burial cairn on the top of the hill in a grove of trees. There is a circular bank of earth and stones enclosing a space 72 paces in diameter. The bank on the outside is nearly 6ft high in places. On the W side it is double, i.e. outside it is a ditch 12 paces wide with another bank. The ditch remains, at least a trace of it does, all round the inner bank. But both banks and ditch have a modern look, as if they had been made up to make field fences some time ago. The inner bank (complete circle) is now a good deal ruined in places: it is 3ft high on the inside in places. At the centre of the space is a low ill-defined mound, 12 to 15 paces in diameter, about 3ft high. The middle has been dug out. There are trees on it and all over the circular space. A disc barrow?

Tipper South townland, parish of Tipper. An old churchyard. Ruin of a large church. Foundations only remaining, except for a piece of barrel vaulting at the W, with one modern wall, and an iron gate closing the opening. A large square granite font is lying in the graveyard about 3ft square. It has a hole in the centre. There is also a piece of a mullion of a Gothic window.

17th April 1937

Co. Kildare, Slieveroe, parish of Tipperkevin. On the top of the hill 1094ft there is a ruined tumulus. Its diameter is 17 to 18 paces, i.e. about 50ft. Circumference about 53 paces. Its height is from 3 to 4ft. It is not a conical or hemispherical mound but flat across the top — but the top is very uneven having been obviously dug into. I think it stands on peat on top of the hill. It is grass-covered, but there were a few stones lying about, which made me think it might be a cairn of stones underneath. The view from it is magnificent, all the Wicklow Mountains, Mount Leinster, Slieve Bloom Mountains, Hill of Allen, all the plain of Meath, the Mote of Ardscull etc.

Tipperkevin old churchyard. The old church is a complete ruin, the interior of it is below the level of the graveyard. Could it have been dug out? The caretaker, Michael Nolan's, son showed me a 17th-century tombstone in the church which he said was that of the Eustaces — and another outside the church, a flat slab, with an incised cross, which looks medieval — also Eustaces' he said.

This boy, aged about 18, said if I took the next road to the left, i.e. the Naas road, and turned to the left at the first turn, I'd come to another graveyard, called 'Calshalocaun' or 'Calchalocaun' ('Caiseal a' lócáin'?) which 'is ten times as old as this one'. (This seems to be in Walshestown townland.) He also said there are caves ½ mile long in the 'Slade of Slieverue'.

28th April 1937

Rampere near Baltinglass. Close to the road which runs from Rampere crossroads to Eldon's Bridge S of the road just before you come to the bend there is a fairly large rath. It is rather ruined but its main features are clear. Sheet 21, 3.8cm W on S edge. Central space about 45 paces across. Inner bank 3 to 5ft on inside, on outside to bottom of ditch 10 to 15ft, outer bank I think gone, and the ditch is filled in on the N and E. Could not measure inner bank (thickness) as it is overgrown, but I'd say it was 20ft or so thick at base.

Continuing this road, crossing railway bridge — and going into field NE of bridge there is a tumulus — about 59 paces in circumference, in Raheen, or about 19 [paces] in diameter. Nine feet high, fairly regular, not much dug away. It is built of gravel: there is a big gravel-pit being worked just the other side of the railway, and I think the land is all gravel here with about 1ft of earth over it. The tumulus is shown on the 1840 6-inch sheet (27).

2nd May 1937

Glenasmole. Walked from Glenasmole Lodge and the Cot Brook up Carrick. On the ridge between Cot and Slade Brooks met a young local farmer who pointed out where I could get a path up it, leading up by the shooting butts. He spoke of 'the Slade', and I asked him what the brook was called and he said 'we just call it "Srugh"'. He called the hill 'the Carrick'. He said 'the hollow over there is "Barnacreel"'(meaning the col between Carrick and Seefingan — he pronounced Seefingan as 'Séefingăn', 'suidhe fingan', stress on middle syllable) — Seefinn he called 'Shangil Chapel' (like 'Seangail', not quite 'ng', 'g' more stressed). He did not know why it was called 'Chapel'. I went on over Carrick to the track along the E side of Seahan [Seechon?]. This track gets lost just about at the townland boundary between Ballymorefinn and Ballinascorney Upper. I went down it and examined it and I am satisfied it is in its present form a modern road — little culverts have been made to carry the streams under it and these are the same level as the road surface, i.e. made when the road was made. It follows the gradient of the mountain. When you get on the N side of the little stream which I think is Glassavullaun Stream, you can see how a path would run straight down to St Ann's (Kilmasantan) and I believe the road follows at least in part an old track, and that this old track then came down here to Kilmasantan. I walked down here, and it is quite practicable for a mountain road, though steep. I feel fairly sure the road went round Seahan [Seechon?] and joined the track which crosses Butter Mountain. It looks to me very much as if the county boundary between Shankill and Ballinascorney Upper marks the track of the old road.

See the description of the county bounds both in the *Carew Calendar* (Lambeth 600, p.143) and in Erck's *Chancery Enrolments I*, i, no. 36. The Lambeth document which is the older speaks of the 'way which leadeth from thence eastward and divideth the Barony of Newcastle from Cowillagh unto Agherillin [Aghfarrell] … and so from thence as the Barony of Rathdown passeth unto Kilmesantan'. This 'way' is this road.

See also Archbishop Alen's note (*c.* 1530) to a document of 1219–1228 in Alen's Reg. fol. 124. He speaks of 'the way from Kilmasanctan to Ballamor, riding on which on the right hand all the intervening land is that of the Church of Dublin'. This 'way' again refers to this road.

283

11th May 1937

St Boodin's Well in Kilbeg. I visited this again today with Mr Michael O'Connor, National Teacher, Lackan. He has been a teacher there for two years, and had visited Leask ten days ago to suggest the excavation of the well. There was much more to be seen than in September 1931: the stems of the thorn trees were bare, and there was of course no growth of bracken. At the S side of the well the earth and stones slope down to the water: at the back there is a lintel stone, which one can see under. It is supported on small stones, but behind these are upright slabs, one on the E and two on the W. Behind these are small stones, and at the back, on the W side is what looked like a small passage — entrance, two uprights and a slab across — about 2ft high. The whole [thing] is completely covered and dark, so it is hard to see. There is water all through it. It looks like a souterrain with water in it. The front lintel is I think about 3ft wide. In the next field to the E is a pile of stones overgrown with thorn bushes. Molloy told O'Connor that this was an old church, and I think this is quite probable. In one place the stones look like a piece of drystone walling. I could see no carved stones. But between the well and this site, just E of the fence between them, is a large granite boulder, with a 'bullán' cavity in it: the hollow is not round but oval, about 18in. x 14in. by about 10in. deep (I had no measure with me).

Notes from Wicklow and Rathdrum court notebook made between 1934 and 1936. Local pronunciations:

Wicklow

5th December 1934	Ballyhara, 'Ballahárra'
16th January 1935	Newrath, 'Newry'
20th February 1935	Timmore, 'Teemore' (this must I suppose be a corruption: it is interesting).
20th February 1935	Ballybeg, 'Ballabeag' (like in 'baile beag')

Rathdrum

6th June 1935	Moneyteige, 'Munštágue'
1935	Ballinaclogh, 'Ballynaclo'
5th March 1936	Templelusk, 'Tamplelusk'

At Wicklow, 2nd October 1935, I got the true form of Glendasan.

Christopher Lawler, carpenter, said in Wicklow Court 'I saw the girl when I was going out the Glinnasaw road — the road leading to Kildare' (from Glendalough) — and again: 'It was on the Glinnasaw road, not the Glinmacanass road'.

'Glinnasaw', perhaps for 'Gleann na samhadh', 'Glen of the Sorrels' — cf. Parknashaw.

Mr Gallagher, County Surveyor, told me he had seen a book called *An exact account of the roads for King William's Army* by Thome.

15th May 1937

Hollywood. Walked with Father W. Hawkes, CC, Hollywood (successor to Father Kavanagh) up Scalp Mountain. The cairn on it is at the SE end of the ridge (boundary of Scalp and Slievecorragh townlands). It is about 24 paces in diameter, and 5ft or so high. It seems to be a good deal ruined. At the centre there is a flat slab lying among the smaller stones, this slab is 5ft x 4ft. There are some three other large stones visible on the edge of the cairn, on the S and E sides — they are not together, and it is difficult to say if they are the remains of a kerb or not. If there was a kerb, why are not more of the stones to be seen? But the cairn has been a good deal knocked about.

In the valley below to the S there is a fairly well-preserved rath with double bank, I think in Toor.

We went back to Hollywood and he showed me a rath which the local people had shown him about 600yds or so NE of the Protestant church (over the 'll' of 'Hollywood' on the 1-inch OS map). Twenty-five paces diameter of inner ring, a ditch round inner bank about 7 or 8yds wide, and perhaps 5 or 6ft deep — but the outer bank has almost all disappeared, and so has most of the ditch. And the inside of the rath is hollow, looking as if it had been dug out. I would not have recognised this place as a rath if it had not been pointed out.

Could the earth in the centre have been dug out and used as top dressing on the field around? There is a very large boulder in it with a flat top which might originally have been level with the floor of the rath.

Father Hawkes said he had been shown a 'dún' at Dunboyke or in the townland of Dragoonhill which he though might be the original 'Dún of Dunboyke'. He says also that between Hollywood and the main road there is a small circle in a marsh, and he wonders could it be a crannog.

16th May 1937

At Fananierin with R.C. Barton. W of the ridge about a mile S of the Avonbeg there are some deserted fields just across the Drumgoff Brook. Barton had been told there was a stone here with a lot of little circles on it and he brought me to see it … .

[There are] small rings of stones some 15ft across, others 7ft across — four or five in all, one or two very much ruined [these are located NW of the stone]. Query, were these sheep folds?

The stone is a flat slab, with a lot of little cups on it, four or five in a row, the others here and there on the surface — mostly about 1½in. in diameter and ½in. or so deep. I do not know what this stone is. I photographed it.

We looked at the old mill in Greenan. The water channel and pond can be seen, but at the mill itself they are nearly filled up. A local man said it was a flour mill used 90 years ago. He didn't know who owned it.

Looked again at the bullauns in Ballintombay Upper. The farmer, Fitzpatrick, said James Byrne of Ballintombay told him that long ago an old man had tilled the rath: he went there one evening and put a spade standing up in it and said 'If you don't want me to dig it, knock the spade down; if you will let me dig it leave the spade standing' — next morning he went to it and the spade was still standing up. So he put down potatoes in the rath, and no harm came to him. Nobody would help him to put in the potatoes, but they ate them all right.

Fitzpatrick had heard some people found two or three stones with writing on them in the rath, and took them away. He thought one was a man named Dunne.

Fitzpatrick looked round the rath and found a small granite stone 6 or 7in. long, rounded, but with one surface ground quite flat. He thought it might be used for fine grinding.

20th May 1937

At Glendalough, 'the Seven Fonts'. Measured the big bullaun stone in Brockagh townland. There are seven bullauns or hollows, not all in the same rock. The big rock has four [hollows], three in a square space hollowed out in the boulder [*D*, *E* and *F*], and one [*C*] outside this space. The three others [*A*, *B* and *G*] are separate, each in one rock, near the big one.

286

The hollowed out space [in the big rock] measures 3ft 3in. x 2ft 6in. x 6in. deep.

Measurements:

A   16½in. x 12½in. x 7in.
B   (circular) 12in. x 4½in.
C   (circular) 15in. x 7in.
D   13½in. x 12in. x 5in.
E   13in. x 12in. x 5½in.
F   17in. x 9in. x 5in.
G   (circular) 15in. x 6in.

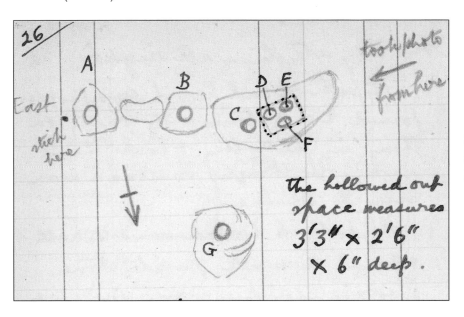

Fig. 113—Sketch of bullaun stones at Brockagh.

I photographed the stone.

Lord Walter Fitzgerald does not mention this stone in *JRSAI* xxxvi, p.198.

I looked at the caher at the place between the two lakes ('the Eeshert'). It measures 16 paces in diameter, and is surrounded by a wall of dry stones built fairly regularly though rather ruined: the wall is from 7 to 10ft thick, and about 4ft or so high. The three crosses each stand in a little heap of stones, the S heap about 12ft in diameter, the middle one 18ft in diameter,

Fig. 114—'The Seven Fonts' at Brockagh (courtesy of the Royal Society of Antiquaries of Ireland ©).

and the N one quite small. At the N heap as well as the cross, there is a stone slab with a hole in it [height 15–28in., width 31in.], standing upright in the heap. The hole measures about 13in. x 4in. x 5in. deep, cut right through the slab. The crosses are all much the same shape, the S one is a thin slab, the others are thicker.

Note that St Kevin's own place at Glendalough was this spot between the two lakes — see the Latin Life (Plummer) sections vi and xvi, and further that he was ordered by an angel to move thence to the E side of the smaller lake, *ibid*. section xxiv. Section xxix which speaks of the men of Dublin shows this life to be at least post-Scandinavian: but it is probably later.

The Irish Life III, section 19, says an angel ordered Caomhgen to go out of the pen in which he lived as an ascetic — this sounds like a recollection of this part of the Latin Life.

This suggests to me that Kevin's original settlement was on the Eeshert (Disert) or beside it. St Kevin's Cell — and that later when the monastery became famous it was moved down to the position between the rivers, a vision of an angel being given out as the reason for the move.

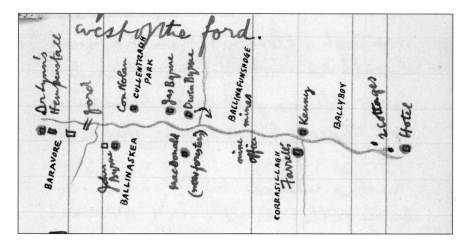

Fig. 115—Sketch-map of houses occupied in Glenmalure.

22nd May 1937

John Byrne of Ballinaskea in Glenmalure pointed me out the hill called 'Coragrainya'. It is the hill at the E end of Baravore, above Dr Lynn's house — about ½ mile W of the ford. The above [Fig. 115] are the only houses now occupied in the glen — the ones marked in red — the others including several not marked are unoccupied or ruined. MacDonald's, now the forester's, is only a cottage. Dr Lynn's bungalow was built 40 years ago. Kenny's is not much more than a cottage. So there are really only five farms now above the hotel.

1st June 1937

Examined a rath which the Reverend J. Robinson mentioned to me — near Castlemacadam. It is at the top of the hill between Castlemacadam and Carty's Corner, where the ruined miners' houses are which are called 'the Ten Houses'. Killeagh, Ballymurtagh and Ballygahan Upper townlands all meet here, and this rath is just on the boundary of the three: I'm not sure which townland it is in. The inside of the rath is flat but it appears to be slightly raised — a bank surrounds it, and *inside* the bank is a ditch. It has the marks of old cultivation in it.

[Total diameter 23 paces, the internal diameter 13 paces.] The bank is 3ft high [9ft wide], and the ditch about 1ft deep [6ft wide]. I do not know if the centre is higher than the level of the surrounding land or not. I could see no sign of an outer ditch. The rath is at the top of the hill.

June 1937

Stone axe found at Knocknaskeagh and forwarded to the Museum by Mr P. O'Toole of Hacketstown. Found by Mr T. Kavanagh at the base of a deep turf bank; and some flint chips of human workmanship nearby. The axe is a small one [about 4in. long] of rather soft grey stone.

1st July 1937

Drove from Glenmacnass to Sally Gap. Between the two brooks which run into the Inchavore River, I spoke to a young man who was spreading turf, his name was Long, and he lives in Killalane, which he said has three or four houses in it, on the right of road as you come up towards Glenmacnass. (That is, in Laragh East.) He said he lived in Glenmacnass near Laragh, and I asked him did he know 'Kill-aylan', and he at once said 'Kill-ə-lāne', correcting me, and said he lived there. I asked him what the bog was called where he was working, and he said 'the Fall ("Fál") Bog' (perhaps from the waterfall?) — that this was the name for all that piece of country (in Cloghoge and Carrigeenduff) (he pointed over as far as the hill I call 'Dalty'). He said the hill beyond 'Ciouc' (Kyowck) was called 'the Lough Flats' (that is the hill E of Lough Ouler, Laragh West). He said 'Lugadruhawn' was in the same place (Laragh West) — he pronounced it 'Lugadrootawn' (the 't' open as if he was saying 'h' with the tip of his tongue very close to the top of his front teeth). He said 'that mountain' (i.e. Scarr) was called 'Kanterch': 'Some calls it "Scarr" but the right name is "Kanturch" ' (the 'ŭ' short, and a hard 'ch' sound instead of a 'k'). He said it was 'right over Drimeen' (Drummin).

Pointing N he said all the country there was called 'Lavarnia' (that is the ridge N of the Cloghoge Brook in Cloghoge). He did not seem to know many names and I couldn't ask him leading questions. He had never been down into 'Duff, and had never been along the road from the Sally Gap past Luggala.

2nd July 1937

Mr Deeley ex National Teacher of Enniskerry lent me some notes on places in the neighbourhood, many of them copied from O'Curry's letters [*OS Letters*]. Today I and Sergeant Duignan went with him to Glencree. We went first to see a cup-marked stone in Tonygarrow (?): we looked for it near Mr Bradner's house (in Cloon?) but could not find it. Query, is this only a stone marked for blasting? There were several boulders blasted by dynamite there. We went on to Kavanagh's of the Relic, in Tonygarrow — one goes down the lane to Noble's house, and Kavanagh's is the house beyond, near the river. It is ¾ mile S of the 'T' of 'Tonygarrow' on the 1-inch OS map and a little to the W. The 'relic' is an irregular space of grass, with trees and bushes. There is a bullaun stone 15in. in diameter, and 8½in. deep, semispherical — it is cut in a large flat rock most of which is covered by grass. Fifteen yards N of this bullaun is a long low mound in the grass, hardly noticeable. It lies E and W. Mr Noble said this was the 'Giant's Grave', and he remembered when there were two small stones, one at each end of it, 11ft apart. He was positive about this distance, though the mound is now 15ft long. He is 79 years of age. He said the stones had been taken away, and he was told that about 75 years ago some men from Kingstown came at night and dug in it, but old Mr Kavanagh came out with two fierce dogs, and they ran away. Mr Noble had heard old men call the place 'the Rossán'.

Near the bullaun, lying loose, was the broken piece of the lower stone of a saddle quern 11in. wide, and about the same length: original size probably 11in. x about 16 to 18in. The end remaining, the thicker end, is 4in. thick. On the round side (not the grinding face) is a cupmark or hollow 3in. diameter x 1in. deep. The grinding side was concave and smooth.

The field W of it is Kavanagh's: it is called 'the Relic Field'. Mr Noble's fields have names — he gave me some:

'Mulligan's Field'
'the Flat'
'Cregg'
'Art's Field.'
(Cregg has a rock in it.)

He named 'Castle Toole' (in Oldboleys) and 'Cloghnagun' (in Tonygarrow) — he had no name for the rock at the E, called on the map 'Prince William's Seat'. The quarries above the bridge in Glencullen he called 'Kearneystown'.

Mr Noble was a stonecutter, and cut the stones for the Museum in Kildare Street, and other buildings in Dublin.

Mr Deeley said there was a pillar stone at Killegar, which fell and was buried in the debris of the sandpit, when the men were digging for sand and gravel. He says the graveyard extended much further N than the present enclosure.

He also heard that one of the Suttons dug sand out of the mote in the NE corner of Glasnamullen, and that his hair turned white in one night, and he never dug any more sand out of it.

4th July 1937

Woodend Hill, in the SW of Oldcourt townland. At the point '997ft', on the OS 1-inch map (or '998ft'), there is a 'rath', or earth monument of some kind. It appears to consist of the ruin of a large low bank of earth and stones about 70 paces in diameter, and inside this, not at the centre, but 40 paces from the W side of the bank, is a small mound in ruins, 21 or 22ft in diameter, and 22 paces in circumference. It is circular and about 3ft high. The centre has been dug out to a level 15 or 18in. below the level of the surrounding ground. In this centre was a circular chamber constructed of stones built like a wall, and in places of large blocks. This chamber appears to be circular and to have an entrance towards the E.

Presumably this is a burial monument of some kind. A field fence [extending N–S] on the E (I had no compass).

On the lower point of Woodend Hill to the SW is a natural outcrop of granite.

I walked then to the W corner of Ballynasculloge Upper, and on, across the S point of Ballynasculloge Lower, down to the ruined house in Ballynatona and straight down to the bend in the Liffey where the Ballylow Brook flows in, and so along the Liffey to Ballysmuttan Bridge.

14th July 1937

Near Baltinglass. While I was examining the milestone on main road in

Castleruddery Lower near Whitestown Bridge, numbered '30', man named Denis O'Toole, of Newtown (age about 50) stopped to speak to me. He asked me did I know the trough nearby, on the side of the road (this is the stone which I believe to be a cross-base, for a termon cross of Baltinglass Abbey). He then told me that when the road was being made, the engineer told the labourers to move the stone, but they couldn't: so next day again he told them to move it, and they could not, every time they stirred it it fell back into the same place: so the engineer said it was not to be moved, and they left it where it was. O'Toole said wasn't that queer, as he was sure if he got a bar, he could move it himself.

This I think shows there was an old tradition that this stone was not to be moved from its place, which I think verifies my conjecture that it may be the base of a termon cross.

I asked him had he ever heard of a holy well in Randalstown, but he said 'No'. He said there was a holy well called 'Knockcorrib Well' in Davidstown, up Germaine Finlay's lane, just beyond the gate on the upper side of Finlay's gate. That there are a lot of tombstones round it. There is a story that a man made nuisance in the well and the well disappeared, and a woman told them to clear the well, and she had a jar of water she got from the priest, and she told them to throw it into the well, and the well spouted up again at once.

O'Toole also told me that he was one of the men who drew the stone to Donard for Father Kavanagh — he called them 'the Piper's Stones' by which he meant the ogham and the other stone still at Ballylion.

He said the two stones were so close together that you could put your hands on the two at the same time — and that as a boy he often vaulted between them. They made a cart for the stone with log wheels, and tried to draw it direct, but it sank in a wet place — and there were two ropes, each with 47 men on it, drawing it out. In the end they had to draw it round by the road by Metcalfe's gate and Phillips'.

18th July 1937

Went with R. Barton to Cloghoge where he showed us a double bullaun stone — it is near the second bridge on the green road. Go in by a gap on the right-hand side of the road just before you come to the second bridge, walk along beside the road for 25 or 30yds, and the stone is in the bracken.

It is a large block of granite, some 3ft each way. From the outside of one hollow to the outside edge of the other is 23in. Each hollow is circular, [one is] 11in. in diameter, and [the other] is 10in. in diameter, each is 6½in. deep, basin-shaped. In the bottom [of one of the basins] a hole has been bored, 5½in. deep and 1½in. in diameter. This is a hole for putting in dynamite for blasting the stone. The worker must have been stopped before he finished the hole. The stones for building the bridge and walls and so on are all blocks made by blasting, and the diameter of the drill-hole on them is 1½in. There is a tiny hollow on the stone, 2in. in diameter, and less than ½in. deep.

25th September 1937
With Dr Macalister at Seefinn Cairn, taking rubbings of the stones in the passage. A young man named McGrath from Cloghleagh came across and spoke to us. He pointed to the clump of trees W of Athdown Mote, near the Liffey, and said 'that's called "the Religeen" '. He told us there was a mote in [Ballyna]brocky called ' "Mótharua" — a great big mote'. He showed us near the road running under Seefinn Mountain on the W a ruined mote. It is about ¾ of a mile S of Shankill crossroads, and a bit N of W of Seefinn Cairn, only about 20yds below the road. It is just a ruined pile of stones, 3 or 4ft over the ground [and] about 10 or 12ft in diameter (estimated) — in the centre is a hole at one side of which, at least, we could see a large stone like the side stone of a cist. McGrath said it had been dug in by boys after rabbits, and that the soldiers had also used it as shelter for putting a machine gun into: manoeuvring, I suppose. McGrath also said that there is a mound of earth outside the churchyard at Cloghleagh.

The place he calls 'the Religeen' is in Athdown townland. It is the church which I suggest was the original church from which Kilbride parish got its name. McGrath also said there is a rath in Lisheens, near the bridge.

5th October 1937
After Tinahely Court went to Kilcromer in Ballynamanoge. The name of the rath is written 'Kilcromer' on the OS map: but this is evidently a surveyor's error. An elderly labourer told me today that an old man named Tom Stafford told him it was called 'Kilcrammin'. This identifies it clearly

with 'Kilcromin' of the 17th-century documents. The rath is 40yds in diameter.

Went and looked at Reilly's excavation at 'Lobnasye'. The monument is curiously small, but it must have had several large capstones on it, which I have no doubt were used for building the house down the lane, formerly Nolan's, and lately occupied by Hughes who married Miss Nolan. The house is now deserted and roofless, and the large slabs at doors and hearth can be seen clearly.

28th July 1937

While waiting for the Kildare Archaeological Society's excursion I looked at the Ball Moat, Donard, and took measurements by pacing. The top is now uneven, but I suspect it was originally flat: it is 22 paces in diameter: there is a bank still standing round it in places, at other parts it has gone. It is now about 2ft high. This top mound is 18 to 20ft above a terrace which varies in width but on an average is 10 paces wide. The terrace is flat.

This [sketch, not reproduced here] is rather too regular, but I think it represents the original appearance, that is when it was a fortified place: query, was it originally a place of burial, i.e. a small tumulus or cairn on the

Fig. 116—Ball Moat, Donard (courtesy of the Royal Society of Antiquaries of Ireland ©).

top of the hill? The hill is of course natural, and has been dug and scarped into its present shape.

2nd January 1938

Ballynerrin near Kilcoole. About 150yds N (or a little E of N) of Ballynerrin House there is a small mound of stones covered by grass at the highest point of the field. This is all very low ground, below 50ft, but this piece between the two outlets of the Killincarrig River is a low sand and gravel hill — the river at least on the N must originally have made a wide marsh beside it. Is this mound of stones the burial mound of some prehistoric settlers on this gravel hill? Only excavation can say, but it looks rather like it. This would perhaps account for the early church (Kilvarnoge) so near, about 500yds to the S. The mound is 9cm from the N edge and 50.7cm from the W edge of Wicklow 6-inch sheet 13. It is only about 3ft high and 15ft or so in length.

9th January 1938

Went to look at Burgage Graveyard etc. Lord Walter Fitzgerald's description of 1913 in *JKAS* vii, p.416–423 is quite accurate for today. The head of a cross and the broken cross-base have been placed together some distance SW of the tower. There is a holy water font, rounded rectangular in shape, near the jamb of the doorway of the church (E side of tower). It has a hole in the bottom: no decoration. A stone which may have an incised cross on it stands on the S side of the tower: it is about 3ft high, tapering upwards to a point.

The well is down near the bridge over the small stream running between Burgage More and Burgage Moyle: it is on the other side of the road SW of the great cross. Just a spring bubbling up. The ground slopes up steeply on the N side, and it is full of banks and lumps, grass-covered. Could the mill have been somewhere here?

Françoise Henry on seeing the photo of the great cross, said there seems to have been a number of undecorated crosses in the west Wicklow–Kildare area, and instanced the Aghowle cross. She thinks it might date back to the 8th century, and compares the boss at the centre of the wheel with that on the cross at Dromiskin, Co. Louth. But note that the Burgage cross is very tall (14ft?) and appears to be cut out of a single block of granite.

Fig. 117—High cross at Burgage (courtesy of Dúchas The Heritage Service ©).

16th January 1938

Ballinacorbeg. Walked with R. Barton up from the main road near Annamoe, to look at a [granite] stone with marks on it (rock on NW brow of Ballinacor over the old hill at Annamoe). The figure resembles a crown ... [with several] indentations about the size of the top of your forefinger. The long horizontal and vertical lines are rock cleavages. There are other markings, but [these are] too indefinite … . The marks do not look very ancient. Barton suggested some stonecutter looking for stones suitable for millstones might have made them.

We went up the boundary between Ballinacorbeg and Tomriland to somewhere near the top of the hill (it was a wet and misty day). There is a road on the E side of the hill, and a ruined house near it. It seems to lead down to Derrylossary Church and Oldtown. The upper part of Tomriland has been tilled and fenced long ago, in big fields: they are still partly clean of furze, but the grass is damp and mossy. There are one or two piles of stones, probably cleared off the fields — but I could see nothing like a cairn.

Fig. 118—Carved boulder at Ballinacorbeg.

5th March 1938

At Glendalough with Françoise Henry. Went first to St Kevin's Cell, the ruins of a beehive hut of the type so common in the west of Ireland. Walls 3ft thick. Diameter about 11ft. About 80yds away, a little S of W, is a cleared and levelled space in the hillside: oblong, about 30yds long. We both thought this artificial — F. H. suggested that as there are no stones lying about, it may have had huts of wood built on it. Not so far from the cell, to the S, is another similar levelled space, round, about 25ft in diameter. It appears also to be artificial; some stones of what look like foundations of the platform are visible on the N side — it was also probably for a wooden hut. A little W of the cell, on the way to St Kevin's Bed, is a flat bluff like the one the cell stands on. This may have had a cell on it, but it shows no signs of remains.

Down at the Reefert Church the Board of Works restorations and buildings of walls have interfered with the appearance of the site. Just outside the SW corner of the graveyard is the mark of a circular foundation only 6 or 7ft in diameter.

Fig. 119—Small cross at Glendalough (referred to as No. 10 in the text) (courtesy of the Royal Society of Antiquaries of Ireland ©).

Went then to Templenaskellig. The church is later than Reefert (F. H.) judging by the doorway. The E window may be as late as Anglo-Norman times. The steps to the W of it lead to a sort of long cell, 4 or 5ft wide, flagged flooring, wall of small stones, with a recess on the N side. Leask's plan in the 1925 ed. of the *Guide* does not show this clearly. ...

It is recessed about 2½ft, and runs along for 6ft — after this the wall is so ruined no feature can be traced. From the recess the 'chamber' goes W for about 15ft. The end is ruined, as though the surrounding platform had slipped in. The whole space of this chamber spreads more widely than would appear from Leask's plan. ... If it was never wider than what Leask calls 'the causeway' then it was a long narrow chamber with perpendicular sides of small stone walling, with a recess (for a bed?) on the N side. Perhaps the large flat stones which lie on the platform formed part of its roof: perhaps it had a wooden roof. We could see the charcoal which the *Guide* mentions, in the wall. The wooden roof may have been burned. This was probably a living room connected with a primitive oratory which existed

Fig. 120—Bullaun stone near the forester's house.

before the present church was built — there are huts facing an oratory in the same kind of way, with perhaps a passage between, at Inishglora, and Teach Molaise on Inishmurray has a bench along one side (F. H.). So it might date back to the 7th century (or possibly earlier?). Some souterrains must have been not unlike this passage. There are no remains of huts here.

We went then to the 'church' ruin near the bridge over the Poulanass River (No. 5 in the map in the *Guide*). It has two well-dressed granite cornerstones one at each end of the bit of wall in which the little cross is stuck. But this wall runs NW–SE. The cross is not old (F. H.). Perhaps this is the ruin of some kind of building connected with the monastery. The caher (No. 7) is probably only a low protecting wall which surrounded a wooden building. If so excavation might reveal post-holes. Between No. 5 and No. 7 are heaps of stones, which may be the ruins of small buildings, perhaps of stone cells. On one is an old cross-slab, which a tree has grown round, so that it can scarcely be seen. The crosses on the piles of stones at No. 6 and No. 8 are not old, or at least show no old characteristics. Near the forester's house SE of No. 6 is a good [double] bullaun stone, sunk in the ground — [stone 4ft long; basin 1: 14in. x 13in. x 7½ –8in. deep; basin 2: 16in. x 13in. x 7½ –8in. deep].

The big cross at No. 9 on the N side of the river is an old one (F. H.). Where the Pilgrims' Road crossed the river, there are no stepping stones, but on the N bank there is a built stone platform: and so probably there was a wooden bridge across the river. I should guess the span at about 15ft.

The little cross at No. 10 is probably old (F. H.). The old road ran just S of it: it is still just visible, and some of the stones which made its foundation can be seen. Perhaps the stones piled up where the cross is are the remains of a hut.

Placenames given to me by Richardson's boatman: 'Camanure' ('Céim an iabhair'?) just W of Templenaskellig. W of it 'Lyreavea'— then the 'Split Stone Lyre', then the 'Slanty Lyre' ('Lyre' is a two-syllable word: 'Radhar'?). The wood there is 'Killagóla Wood'.

The brook at the end is 'Glánavdlá Brook' (it is very hard to represent the syllable I have written 'vdl' but it sounds rather like a very broad Irish 'l' after the 'v' — the way he pronounced might be written 'v-l' with a hesitation between and a broad guttural 'l'. Stress on last syllable and almost equally strong on the first). A number of people lived there in the days of the mines. He never heard of people called McCabe living there, but there are McCabes now living up in Brockagh.

On N side of lake, in Camaderry — 'the Long Bench' — a long line of rock up at the top. 'The Burnt Lyre'. 'Carrigaféen', on the flat above the Burnt Lyre. 'Kathleen's Rock', near where the boats are kept. Kathleen's ghost is seen there. On the Wicklow Gap road, the mines of 'Luganure' are on the S side, below Lough Nahanagan. The mines on the opposite, N, side of the road are called 'the Hairo' (pronounced like the Irish pronunciation of the word 'hero'). He spoke of 'Lough Ferb' (Fer pronounced like 'fir', the name of the tree).

The plantation in Lugduff covers:

1. 'the pasture' (of the mountain), just at the back of the cliff,
2. 'the middle hill', next S of 1,
3. Slayfonn next S of 2.

On the hill above Poulanass where the houses were, the field is called 'Bunnagore Field'.

We went on to St Mary's Church — originally it had no chancel, like the Cathedral and St Kevin's 'Kitchen'. The door can be dated from its framework and cross, by analogy from Maghera, Fore, etc. Also the style of building, with well-cut large stone blocks. The date may be last quarter of the 7th century (F. H.). The Cathedral also has the large stone, ashlar, masonry, but is perhaps a little later than St Mary's — say about 700 or a little earlier (F. H.). Note that the rounded stone of a pilaster or column, now in St Kevin's 'Kitchen' comes out of the wall of the Cathedral. The tower of St Kevin's 'Kitchen' is an addition: it was *originally* a rectangular building (no choir), with a wooden floor, and a third storey consisting of the croft. Perhaps a residential building like St Columba's House, Kells, and not a church (F. H.).

Aghowle Church and these three are of approximately the same date: early 8th century or late 7th (F. H.).

The arch over the lintel of the W door of the Cathedral is probably a feature of the rebuilding of the church after it had been burned and ruined: the lintel was thought to have perhaps been weakened by fire (F. H.).

None of the fragments in St Kevin's 'Kitchen' is older than the end of the 7th century.

John Richardson and his brother both told me that there is a passage at the N side of St Kevin's 'Kitchen', leading under the graveyard towards the Cathedral: and that their father had been down it. The entrance is now covered up: it was near a bush.

21st March 1938

Leask was down seeing about the waterproofing of the roof of St Kevin's 'Kitchen'. He said that the big 'ashlar' blocks in the front of the Cathedral are really slabs 6in. or so thick, placed on the front of the wall to improve its appearance — and that really the wall higher up than this is a better piece of building.

The round pilaster in St Kevin's 'Kitchen' was taken out of the wall of the Cathedral. There are other pieces in the wall. It was part, he says, of an early chancel arch.

30th March 1938

Went with Françoise Henry to Burgage. She thinks the great cross is in its original shape — the tenon on the top arm was made like that, and the arm has not been broken. But she says, query, could there ever have been an urn-shaped finial on top of it, as for instance at Ahenny, or could there have been some idea that the cross, or the pillar stone out of which it developed,

Fig. 121—Burgage cross-inscribed slab.

was a living thing, and the unshaped tenon be a sign of growth? Note that this cross is formed out of one stone, as a pillar stone would be.

She photographed the incised cross on the stone near the church building — in outline it has a design curiously reminiscent of the shape of the great cross.

Across the road to the W of the churchyard the grass-covered banks in the field suggest some kind of square enclosure.

We went on to Ballintober, and looked at the broken cross, which is only about 100yds or so WSW of Byrne's house. F. H. said it was clearly

303

being cut on the site, as the back of it is still quite unshaped. It must have broken while being moved, i.e. turned over, in the course of the cutting. It might be of any date. There are a lot of large granite blocks on the hill.

We went on to Lockstown. The place where the Labyrinth Stone was is well known locally — one man called it 'the stone with "the Walls of Troy" on it'. [Went to a house near the Robbery House where the stone used to be.] The house was locked up. The woman's brother Tom Carroll lives a little way up the Blackditches road, but that house was also locked. A man cutting stone nearby said he remembered the stone being taken to the Museum about 12 years ago. He knew the Robbery House and pointed it out to me. But neither he nor the other two or three men I saw had ever heard of a stone with a cross cut on it, much less knew where it was. We looked at the walls and the stones lying round, but could see no carving. The place is full of granite blocks, suitable for cutting. Many have been cut, others have wedge marks left by cutters who for some reason did not go on with the cutting. The walls of the lane are very thick, and are built of blocks of granite which look as if they'd been broken long ago with sledges. We only saw dynamite marks round the house. The Labyrinth Stone might well have been broken up if it hadn't been taken to the Museum.

The Robbery House is a natural crevasse between two very large granite boulders. The front of it towards the E has been built up with stones so as to make a small entrance — I could just fit through. The chamber inside must be 10 or 12ft long, nearly 6ft wide, and I think about 4ft high (all estimated). A few ferns, or stones rolled over the entrance part, would hide it completely. F. H. says this kind of place is still used in Connemara to hide poteen. I should say it is either for this purpose, or to hide stolen goods. Nothing prehistoric about it.

Went on to Killerk. F. H. [would date the cross] very early — in fact she even thought it might have been pagan, and have had a head on the top.

The Burgage Cross she would date as at least pre-Scandinavian, not later than [AD] 850.

7th April 1938
Lunched at Cronroe (the Bel Air Hotel). I found two granite blocks — a large one with a bullaun about 13in. x 11in. and 4in. deep — in this large

block there is another slight hollow, you could not call it a 'bullaun', but it is like the beginning of one. In the smaller block there is a bullaun about 13in. in diameter, circular, 4in. deep. Both blocks are near a thorn tree, about 150yds ESE of the house. (The bullauns are bowl-shaped.) Near them is a well, neglected and rather dirty, and a little further away is a small artificial pond, also dirty. Mr Huband speaks of 'several cavities'. I could only see the two blocks. Presumably the well is what he refers to as 'the Priest's Well', but there is no wall between it and the stones.

5th April 1938

Went along the upper road leading from the Wicklow Gap past Glenbride to Valleymount. At the highest point of this road, about 1230ft [OD], on the N side there is a stone on the bank, granite, with an incised cross cut on it, 10in. long by 7¾in. wide. The right-hand transverse cut at the top has a distinct extension downwards. This cross is in the townland of Togher.

9th April 1938

In Granabeg there is a green track leading downhill towards the bog, about ½ mile S of the junction of the Togher road and the road to Granabeg School. About 200yds down from the road there is another cross. It is on a pillar of granite, much buried in heather. The cross is in low relief. The stone now stands about 2½ft above ground. The arms of the cross are 5in. wide. The top arm is 9in. long. The stone is about 1ft 1in. wide.

A man named Miley, of Hollywood I think, told me the road is called 'the old green road'. It went on through the bog round Lockstown Hill, then he thinks it went N.

Eastward it leads up to the Wooden Cross which is the local name for the highest point of the Togher, where the other cross is. He said it was the continuation of St Kevin's Road.

FIELD NOTEBOOK 17:
April 1938–April 1939

17th March 1938

Templeteenan is a little E of the house near Ballinagee Bridge. It is on the old road (St Kevin's Road) which is clearly marked, grass-covered, on the N side of this house. It seems to be a quite featureless site. I was not able to distinguish even a church ruin from the piles of granite stones covering the hillside. Another name for it is 'the Church Park' [see pp 311–12 below].

Walked across the ford between Garryknock and Oakwood, and on to Knocknadroose. There seems to be only one inhabited house in Oakwood. Cornagrus is in Knocknadroose, a man pointed it out to me as being on the slope S of the bog, just W of a drystone fence. Here I found a granite stone with a natural cross on it, hard ridges standing out from the granite — about 24in. x 18in. When I got back to the road another man told me that the cemetery was higher up on this hill. He said the hill was called 'Cornagrus', and the hill above it to SW was 'Coontia'. The path to Glenmalure went between them and on towards Conavalla — by a place which he called 'Oonacleebawn' which he said was to the right of Conavalla. There are only three inhabited houses in Knocknadroose as far as I could see. This road from the ford is now broken up but it was a made road, with granite blocks forming fences on each side. 18th century?

18th March 1938

Walked by the green road to the forester's house and then up the zigzag to the ruined houses. The first, near a few oak trees, must have been a big one, but it is impossible to see exactly where its windows and doors were. In fact as the doorway on the N was 6ft wide, one wonders was it an enclosure rather than a house. Perhaps the house was on the E side, its back excavated out of the hill.

Further up are the walls of a cottage, and a pile of stones which may have been another. Further S again, but more towards the Lugduff Brook are two more rectangles of piled stones — perhaps ruins of two cottages? I walked on up to the wide fence or roadway which is the boundary of Derrybawn and Ballybraid — going up I kept on the E side, under the ridge of Derrybawn — and I came down by the Lugduff Brook. There is no track or pathway — but it is not a difficult walk. From the large house (No. 1) to the boundary on the ridge only took me about ¾ of an hour. The zigzag path at the beginning is a properly built road, the continuation of the green road. It dies out after the first house ruin. This road is probably an 18th-century road built to lead up to these houses and the land, which was most likely only then put under modern cultivation — like the Lime Fields in Fananierin.

20th March 1938

[Glendalough.] The [rectangular stone] containing three bullauns, which are three of the 'Seven Fonts': [dimensions:] at top 29in. x 40in., at bottom 27in. x 38in., 7in. deep.

Looked for St Kevin's Keeve. Mrs O'Neill of Brockagh pointed out to me where it was — it was a well by the N side of the river, under a tree, opposite the side of Wynne's house. Mrs O'Neill (a woman of 55 or so, at a guess) said she remembered the trees all hung over with rags when she was a child: that lots of people used to come there to be cured, and would wash their legs or whatever part it was in the well. But she says nobody goes there now. I could see no rags anywhere: but I did not go back and examine the spot closely.

In the field SW of the Lady Church a pit has been opened. There is only a very shallow layer of earth or clay on top, 10in. or 12in. Below it is all yellow sand, some of it very fine sand: deposited either by a lake or under a glacier. They are making concrete blocks out of it. At one point you could see in the side of the pit where a hole had been dug, about 4ft deep: it was filled in with burned (or blackened) stones, and some charcoal, and I saw two little bits of burned bones which looked to me like the bones of a rabbit. I don't know what this hole was — it was some 3ft across at the top of the sand.

21st March 1938

Glenmalure. Walked from the empty forester's house in Ballinaskea or Clonkeen up the path made by the foresters. It leads W up to the cliff in front of Art's Lough. From the top there is a view right up and down the valley. Lodarrig is straight opposite, at the back of Cullentragh Park. The raheen down by the river is just beneath. From it a diagonal line starts to run up the N side of the valley towards Mullacor. It does not go far but it would be quite feasible to walk in a continuation of its line across the scree up to the grassy top of the cliff. This route would not however go to Lodarrig, but a good deal E of it, to the slope of Mullacor itself. But if instead of going diagonally one clambered straight up one would come directly to Lodarrig and the white stones (which are clearly visible from the opposite side) here and there in the grass.

Afternoon, with Paddy Byrne [of Glendalough]. I took notes in pencil while Paddy Byrne was talking. [These notes are not reproduced here, as the following is a clearer version.] He is an elderly man about 60 or more who was gamekeeper to Mr Wynne, and who before that seems to have been employed by the mining company. He lost his left leg about 10 years ago, was sent to Dublin and had to have it amputated.

He was born in Glenbride. His mother came from Brockagh, near the Chapel. She died some 5 or 6 years ago in Philadelphia where she was with his brother.

I asked him first if he knew a place where they put the coffins down coming from Laragh. He said yes, it was called 'Cushóona Bush', that it was where an old woman hanged herself — that it was the custom to halt a funeral wherever a person had killed himself. He pointed me out the spot,

Fig. 122—Paddy Byrne of Glendalough.

between the Post Office (Dolan's) and the old school, now the Youth Hostel, on the lower side of the road.

We drove up then over the Wicklow Gap. He said: St Kevin's Road started from the monastery (i.e. St Saviour's). He could show it different places up the gap. It ran behind Kavanagh's house where the five querns were in one stone — and on past St Kevin's Keeve. The Keeve is a little well on the N bank of the river — (he called it 'Glendasan River'). A man named 'Squint' Mahon cut down the old thorn bush — he said he wouldn't be having people putting rags on his tree. Mahon was 'thick'. The Hotel was built on St 'Kavan's' Road. It was Dolan's long ago. Then a man named Jordan got it and pulled down Dolan's house, and built the present hotel or at least the oldest part of it. There is a piece of St Kavan's Road very clear, a little above the houses in Glendasan — he showed it to me (just above the wall leading down to the river, near a big granite rock — at the 'Hollyrock' Mine). All St Kavan's Road was paved like this bit. The road round Camaderry was made by the mining company — so was the bridge which was broken down in the big rain last summer. The 'Háiro' Mine is at the place where the road bends to the right. The county road was made in 1829. 'Ruppla' is a little further on (where the track to Lough Nahanagan goes off to the left). The brook there is called 'the Soger's (Soldier's) Brook'. The next two mines were called 'Cape Horn' and 'the North Mine'. All the mineworks on the left were part of the Luganure mines. (Boleybeg) 'Bóliabeg' is on the N slope of Camaderry Mountain. 'Coolmoon' and 'Lugburnoran' are other places on Camaderry, but on the other side. 'Tomanéena' is the hill S of the Wicklow Gap. The gap between Tomaneena and Lough Nahanagan is 'Lýravawn'. 'The Fair' is the next hill to the W — still in Sevenchurches. There were robbers on the Kildare side who used to meet robbers from the Wicklow side there with the cattle they had stolen, and exchanged them there — that's why it's called 'the Fair'. 'The Bench of the Fair' is below it towards the river. Where the Glanakeera Brook meets the King's River and Glashawee is called 'Inchagurnyáwn'. 'There was a house there — there were wicked fellows there.' ('Why were they wicked?'). There were Normans there long ago and 'they stole this fellow's daughter living in Imaal, and they were killed' (he got confused about this).

A 'gurnyawn' is the tuft of wool that you sometimes see on a sheep's rump over its tail. (He then spoke about the Madman's Road, but afterwards said more about Inchagurnyawn.) A big rock there is called 'Corrigaphreéchaun': in English that's 'the Fraughan Rock'. The last wolf was killed in Tomaneena and he's buried here in Inchanagurnyawn. A 'gurnyawn' is made of mud or turf, it represents those stone things you find on the mountains, what do you call them? ('Cairns'?) Yes, cairns — not keerawns. A 'keerawn' is a broken turf. ('Keerawn' or 'cawrawn'.)

The Madman's Road runs straight along the hillside above St Kevin's Road. It was a Colonel Smith of Baltyboys that built it. It was one of these Smiths that married Mr Stannus. ('When did he build it? was it 100 years ago?') Oh more, it might be 200. The Wooden Cross road (i.e. the road to Valleymount) is built on his road. At the top of the Wooden Cross road (i.e. at the top of the ridge) just going down to the Tōgher, there's a big stone on the side of the road with a cross cut on it. It's on the N side of the road.

All the Glendalough people call Valleymount 'the Cross', not 'Valleymount'.

The hill on the N side of Tonelegee (which you see on the right just after passing the top of the gap) is 'Crickgarr'. It's also called 'the Black Hill'. The slope of the mountain on this side of it (i.e. S of Crickgarr) is 'Bláneloss' ('bléan'): (this is E of Glashawee Bridge). The next hill N of Crickgarr is 'Barnaweelyeen' (this is the hill called 'Barnacullian' on the OS map). (It is the hill you see at the back of the valley which is on your right front as you go down to Glashaboy Bridge.) I said 'Glashawee' and he said 'Some people call it "Glashaboy" now'.

'The Thorn Brook' leads up from Annalecky Brook — it leads up to Mullaghcleevaun.

(What he called 'Barnaweelyeen' is evidently what the Ordnance map has as 'Barnacullian'; I am sure his version of the name is the correct one.)

Further down the King's River from Inchanagurnyawn is an old field called 'Inchanamulloge', that is on the S side of the river. On the N side, opposite it and not very far from the road is a rock called 'the Piper's Rock'. The people used to stop there on their way to the pattern at the Churches; they'd have tents there, and dancing and music. The pattern itself used to last three days. He didn't know if it began on the Saint's day (3rd June) or not.

We went on then to Templeteenawn, where he showed me where the old church ruin is. (I have already drawn the plan to scale.) It is just where

Fig. 123—Sketch-plan of Templeteenawn Church.

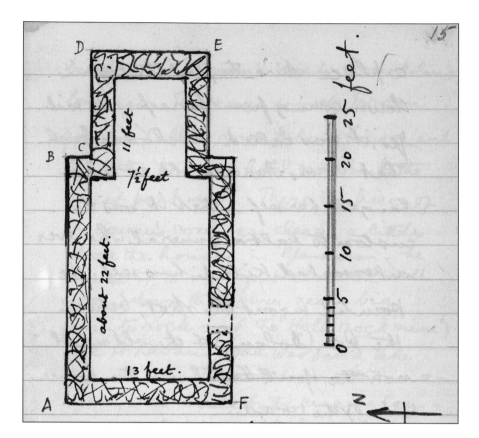

the Church Park is on the road, but up a little on the N side of the road, at the back of a knoll. The old road which he says is 'the Madman's Road' leads in here towards the house (now Reilly's). There is a roadway leading down from the graveyard towards this road, but it doesn't go quite all the way. The gateway into the graveyard is 3½ft wide. It is about 6ft to the S of the church wall.

[Dimensions of church: length of nave 22ft; width of nave 13ft; length of chancel 11ft; width of chancel 7½ft. Thickness of walls: nave 2ft 9in., chancel 2½ft, but the E gable is 3ft thick.] The door is about 6ft from the W wall but it is not clear; I think however I could see the doorway.

I looked for carved or inscribed stones in the church or churchyard but could see none. The church is built of granite blocks, many of them squared. The walls are now about 2ft high.

He gave me some names in Oakwood, going up to Lough Firrib. After Corrigaphreeghaun is 'Cláhoppéen'. Outside that is 'the Coob' (it sounded

312

a little like 'Coomb' but he didn't say 'Coomb', he pronounced the 'b' distinctly). Then there's 'Coolcawm' ('cúlcám'), and 'Córrignamáddra', and 'Glanacéera' is at the upper end. The head of Corrignamaddra is 'this side' (i.e. N) of Lough Firrib.

The spot just W of Glashawee Bridge (in Brockagh) is called 'Corrignamuck'.

La Touche of Laragh, the same family as the La Touches who carried out the evictions at Cloghoge, had 700 pigs grazing in 'Lugadroóchawn' [Lugadroohaun], and 400 of them were swept down the Glenmácanáss waterfall in a flood, and the rest went wild and rushed over the hill to 'Ballinountagh', and the Ballinountaghs [i.e. the people from Ballynultagh?] drove them to Naas and sold them — and why not?

The mountain at the back of (i.e. S of) the Fair is 'Corriglusk'. The flat W of the gap where the three brooks meet is called 'Tomsesk' (that is the whole area).

I asked him then about the valley between Derrybawn and Lugduff, that I walked up on Friday the 18th. He said it was 'the Bookeys' who made the green road and the zigzag. The first house, near the trees, is called 'Baker's Walls'. It is in ruins a long time. Gunsmiths lived above Baker's. In Lugduff (where the houses are now hidden by trees) there were at least five families. He remembers Tom Byrne living there. Tom and his brother John owned the Middle Hill. One house was Matt Byrne's, and there were two other Byrnes, and Quins. I asked him the name of the village: he said it wasn't called anything except 'Uppertown'. 'The Prison' (he pronounced it 'Prezen') is at the head of the brook going up to 'Mullaghmore', that is the brook on the N side of the Middle Hill (what he calls 'Mullaghmore' is the top of Lugduff or at least the E end of it).

The hill NW of the shooting lodge he called 'Kyowk Rock' ('ciabhc', one syllable).

He then spoke about Glenmalure: he said the old raheen there was called 'Bóliacróne', and that the plains of Lodarrig was where Feagh McHugh O'Byrne and the English fought a battle.

22nd March 1938

The Cushoona Bush was an old thorn bush on the N side of the road from Laragh to Glendalough. It is between Dolan's (the Post Office) and the

Youth Hostel, which was the old school, nearer to the hostel. Mr Kavanagh showed me the place, just where a stream runs down from the road towards St Saviour's. The bush died and fell down. An old woman is supposed to have hanged herself there. In the field above the road, 20yds up or so, there is a place where water runs out, not exactly a well, but a little spring I think — at least a wet place in the field, among some big stones.

Another day (19th) Paddy Byrne gave me a few other names — towards Glenmalure side: 'Slayfonn', then 'Mullacor', 'Mullaghmore', 'Corrig', 'the Hag's Sloughs' (pronounced like 'plough'), then 'Conavalla'.

NW of the Upper Lake are 'the Troman Loughs', then 'Glánavlágh Beg', then 'Glánavlá'.

11th April 1938

Blessington. After the court I went and saw Mr Michael O'Connor National Teacher of Lackan. He brought me to see Mr John Lennon of Kilbeg — house on left of the byroad leading up to Kilbeg Lodge. He gave us a number of local names … I am publishing them for Mr O'Connor in *JRSAI* June 1938 [see below].

He knows the old well with the roofing stones over it — he said it was called simply 'Mack's Blest Well' from the man who owned the land. There's a 'raw' up against it, in the field E of it. It's supposed there was an old church there. The well below is called 'St Boodin's Well'.

The rath a little bit W of the old well he called 'the Round Garden', and he said the boys used to play football there, and there used to be 'rasslin' (i.e. wrestling) there in old days, but that has died out. He remembers when he used to have to go and milk the cows on the mountain above the lodge and carry back the milk, and he remembers his mother carrying back the milk from the mountain S of Black Hill in a side pail. He used to cut the oats with a reaping hook, and he remembers it being threshed with a flail — or even with a handstick — his mother used to thresh it with a handstick, kneeling down with the oats in front of her: and as she threshed it she threw it up over her head (I think he said into the room above). You could only thresh with a flail if you had a good barn.

Not many houses have gone into ruin round him in his lifetime — he showed me two or three further up the byroad than his house. The little lane going to the right to the mountain a little bit W of his house is called

'Pound Lane' — there's a round place on it where they used to count the sheep.

He spoke of 'Glanmicanass', 'Lugadroochawn', 'Glanagoppul' (in Ballinoultagh [Ballynultagh?]), 'Glanakee' (in Ballinoultagh [Ballynultagh?]), 'Blaneloss' (in Ballinoultagh, W of Black Hill [Ballynultagh?]), 'Lugacullyeen', 'Krucknagark', 'Krucknanob'. He knew the mountains well going after sheep.

[Local names given by John Lennon of Kilbeg:]
'The Stonecutter's Rocks', 'Tor Stone', 'the head of the spring well', 'Glanmore', 'Corrnahorny', 'the head of the nigh brook' and 'the head of the far brook', then 'Whelp Rock' is next, 'Corrnamuck' is next, 'Brushy' is next, 'Billy Byrne's Gap' (aged 96, [he said the] mountain is 'full of blind holes') is next, that finishes our boundary, 'Kylebeg', 'The Tredders' — a pasture ('Tradders' or 'Trudders').

Kylebeg
1. 'Bunnagbawn' grazing, back of Black Hill.
2. 'The Cunnakus', into (1).
3. 'Buddyock', 'Budgach' this side of (1).
4. 'Ballnaskoob' — turf, this side of Black Hill.
5. 'Shanavalya', this side of Sorrel Hill.
6. 'Bognahown', this side of the brook towards Sorrel.

'The Tick Rock' this side of Glanmore, 'the Moonroo', 'Thrumawn' near Shanavalya, 'Ballinaslōckan', 'Knickeen', 'Shanyharch', 'the Coon', 'Thoor', 'Moanvayn', 'Codderawaddra', 'Kricknaweena', 'Bawnagrash', 'Drimroo', 'Shileshawn', 'Gornaweena', 'Klucknagollyeen', 'Tubberanarawn', 'Lackan', 'Koolyamoon', 'Kishnagolleen', 'Clorenawn' (unbaptised children buried there), 'Gornathro'.

13th April 1938
Tuckamine, Co. Carlow. Edward O'Toole of Rathvilly told me of an ogham stone, 200yds E of Rathmore Bridge, on the boundary between Tuckamine and Ballybit. I saw it today. The ogham inscription is on the rounded surface, not on an angle. This might read: 'MUCU IBUCT'.

Mr O'Toole says that some years ago he saw this stone built into a gap, and that the portion which could be seen appeared to have ogham markings on it. Recently a labourer's cottage has been built on the spot, and the stone was taken out and left on the grass margin by the road. I should say there is danger that the stone might be broken up.

I also saw at Broughillstown, Co. Carlow, a pillar stone in a field. It is 4ft high and trapezoidal in section — with groovings on it like the Ardristan stone. All the sides show groovings, but only two … go all the way down, the others die out some way below the top. It is of granite. The similarity to the Ardristan pillar makes me wonder if the groovings could be artificial. I spoke to the woman of the house who was drawing water in the yard on the other side of the road. She said her husband's father used to say that some old walls or old ruins had been cleared away there long ago — and that they found skulls there, when making ditches. This place is about two miles S of Clogh.

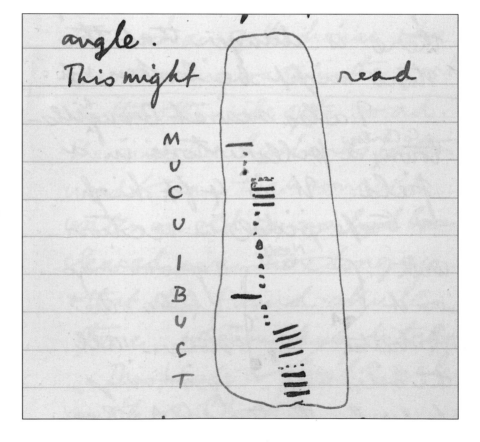

Fig. 124—Sketch of ogham inscription on stone at Tuckamine, Co. Carlow.

14th April 1938

Calary Lower. Excavated the cist at Agower, with Sergeant Heaney, Garda Tuite and Miss Mary Bermingham, a 'freelance' in the Museum. Jack Carey, ploughman to Fox, found it when ploughing. He saw the pot when they lifted the flag, and didn't know what it was: he said he thought it might be metal. One of the Foxes was with him. He said the spade fell against it, but as he also told me, before I started to dig, that there was a flag at the bottom of the grave, it is clear that they put a spade right down to the bottom, and I am pretty sure they broke the pot to see what was in it. Most of the rim was in position, to a depth of 6in.: the rest of the pot was in bits, the pieces all through the cist mixed with earth and grass. All showed fresh breaks. The outer surface was a very fresh red-brown colour, the inside was black. When it dried, the outside turned yellowish-brown and the inside grey. All the cremated bone was at the bottom: even in disturbing the cist they had hardly scattered more than one or two fragments of bone. There was very little bone, not much more than would fill a teacup.

Carey said that an old man named Sutton, over 80, who lives near there, said he had never heard of anything of the sort being found in the district.

Mr Fox presented the pieces of the urn to the National Museum.

I got the name of the little hill on the W boundary of Calary from both

Fig. 125—Cist at Agower, Calary Lower, during excavation (courtesy of the Royal Society of Antiquaries of Ireland ©).

Fig. 126—Reconstructed encrusted urn from cist at Agower, Calary Lower (courtesy of the Royal Society of Antiquaries of Ireland ©).

Carey and Fox. They call it 'Knuckdauy' — not quite '-doy', the 'o' is more like 'aw', and makes a very long syllable. This is quite clearly O'Curry's 'Knockdaee', and represents 'Cnoc Dáithi'.

3rd May 1938
Crosspatrick. The churchyard is clearly an old one, though there are not any old stones visible in it. One stone probably part of the jamb of a door is built into the road wall: it shows a chamfered edge. I should say the site is probably long pre-Norman though there is nothing above ground to prove it. Its foundation may have had some relation to the prominent Anglo-Norman mote about a mile away, in the townland of Loggan Lower, Co. Wexford, which is in the parish of Crosspatrick. One gravestone reads:

'HERE LIETH THE BODY OF JOHN FIFGARROLL NITE OF GLINWORTH,
LORD HAVE MERCY ON HIS SOUL.
ALSO HIS DAUTER.'

No date [on the gravestone].

April 1938

A Bronze Age cist was found at Aghfarrell, Co. Dublin, just beside the Co. Wicklow border, and I brought J. Raftery out to investigate it. It contained a crouched burial lying on its right side with a food vessel behind the head. Raftery took particulars and brought skeleton and pot to the Museum [see p.321 below].

5th May 1938

The old road led up from Glenealy by Ballydowling, and then by Barnbawn, Garryduff, Moyntiagh (past the old mill) and Parkroe to Trooperstown and so down to Killafeen. The old mill at Moyntiagh near Garryduff crossroads had a long mill-race carefully built, bringing the stream in from the N: there must have been a fall of 15 or 20ft for the water at the mill building.

22nd May 1938

Photographed the cross inscribed on the stone at Togher ('the Wooden Cross') near Valleymount. 'The Wooden Cross' is the piece of road consisting of the hill leading up from Togher to this spot and this bit of road where the stone is. It is only the piece of road. The hill beside it is called 'Togher Hill'. Went down the green road in Granabeg and photographed the cross there. I believe this was a chapel or rather church site. Note that O'Connor (*Wicklow OS Letters* p.317) says Granabeg parish is in Lower Talbotstown barony, but that there is no church in ruins or no old churchyard in the parish.

I walked over Lockstown Hill. A young chap named Farrington who lives in Lockstown said the green road that I had come down was called 'the Coantagh road', that it had come down from 'Coantagh' (Quintagh). This agrees with A.R. Nevill's map, though the road he gives is evidently

Fig. 127—Cross-inscribed boulder at Togher (courtesy of the Royal Society of Antiquaries of Ireland ©).

only roughly mapped, drawn as a straight line, without showing bends. One can still trace it after crossing the fence between Granabeg and Lockstown, in the heather: it bends N towards the houses on the N side of Lockstown Hill. But after about 300yds or so the trace here is lost. Whatever way it went, it clearly came down beside the house in Lockstown where the Labyrinth Stone came from (Farrington called it 'Quinn's'). I conclude that it came this way because of the way the road is drawn on Nevill's map — coming from Togher Bridge, crossing the King's River where the bridge is now and going straight W over Lockstown Hill. The old walls of the road or lane which leads past this house ('Quinn's') are built just like the old

320

walls of the bit of green road in Granabeg: big granite stones either unbroken or broken with sledges — no dynamite used.

Farrington said the big rock on the top of Lockstown Hill was called 'the Mass Rock' and that his father said there was a chapel there. I looked at it: it is a big rock of granite, all breaking up through weathering. No marks at all on it, and no signs of a chapel or a building. Possibly he was really thinking of the Granabeg stone? Query this.

There can be no doubt about the existence of a road joining the Wooden Cross, the cross in Granabeg, the Labyrinth Stone and going on to Togher Bridge between Coonmore and Slievecorragh. It was a road 12ft wide or so, and in the boggy parts had a ditch dug beside it. How old is it? Even if it is a 17th- or 18th-century road, was it on the track of an older road?

24th May 1938

Aghfarrell. Another burial was found in the sandpit, an urn inverted over cremated bones. Two urns were found, without any protecting stones. One was broken, the other was preserved. I got it from Patrick Healy and brought it to the Museum. It was found some 20ft or so from where the cist was found. I sent a full report to the Museum.

The urn is rather like one of the Burgage More urns.

A few pieces of cremated bone found with the urns were shown to Professor Jamieson on 17th June 1938. He said they were the bones of a small adult person.

15th June 1938

Mr John Crammond of Threemilewater reported the find of a skull in a sandpit. I went out there today. The pit is on the little hill ⅜ of a mile W of the word 'Maghera' on the 1-inch map. A lot of digging had gone on in it long ago. We could trace an old fence of stones running across it N and S down to the river. The skull was under this fence — the boy who found it Myles Hughes said it was some feet below the sod, i.e. 6ft or so, and perhaps 2ft below the fence. No stones round it — it was not a prehistoric burial. Perhaps someone killed at the defeat of Sir Henry Harrington in 1599?

17th June 1938

Professor Jamieson examined the skull. He said it was an elderly person, about 50, probably male. Teeth not worn at all, the skull of a common man — the type found among the Saxon serfs. Irregularities and unevenness in the skull are indicative of this. Perhaps he suffered from rickets in childhood, as the forehead was rather bulging. No evidence that it was prehistoric. I left the skull with him.

21st June 1938

With Professor MacNeill. First to Dunboyke. [The cross-slab] is outside the church, the bottom is buried in the ground, so it is hard to see and measure it. There is a round stone, in two parts, with a hole in centre, at N side of graveyard. Mr Thomas Mason photographed these. For measurements of the church see Walshe, *JRSAI* vol. 61, p.140.

Professor MacNeill thinks the church is on the old site of the dún.

Went on to Kilbaylet. In the extreme N of Kilbaylet Upper, on the W side of the road, is a small rath: its measurements are as follows: fort 25 paces internal diameter. Inner bank 6ft high over ditch. A small outer bank. Ditch about 15ft wide.

Professor MacNeill considers that this may have been Dunbolg, as he thinks this is the position Dunbolg should be in, at the S entrance to the defile. It is just S of the last house in Woodenboley.

We went on to Crossoona Rath. He considers that this is very old: is it Dun Buchat? We went finally to Kilranelagh, where I showed him St Bridget's Well, and the 'Gates of Heaven'. The graveyard is very large and full of little enclosures made of lines of stones like ruined walls. They may be only boundaries of family graves. There is one old cross, decorated on one face with a boss. Mason photographed it.

Ned Stephens lent me some maps of the Synge properties — one is a map of Glanmore. It seems to have been made for a lawsuit as it shows 'plf's mill'; but it is not signed or dated. It shows a road coming up from the bridge at Clora. This road curved round W from the bridge, then NW, and crossed the avenue a little to the SW of the house. Then it stops, but further NW in the same line a track zigzags up the hill, and goes about halfway to the waterfall — no further. The house at the W end of Ballymaghroe near Tiglin is not shown on this map, but a road runs off the present Ballymaghroe Hill road, at about the middle of Tiglin, towards Ballycullen: and joins the old road to Ballycullen that is shown on the OS 1-inch map.

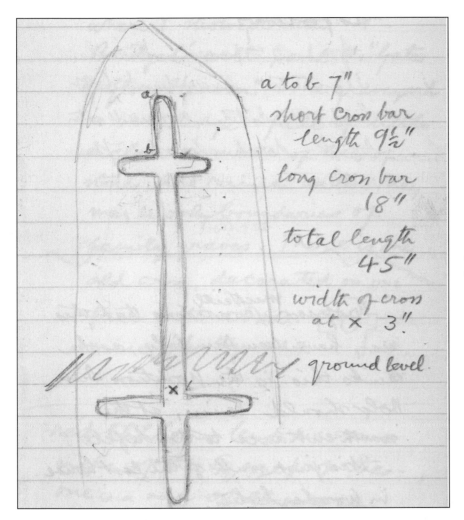

a to b 7"
short cross bar
length 9½"
long cross bar
18"
total length
45"
width of cross
at x 3"
ground level.

Fig. 128—Sketch of cross-slab at Dunboyke.

But the map does not distinguish between old roads, new roads and tracks. It also shows an old road running along the SE boundary of Ballycullen.

Next is a 'Map of part of the lands of Upper Aghoul surveyed for Francis Synge Esquire, by Bartholomew Swiney, December 1813'. It shows the old road through Aghowle village … . The existing road … is not shown: on the map the brook ends in a patch of bog containing seven acres. The place where the two main roads join is just outside the map so that the place where the bullaun stone is does not come into the map. The name Sleanaglogh is spelled 'Slevenaclogh'.

Next is a 'Survey of the Lands of Killfee and Cloragh etc. … surveyed for Francis Synge Esquire by Brownrigg and Co., 1804'. Total of Killfee 130

Irish acres and 28 perches. Ballardbeg is called Killfee, and the rest of it is the piece now in Ballymaghroe adjoining Nunscross Bridge and the river. The bounds are the same as on the map of 1776 by Nevill of which I have a tracing.

But the position of Kilfee Church and the old road beside it is more correctly shown. This is called 'private road' on Nevill's map, but on this map it is 'Road from Wicklow'. I have marked it in pencil on my tracing. Ballymaghroe is spelled 'Ballymurroghroe'.

25th June 1938

Went up the hill at Ballymanus from the W, from the road that goes W from Ballymanus House. The top of the hill is contoured .... There is nothing on the top of the hill but little outcrops of rock here and there.

The church ruin at Killaduff is not up here at all, but away down, 400 or 500yds from the river, opposite Craffield.

26th June 1938

Went back to the top of the Wicklow Gap, and looked to see if there was any boulder there on or near St Kevin's Road showing any mark of decoration. There is not. A man following sheep told me that the straight line through the bog, which I walked on the previous Saturday, 18th June, is supposed to be St Kevin's Road. He said it went to 'the Churchyard', meaning Templeteenawn, and that it then went up the hill, not the way the old road to Valleymount goes: but he couldn't tell me where it went.

On Saturday 18th June I walked up Tomaneena and across to the Fair (where there is a small heap of stones on the very top) then down to Inchagurnyawn — then back to the top of the Wicklow Gap by the straight line through the bog, which you can see quite clearly looking down from the Fair. But it is all bog, and I could not see any remains of the road, though the line is visible and one can follow it.

24th June 1938

Received a letter from Christopher Cullen, Donard, dated 22nd June 1938. We met him when out with Professor MacNeill on Tuesday, and asked him about placenames in Mullycagh. He says:

'As far as I can trace the battle which was fought about Hollywood Glen was nearer Hollywood village. The place is called the (Bloody Vales) it must be near St Kevin's Chair that's where the red girl haunted St Kevin he flew then to Glendalough and [took] rest in the cave. He said "By that lake whose gloomy shore …" .' (He quotes the whole poem.) 'People come from far parts of the country and sit in this chair in Hollywood Glen and say some prayer to St Kevin, it cures a pain in the back … .' (He tells the story of St Kevin and the woman with the loaves which were turned into stones.) 'Those stones are now steps across a small lake in the Churches called "the big bawns" near the old churchyard … . There is a shaking stone up in Scalp where there is supposed to be a lot of money hid in it. There is an old man named Pat Hegarty, Scalp, who would give you its history, beside this stone he lives. He would tell you about a man who held up the long car years ago and was tried in Baltinglass and before he was hung he shouted in the court house was there anybody from Scalp in the Court, he said my treasure lies in it and people were afraid to go near him. Hollywood Glen in those days was a den for highway robbers. The carriers had to pass through it before the other road was made.'

(I sent the letter to the Folklore Commission.)

1st July 1938

(ex relatione Ned Stephens) Mary Ark's Well is in the wood above the farm buildings of Glanmore on Ballymaghroe Hill. It is used to bring water to these buildings. The people said it was wrong to interfere with it. That was about 50 years ago.

2nd July 1938

The site which is called a graveyard in Killaduff is a featureless raheen, part of the wall of which has been removed and rebuilt in straight lines: perhaps to make a field fence or the wall of a lane? The encircling wall is stone-built, about 2ft high and 3ft thick. Rock outcrops here and there inside. There are also loose stones inside — no cut stones that I could see and no trace of a church. NE of it in the same field is a pile of stones 20ft long or so, some of them big stones. This could possibly be the ruin of a cairn, but it might also be merely a pile of field stones.

9th July 1938

At Preban. The old graveyard is just near the road opposite the modern church. All the graves in it seem to me to be Catholic. The headstone is there to Philip and Patrick Leacy:

'DEPTd THIS LIFE 21 JUNE 1798'

(two men killed at the bridge in 1798). The remains of the foundation of a church are there — I think it was a church with a chancel, but even that is not clear. Could not take measurements. I think the wall of the graveyard is that of an old circular rath. I looked at the old headstones, but there are no ancient sculptures — one or two blocks of stone seem to show a chamfered angle, and perhaps came out of the old church. The caretaker, an old man, pronounced it 'Príbawn', accent on first syllable.

Miss Hanbidge, whose father lived at Tinnehinch in Glen Imaal, sent me a story she got from a relative about Ballintruerbeg Castle, 'written down by John Hanbidge aged 77, born at Ballintruer. Father of the Reverend A.A. Hanbidge of Dundalk Grammar School. July 1938'.

'The following is an old story of long ago. There is an old Danish castle a short distance (from) Hanbidge's house at Ballintruer. In about 1750 a man in that locality had a dream on three nights in succession, that if he went to the Dane's castle in the night time and dig a hole in [the] floor he would get a chest of gold. He should observe two conditions strictly to be observed. First no one of the party to speak a word until the gold was found. A party was made up. They were to take a live cock with them and kill it when the gold was discovered. The party went to the old castle and dug the hole four feet down when the man that was using the fack (a spade) hit an iron box, he gave a great shout and a curse, the fack fell out of (his) hand and the iron box receded from him. They got a great fright and ran away. Next day a man went to see the digging, he found a large lump of gold worth several pounds.

'I visited this old castle in 1934. Portion of one side wall was standing and one gable end. The standing walls are 12ft high and 3½ft thick. The hole in the centre of the floor is there to this day is about 4ft by 2½ft. There is also a hollow in the ground around the castle like a dyke where water was let in from an adjoining stream. From this account one could think the Danes had the best of the fight for the chest of gold.'

16th July 1938

Walked from Glenmalure Hotel to the top of Kirikee where it bounds Ballinabarny and Ballintombay Upper. The top is flat. There is a very wide distant view, mountains on the W, sea on the E. There are two small Ordnance Survey cairns on it — a small outcrop of rock and boundary fences, mere banks. I spoke to an elderly man named Byrne, I think his Christian name is Mick. He lives in the highest-up house on the roadway that runs up through Carriglinneen near the boundary of Kirikee. He says Russacoose (he pronounced it something like 'Réssacoórse') is the part of Carriglinneen on the road near the hotel. This is where the road runs under the cliff — so I feel pretty sure that '-coose' = 'cuas', 'a cave'.

Coolnahoóry is the part of Carriglinneen beside the bounds of Kirikee (pronounced 'Keérakeé'). The cairn (which C.M. Byrne calls 'Art O'Neill's Grave') is called 'the Cloughraun' — Byrne always heard it so called.

I think that Carriglinneen is 'Carraig glinnín', 'the little glen', meaning what the State Papers call 'the mouth of the glen' (*JKAS* vol. xi, p.149). 'The mouth of the glen', or 'the little glen', would mean the place where the spur of Fananierin and the side of Carriglinneen Hill come fairly close to one another, after which there is a widening at Drumgoff before the glen proper begins.

17th July 1938

At Mullans near Tinahely. Pronounced 'Moólins'. Walked up to Mr Byrne's third field as I thought I saw a rath there, but it was only a rock outcrop. Mr Byrne said there was a little raheen in a field to the N, so I went on through the fields but I missed it. It must be quite small. The fields are big, well fenced, wide courses left for the streams, some ruins of houses — a bit of bog where the rath is. [There is] a big ruined house standing among trees, with ruined outbuildings.

I met Mr Collins aged 77 on the road. He said this house goes by the name of 'Ebbs's outbuildings'. Ebbs used it for foddering cattle. I asked him was it a mill, he said 'No', asked him did he know any mill anywhere near, he said he didn't. He said there are two more raths in Mullans to the N. There was quite a good roadway from [Ebbs's house] to the old road — but it is all grassed over. I'd say this was an 18th-century house, of a fairly large farm. Who was Ebbs? Mr Collins pronounced Curravanish 'Co̊oraváhnish', 'cúra mhágnuis' (the short double 'o' sound, not exactly long 'ú').

The OS map marks 'site of raheen' in Mullans North, just N of this ruined house.

Mr William Deeley, ex National Teacher, of Enniskerry, wrote me a letter in July 1937 adding some details to what he told me when I went to Glencree with him:

'(1) The late Father O'Dwyer, first parish priest of the new Enniskerry parish which was established in 1860, one day visited the Killager [Killegar?] burial ground accompanied by a couple of labourers with spades. He took with him a rough map of the graves. It is alleged that this map was sent to him from the Vatican Archives. The labourers proceeded to excavate the grave indicated in the "V.A." map, and soon discovered a "large" gold cross which was immediately taken possession of by the reverend gentleman. Nothing ever afterwards was heard of the "large" gold cross, in this parish by the people.

(2) Up to 29 or 30 years ago the old people of the district enclosing the [Powerscourt] waterfall were in the habit of showing visitors to the fall what was known as the "Kneeling" or "Praying Stone", which had I am informed two hollow marks, made it is alleged by the continual marking of the persons praying while kneeling thereon. The use of this stone by the penitents may have been a source of revenue to the holy men of the monastery or church reputed to have been in this secluded district in ancient times. This stone was dislodged owing to the terrible rush of water caused by a "cloudburst" in the mountains about 29 or 30 years ago and was supposed to have been carried down the small river for some distance. My informant believes it is still possible to recover it from the river.

(3) A flint arrowhead is in the possession of a gamekeeper named MacLauren who resides somewhere up in the mountains near the Seven Churches … (at Lough Bray).'

He does not say who his informants were. The stone mentioned in (2) is of course the 'Praying Stone' in Deerpark, Powerscourt … .

11th September 1938

At Kilmalum, Co. Kildare, with Professor MacNeill and Michael O'Connor National Teacher of Lackan. In that part of Kilmalum which is near Glenmore there is a place which is said to be an old burial ground. There is nothing there but a couple of low grassy banks, quite shapeless, and a couple of granite boulders: beside one of the banks is a small hollow with nettles in it, and in this there was a small rough stone cross, which was taken out of the hollow a few years ago and set up beside the fence near the place: it is broken in two, and the break looks recent, so perhaps it was broken in being moved. One arm of the cross is broken off; a very old break, I should say… . The shaft is oblong 9in. wide and 5in. deep. There is a small cupmark near the bottom and what looks like a raised line near the break, but the granite is too worn to know if this is a pattern or not. [Height of cross 41in.]

The church site according to a man named Creighton who showed it to us [is in a field called 'the Hollow Field': and the field directly S is called 'the Relickeen': the field to E is called 'the Slang']. There was a house just NW of the church site in the Hollow Field, but its walls have now completely disappeared. It is marked on the old OS map (1-inch 1860 ed.) so it has disappeared since then. From the fact that the field next to S is called the Relickeen I suspect that the church site was there and not where the cross is.

In the SW corner of the Hollow Field is a big hollow with sides which look as if they had been artificially shaped, and the dried-up bed of a stream — a sort of steep grassy glen — runs down to it from the SW. Could this have been the fish pond of a monastery?

Perhaps this is the place which Mr Henry said was called 'Mudyeenacrow'. Could this name be a corruption of 'Bótharín na gCró'? There is an old roadway, or there was one, leading in from the E, and it would have led across the hill towards old Tipperkevin Church. Creighton's pronunciations: 'Tubber kevin', 'Glan Ding'.

Professor MacNeill said an old Irish territory was divided into three kinds of land: 'Magh', meaning cleared land; 'Sliabh', moorland; and 'Fidh' or 'Coill', woodland.

He said 'Domhnach' definitely meant an early church of importance —
5th, 6th or 7th century. He also said 'Seipéal' was a derivative of the French
'chapelle', not the Latin 'capella' — so that it (the Irish word) means a
subordinate church built after the Anglo-Norman invasion.

September 1938
Ned Stephens says there are three bullaun stones near Derrylossary
Church, three in one stone, and two single ones.

14th September 1938
A man named Ghent giving evidence at Castledermot Court said he lived
at Rahoonbeak; he pronounced it 'Rahoonbake' (written in Irish
'Ráthúnbéic' or 'Ráthúnbéac', I could not hear which) stress about equal
on the three syllables, perhaps more on the first and third. There are four
houses in the townland and about twenty people.

30th September 1938
Mr Michael O'Connor, National Teacher, Lackan, who is arranging to
excavate the raths in Ballinahown etc. before they are flooded by the Liffey
scheme, and is now measuring and planning the rath marked 'No. 4' in
Lackan in my notebook writes:

'I got a name for it from the owner of the land James Cullen: "Rath na
Frishteáin", "Rath na Fristawn", "Raw na Frichtawn": he heard all three
names from the old people who lived there years ago.'

It was formerly Tobin's [land], now called 'Tobin's Rath'.

Michael Duignan was told of the finding of a flint arrowhead near
Lough Bray. We went to see where it had been found. The spot was at the
head of the cliff or amphitheatre surrounding Lough Bray Lower. Mr
George McLaren, gamekeeper and steward employed by the Guinnesses
who own Lough Bray House, found it some time ago when out on the
mountain. He saw a small white thing on the black turf (peat), where the
grassy top had broken away and one of the turf banks was forming which
one finds all over the mountains: caused by the turf being stripped off by
the weather? The turf here must be 9 or 10ft deep. The spot is on the NE
side of a sort of pass up the cliff, where the turf is gone and the gravel
shows. This pass has the name of 'the Cat's Walk' or 'Cat's Ladder'. McLaren

got this name from the old people. He says it is just the kind of place which deer would use as a pass: and he suggested a man was lying in wait for them to shoot at the deer, and the arrow may have wounded one of the deer: or perhaps been lost … . I brought down a little bit of the turf. The arrowhead was [found] about 2ft below the grassy top. From below, the place is a little bit to the right of a scar on the face of the cliff. The arrowhead … is made of greyish white quartz, not of flint.

9th October 1938

With W.J. Hemp and his assistant Gresham. First, visited the big rath in Glasnamullen. Mr Sutton of 'Sutton's of the Fort' pointed out its boundaries — it is only on the W side that the bank and ditch remain, and on the S. On the E and N it has been levelled and the fences are modern. It is divided in two by a modern fence running E and W: Mr Sutton calls the two fields 'Little Fort' and 'Big Fort'. (He calls a field over on the W of his farm 'the Summer House'). Mr Sutton said his family are there since 1690.

Hemp did not think this had the appearance of a military work: it is not defensible — low bank, narrow and shallow ditch. He suggests it is a cattle enclosure.

Mr Sutton showed me a lead bullet … . Spherical, with a slight raised line surrounding it, showing the join of the two sides of the mould. It is flattened on one side where it struck something. It was found in the turf in a field next the road on his farm, by his sister-in-law — she was getting in some turf and broke one, and the bullet fell out. He said it was about 1½ft down in the turf.

We went on to Glendalough, where Hemp looked at my two platforms above St Kevin's Cell and said they were certainly hut sites. He also showed me what he believes to be the old cashel wall surrounding Rhefeart [Reefert].

Afterwards he and Gresham spent two days round the Upper Lake and found hut sites all round it. He suggests they are older than St Kevin's time. *Sed quaere.*

12th October 1938

Visited a group of standing stones in Co. Carlow with Edward O'Toole.

Some are grooved stones like the Ardristan stone — see E. O'Toole's photo of one at Glenogue, Co. Carlow, in *JKAS* vol. xi (1933) p.298.

1. Straboe: the stone is in the second field from the crossroads. It is not tall, 4ft or so, and it is wide — (4ft) at the base. I thought first it was part of a megalith, but afterwards on seeing others, I assume it to be a gallán.

2. Tankardstown: Stone (1) is marked on the 6-inch map. I photographed it. It is 5½ or 6ft high, and has five grooves at the top. [It is E of the crossroads.] No. (2) is a slab like that at Straboe. No. (3) [is W of the T-junction, SE of Tankardstown crossroads] — I did not see it as it was raining.

3. Williamstown: marked on the 6-inch map. A fine fluted stone. It was too wet to photograph it. Long flutings.

4. Tombeagh: we did not go to see this one on account of the bad weather — Edward O'Toole had seen it and pointed out its position on the 6-inch map. It is fluted.

For a similar stone at Broughillstown see [p.316 above].

14th October 1938

On Monday 10th Sergeant B.J. Duignan of Enniskerry showed me a piece of copper found in a sandpit at Monastery. It turned out to be the broken top half of a flat copper axe. I visited the pit today. It is on the land of Miss Lang. A workman named Thomas Bradshaw, [from] Kiltiernan, Co. Dublin, found it a few days ago on the floor of the pit when he was screening some sand and gravel mixed with earth which had fallen down from the top of the pit. The face here is about 80ft high, and at the top there is about 7ft of earth. This had slipped down. At the same place and about the same time (a couple of days later) he found a thin cake of melted copper. The pit is in a steep slope running down from the high part of Monastery townland (the fields S of Rannock House) to the Cookstown River. The place where the earth slipped from is about 20ft below the top of the slope: and the spot is about 150yds NE of Enniskerry Bridge (behind Tallon's Hotel).

This spot is about 300yds or so to the W of the tumulus on the ridge in Monastery, in John Fisher's land, and some 600yds or so WSW of the site of the Fassaroe cist.

Notes taken, summer 1938, at Tuckamine with Edward O'Toole. The ogham stone may have come from a graveyard on Miss Hopkins' land, a field in Kilmagarvoge Upper, only two fields away (½ mile?), called 'the

Churchyard Field'. Miss Hopkins who is over 80 said her father or grandfather may have brought it over to put as a gatepost there. She remembers her father fencing there, in the upper corner of the field joining Bolger's: they dug up a lot of human bones and buried them down again, it would be 60 years ago.

Tuckamine is part of Ballybit, the local people say. The Ballybit urn was found on the lawn at her uncle Mr Salter's place, on the pathway between the pen and the big gate.

1st November 1938

Photographed the Williamstown and Tombeagh stones. The Williamstown stone is 6ft 2in. high, 4ft 8in. broad at base, and 2ft 6in. thick. It is rounded on the S side, where the grooves are.

4th November 1938

Sergeant Duignan brought me in two pieces of copper axes, both the cutting parts, neither fitting the previous fragment: they were found in the same place as the other, on the floor of the sandpit at Monastery.

6th November 1938

Roundwood. Mr Redmond, National Teacher, Roundwood, told me a burial had been found in a sandpit at Tomriland. I went to Tomriland. A man named James Walker, a labourer, brought me to Armstrong's sandpit and showed me where he and Thomas Healy found burned bones some 5 or 6 years ago, a human skull, with a heap of burned bones near it: 3ft below the grass, in the sand. They gave the skull to the Guards in Roundwood, and heard nothing more about it.

He also brought me to Burke's sandpit, a little to the E. There we found two or three fragments of cremated bone in the sand. Mr Freeman of Tomdarragh had got gravel from this pit. I went to him and he told me that some years ago they had found bones there. He knew that a skull had been found in Armstrong's.

In neither case were there any surrounding stones, nor as far as I could make out, any pottery. These therefore appear to have been cremations buried without any cists in the sand.

The roadway to Mr Freeman's house leads towards the plank bridge at

Knockadreet. I am sure it is the old road. He said his house was built in 1765. In his haggard is a stone about 2ft high, a sort of slaty stone. On it are five concentric circles, the outer about 5in. diameter. They are very regular. Perhaps an 18th-century carving: but what was its purpose? Mr Freeman said all the other stones there are granite. Glacial boulders? (Yes: authority A. Farrington.)

31st October 1938
Letter from Edward O'Toole, of Rathvilly.

' … Frank McDonnell (of Ballyredmond) told me he had discovered an ogham stone in the townland of Orchard near Clonegal … .'

14th November 1938
Ballinascorney Upper. About ½ mile NE of the Aghfarrell sandpits, not far up from the E bank of the little river (which later on is led into the Brittas Reservoir) are three standing stones of granite. They are in a large field which has just been planted with trees. They stand in a row NE to SW at the SE side of a hollow or depression in the field which is 15 or 20ft across. They are rather rectangular-shaped blocks, each about 4ft high and about 3ft wide. The one to the SW has I think fallen over. It has a cupmark (1in. diameter) on what was the top — the one to the NE has a similar cupmark on the top. Three to 4ft between this one and the next: 6ft or so between the middle one and the one that has fallen.

Some 80yds E or SE of these in a higher part of the field is a small irregular circle of stones, five quite small stones about 2ft high. E to W about 11ft across, NE to SW about 12ft. [The distances between the stones range from 3ft to 9ft.]

There is a road here in Ballinascorney Upper which lorries are at present using to go to a sandpit. It leads S from the present road to Ballinascorney House crossing the stream by a small concrete and wooden bridge: then it goes on SW to a farm. This must be the old road, connecting with Kilbride to the SW and with the road going over the hill, W of Knockannavea and down to Killinardan on the N. Petty's 'Lower way from Dublin to Ballimore Eustace' would meet it about in Jobstown.

3rd January 1939

Went to Armagh with S.H. Delargy, and saw Mr T.G. Paterson, curator of the Armagh County Museum. He brought us out and showed us the ruin of the Navan Fort, a large oval enclosure bounded by a high rampart built of stones and earth, with an internal ditch. Inside it at the highest point is a raised circular platform; no ditch round it. The site of a house? Or a place for ceremonials? The Protestant Cathedral of Armagh is about two miles away, standing up on its hill. Paterson said it was supposed that there was some sort of pre-Christian interment place there originally; and that there had been a stone circle in the town, which had been destroyed when the gas works were made. He brought us out then and showed us the ditch which local tradition says was the S boundary of Emania. A bank with a ditch on the S side of it. He said possibly this had originally gone right round Emania, but it may have been only a defence on the S. Where he showed it to us was at a place called 'Lisnadill', and he said the farmer when digging in it to make a shed found several beads, which he gave to his children and they were all lost. It is called locally 'Luig na muc' ('Lig na mŏock'). Then he brought us to the Dorsey, and showed us where he and Davies excavated. They uncovered the site of a house beside the road which is an old road, said to have led from Tara to Armagh. They found post-holes and I think a floor. Paterson believes it was a guardhouse at the S gate of the Dorsey.

For all these fortifications see de Vismes Kane's papers in: *PRIA* 27**C**, 14 (1909), p.301; *PRIA* 32**C**, 20 (1915), p.324; *PRIA* 33**C**, 19 (1917), p.539. But his historical remarks cannot be relied on at all.

18th February 1939

In Glencullen. Walked up the track to Glendoo House (on the S side of the main road), just SE of it two streams join, on the boundary of Boranaraltry townland. I crossed where they join, went a little way up the hill, and followed a boundary ditch which runs beside an old track that goes uphill in a SE direction across Boranaraltry. I left it and went down below the highest-up house in Boranaraltry: in the heather there is a circular stone wall enclosing a space about 20ft (?) across; site of a circular hut or house? Went down then to the bridge and up the road to Ballybrack. I spoke to an elderly man named Christopher Mulvey who lives alone in Ballybrack, about 65 years of age. I asked him what the village opposite was called, and he said 'Boranaraldha': I got him to repeat it several times as it was difficult to catch: it varied between 'Bohanuralda' and 'Bohernaraldha' or as above: the final 'd' was a 'dh' sound, like 'th' in 'they', stress on '-ál-' and also a strong stress on 'Bó-': he pronounced five syllables, but the second syllable was very indeterminate, almost like Bo-ə-nə-ral-dha. 'Bóthar na Aralta' or 'Bóthar na hAralta': 'the road of the Harolds' or 'Harolds' Road'.

He gave me some other names: on the stream between Boranaraltry and Glencullen Mountain, a glen is called 'Lugmore', some way up the mountain. Glencullen Mountain he called 'Glencullen Bog'. 'Kearneystown' is the upper part of Ballybrew on the county boundary. 'Ballinoúntha' (or 'Ballinoultha') is the hill above it where the trees are cut down. [Ballyna]brockey in Ballybrew he called 'Knŏockanabrŏokey' ('Cnúc an a brúccaidh', 'oo' is a short 'u' sound): there are only three houses in it. The boundary between Glendoo and Killakee mountain (i.e. Cruagh) is 'Owenthrasna', or it is sometimes called 'Crossowen' — that is above where the people camp. There's only the one house in Glendoo, a man called Mahon lives in it. He was a yearly tenant of Massey's. Boranaraltry belonged to Fitzsimons of Killiney.

In Ballybrack above the road (i.e. on the slope leading up towards the Two Rock) there's a place called 'Corrigónigee' (long 'o', accented): and 'Taylor's Rocks': and 'Boherthóllin' (short 'o', accented or stressed). There's a giant's grave on Tibradden, Colonel Guinness's mountain.

He said the ditch in Boranaraltry that I was walking along was a bounds ditch between the mountain and the pasture: but later he said it was a way up to the bog. I think it is an old track.

His great-grandfather lived in the house he lives in: he said the house was 200 years old.

22nd February 1939

Ballinacrow and Saundersgrove Hill. I walked up Ballinacrow Hill from the main road at Saundersgrove gate. First, the avenue of Saundersgrove continues on the E side of the main road, a wide grassy avenue bordered by old beech trees. This runs as far as the E boundary of Saundersgrove Hill townland where it ends in a poorly built but solid stone wall. As the fence on the N and S is the usual type of earth and stone bank, it is clear that the end of the avenue was walled up; the wall is clearly more recent than the fences which continue its line to N and S. Where Ballinacrow Lower and Upper adjoin one another and adjoin Saundersgrove, there was a wood, which is marked on the 1911 revise of the OS map. The wood is all cut down: the stumps are still there. I assume therefore that it was cut down during the war, I suppose 23 or 24 years ago. Most of the stumps are rotting away. I would not know how old the trees were, but they were well grown.

Apparently Nevill's map of 1760 already shows that piece of the main road which runs from near Manger Bridge to Tuckmill crossroads. But I should say the beech trees bordering the avenue are older than 1760: they are very big old trees, much older than the cut-down trees of which the stumps remain.

I would not like to be positive that there was a road running along between Saundersgrove Hill and Ballinacrow Upper and Lower, but (1) the fence looks as if it was the fence of an old road; (2) it is just in line with the piece of road which runs S from the Tuckmill to Kill (Kyle) road and then bends E, forming the boundary between Tuckmill Upper and Tuckmill Lower; (3) while this part of Ballinacrow Lower is all overgrown with furze bushes and brambles, I could see the marks of old cultivation (potato ridges) a little bit to the E of the boundary of Saundersgrove Hill, and they seemed to occupy a fairly narrow strip — the suggestion to my mind being that they were small plots, perhaps with houses on them, on the E side of the suggested line of road.

The fence which makes the boundary between Ballinacrow Upper and Lower leading over towards Eadestown is a fairly good fence of stones and earth. Right on the top of Ballinacrow Hill there was a good wall running N and S. It is now very much knocked down. All the hill is divided into large pasture fields. I should think the wall and the fences were built out of the stones cleared off these fields when they were made.

I should think it is very likely that it was when these fields were being made that the graves containing ashes and burned bones were found, in 1787 (see *Ages of Stone and Bronze in Co. Wicklow,* p.46).

The rath which is marked on the map in the N part of Ballinacrow Lower near the top of the hill is quite visible, though nearly level with the field. It was surrounded by a ditch with a bank inside and outside. Width of ditch about 4yds: diameter of rath from top of inner bank about 35yds. The bank was of stones and earth.

4th March 1939

Visited Christopher Mulvey again, with Sean O'Sullivan. He had not much folk material, but I got several placenames. His pronunciation of Boranaraltry is really 'Bō·naraldha not 'Bona·raldha'.

Names in Tibradden (a dot in front of a syllable means the syllable is stressed.)

'·Cruckawn' in the boundary of Tibradden, a rising bank; a sheep run.

'The ·Buggans' — adjoining it.

'The Bush Field', 20 or 30yds from the boundary. The bush is supposed to be a '·rawheen' — it's not lucky to meddle with them.

'The ·Astree' or '·Astry Park'.

'Con's Hill', remains of old houses there on the mountain. It's now Casey's land.

'Rooney's Corner', there are no Rooneys there now — remains of old walls there.

'The Old Pound', on the main road, near the Crooked Bridge — it's near the new cottage. Sheep were pounded in there at night.

'The Sandy Gardens': another field in Tibradden near the Bush Field.

'Finn's Chair' on Colonel Guinness's boundary, an ordinary rock or big stone at the back of the big wood. People sit on it — there are small stones round about it.

'Nick's Chapel', a big stone you could turn a coach and four under. They say it was a chapel in troubled times. It's on the road up to Mahon's (that is, on the W side of the main road) still in Tibradden.

'·Lugana·gurnan' (or '–·gurnawn' or '·Lug na ·gurlawn') beyond the gamekeeper's house, on the bend of the road: this side of the gate leading up to Mahon's.

Names in Ballybrack

'Hanlon's Green', over the road.

'·Cammels Rocks'; these two are nearly together. There was Campbells living about there.

'Cloch·wán (–·wawn) Stone', a great big mossy stone.

'Red Scar' — opposite the house (Mulvey's house).

'The ·Corrig·eens'

'The ·Muiliuc' (or '·Meelick' or '·Muilleack'), an old rough field here on the main road, on Ballybrack.

'·Gornago·bawstha' — a field opposite the door. ('Gort na gcabáiste'?)

'The Stony Road' in Ballybrack, here over the house on this side of the mountain, over the main road — ten minutes' walk from the house.

'The Old Crow', up on this mountain, an old bog, a sheep pen — there's an old habitation in it.

'The Old Pin', near it. These are seven or eight minutes' walk from one another, all surrounding the Stony Road.

'Nanny's House' — near the mud-hole over the road. All occupied years ago.

'Tall Boy', a big rock standing about 12ft high, up on the mountain.

'The Fair Cord', the name of a field.

'·Boreen' ('·Boareen'), a field under the house.

In Glendoo

'The Glen·doo Brook' divides 'Glen·doo' and '·Killa·kee'.

'Dead Man's Hollow', on Glendoo — out at the house on the mountain (Mahon's) men were benighted and drowned in it.

'The Middle Brook' — over Mahon's house.

'Porke·racy' (or '-·razy') ('pórc-ɔ-·réasai'), under the gamekeeper's house.

'The Rye Bank', on Mahon's. An old bank, there was rye grown on it.

'·Aska', the name of a brook over Mahon's: it branches off into the Dead Man's Hollow.

Other localities

'The Fol·bólia Brook' ('fal·bóilia' or '·fol·boulye') ('Ғál-buaileadh') at the top of the bog between 'Glan·cree' and Dublin. It's out over the boundary of the 'Owen·trasna Brook'.

'Fitzwilliam's Seat' hits on the Bonaralda side, joining Wicklow; a big rock, a resting place for the gentlemen when fowling on the top.

'The Whistling Stone', on Bonaralda side.

'·Toma·leen Bog' (or 'Thomaleen'), near the granite quarries, on this side of 'Ballyn·oultha' (i.e. Glencullen Mountain), a 'ma'shy old place' (i.e. marshy).

'The Red River', underneath the road going to the granite quarries.

'·Mónialig' ('móin a' luig'), 'a rale ould ould name, an old coarse pastury field'.

'·Inchy', a field on the 'Bonaralda' estate (meaning in Boranaraltry townland), the river runs beside it.

'The ·Bō-er Ditch' ('bó' and 'er', two syllables), on a field underneath the
house on the Bonaralda side.

'The Cosheer' or 'Casheer' (equal stress), the name of a field on Bonaralda,
an ordinary grazing or tillage field (meaning? 'caise iar' or 'iarthach', 'the
boundary stream').

'Scully's Top', 'convaynient to the wood this side of the granite quarries;
there was Scullys lived here'.

'The ·Eska·law Brook', at the top of Glendoo Mountain, joining Glencree.

'Bradley's Turn', on the bounds between Glenasmole and Glencree, in off
the road, in on the mountain, near Lemass's Cross.

'·Lugawns', up over Fox's house in Glencullen.

'·Corrigeena·roe', opposite Fox's. Kip Field adjoining it.

'Lough Greens', a field belonging to Roe of Ballybetagh.

'Lugdoo', on the Ticknock estate, convenient for the Lamb Doyle's.

'·Lackan', under the house (in Ballybrack or Bonaralda, I'm not sure which
he said).

Mulvey said he thought the circular stone wall in Boranaraltry was a place
where a man had died, and they made a cairn of stones at the place: but it
had got knocked about since.

He spoke of '·Shangill', where Eustace lives (Shankill, Co. Wicklow),
'Bally·mofinn', '·Glassa·muilyawn' (Glassavullaun) and 'Corragower' (i.e.
Carrigower near Kilbride, Co. Wicklow).

Asked was there any St Patrick's Well in Glencullen, he said 'No, but
there is a well called "St Columcille's Well", below Woodtown — to get to
it you'd cross Billy's Bridge from Ballyboden, and go straight on through
Scholarstown. Cattle used to drink out of the well, but now it has been
built round and preserved. People go there to pray and to use the water.'

'·Boher·thollin' ('bóthar talainn') in Ballybrack, runs to the boundary of
Ticknock.

An old boreen runs from near Mulvey's house to Kilmashogue. The
White Houses are on this road between Ballybrack and Kilmashogue. An
old woman, Miss Hannah Farrell, 113 years old, now in the Hospice for the
Dying, lived near White Houses. Her memory isn't good.

18th March 1939

Deputy's Pass. The blue pencil lines [on Fig.129] are the little head streams of the Potter's River, which meet and flow down Deputy's Pass. I walked from *A* to *B* up the hill [from the Kilnamanaghmore/Ballygannon crossroads]: this is supposed to be the old road from Dublin to Arklow passing Kilmacurra. A very steep hill. When you get to the top, the road goes right, leading along the ridge back towards Red Peg's crossroads: it is this road which is called 'the Black Road', over Glenealy. It also goes left, down to Deputy's Pass at *C* [at the boundary between Ballinacooley and Ballygannon]: this was the way I walked. This road looks as if it had been made by digging out two big ditches 20ft or so apart and piling the material out of the ditches on to the space between, so making a raised bank or causeway. This bank is all overgrown and the road is now in the W ditch, a metalled road, which has in places destroyed the trace of the ditch. The bank in the middle is also much destroyed. Continuing on from *C* to *D* [SW], at first the road looks the same, two ditches and a bank between — but after a couple of hundred yards the E ditch gets shallow and then it disappears (after reappearing for a little bit) —and the bank becomes a big bank bordering the road on the E side. It goes straight to where the two streams join at the boundary of Drumdangan and Ballygannon. I feel pretty sure this is the Long Ford at Ballygannon, for before the little bridges were made the roadway must have run for about 200yds through the water.

I believe a road must at one time have gone from *B* down to what is called on the map 'Ballinacooley House', and on then down to the gate of

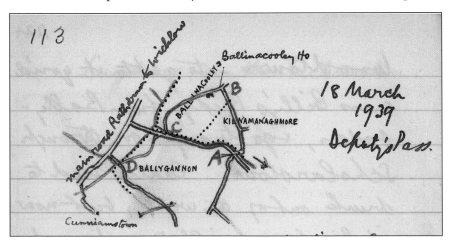

Fig. 129—Sketch-map of Deputy's Pass.

Glascarrig House, and so in by the avenue, which is the old road. So the road along the ridge may be more recent than the road going down through Ballinacooley to Glenealy. The road *B–C–D* is where I think Russell made his 'pass'.

19th March 1939
Mr Byrne of Drumgoff told me that the long ditch at Fana·neerin (running from the ridge down W to the stream) is called 'the ·Pasther Ditch' ('pasture'): it divided the enclosed pasture from the mountain. A green patch a bit to the N side of this wall, in the big enclosed field that has now gone back out of cultivation, is called '·Lyre-a·greech' ('Labhar a gcrích') and the high point of Fananierin he called 'Scro·hoge' ('Scro-hóg').

Also saw Brian Farrell of Corrasillagh, who had been ill. He mentioned some placenames:

'·Lōgar Brook', running down to the Ass, between Conavalla and
    Ballinagoneen.
'Badger Burrow Brook' (pronounced '·Badgə·burrə'), so called because
    there are a lot of badgers there: running into Kelly's Lake.
'Cora·greinge' is in Corrasillagh.

A copper pot was found high up in '·Clōnakeen' [Clonkeen] above the Been Rock — no houses ever there, but there's a cave there called 'Dwyer's Cave'. Perhaps he used it for cooking, Farrell said. (Dr Lynn reported the find of this pot to me, and I was to get it, but did not. I think it's modern.) There's another Dwyer's Cave in Coragreinge.

The Forestry have bought Ballinafunshoge, so Odie Byrne's house and the Kennys' house will both be shut up — two more families leaving the glen. The Kennys are only caretakers. Odie Byrne is not married, he may go to England.

2nd April 1939
At Redbog, Co. Kildare: the hill NW of Blessington. There is a mote on the top, much of it has been dug away. It is now about 53 paces in circumference and at its highest 6ft above ground level. The middle has been dug into. The hill is called 'Caween', pronounced '·Cawryeen' (slight 'y' sound).

3rd April 1939

Chapel near Redcross. Went again to look at the raheen. The walls of the old church are there, almost completely ruined, and overgrown. Approximate measurements outside: 21 or 22ft long and 14 or 15ft wide, walls about 2ft thick, but I could not measure at all accurately. The field is called 'the Churchyard'. The stream between it and Crone bounds the field on the N side: the banks in the Camp Field, which evidently formed a square, are quite close to it, just across the hedge. The enclosure round the church is square, not round. Some 14 years or so ago a man ferreting for rabbits dug up a human skull in it: the enclosure is full of rabbit-holes. I could see no carved or cut stones either in the walls or lying about in the enclosure.

Redcross old graveyard. Behind, that is E of, the Protestant church. An old mixed graveyard, full of graves: no sign of a church or of its site. Still used occasionally by a few old families. The new Protestant graveyard is beside the church. The old graveyard is enclosed by an approximately circular wall or bank. In it rather to the NE of the centre is a large granite stone embedded in the ground, with a large hole in it … the hole is not bored quite perpendicular, 18in. wide at mouth, then a step about 7in. down [below the mouth], then 12in. in diameter. It goes through the stone but I could not see the outline of the stone itself. Query, some part of a water-mill?

There were some nondescript pieces of stone lying under a small tree, one at least was rounded as though by cutting or grinding. Perhaps a piece of a pillar?

8th April 1939

Drove to Seir Kieran, that is Clareen, near Birr, with H.E. Kilbride-Jones. The Reverend F.H. Gilling had started digging in a mound outside the churchyard, having got a diviner to go over the ground: the diviner said there was metal at a certain spot, so he started to dig there. Miss Roe told Dr Mahr, and he sent us down to get the man to stop. He agreed to stop, to do no more digging till he heard from Dr Mahr (he'd found nothing).

There are very interesting and curious remains at Seir Kieran. A very large double rampart, I should say 400yds across: the church and graveyard are in the middle of it. It probably ended on the E in a lake or marsh: was never a full circle. The mound where he was digging sticks out on the inside: it is square: query, site of an Anglo-Norman building? On the W side of the road is a big four-ringed enclosure, not round, but I think roughly rectangular. Mr Gilling said there was a holy well, with hut sites around it, down to the SE of the graveyard: we did not go to look at it. For his discoveries of monuments in the graveyard see *JRSAI*.

16th April 1939

Looked at St Anne's churchyard, Glenasmole ('Killmasanctan' or 'Killepscopsantan'). There are no old tombstones in it (i.e. pre-17th century) that I could see. A small piece of the church wall is standing — not very old-looking. The old font is standing inside the gate, against the E wall of the graveyard. [It is] granite [with] a square opening 2 or 2½ft — about 3ft high — a hole in one corner to let the water out. It is all covered with briars. I don't think it is decorated. The measurements are only guesses.

The fields round the graveyard are all on a slope — above it there are grass-covered banks and mounds, a couple of fields away. Could trace no plans of houses. The field on the N side is circular in shape, but has no bank or fosse: only an ordinary field ditch round it.

17th April 1939

Visited Dunganstown Castle. It is a very fine ruin. O'Curry's plan and elevation, though not incorrect, don't do it justice at all. It is late Elizabethan or early Jacobean in style with cut-stone window frames and gable ornaments.

[Later note, no date]

I asked Ned Stephens when did Paddy Byrne die: he asked Mrs Wynne of Glendalough, and she wrote to me on 13th December 1944 that he died on 11th February 1942. She says 'What a grand old man he was ... no one like him left here now'.

Fig. 130—
Dunganstown Castle
(courtesy of the Royal
Society of Antiquaries of
Ireland ©).

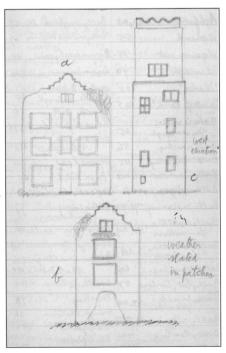

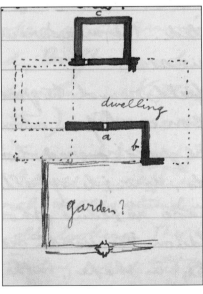

Fig. 131—Sketch-plan
and elevations of
Dunganstown Castle.